SCHAUM'S OUTLINE OF

Theory and Problems of MANAGERIAL ACCOUNTING

Second Edition

JAE K. SHIM, Ph.D

Professor of Accountancy
California State University at Long Beach

JOEL G. SIEGEL, Ph.D., CPA

Professor of Accounting and Finance
Queens College, City University of New York

Schaum's Outline Series

McGRAW-HILL

New York San Francisco Washington, D.C. Auckland Bogotá Caracas Lisbon
London Madrid Mexico City Milan Montreal New Delhi
San Juan Singapore Sydney Tokyo Toronto

JAE K. SHIM is currently Professor of Business Administration at California State University at Long Beach. He received his M.B.A. and Ph.D. from the University of California at Berkeley. Professor Shim has published over 40 articles in accounting, finance, economics, and operations research journals. He is a coeditor of *Readings in Cost and Managerial Accounting*. He is also a coauthor of the Schaum's Outlines of *Financial Accounting*, *Personal Finance*, and *Managerial Finance*, and of the AICPA's *Variance Analysis for Cost Control and Profit Maximization* and *Accounting for and Evaluation of Process Cost Systems.* Dr. Shim was the recipient of the 1982 Credit Research Foundation award.

JOEL G. SIEGEL is Professor of Accounting and Finance at Queens College of the City University of New York. He possesses a Ph.D. in accounting from the Bernard M. Baruch College of the City University of New York and a CPA certificate from New York. In 1972, Dr. Siegel was the recipient of the Outstanding Educator of America Award. He was employed as a staff accountant with Coopers & Lybrand, CPAs. Professor Siegel is a coauthor of the Schaum's Outlines of *Financial Accounting* and *Managerial Finance.* He has also written *How to Analyze Businesses, Financial Statements and The Quality of Earnings*, published by Prentice-Hall. Dr. Siegel is the author of five publications in continuing professional education published by the AICPA.

Schaum's Outline of Theory and Problems of
MANAGERIAL ACCOUNTING

3 4 5 6 7 8 9 10 11 12 13 14 15 16 17 18 19 20 PRS PRS 9 0 2 1 0

ISBN 0-07-058041-3

Sponsoring Editor: Barbara Gilson
Production Supervisor: Sherri Souffrance
Editing Supervisor: Maureen B. Walker

Library of Congress Cataloging-in-Publication Data

Shim, Jae K.
Schaum's outline of theory and problems of managerial accounting/
Jae K. Shim, Joel G. Siegel. — 2nd ed.
p. cm. — (Schaum's outline series)
Includes index.
ISBN 0-07-058041-3
1. Managerial accounting. 2. Managerial accounting—Problems, exercises, etc. I. Siegel, Joel G. II. Title. III. Series.
HF5635.S5529 1998
658.15'11—dc21 98-27629
CIP

McGraw-Hill
A Division of The McGraw-Hill Companies

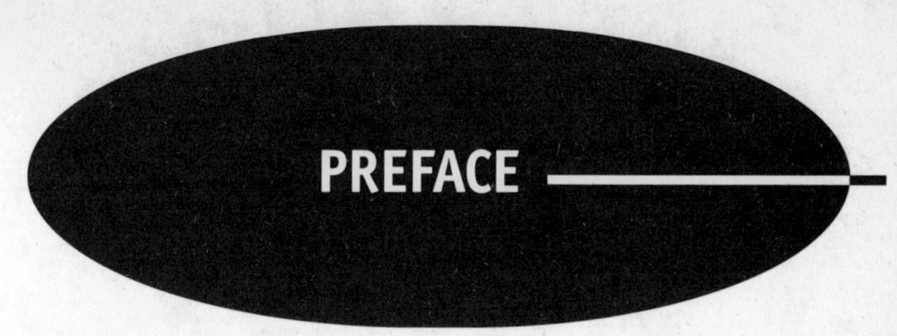

PREFACE

Managerial Accounting is designed for accounting and nonaccounting business students. It covers the managerial use of accounting data for planning, control, and decision making. As in the preceding volumes in the Schaum's Outline Series in Accounting, the *solved problems* approach is used, with emphasis on the practical application of managerial accounting concepts, tools, and methodology. The student is provided with the following:

1. Definitions and explanations that are understandable
2. Examples illustrating the concepts and techniques discussed in each chapter
3. Review questions and answers by chapter
4. Detailed solutions to representative problems covering the subject matter
5. Comprehensive examinations with answers and solutions to test the student's knowledge of each chapter. The exams are representative of those used by two- and four-year colleges and MBA programs.

Managerial Accounting covers a wide variety of managerial uses of accounting data. In line with the ever-changing, dynamic nature of the subject, the Institute of Management Accountants (IMA) has established the Certified Management Accountants (CMA), which is being widely recognized by academicians as well as practitioners. This book is written with the following objectives in mind:

1. It supplements formal training in management accounting courses at the *undergraduate* and *graduate* levels. It may well be used as a study guide.
2. It provides excellent preparation and review in the cost/managerial accounting portion of such professional examinations as the CPA, CMA, SMA, and CGA examinations.
3. Financial accounting is not a prerequisite. Without much knowledge of financial accounting, students and practitioners engaged in fields other than accounting can gain knowledge about managerial accounting.

Managerial Accounting was written to cover the common denominator of managerial accounting topics after a thorough review was made of the numerous managerial accounting texts available in the market. It is, therefore, comprehensive in coverage and presentation. Particularly, in an effort to give readers a feel for what types of problems are asked on the CPA, CMA, SMA, and CGA examinations, problems have been taken from those exams and incorporated within.

Our appreciation is extended to the American Institute of Certified Public Accountants, the National Association of Accountants, the Society of Management Accountants of Canada, and the Canadian Certified General Accountants' Association, for their permission to incorporate their examination questions in this book. Selected materials from the CMA Examinations, copyright © by the National Association of Accountants, bear the notation "(CMA, adapted)." Problems from the Uniform CPA Examinations bear the notation "(AICPA, adapted)," problems from the SMA Examinations are designated "(SMA, adapted)," and problems from CGA Examinations bear the notation "(CGA, adapted)."

Finally we would like to thank our assistants, Allison Shim and Paul Chun, for their enormous contribution and assistance. We also would like to extend our gratitude to Maureen Walker and Richard Cook for their outstanding editorial contribution to the manuscript.

JAE K. SHIM
JOEL G. SIEGEL

CONTENTS

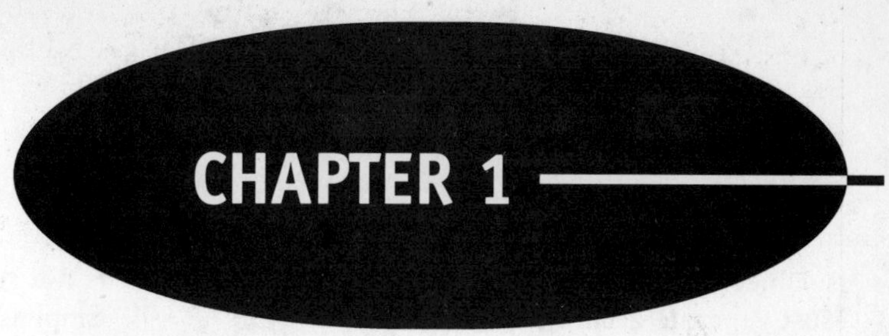

Management Accounting—A Perspective

1.1 THE ROLE OF MANAGEMENT ACCOUNTING

Management accounting as defined by the National Association of Accountants (NAA) is the process of identification, measurement, accumulation, analysis, preparation, interpretation, and communication of financial information, which is used by management to plan, evaluate, and control within an organization. It ensures the appropriate use of and accountability for an organization's resources. Management accounting also comprises the responsibility for the preparation of financial reports for nonmanagement groups such as regulatory agencies and tax authorities. Simply stated, management accounting is the accounting for the planning, control, and decision-making activities of an organization.

1.2 FINANCIAL ACCOUNTING VS. MANAGEMENT ACCOUNTING

Financial accounting is concerned mainly with the historical aspects of external reporting, that is, providing financial information to outside parties such as investors, creditors, and governments. To protect those outside parties from being misled, financial accounting is governed by what are called *generally accepted accounting principles* (GAAP). Management accounting, on the other hand, is concerned primarily with providing information to internal managers who are charged with planning and controlling the operations of the firm and making a variety of management decisions. Because of its internal use, management accounting is not subject to GAAP. More specifically, the differences between financial and management accounting are summarized below.

Financial Accounting	Management Accounting
1. Provides data for *external* users	1. Provides data for *internal* users
2. Is required by the law	2. Is not mandatory by law

Financial Accounting	Management Accounting
3. Is subject to GAAP	3. Is not subject to GAAP
4. Must generate accurate and timely data	4. Emphasizes relevance and flexibility of data
5. Emphasizes the past	5. Has more emphasis on the future
6. Looks at the business as a whole	6. Focuses on parts as well as on the whole of a business
7. Primarily stands by itself	7. Draws heavily from other disciplines such as finance, economics, and operations research
8. Is an end in itself	8. Is a means to an end

1.3 COST ACCOUNTING VS. MANAGEMENT ACCOUNTING

The difference between cost accounting and management accounting is a subtle one. The NAA defines *cost accounting* as "a systematic set of procedures for recording and reporting measurements of the cost of manufacturing goods and performing services in the aggregate and in detail. It includes methods for recognizing, classifying, allocating, aggregating and reporting such costs and comparing them with standard costs." From this definition of cost accounting and the NAA's definition of management accounting, one thing is clear: the major function of cost accounting is cost accumulation for inventory valuation and income determination. Management accounting, however, emphasizes the use of the cost data for planning, control, and decision-making purposes.

EXAMPLE 1.1 Management accounting typically does not deal with the details of how costs are accumulated and how unit costs are computed for inventory valuation and income determination. Although unit cost data are used for pricing and other managerial decisions, the method of computation itself is not a major topic of management accounting but rather of cost accounting.

1.4 THE WORK OF MANAGEMENT

In general, the work that management performs can be classified as (*a*) planning, (*b*) coordinating, (*c*) controlling, and (*d*) decision making.

Planning. The planning function of management involves the selection of long-range and short-term objectives and the drawing up of strategic plans to achieve those objectives.

Coordinating. In performing the coordination function, management must decide how best to put together the firm's resources in order to carry out established plans.

Controlling. Controlling entails the implementation of a decision method and the use of feedback so that the firm's goals and specific strategic plans are optimally obtained.

Decision making. Decision making is the purposeful selection from among a set of alternatives in light of a given objective.

Management accounting information is important in performing all of the aforementioned functions.

1.5 THE ORGANIZATIONAL ASPECT OF MANAGEMENT ACCOUNTING

There are two types of authorities in the organizational structure: line and staff.

Line authority is the authority to give orders to subordinates. Line managers are responsible for attaining the goals set by the organization as efficiently as possible. Production and sales managers typically possess line authority.

Staff authority is the authority to give advice, support, and service to line departments. Staff managers do not command others. Examples of staff authority are found in personnel, purchasing, engineering, and finance. The management accounting function is usually a staff function with responsibility for providing line managers and also other staff people with a specialized service. The service includes (*a*) budgeting, (*b*) controlling, (*c*) pricing, and (*d*) special decisions.

1.6 CONTROLLERSHIP

The chief management accountant or the chief accounting executive of an organization is called the *controller* (often called *comptroller*, especially in the government sector). The controller is in charge of the accounting department. The controller's authority is basically staff authority in that the controller's office gives advice and service to other departments. But at the same time, the controller has line authority over members of his or her own department such as internal auditors, bookkeepers, budget analysts, etc. (See Fig. 1-1 for an organization chart of a controllership situation.) The principal functions of the controller are:

1. Planning for control
2. Financial reporting and interpreting
3. Tax administration
4. Management audits, and development of accounting systems and computer data processing
5. Internal audits

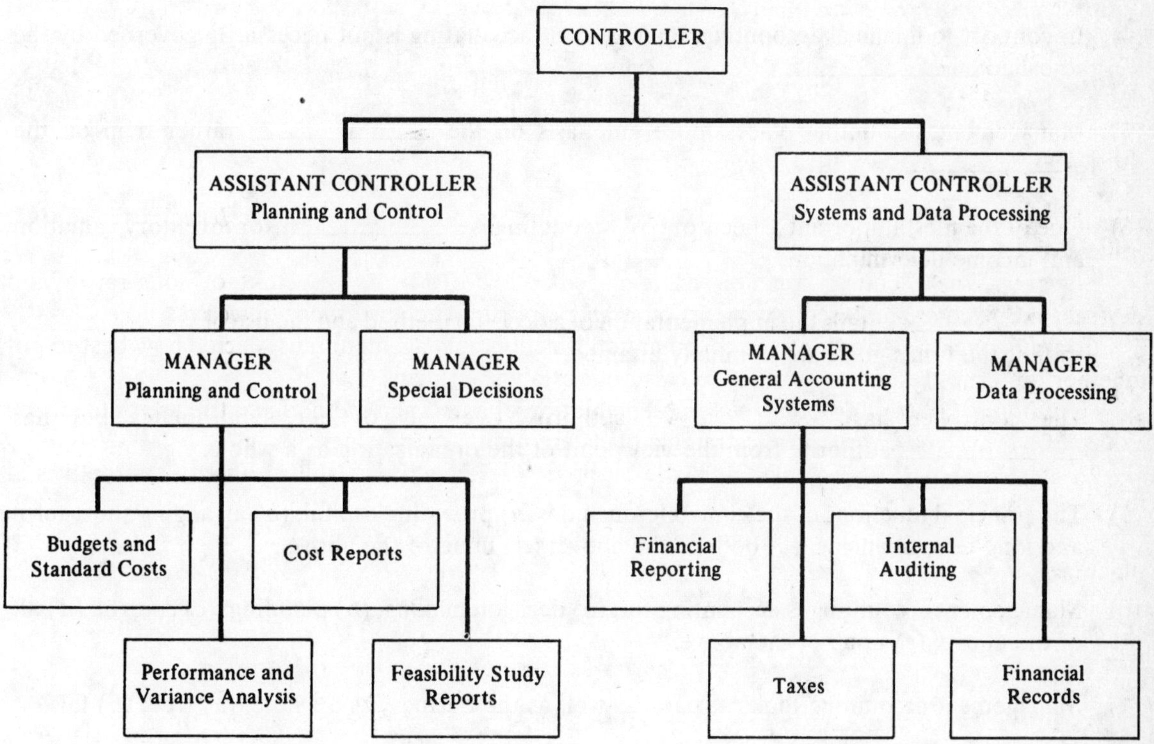

Fig. 1-1

1.7 THE CERTIFIED MANAGEMENT ACCOUNTANT (CMA)

Management accounting has expanded in scope to cover a wide variety of business disciplines such as finance, economics, organizational behavior, and quantitative methods. In line with this development, the National Association of Accountants (NAA) has created the Institute of Management Accounting, which offers a program for becoming a Certified Management Accountant (CMA). The CMA program requires candidates to pass a series of uniform examinations covering a wide range of subjects. (See Problem 1.3 for the subjects covered in the CMA examination.) The objectives of the program are fourfold: (1) to establish management accounting as a recognized profession, (2) to foster higher educational standards in the area of management accounting, (3) to establish objective measurement of an individual's knowledge and competence in the area of management accounting, and (4) to encourage continued professional development by management accountants.

Summary

(1) Management accounting provides data for ____________ uses.

(2) The chief accounting executive in an organization is often called the ____________.

(3) The Institute of Management Accounting, created by the National Association of Accountants, offers a program for becoming a ____________, indicating professional competence in this expanding field.

(4) In contrast to financial accounting, management accounting is not necessarily governed by the so-called ____________.

(5) Management accounting places more emphasis on the ____________ rather than on the ____________.

(6) One of the most important aspects of cost accounting is ____________ for inventory valuation and income determination.

(7) ____________ entails the implementation of a decision method and the use of ____________ so that the firm's goals are optimally attained.

(8) The controller has ____________ authority over his or her subordinates but has ____________ authority from the viewpoint of the organization as a whole.

(9) The principal functions of the controller include: (*a*) providing capital; (*b*) arranging short-term and long-term financing; (*c*) both of the above; (*d*) none of the above.

(10) Management accounting is accounting for: (*a*) decision making; (*b*) planning; (*c*) control; (*d*) all of the above; (*e*) none of the above.

(11) Management accounting looks at parts as well as the business as a whole: (*a*) true; (*b*) false.

(12) Management carries out four broad functions in an organization. They are planning, ____________, controlling, and decision making.

(13) ______________ is mainly concerned with providing information for external users such as stockholders and creditors.

Answers: (1) internal; (2) controller; (3) Certified Management Accountant (CMA); (4) generally accepted accounting principles (GAAP); (5) future, past; (6) cost accumulation; (7) controlling, feedback; (8) line, staff; (9) (*d*); (10) (*d*); (11) (*a*); (12) coordinating; (13) financial accounting.

Solved Problems

1.1 For each of the following, indicate whether it is identified primarily with management accounting (MA) or financial accounting (FA):

1. Draws heavily from other disciplines such as economics and statistics
2. Prepares financial statements
3. Provides financial information to internal managers
4. Emphasizes the past rather than the future
5. Focuses on relevant and flexible data
6. Is not mandatory
7. Focuses on the segments as well as the entire organization
8. Is not subject to generally accepted accounting principles
9. Is built around the fundamental accounting equation of debits equal credits
10. Draws heavily from other business disciplines

SOLUTION

1. MA; 2. FA; 3. MA; 4. FA; 5. MA; 6. MA; 7. MA; 8. MA; 9. FA; 10. MA.

1.2 For each of the following pairs, indicate how the first individual is related to the second by writing (L) line authority, (S) staff authority, or (N) no authority.

(*a*) Controller; internal auditor
(*b*) VP, production; accounts receivable bookkeeper
(*c*) VP, finance; personnel director
(*d*) Controller; budget analyst
(*e*) VP, finance; treasurer
(*f*) Treasurer; controller
(*g*) Controller; assistant controller
(*h*) Controller; shipping clerk
(*i*) Assistant controller, computer; data processing clerk
(*j*) Production supervisor; foreman
(*k*) VP, manufacturing; payroll clerk
(*l*) Controller; VP, production

SOLUTION

(*a*) L; (*b*) N; (*c*) S; (*d*) L; (*e*) L; (*f*) S; (*g*) L; (*h*) N; (*i*) L; (*j*) L; (*k*) N; (*l*) S.

1.3 What are the objectives of the program for Certified Management Accountants (CMAs), and what topics are covered in the examination for this certificate?

SOLUTION

The objectives of the CMA program are fourfold: (1) to establish management accounting as a recognized profession by identifying the role of the management accountant and financial manager, the underlying body of knowledge, and a course of study by which such knowledge is acquired; (2) to encourage higher educational standards in the management accounting field; (3) to establish an objective measure of an individual's knowledge and competence in the field of management accounting; and (4) to encourage continued professional development by management accountants.

The CMA program requires candidates to pass a series of uniform examinations covering a wide range of subjects. The examination consists of the following four parts: (1) economics, finance, and management (3 hours); (2) financial accounting and reporting (3 hours); (3) management reporting analysis, and behavioral issues (3 hours); and (4) decision analysis and information systems (3 hours).

1.4 Management accounting is not as important or useful in nonprofit organizations such as hospitals and government as it is in private business firms, since these organizations do not strive to make profits. Comment on this statement.

SOLUTION

This statement is *not* true. Management accounting is useful in planning, controlling, and decision making. Whether the object of an organization is to make a profit or not, the concepts of planning, control, and decision making are the same in both profit-oriented businesses and nonprofit organizations. Nonprofit organizations need financial and accounting information in meeting their objectives and in allocating their resources. They are concerned with such matters as control of revenue and costs and making economical decisions.

1.5 Prepare an organization chart (highlighting the accounting functions) of J. Company, which has the following positions:

Special reports and studies manager	VP, sales
Billing clerk	Cost systems analyst
VP, finance	Assistant controller
Assistant treasurer	Systems and data processing manager
Accounts receivable clerk	General accounting manager
Budget and standard cost analyst	Treasurer
Controller	Payroll clerk
VP, production	Internal audit manager
Tax manager	Performance analyst
Cost accounting manager	General ledger bookkeeper
Cost clerk	Accounts payable clerk

SOLUTION

See Fig. 1-2.

1.6 Successful business organizations have clearly defined long-range goals and a well-planned strategy to reach them. These organizations understand the markets in which they operate as well as their own internal strengths and weaknesses. They grow through internal development or acquisitions in a consistent and disciplined manner.

(*a*) Discuss the need for long-range goals in business organizations.

(*b*) Discuss how long-range goals are established.

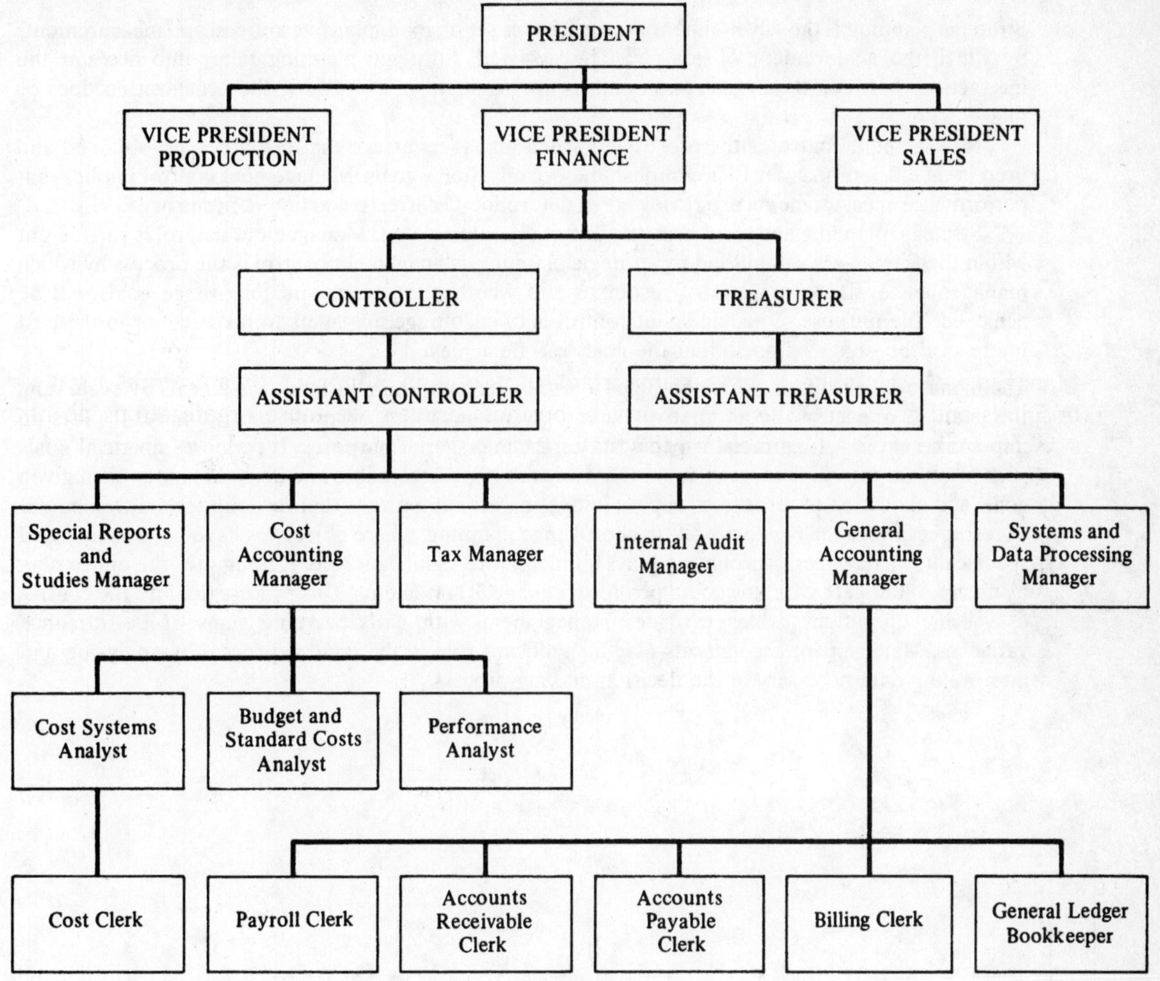

Fig. 1-2

(*c*) Define strategic planning and management control. Discuss how they relate to each other and contribute to the attainment of long-range goals.

(*d*) How does management accounting help a firm in accomplishing its long-range goals? (CMA, adapted)

SOLUTION

(*a*) Long-range goals enable an organization to develop a business philosophy regarding the direction of the organization and the limits within which the management is free to exercise discretion. The development of long-range goals is important for providing the basis for plans, enhancing the efficiency of the organization's decision makers, and providing a basis for evaluating alternate courses of action.

Long-range goals serve as a basis for individual goals and goal congruence. Goals also serve as standards against which long-term progress can be measured and evaluated.

(*b*) Long-range goals are normally set by persons at the highest level of the organization. However, input should be solicited from employees at all levels of the organization. The goals are developed by weighing various constraints such as:
— Economic conditions (present and future)
— The desires of the owners and management
— The resources of the firm

(*c*) Strategic planning is the development of a consistent set of goals, plans, resources, and measurements by which the achievement of goals can be assessed. Strategic planning takes into account the interactions between the organization and its environment in everything the organization does or plans.

Management control is the process by which managers assure that resources are obtained and used in an efficient manner to accomplish the organization's goals. Management control implies that performance measurements are reviewed to determine if corrective action is necessary.

Strategic planning and management control are interrelated. Management control is carried out within the framework established by strategic planning. Management control is the process by which management evaluates the use of resources and whether the plans and long-range goals will be achieved. The purpose of management control is to encourage managers to take actions in the best interest of the organization so that the goals can be achieved.

(*d*) The managerial accounting function helps a firm in accomplishing its long-range goals by evaluating the financial impact of the alternatives within given constraints on profit performance. It plays an important role in setting certain specifications for managerial purposes. It proposes financial goals such as rate of return, debt, cash, and other ratios that are acceptable and desirable in terms of given goals and allocation of resources. Capital budgeting is an important tool for long-term development of resources for capacity expansion. In short-range planning, where objectives have been established specifically, management accounting plays a much more significant role. It integrates the entire plan by means of budgets, cash flows, and pro-forma financial statements. This process ties into the control of specific operations, which provides management with early warning signs of performance variances. Management accountants play a significant role in the control process by analyzing and interpreting data necessary in the decision-making process.

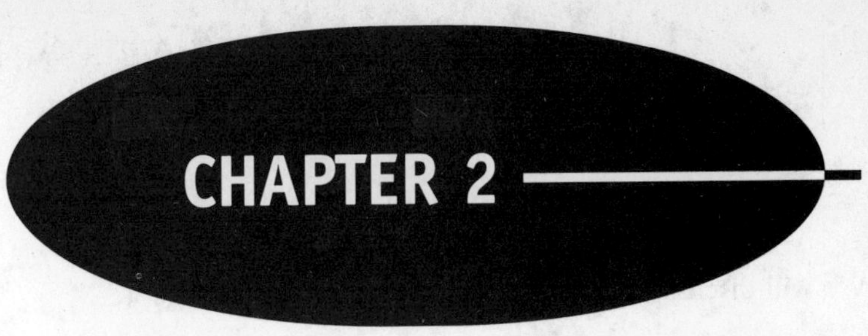

Cost Concepts, Terms, and Classifications

2.1 DIFFERENT COSTS FOR DIFFERENT PURPOSES

In financial accounting, the term *cost* is defined as a measurement, in monetary terms, of the amount of resources used for some purposes. In managerial accounting, the term *cost* is used in many different ways. That is, there are different types of costs used for different purposes. Some costs are useful and required for inventory valuation and income determination. Some costs are useful for planning, budgeting, and cost control. Still others are useful for making short-term and long-term decisions.

2.2 COST CLASSIFICATIONS

Costs can be classified into various categories, according to

1. Their management function
   (*a*) Manufacturing costs
   (*b*) Nonmanufacturing costs
2. Their ease of traceability
   (*a*) Direct costs
   (*b*) Indirect costs
3. Their timing of charges against sales revenue
   (*a*) Product costs
   (*b*) Period costs
4. Their behavior in accordance with changes in activity
   (*a*) Variable costs
   (*b*) Fixed costs
   (*c*) Semivariable costs
5. Their relevance to control and decision making
   (*a*) Controllable and noncontrollable costs
   (*b*) Standard costs
   (*c*) Incremental costs
   (*d*) Sunk costs

(*e*) Opportunity costs
(*f*) Relevant costs

We will discuss each of the cost categories in this chapter.

2.3 COSTS BY MANAGEMENT FUNCTION

In a manufacturing firm, costs are divided into two major categories, by the functional activities they are associated with: (1) manufacturing costs and (2) nonmanufacturing costs, also called *operating expenses*.

MANUFACTURING COSTS

Manufacturing costs are those costs associated with the manufacturing activities of the company. Manufacturing costs are subdivided into three categories: direct materials, direct labor, and factory overhead.

Direct materials are all materials that become an integral part of the finished product. Examples are the steel used to make an automobile and the wood to make furniture. Glues, nails, and other minor items are called *indirect materials* (or supplies) and are classified as part of factory overhead, which is explained later.

Direct labor is the labor that is involved directly in making the product. Examples of direct labor costs are the wages of assembly workers on an assembly line and the wages of machine tool operators in a machine shop. *Indirect labor*, such as wages of supervisory personnel and janitors, is classified as part of factory overhead.

Factory overhead can be defined as including all costs of manufacturing except direct materials and direct labor. Some of the many examples include depreciation, rent, taxes, insurance, fringe benefits, payroll taxes, and cost of idle time. Factory overhead is also called *manufacturing overhead*, *indirect manufacturing expenses*, and *factory burden*.

Many costs overlap within their categories. For example, direct materials and direct labor when combined are called *prime costs*. Direct labor and factory overhead are combined into *conversion costs* (or processing costs).

One important category of factory overhead is *quality costs*. Quality costs are costs that occur because poor quality may exist or actually does exist. These costs are significant in amount, often totaling 20 to 25 percent of sales. The subcategories of quality costs are prevention, appraisal, and failure costs. *Prevention costs* are costs incurred to prevent defects. Amounts spent on quality training programs, researching customer needs, quality circles, and improved production equipment are considered prevention costs. Expenditures made for prevention will minimize the costs that will be incurred for appraisal and failure. *Appraisal costs* are costs incurred for monitoring or inspection; these costs compensate for mistakes that are not eliminated through prevention. *Failure costs* may be internal (such as scrap and rework costs and reinspection) or external (such as product returns or recalls due to quality problems, warranty costs, and lost sales due to poor product performance).

NONMANUFACTURING COSTS

Nonmanufacturing costs (or operating expenses) are subdivided into selling expenses and general and administrative expenses.

Selling expenses are all the expenses associated with obtaining sales and the delivery of the product. Examples are advertising and sales commissions.

General and administrative expenses include all the expenses that are incurred in connection with performing general and administrative activities. Examples are executives' salaries and legal expenses.

Many other examples of costs by management function and their relationships are found in Fig. 2-1.

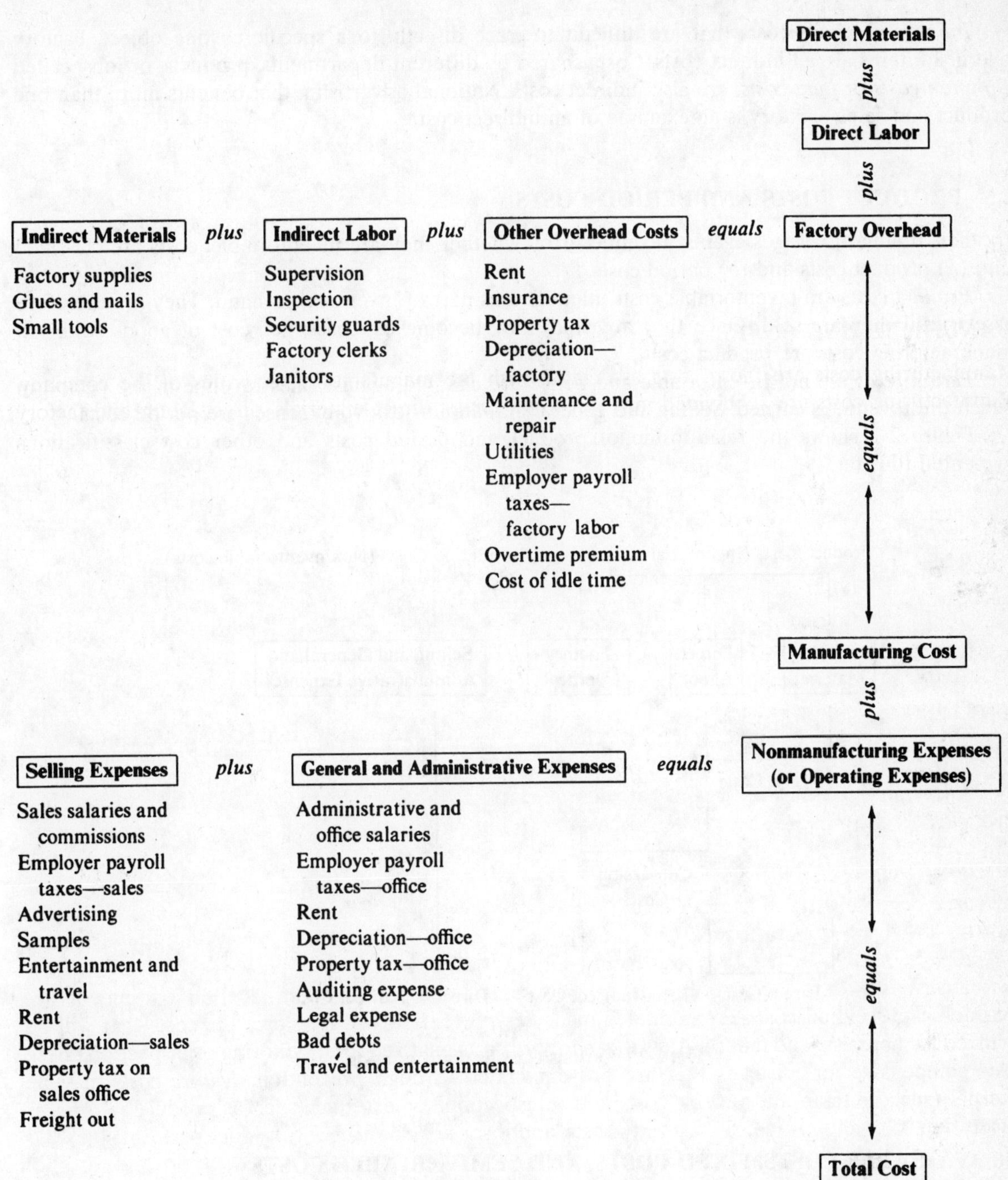

Fig. 2-1 Costs by management function.

2.4 DIRECT COSTS AND INDIRECT COSTS

Costs may be viewed as either *direct* or *indirect* in terms of the extent to which they are traceable to a particular object of costing, such as products, jobs, departments, or sales territories.

Direct costs are those costs that can be traced directly to the costing object. Examples are direct materials, direct labor, and advertising outlays made directly to a particular sales territory.

Indirect costs are costs that are difficult to trace directly to a specific costing object. Factory overhead items are all indirect costs. Costs shared by different departments, products, or jobs, called *common costs* or *joint costs*, are also indirect costs. National advertising that benefits more than one product and sales territory is an example of an indirect cost.

2.5 PRODUCT COSTS AND PERIOD COSTS

By their timing of charges against revenue or by whether they are inventoriable, costs are classified into (*a*) product costs and (*b*) period costs.

Product costs are inventoriable costs, identified as part of inventory on hand. They are therefore assets until they are sold. Once they are sold, they become expenses, i.e., cost of goods sold. All manufacturing costs are product costs.

Period costs are not inventoriable and hence are charged against sales revenue in the period in which the revenue is earned. Selling and general and administrative expenses are period costs.

Figure 2-2 shows the relationship of product and period costs and other cost classifications presented thus far.

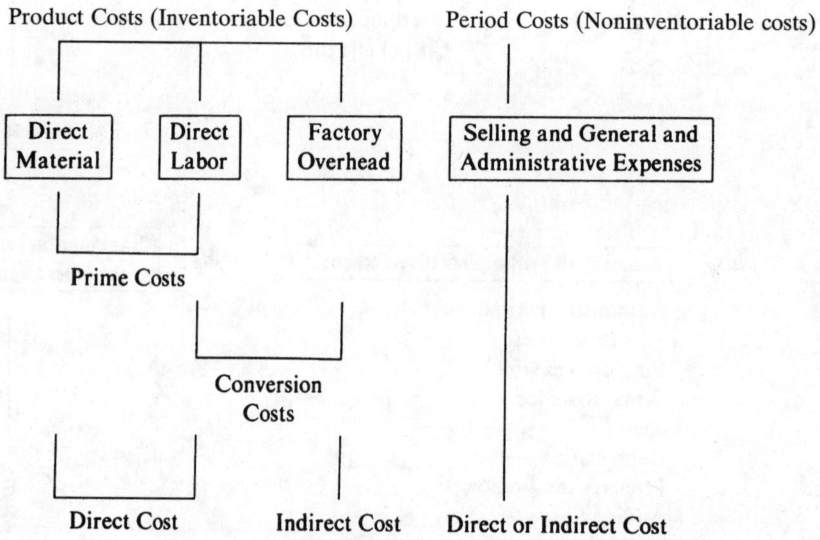

Fig. 2-2 Various classifications of costs.

2.6 VARIABLE COSTS, FIXED COSTS, AND SEMIVARIABLE COSTS

From a planning and control standpoint, perhaps the most important way to classify costs is by how they behave in accordance with changes in volume or some measure of activity. By behavior, costs can be classified into three basic categories.

Variable costs are costs that vary *in total* in direct proportion to changes in activity. Examples are direct materials and gasoline expense based on mileage driven.

Fixed costs are costs that remain constant *in total* regardless of changes in activity. Examples are rent, insurance, and taxes.

Semivariable (or mixed) costs are costs that vary with changes in volume but, unlike variable costs, do not vary in direct proportion. In other words, these costs contain both a variable component and a fixed component. Examples are the rental of a delivery truck, for which a fixed rental fee plus a variable charge based on mileage is made; and power costs, for which the expense consists of a fixed amount plus a variable charge based on consumption.

The breakdown of costs into variable and fixed components is very important in many areas of management accounting, such as flexible budgeting, break-even analysis, and short-term decision making.

2.7 COSTS FOR PLANNING, CONTROL, AND DECISION MAKING

CONTROLLABLE AND NONCONTROLLABLE COSTS

A cost is said to be *controllable* when the amount of the cost is assigned to the head of a department and the level of the cost is significantly under the manager's influence. *Noncontrollable* costs are those costs that are not subject to influence at a given level of managerial supervision.

EXAMPLE 2.1 All variable costs, such as direct materials, direct labor, and variable overhead, are usually considered controllable by the department head. Further, a certain portion of fixed costs may also be controllable. For example, depreciation on equipment used specifically for a given department is an expense that is controllable by the head of the department.

STANDARD COSTS

The standard cost is a production or operating cost that is carefully predetermined. It is a target cost that should be achieved. The standard cost is compared with the actual cost in order to measure the performance of a given costing department.

EXAMPLE 2.2 The standard cost of material (per pound) is obtained by multiplying standard price per pound by standard quantity per unit of output (in pounds).

Purchase price	$ 3.00
Freight	0.12
Receiving and handling	0.02
Less: Purchase discount	(0.04)
Standard price per pound	$ 3.10

Per bill of materials in pounds	1.2
Allowance for waste and spoilage in pounds	0.1
Allowance for rejects in pounds	0.1
Standard quantity per unit of output	1.4 pounds

The standard cost of material is 1.4 pounds × $3.10 = $4.34 per unit.

INCREMENTAL (OR DIFFERENTIAL) COSTS

The incremental cost is the difference in costs between two or more alternatives.

EXAMPLE 2.3 Consider the two alternatives *A* and *B*, whose costs are as follows:

	A	*B*	Incremental Costs ($B - A$)
Direct materials	$10,000	$10,000	$ 0
Direct labor	10,000	15,000	5,000

The incremental costs are simply $B - A$ (or $A - B$), as shown in the last column.

SUNK COSTS

Sunk costs are the costs of resources that have already been incurred whose total will not be affected by any decision made now or in the future. They represent past or historical costs.

EXAMPLE 2.4 Suppose you acquired an asset for $50,000 three years ago which is now listed at a book value of $20,000. The $20,000 book value is a sunk cost which does not affect a future decision.

OPPORTUNITY COSTS

An opportunity cost is the net revenue forgone by rejecting an alternative.

EXAMPLE 2.5 Suppose a company has a choice of using its capacity to produce an extra 10,000 units or renting it out for $20,000. The opportunity cost of using the capacity is $20,000.

RELEVANT COSTS

Relevant costs are expected future costs that will differ between alternatives.

EXAMPLE 2.6 The incremental cost is said to be relevant to the future decision. The sunk cost is considered irrelevant.

2.8 INCOME STATEMENTS AND BALANCE SHEETS—MANUFACTURER'S VS. MERCHANDISER'S

Figure 2-3 compares the income statement of a merchandiser to that of a manufacturer. The important characteristic of the income statement for a manufacturer is that it is supported by a schedule of cost of goods manufactured (see Fig. 2-4). This schedule shows the specific costs (i.e., direct materials, direct labor, and factory overhead) that have gone into the goods completed during the period. Since the manufacturer carried three types of inventory (direct materials, work-in-process, and finished goods), all three items must be incorporated into the computation of the cost of goods sold. These inventory accounts also appear on the balance sheet for a manufacturer (see Fig. 2-5).

Income Statements
Manufacturer's vs. Merchandiser's

Manufacturer's		*Merchandiser's*	
For the Year Ended December 31, 19X1		For the Year Ended December 31, 19X1	
Sales	$320,000	Sales	$1,125,000
Less: Cost of Goods Sold		Less: Cost of Goods Sold	
Finished Goods, Dec. 31, 19X0	$ 18,000	Merchandise Inventory,	
Cost of Goods Manufactured		Dec. 31, 19X0	$ 68,000
(see Schedule, Fig. 2-4)	121,000	Purchases	925,000
Cost of Goods Available for Sale	$139,000	Cost of Goods Available for Sale	$ 993,000
Finished Goods, Dec. 31, 19X1	21,000	Merchandise Inventory, Dec. 31, 19X1	63,000
Cost of Goods Sold	$118,000	Cost of Goods Sold	$ 930,000
Gross Margin (or Gross Profit)	$202,000	Gross Margin (or Gross Profit)	$ 195,000
Less: Selling and Administrative		Less: Selling and Administrative	
Expenses (detailed)	60,000	Expenses (detailed)	54,000
Net Income	$142,000	Net Income	$ 141,000

Fig. 2-3

Manufacturer's
Schedule of Cost of Goods Manufactured

Direct Materials:		
Inventory, Dec. 31, 19X0	$23,000	
Purchases of Direct Materials	64,000	
Cost of Direct Materials Available for Use	$87,000	
Inventory, Dec. 31, 19X1	7,800	
Direct Materials Used		$ 79,200
Direct Labor		25,000
Factory Overhead:		
Indirect Labor	$ 3,000	
Indirect Materials	2,000	
Utilities	500	
Depreciation—Plant, Building, and Equipment	800	
Rent	2,000	
Miscellaneous	1,500	9,800
Total Manufacturing Costs Incurred During 19X1		$114,000
Add: Work-in-Process Inventory, Dec. 31, 19X0		9,000
Manufacturing Costs to Account for		$123,000
Less: Work-in-Process Inventory, Dec. 31, 19X1		2,000
Cost of Goods Manufactured (to income statement)		$121,000

Fig. 2-4

Current Asset Section of Balance Sheets
Manufacturer's vs. Merchandiser's

Manufacturer's

Current Assets:		
Cash		$ 25,000
Accounts Receivable		78,000
Inventories:		
Raw Materials	$ 7,800	
Work-in-Process	2,000	
Finished Goods	21,000	30,800
Total		$133,800

Merchandiser's

Current Assets:	
Cash	$ 20,000
Accounts Receivable	90,000
Merchandise Inventory	63,000
Total	$173,000

Fig. 2-5

Summary

(1) Historical costs that cannot be recovered by any decision made now or in the future are called ____________.

(2) Factory overhead costs are all manufacturing costs incurred in the factory except for ____________ and ____________.

(3) The sum of direct labor and factory overhead is termed ____________.

(4) Product costs are ____________ costs, that is, they are ____________ until they are sold; whereas period costs are matched immediately against the ____________ in the period in which it is earned.

(5) Variable costs change ____________ in direct proportion to changes in output.

(6) The net revenue forgone as a result of the rejection of an alternative is called an ____________.

(7) Three inventory accounts are commonly used in manufacturing firms. They are raw materials, ____________, and finished goods.

(8) The terms *cost of goods manufactured* and *total manufacturing costs* are used interchangeably: (*a*) true; (*b*) false.

(9) Prime cost includes direct materials, direct labor, and a fair share of factory overhead: (*a*) true; (*b*) false.

(10) The beginning finished goods inventory plus the ____________, minus the ending finished goods inventory equals the cost of goods sold for a manufacturer.

(11) The cost of direct materials used is the ____________ plus ____________ minus the ending inventory of direct materials.

(12) A variable cost is ____________ per unit.

(13) The incremental cost is the ____________ between two or more alternatives.

(14) Payroll fringe benefits are generally classified as ____________.

(15) The ____________ is a production or operating cost that is carefully predetermined. It is compared with the actual cost in order to measure the ____________ of a given costing department.

(16) Selling and administrative expenses are period expenses: (*a*) true; (*b*) false.

Answers: (1) sunk costs; (2) direct materials, direct labor; (3) conversion cost; (4) inventoriable, assets, revenue; (5) in total; (6) opportunity cost; (7) work-in-process; (8) (*b*); (9) (*b*); (10) cost of goods manufactured; (11) beginning inventory of direct materials, purchases; (12) constant; (13) difference; (14) factory overhead; (15) standard cost, performance; (16) (*a*).

Solved Problems

2.1 Classify the following costs as direct (D) or indirect (ID) costs.

(*a*) The foreman's salary
(*b*) Supplies
(*c*) Depreciation of factory equipment
(*d*) Leather used in the manufacture of shoes
(*e*) Lubricants for machines
(*f*) Fringe benefits
(*g*) Wood in making furniture
(*h*) Glue in tube making
(*i*) FICA tax
(*j*) Janitorial supplies

SOLUTION

(*a*) ID; (*b*) ID; (*c*) ID; (*d*) D; (*e*) ID; (*f*) ID; (*g*) D; (*h*) ID; (*i*) ID; (*j*) ID.

2.2 Classify the following costs as variable (V), fixed (F), or semivariable (S) in terms of their behavior with respect to volume or level of activity.

(*a*) Property taxes
(*b*) Maintenance and repair
(*c*) Utilities
(*d*) Sales agent's salary
(*e*) Direct materials
(*f*) Insurance
(*g*) Depreciation by straight-line
(*h*) Sales agent's commission
(*i*) Depreciation by mileage—automobile
(*j*) Rent

SOLUTION

(*a*) F; (*b*) S; (*c*) S; (*d*) F; (*e*) V; (*f*) F; (*g*) F; (*h*) V; (*i*) V; (*j*) F.

2.3 Classify the following costs as either manufacturing (M), selling (S), or administrative (A) expenses in terms of their functions.

(*a*) Factory supplies
(*b*) Advertising
(*c*) Auditing expenses
(*d*) Rent on general office building
(*e*) Legal expenses
(*f*) Cost of idle time
(*g*) Entertainment and travel
(*h*) Freight-out
(*i*) Bad debts
(*j*) Freight-in
(*k*) Employer's payroll taxes—factory
(*l*) Employer's payroll taxes—sales office
(*m*) President's salary
(*n*) Samples
(*o*) Small tools
(*p*) Sanding materials used in furniture making
(*q*) Cost of machine breakdown

SOLUTION

(*a*) M; (*b*) S; (*c*) A; (*d*) A; (*e*) A; (*f*) M; (*g*) S or A; (*h*) S; (*i*) A; (*j*) M; (*k*) M; (*l*) S; (*m*) A; (*n*) S; (*o*) M; (*p*) M; (*q*) M.

2.4 Classify the following costs as product costs (PC) or period expenses (PE).

(*a*) Pears in a fruit cocktail
(*b*) Overtime premium
(*c*) Legal fees
(*d*) Insurance on office equipment
(*e*) Advertising expenses
(*f*) Fringe benefits—general office
(*g*) Workers' compensation
(*h*) Social Security taxes—direct labor
(*i*) Travel expenses
(*j*) Rework on defective products

SOLUTION

(*a*) PC; (*b*) PC; (*c*) PE; (*d*) PE; (*e*) PE; (*f*) PE; (*g*) PC; (*h*) PC; (*i*) PE; (*j*) PC.

2.5 Ron Weber is considering replacing an old machine, which he purchased for $15,000 three years ago, with some labor-saving equipment. The old machine is being depreciated at $1,500 a year. The following alternative equipment options are available *for consideration.*

Machine A. The purchase price of machine A is $25,000, and yearly cash operating costs are $5,000.

Machine B. The purchase price of machine B is $28,000, and yearly cash operating costs are $4,500.

(*a*) What are the incremental costs, if any, in this alternative-choice situation?
(*b*) What are the sunk costs, if any, in this situation?

SOLUTION

(*a*) The following schedule will identify the incremental costs in this decision problem.

	Machine A	Machine B	Incremental Costs ($B - A$)
Purchase price	$25,000	$28,000	$3,000
Cash operating costs	5,000	4,500	(500)
Depreciation of old equipment	1,500	1,500	—

The incremental costs are purchase price ($3,000) and cash operating costs ($500).

(*b*) The depreciation on old equipment, $1,500 (or the total purchase price of $15,000), is a sunk cost because it represents an investment outlay made in the past.

2.6 John Jay is a full-time student at a local university. He wants to decide whether he should attend a four-week summer school session, where tuition is $250, or take a break and work full time at a local delicatessen, where he could make as much as $150 a week. How much would going to the summer school cost him from a decision-making standpoint? What is the opportunity cost?

SOLUTION

The total cost of going to summer school would be $850, that is, $250 tuition plus $600 which he would give up by attending the school. The opportunity cost would be $600, since this is the amount he gives up by rejecting the alternative of working full time.

2.7 Which of the following costs are likely to be *fully* controllable, *partially* controllable, or *not* controllable by the chief of the production department?

(*a*) Wages paid to direct labor
(*b*) Rent on factory building
(*c*) Chief's salary
(*d*) Utilities
(*e*) Direct materials used
(*f*) Supplies
(*g*) Insurance on factory equipment
(*h*) Advertising
(*i*) Price paid for materials and supplies
(*j*) Idle time due to machine breakdown

SOLUTION

(*a*) fully; (*b*) not; (*c*) not; (*d*) partially; (*e*) fully; (*f*) partially; (*g*) not; (*h*) not; (*i*) not; (*j*) partially.

2.8 The Ellis Machine Tool Company is considering production for a special order for 10,000 pieces at $0.65 apiece, which is below the regular price. The current operating level, which is below full capacity of 70,000 pieces, shows the operating results as contained in the following report.

The regular production during the year was 50,000 pieces.

Sales @ $1			$50,000
Direct materials		$20,000	
Direct labor		10,000	
Factory overhead:			
Supervision	$3,500		
Depreciation	1,500		
Insurance	100		
Rental	400	5,500	35,500
			$14,500

Factory overhead costs will continue regardless of the decision.

(*a*) What are the incremental costs, if any, in this decision problem? Prepare a schedule showing the incremental cost.

(*b*) Which costs, if any, represent sunk costs?

(*c*) What would be the opportunity cost, if any, associated with the special order?

SOLUTION

(*a*)

	Cost per Unit	*A* w/o Special Order (50,000 pieces)	*B* with Special Order (60,000 pieces)	Incremental Costs ($B-A$)
Price	$1.00	$50,000	$56,500	$6,500
Direct materials	0.40	20,000	24,000	4,000
Direct labor	0.20	10,000	12,000	2,000
Factory overhead:				
Supervision	0.07	3,500	3,500	—
Depreciation	0.03	1,500	1,500	—
Insurance	0.002	100	100	—
Rental	0.008	400	400	—
Income		$14,500	$15,000	$ 500

Direct materials and direct labor are incremental costs.

(*b*) The depreciation expense is a sunk cost.

(*c*) The opportunity cost is $500, since by rejecting the special order, the company would give up an opportunity of making $500 more with this special order.

2.9 Some selected sales and cost data for job order 515 are given below.

Direct materials used	$100,000
Direct labor	150,000
Factory overhead (all indirect, 40% variable)	75,000
Selling and administrative expenses (50% direct, 60% variable)	120,000

Compute the following: (*a*) prime cost, (*b*) conversion cost, (*c*) direct cost, (*d*) indirect cost, (*e*) product cost, (*f*) period expense, (*g*) variable cost, and (*h*) fixed cost.

SOLUTION

(*a*) Prime cost = Direct materials used + Direct labor
= \$100,000 + \$150,000 = \$250,000

(*b*) Conversion cost = Direct labor + Factory overhead
= \$150,000 + \$75,000 = \$225,000

(*c*) Direct cost = Direct materials used + Direct labor
+ 50% of selling and administrative expenses
= \$100,000 + \$150,000 + \$60,000 = \$310,000

(*d*) Indirect cost = 100% of factory overhead + 50% of selling and administrative expenses
= \$75,000 + \$60,000 = \$135,000

(*e*) Product costs = Direct materials used + Direct labor + Factory overhead
= \$100,000 + \$150,000 + \$75,000 = \$325,000

(*f*) Period expenses = Selling and administrative expenses = \$120,000

(*g*) Variable cost = Direct materials used + Direct labor + 40% of factory overhead
+ 60% of selling and administrative expenses
= \$100,000 + \$150,000 + \$30,000 + \$72,000 = \$352,000

(*h*) Fixed cost = 60% of factory overhead + 40% of selling and administrative expenses
= \$45,000 + \$48,000 = \$93,000

2.10 Selected data concerning the past fiscal year's operations (000 omitted) of the Televans Manufacturing Company are presented below.

	Inventories	
	Beginning	Ending
Direct materials	\$75	\$ 85
Work-in-process	80	30
Finished goods	90	110
Other data:		
Direct materials used		326
Total manufacturing costs charged to production during the year (includes direct materials, direct labor, and factory overhead applied at a rate of 60% of direct labor cost)		686
Cost of goods available for sale		826
Selling and general expenses		25

1. The cost of direct materials purchased during the year amounted to
   (*a*) \$411 (*d*) \$336
   (*b*) \$360 (*e*) Some amount other than those shown above
   (*c*) \$316
2. Direct labor costs charged to production during the year amounted to
   (*a*) \$135 (*d*) \$216
   (*b*) \$225 (*e*) Some amount other than those shown above
   (*c*) \$360
3. The cost of goods manufactured during the year was
   (*a*) \$636 (*d*) \$716
   (*b*) \$766 (*e*) Some amount other than those shown above
   (*c*) \$736

4. The cost of goods sold during the year was
   (*a*) \$736 (*d*) \$805
   (*b*) \$716 (*e*) Some amount other than those shown above
   (*c*) \$691 (CMA, adapted)

SOLUTION

1. (*d*) Direct materials used = Beginning inventory + Purchases − Ending inventory

$$\$326 = \$75 + x - \$85$$
$$x = \$336$$

2. (*b*) Total manufacturing costs charged = Direct materials used + Direct labor + Factory overhead (60% of direct labor cost)

$$\$686 = \$326 + x + 0.6x$$
$$x = \$225$$

3. (*c*) Cost of goods manufactured = Beginning work-in-process + Total manufacturing costs − Ending work-in-process

$$= \$80 + \$686 - \$30 = \$736$$

4. (*b*) Cost of goods sold = Cost of goods available for sale − Ending finished goods inventory

$$= \$826 - \$110 = \$716$$

2.11 A manufacturing company shows the following amounts in the income statement for 19B:

Materials Used	\$590,000
Cost of Goods Sold	750,000
Cost of Goods Manufactured	800,000
Total Manufacturing Costs	790,000

1. Determine the amounts of (*a*) and (*b*) in the balance sheets of 12/31/19A and 12/31/19B.

	Inventories	
	12/31/19A	12/31/19B
Materials	\$100,000	\$150,000
Work-in-process	(*a*)	87,000
Finished goods	80,000	(*b*)

2. Compute the amount of materials purchased in 19B.

SOLUTION

1. (*a*) Cost of goods manufactured = Beginning work-in-process inventory + Total manufacturing costs − Ending work-in-process inventory

$$\$800,000 = x + \$790,000 + \$87,000$$
$$x = \$97,000$$

(*b*) Cost of goods sold = Cost of goods manufactured + Beginning finished goods inventory − Ending finished goods inventory

$$\$750,000 = \$800,000 + \$80,000 - x$$
$$x = \$130,000$$

2. Materials used = Beginning materials inventory + Purchases − Ending materials inventory

$$\$590,000 = \$100,000 + x - \$150,000$$
$$x = \$640,000$$

2.12 For each of the following cases, find the missing data. Each case is independent of the others.

	Case 1	Case 2	Case 3
Beginning direct materials	$ 5,000	$ 3,000	$ 3,000
Purchases of direct materials	17,000	45,000	10,000
Ending direct materials	(*a*)	7,000	(*m*)
Direct materials used	(*b*)	(*f*)	6,000
Direct labor	16,000	(*g*)	4,000
Factory overhead	3,000	20,000	6,000
Total manufacturing costs	(*c*)	85,000	(*n*)
Beginning work-in-process	6,000	6,000	5,000
Ending work-in-process	6,000	4,000	(*o*)
Cost of goods manufactured	23,000	(*h*)	10,000

	Case 1	Case 2	Case 3
Sales	52,000	125,000	23,000
Beginning finished goods	8,000	7,000	7,000
Cost of goods manufactured	23,000	(*i*)	10,000
Ending finished goods	(*d*)	(*j*)	6,000
Cost of goods sold	27,000	(*k*)	(*p*)
Gross profit	(*e*)	60,000	(*q*)
Selling and administrative expenses	5,000	8,500	4,000
Net income	20,000	(*l*)	8,000

SOLUTION

(*a*) $18,000; (*b*) $4,000; (*c*) $23,000; (*d*) $4,000; (*e*) $25,000; (*f*) $41,000; (*g*) $24,000; (*h*) $87,000; (*i*) $87,000; (*j*) $29,000; (*k*) $65,000; (*l*) $51,500; (*m*) $7,000; (*n*) $16,000; (*o*) $11,000; (*p*) $11,000; (*q*) $12,000.

The answers above are computed as

CASE 1

Cost of goods manufactured	$23,000	
− Beginning work-in-process	6,000	
+ Ending work-in-process	6,000	
Total manufacturing costs	$23,000	(*c*)
Total manufacturing costs	$23,000	
− Direct labor	16,000	
− Factory overhead	3,000	
Direct materials used	$ 4,000	(*b*)
Beginning direct materials	$ 5,000	
+ Purchase of direct materials	17,000	
− Direct materials used	4,000	
Ending direct materials	$18,000	(*a*)
Beginning finished goods	$ 8,000	
+ Cost of goods manufactured	23,000	
− Cost of goods sold	27,000	
Ending finished goods	$ 4,000	(*d*)
Sales	$52,000	
− Cost of goods sold	27,000	
Gross profit	$25,000	(*e*)

CASE 2

Beginning direct materials	$ 3,000	
+ Purchase of direct materials	45,000	
− Ending direct materials	7,000	
Direct materials used	$ 41,000	(*f*)
Total manufacturing costs	$ 85,000	
− Direct materials used	41,000	
− Factory overhead	20,000	
Direct labor	$ 24,000	(*g*)
Total manufacturing costs	$ 85,000	
+ Beginning work-in-process	6,000	
− Ending work-in-process	4,000	
Cost of goods manufactured	$ 87,000	(*h*) = (*i*)
Sales	$125,000	
− Gross profit	60,000	
Cost of goods sold	$ 65,000	(*k*)
Beginning finished goods	$ 7,000	
+ Cost of goods manufactured	87,000	
− Cost of goods sold	65,000	
Ending finished goods	$ 29,000	(*j*)
Gross profit	$ 60,000	
− Selling and administrative expenses	8,500	
Net income	$ 51,500	(*l*)

CASE 3

Beginning direct materials	$ 3,000	
+ Purchases of direct materials	10,000	
− Direct materials used	6,000	
Ending direct materials	$ 7,000	(*m*)
Direct materials used	$ 6,000	
+ Direct labor	4,000	
+ Factory overhead	6,000	
Total manufacturing costs	$16,000	(*n*)
Total manufacturing costs	$16,000	
+ Beginning work-in-process	5,000	
− Cost of goods manufactured	10,000	
Ending work-in-process	$11,000	(*o*)
Beginning finished goods	$ 7,000	
+ Cost of goods manufactured	10,000	
− Ending finished goods	6,000	
Cost of goods sold	$11,000	(*p*)
Sales	$23,000	
− Cost of goods sold	11,000	
Gross profit	$12,000	(*q*)

2.13 For each of the following cases, find the missing data. Each case is independent of the others.

	Case 1	Case 2	Case 3
Sales	$15,000	$35,000	(*g*)
Direct materials used	5,000	2,000	$ 3,700
Gross profit	6,000	27,000	10,000
Accounts payable, beginning	5,300	4,000	2,300
Accounts payable, ending	4,200	5,000	2,600
Beginning finished goods	1,500	4,000	8,000
Ending finished goods	2,000	(*d*)	6,000
Cost of goods sold	(*a*)	8,000	30,000
Total manufacturing costs	(*b*)	10,000	33,700
Direct labor	2,500	(*e*)	9,000
Factory overhead	2,000	3,500	21,000
Accounts receivable, beginning	6,200	5,000	4,200
Accounts receivable, ending	7,100	6,000	4,300
Beginning work-in-process	5,000	5,000	(*h*)
Ending work-in-process	4,000	(*f*)	6,700
Purchase of direct materials	6,000	2,500	500
Cost of goods manufactured	(*c*)	12,000	28,000

SOLUTION

(*a*) $9,000; (*b*) $9,500; (*c*) $10,500; (*d*) $8,000; (*e*) $4,500; (*f*) $3,000; (*g*) $40,000; (*h*) $1,000.

Supporting computations are

CASE 1

	Sales	$15,000	
−	Gross profit	6,000	
	Cost of goods sold	$ 9,000	(*a*)
	Direct materials used	$ 5,000	
+	Direct labor	2,500	
+	Factory overhead	2,000	
	Total manufacturing costs	$ 9,500	(*b*)
	Total manufacturing costs	$ 9,500	
+	Beginning work-in-process	5,000	
−	Ending work-in-process	4,000	
	Cost of goods manufactured	$10,500	(*c*)

CASE 2

	Beginning finished goods	$ 4,000	
+	Cost of goods manufactured	12,000	
−	Cost of goods sold	8,000	
	Ending finished goods	$ 8,000	(*d*)
	Total manufacturing costs	$10,000	
−	Direct materials used	2,000	
−	Factory overhead	3,500	
	Direct labor	$ 4,500	(*e*)
	Total manufacturing costs	$10,000	
+	Beginning work-in-process	5,000	
−	Cost of goods manufactured	12,000	
	Ending work-in-process	$ 3,000	(*f*)

CASE 3

Gross profit	$10,000	
+ Cost of goods sold	30,000	
Sales	$40,000	(*g*)
Cost of goods manufactured	$28,000	
+ Ending work-in-process	6,700	
− Total manufacturing costs	33,700	
Beginning work-in-process	$ 1,000	(*h*)

2.14 Jung Stores, Inc., shows the following accounting records for 19X2:

Sales commissions	$ 15,000
Beginning merchandise inventory	16,000
Ending merchandise inventory	9,000
Sales	185,000
Advertising	10,000
Purchases of merchandise	85,000
Employees' salaries	20,000
Other operating expenses	30,000

Prepare an income statement for 19X2.

SOLUTION

JUNG STORES INC.
Income Statement
For the Year Ended December 31, 19X2

Sales		$185,000
Less: Cost of Goods Sold		
Beginning Inventory	$ 16,000	
Purchases	85,000	
Cost of Goods Available for Sale	$101,000	
Ending Inventory	9,000	
Cost of Goods Sold		92,000
Gross Profit		$ 93,000
Less: Selling and Administrative Expenses		
Sales Commissions	$ 15,000	
Advertising	10,000	
Employees' Salaries	20,000	
Other Operating Expenses	30,000	75,000
Net Income		$ 18,000

2.15 In April, Steinhardt, Inc., sold 50 air conditioners for $200 each. Costs included material of $50 per unit, direct labor of $30 per unit, and factory overhead at 100 percent of direct labor cost. Effective May 1, material costs decreased 5 percent per unit and direct labor costs increased 20 percent per unit.

Assume that the expected May sales volume is 50 units, the same as for April.

(*a*) Calculate the sales price per unit that will produce the same ratio of gross profit, assuming no change in the rate of factory overhead in relation to direct labor costs.

(*b*) Calculate the sales price per unit that will produce the same ratio of gross profit, assuming that $10 of the April factory overhead consists of fixed costs and that the variable factory overhead ratio to direct costs is unchanged from April.

(AICPA, adapted)

SOLUTION

(*a*) and (*b*)

April gross profit:

Sales price		$200.00
Less: Cost of goods sold		
Materials	$50.00	
Labor	30.00	
Factory overhead	30.00	110.00
April gross profit		$ 90.00

The April gross profit of $90.00 is 45 percent of April sales. The cost of goods sold of $110 is 55 percent of April sales.

	Questions (*a*)	Questions (*b*)
Cost of goods sold:		
Materials (95% of $50.00)	$ 47.50	$ 47.50
Labor (120% of $30.00)	36.00	36.00
Factory overhead:		
(*a*) (100% of $36.00)	36.00	
(*b*) Fixed costs		10.00
Variable costs (⅔ of $36.00)*		24.00
Total cost (55% of sales price)	$119.50	$117.50
Sales price:		
(*a*) $119.50 ÷ 55%	$217.27	
(*b*) $117.50 ÷ 55%		$213.64
	$217.00	$214.00

*Variable overhead:
$ 30 total overhead
−10 fixed overhead
$ 20 variable overhead
$20 ÷ $30 or ⅔ of total labor is variable overhead = ⅔ × $36 = $24

2.16 The Shim Refrigerator Co. shows the following records for the period ended December 31, 19A:

Materials purchased	$ 550,000
Inventories, Jan. 1, 19A:	
Materials	$ 20,000
Work-in-process	$ 200,000
Finished goods	1,000 units
Direct labor	$1,050,000
Factory overhead (40% variable)	$ 750,000
Selling expenses (all fixed)	$ 500,750
General and administrative (all fixed)	$ 385,230
Sales (7,500 units at $535)	
Inventories, Dec. 31, 19A:	
Materials	$ 50,000
Work-in-process	$ 100,000
Finished goods	1,000 units

Assume that finished goods inventories are valued at the current unit manufacturing cost.

1. Prepare a schedule of cost of goods manufactured.
2. Find the number of units manufactured and unit manufacturing cost.
3. Prepare an income statement for the period.
4. Find the total variable and fixed costs.

SOLUTION

1.

SHIM REFRIGERATOR CO.

Schedule of Cost of Goods Manufactured
For the Year Ended December 31, 19A

Direct Materials Used:		
Beginning Inventory	$ 20,000	
Purchases	550,000	
Ending Inventory	(50,000)	$ 520,000
Direct Labor		1,050,000
Factory Overhead		750,000
Total Manufacturing Costs during 19A		$2,320,000
Add: Beginning Work-in-Process		200,000
Less: Ending Work-in-Process		100,000
Cost of Goods Manufactured		$2,420,000

2. Unit manufacturing cost = $2,420,000 ÷ 7,500 units manufactured = $322.67

3.

SHIM REFRIGERATOR CO.

Income Statement
For the Year Ended December 31, 19A

Sales		$4,012,500
Less: Cost of Goods Sold		
Beginning Finished Goods	$ 322,670	
Cost of Goods Manufactured	2,420,000	
Ending Finished Goods	(322,670)	2,420,000
Gross Profit		$1,592,500
Less: Selling and Administrative Expenses		
Selling Expenses		(500,750)
General and Administrative Expenses		(385,230)
Net Income		$ 706,520

4. Total fixed costs = 60% of factory overhead + Selling expenses (all fixed) + General and administrative expenses (all fixed)
= $450,000 + $500,750 + $385,230 = $1,335,980

Total variable costs = Direct materials used + Direct labor + 40% of factory overhead
= $520,000 + $1,050,000 + $300,000 = $1,870,000

2.17 The Montreal Manufacturing Company incurred the following costs for the month of June:

Materials used:	
Direct materials	$6,600
Indirect materials	1,200
Payroll costs incurred:	
Direct labor	6,000
Indirect labor	1,700
Salaries:	
Production	2,400
Administration	5,100
Sales	3,200
Other costs:	
Building rent (production uses one-half of the building space)	1,400
Rent for molding machine (*per month, plus $0.50 per unit produced)	400*
Royalty paid for the use of production patents (calculation based on units produced, $0.80 per unit)	
Indirect miscellaneous costs:	
Production	2,700
Sales and administration	1,800

The beginning work-in-process inventory was $6,000; the ending work-in-process inventory was $5,000. Assume that 1,000 units were produced during the month.

1. Prepare a statement of cost of goods manufactured for the month.
2. Compute the cost to manufacture one unit of product.

(CMA, adapted)

SOLUTION

1.

THE MONTREAL MANUFACTURING COMPANY

Statement of Cost of Goods Manufactured
For the Month of June

Direct Materials		$ 6,600
Direct Labor		6,000
Manufacturing Overhead:		
Indirect Materials	$1,200	
Indirect Labor	1,700	
Production Salaries	2,400	
Building Rent (50% × $1,400)	700	
Machine Rent [$400 + ($0.50 × 1,000 units)]	900	
Patent Royalty ($0.80 × 1,000 units)	800	
Other Overhead Costs	2,700	10,400
Total Manufacturing Costs		$23,000
Add: Beginning Work-in-Process		6,000
Total		$29,000
Less: Ending Work-in-Process		5,000
Cost of Goods Manufactured		$24,000

2. Manufacturing cost per unit: $24,000 ÷ 1,000 units = $24 per unit

2.18 Heaven Consumer Products, Inc., has the following sales and cost data for 19A:

Selling and administrative expenses	$ 25,000
Direct materials purchased	12,000
Direct labor	18,000
Sales	160,000
Direct materials inventory, beginning	3,000
Direct materials inventory, ending	2,000
Work-in-process, beginning	14,000
Work-in-process, ending	13,500
Factory depreciation	27,000
Indirect materials	4,000
Factory utilities	2,000
Indirect labor	5,500
Maintenance	2,000
Insurance	1,000
Finished goods inventory, beginning	6,000
Finished goods inventory, ending	4,000

1. Prepare a schedule of cost of goods manufactured for 19A.
2. Prepare an income statement for 19A.
3. Assume that the company manufactured 5,000 units during the year. What was the unit cost of direct materials? What was the unit cost of factory depreciation? (Assume that depreciation is computed by the straight-line method.)
4. Repeat the computation done in part 3 for 10,000 units of output. How would the total costs of direct materials and factory overhead be affected?
5. Comment on the results you obtained in parts 3 and 4 in terms of how they affect the possible sales price.

SOLUTION

1.

HEAVEN CONSUMER PRODUCTS, INC.

Schedule of Cost of Goods Manufactured
For the Year ended December 31, 19A

Direct Materials:		
Beginning Materials Inventory	$ 3,000	
Add: Purchases	12,000	
Cost of Materials Available for Use	$15,000	
Less: Ending Materials Inventory	2,000	
Direct Materials Used		$13,000
Direct Labor		18,000
Factory Overhead:		
Factory Depreciation	$27,000	
Indirect Materials	4,000	
Factory Utilities	2,000	
Indirect Labor	5,500	
Maintenance	2,000	
Insurance	1,000	41,500
Total Manufacturing Costs		$72,500
Add: Beginning Work-in-Process		14,000
Less: Ending Work-in-Process		13,500
Cost of Goods Manufactured		$73,000

2. **HEAVEN CONSUMER PRODUCTS, INC.**

Income Statement
For the Year Ended December 31, 19A

Sales		$160,000
Less: Cost of Goods Sold		
Beginning Finished Goods Inventory	$ 6,000	
Add: Cost of Goods Manufactured	73,000	
Cost of Goods Available for Sale	$79,000	
Less: Ending Finished Goods Inventory	4,000	
Cost of Goods Sold		75,000
Gross Profit		$ 85,000
Less: Selling and Administrative Expenses		25,000
Net Income		$ 60,000

3. Unit cost of materials = $13,000 ÷ 5,000 units = $2.60 per unit
Unit cost of depreciation = $27,000 ÷ 5,000 units = $5.40 per unit

4. The unit cost of materials would stay the same at $2.60 per unit. The unit cost of depreciation would be $27,000 ÷ 10,000 units = $2.70 per unit. Total material costs would go up by 100 percent to $26,000, whereas total factory depreciation would be unchanged at $27,000.

5. Changes in volume will affect *total* variable costs but not *total* fixed costs. Unit variable and fixed costs differ, however. No matter what the volume, the *unit* variable cost would be constant, whereas the *unit* fixed cost such as factory depreciation would be changed. The sales price, however, would be affected by the change in unit fixed cost, which is caused by the change in volume or level of activity.

Determination of Cost Behavior Patterns

3.1 ANALYSIS OF COST BEHAVIOR

Not all costs behave in the same way. Certain costs, such as labor hours and machine hours, vary in proportion to changes in volume or activity. Other costs do not change regardless of the volume. An understanding of costs by behavior is very useful:

1. For break-even and cost–volume–profit analysis
2. To make short-term special decisions such as the make-or-buy decision and the acceptance or rejection of a special order
3. For appraisal of managerial performance by means of the contribution approach
4. For flexible budgeting

3.2 A FURTHER LOOK AT COSTS BY BEHAVIOR

As noted in Chapter 2, costs are classified in terms of their behavior into three basic categories: variable costs, fixed costs, and semivariable costs. The classification is made with a specified range of activity, called a *relevant range*. The relevant range is the range over which volume is expected to fluctuate during the period of time being considered.

VARIABLE COSTS

Variable costs are those costs that vary *in total* with change in volume or level of activity. Examples of variable costs include the costs of direct materials, direct labor, sales commissions, and gasoline expenses. The following factory overhead items fall into the variable-costs category:

Variable Factory Overhead	
Supplies	Receiving costs
Fuel and power	Overtime premium
Spoilage and defective work	

FIXED COSTS

Fixed costs are costs that do not change *in total* regardless of the volume or level of activity. Examples include rent, property taxes, insurance, and, in the case of automobiles, license fees and annual insurance premiums. The following factory overhead items fall into the fixed-costs category:

Fixed Factory Overhead	
Salaries of production supervisors	Rent on warehouse and factory building
Depreciation (by straight-line)	Salaries of indirect labor
Property taxes	Property insurance
Patent amortization	

SEMIVARIABLE (OR MIXED) COSTS

Semivariable costs are costs that contain both a fixed element and a variable element. Salespersons' compensation including salary and commission is an example. The following factory overhead items may be considered semivariable costs:

Semivariable Factory Overhead	
Supervision	Maintenance and repairs
Inspection	Compensation insurance
Service department costs	Employer's payroll taxes
Rental of delivery truck	Utilities
Fringe benefits	

Note that factory overhead, taken as a whole, is an example of a semivariable cost.

Figure 3-1 displays how each of these three types of costs varies with changes in volume or level of activity.

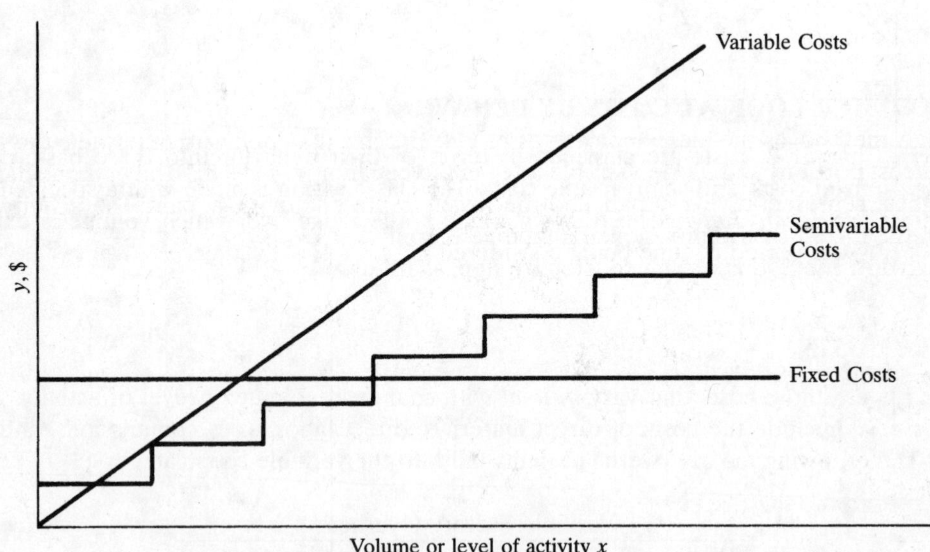

Fig. 3-1 Cost behavior patterns.

3.3 TYPES OF FIXED COSTS—COMMITTED OR DISCRETIONARY

Strictly speaking, there is no such thing as a fixed cost. In the long run, all costs are variable. In the short run, however, some fixed costs, called *discretionary* (or *managed* or *programmed*) fixed costs, change because of managerial decisions or changes in volume. Examples of this type of fixed costs are advertising outlays, training costs, and research and development costs. Another type of fixed costs, called *committed* fixed costs, are those costs that are the results of commitments made previously. Fixed costs such as rent, depreciation, insurance, and executive salaries are committed fixed costs, since management has committed itself for a long period of time regarding the company's production facilities and labor requirements.

3.4 ANALYSIS OF SEMIVARIABLE COSTS (OR MIXED COSTS)

For purposes of various types of cost analyses, semivariable costs (or mixed costs) must be broken down into their fixed and variable elements. Since semivariable costs contain both fixed and variable components, the analysis takes the following mathematical form, which is called a *cost–volume* formula:

$$y = a + bx$$

where y = the semivariable cost to be broken up

x = any given measure of activity, such as production volume, sales volume, or direct labor hours

a = the fixed cost component

b = the variable rate per unit of x

Several methods are available to separate a semivariable expense into its variable and fixed components, including

1. The high–low method
2. The scattergraph method
3. The method of least squares (regression analysis)

3.5 THE HIGH–LOW METHOD

The high–low method, as the name indicates, uses two extreme data points to determine the values of a (the fixed cost portion) and b (the variable rate) in the equation $y = a + bx$. The extreme data points are the highest representative x–y pair and the lowest representative x–y pair. The activity level x, rather than the mixed cost item y, governs their selection.

The high–low method is explained, step by step, as follows.

Step 1 Select the highest pair and the lowest pair.

Step 2 Compute the variable rate, b, using the formula

$$\text{Variable rate} = \frac{\text{Difference in cost } y}{\text{Difference in activity } x}$$

Step 3 Compute the fixed cost portion as

$$\text{Fixed cost portion} = \text{Total semivariable cost} - \text{Variable cost}$$

EXAMPLE 3.1 Flexible Manufacturing Company decides to relate total factory overhead costs to direct labor hours (DLH) to develop a cost–volume formula in the form of $y = a + bx$. Twelve monthly observations are collected. They are given in Table 3-1.

Table 3-1

Month	Direct Labor Hours x (000 omitted)	Factory Overhead y (000 omitted)
January	9 hours	$ 15
February	19	20
March	11	14
April	14	16
May	23	25
June	12	20
July	12	20
August	22	23
September	7	14
October	13	22
November	15	18
December	17	18
Total	174 hours	$225

The high–low points selected from the monthly observations are

	x	y	
High	23 hours	$25	(May pair)
Low	7	14	(September pair)
Difference	16 hours	$11	

Thus,

$$\text{Variable rate } b = \frac{\text{Difference in } y}{\text{Difference in } x} = \frac{\$11}{16 \text{ hours}} = \$0.6875 \text{ per DLH}$$

The fixed cost portion is computed as

	High	Low
Factory overhead (y)	$25	$14
Variable expense ($0.6875/DLH)	(15.8125)	(4.8125)
	$ 9.1875	$ 9.1875

Therefore, the cost–volume formula for factory overhead is $9.1875 fixed, plus $0.6875 per DLH. Or, alternatively,

$$y' = \$9.1875 + \$0.6875x$$

where y' = estimated factory overhead
x = DLH

Note that the reason for using a new symbol y' (read as *y-prime*) is that the cost–volume formula just obtained gives an *estimated* value of y.

The high–low method is simple and easy to use. It has the disadvantage, however, of using two extreme data points, which may not be representative of normal conditions. The method may yield unreliable estimates of a and b in our formula. In such a case, it would be wise to drop them and choose two other points that are more representative of normal situations.

3.6 THE SCATTERGRAPH METHOD

In the scattergraph method, a semivariable expense is plotted on the vertical axis (or y axis) and an activity measure is plotted on the horizontal axis (or x axis). Then, a *regression line* is fitted by visual inspection of the plotted x–y data. The method is best explained by the following example.

EXAMPLE 3.2 For purposes of illustration, let us use the data in Example 3.1. The factory overhead and direct labor hours are plotted in Fig. 3-2.

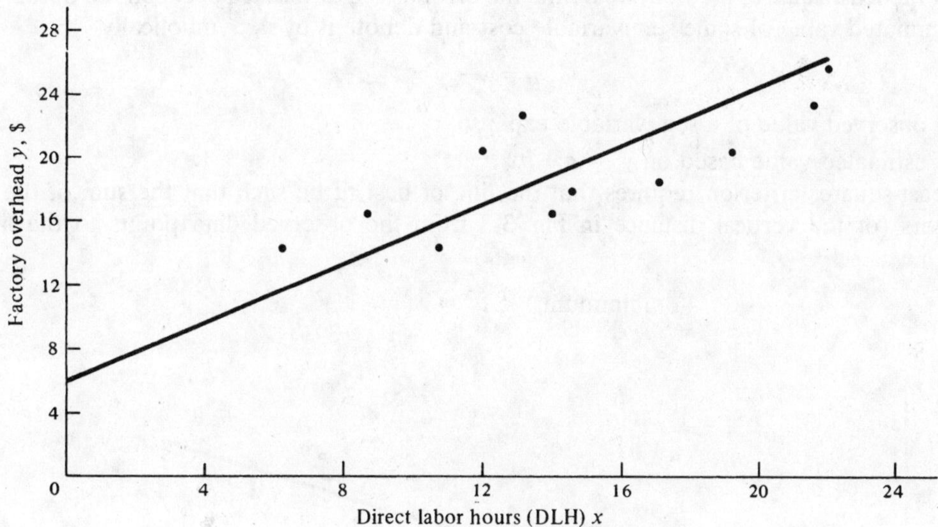

Fig. 3-2 The scattergraph method.

Since the regression line obtained by visual inspection strikes the factory overhead axis at the $6 point, that amount represents the fixed cost component. The variable cost component is computed as

Factory overhead at 23 hours of direct labor	$25
Less: Fixed cost component	6
Variable cost component	$19

Therefore, the variable rate per hour is $19/23 hours = $0.8261 per DLH.

In summary, based on the scattergraph method, we obtain

$$y' = \$6 + \$0.8261x$$

where y' = estimated factory overhead
x = DLH

The scattergraph method is relatively easy to use and simple to understand. However, it should be used with extreme caution, because it does not provide an objective test for assuring that the regression line drawn is the most accurate fit for the underlying observations.

3.7 THE METHOD OF LEAST SQUARES (REGRESSION ANALYSIS)

One popularly used method for estimating the cost–volume formula is regression analysis. Regression analysis is a statistical procedure for estimating mathematically the average relationship between the dependent variable y and the independent variable(s). *Simple regression* involves one independent variable, such as DLH or machine hours alone, whereas *multiple regression* involves two or more activity variables. (We will assume simple *linear* regression throughout this chapter, which means that we will maintain the $y = a + bx$ relationship.)

Unlike the high–low method, in estimating the variable rate and the fixed cost portion, the regression method does include all the observed data and attempts to find a line of *best fit*. To find the line of best fit, a technique called the *method of least squares* is used.

THE METHOD OF LEAST SQUARES

To explain the least-squares method, we define the error as the difference between the observed value and the estimated value of some semivariable cost and denote it by u. Symbolically,

$$u = y - y'$$

where y = observed value of a semivariable expense

y' = estimated value based on $y' = a + bx$

The least-squares criterion requires that the line of best fit be such that the sum of the squares of the errors (or the vertical distance in Fig. 3-3 from the observed data points to the line) is a minimum, i.e.,

$$\text{minimum:} \quad \Sigma u^2 = \Sigma(y - y')^2$$

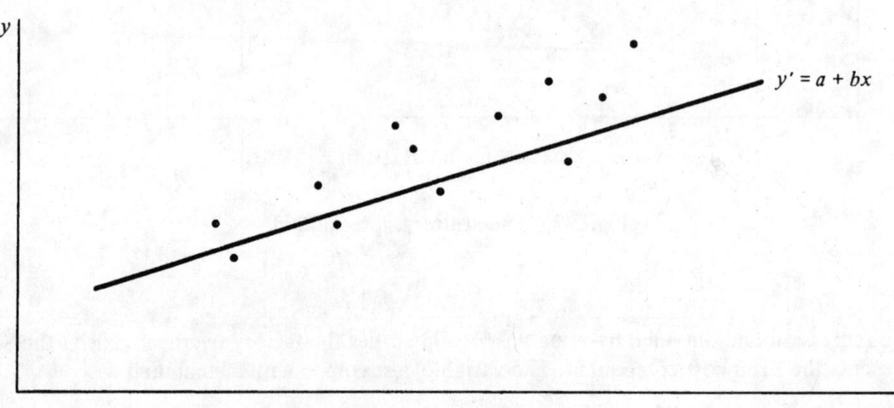

Fig. 3-3 ***y* and *y*′.**

Using differential calculus, we obtain the following equations, called *normal equations*:

$$\Sigma y = na + b\Sigma x$$
$$\Sigma xy = a\Sigma x + b\Sigma x^2$$

Solving the equations for b and a yields

$$b = \frac{n\Sigma xy - (\Sigma x)(\Sigma y)}{n\Sigma x^2 - (\Sigma x)^2}$$

$$a = \bar{y} - b\bar{x}$$

where $\bar{y} = \Sigma y/n$ and $\bar{x} = \Sigma x/n$.

The formula for a is a short-cut formula which requires the computation of b first. This will save a considerable amount of time. If the data collected are too voluminous to fit into a calculator, b can be computed using

$$b = \frac{\Sigma(x - \bar{x})(y - \bar{y})}{\Sigma(x - \bar{x})^2}$$

$$a = \text{the same as above}$$

EXAMPLE 3.3 To illustrate the computations of b and a, we will once again refer to the data in Table 3-1. All the sums required are computed and shown below.

Direct Labor Hours x	Factory Overhead y	xy	x^2	y^2
9 hours	$ 15	135	81	225
19	20	380	361	400
11	14	154	121	196
14	16	224	196	256
23	25	575	529	625
12	20	240	144	400
12	20	240	144	400
22	23	506	484	529
7	14	98	49	196
13	22	286	169	484
15	18	270	225	324
17	18	306	289	324
174 hours	$225	3,414	2,792	4,359

From the table above,

$$\Sigma x = 174 \qquad \Sigma y = 225 \qquad \Sigma xy = 3{,}414 \qquad \Sigma x^2 = 2{,}792$$

$$\bar{x} = \frac{\Sigma x}{n} = \frac{174}{12} = 14.5 \qquad \bar{y} = \frac{\Sigma y}{n} = \frac{225}{12} = 18.75$$

Substituting these values into the formula for b first:

$$b = \frac{n\Sigma xy - (\Sigma x)(\Sigma y)}{n\Sigma x^2 - (\Sigma x)^2} = \frac{(12)(3{,}414) - (174)(225)}{(12)(2{,}792) - (174)^2} = \frac{1{,}818}{3{,}228} = 0.5632$$

$$a = \bar{y} - b\bar{x} = 18.75 - (0.5632)(14.5) = 18.75 - 8.1664 = 10.5836$$

Note that Σy^2 is not used here but rather is computed for future use.

3.8 REGRESSION STATISTICS

Unlike the high–low method, regression analysis is a statistical method. It uses a variety of statistics that tell us about the accuracy and reliability of the regression results. They include:

1. Correlation coefficient (r) and coefficient of determination (r^2)
2. Standard error of the estimate (s_e)
3. Standard error of the regression coefficient (s_b) and t-statistic

CORRELATION COEFFICIENT (r) AND COEFFICIENT OF DETERMINATION (r^2)

The correlation coefficient r measures the degree of correlation between y and x. The range of values it takes on is between -1 and $+1$. More widely used, however, is the coefficient of determination, designated r^2 (read as r-squared). Simply put, r^2 tells us how good the estimated regression equation is. In other words, it is a measure of "goodness of fit" in the regression. Therefore, the higher the r^2, the more confidence we can have in our estimated cost formula.

More specifically, the coefficient of determination represents the proportion of the total variation in y that is explained by the regression equation. It has the range of values between 0 and 1.

EXAMPLE 3.4 The statement "Factory overhead is a function of machine hours with $r^2 = 70$ percent," can be interpreted as "70 percent of the total variation of factory overhead is explained by the regression equation or the change in machine hours and the remaining 30 percent is accounted for by something other than machine hours."

The coefficient of determination is computed as

$$r^2 = 1 - \frac{\Sigma(y - y')^2}{\Sigma(y - \bar{y})^2}$$

In a simple regression situation, however, a short-cut method is available:

$$r^2 = \frac{[n\,\Sigma xy - (\Sigma x)(\Sigma y)]^2}{[n\,\Sigma x^2 - (\Sigma x)^2][n\,\Sigma y^2 - (\Sigma y)^2]}$$

Comparing this formula with the one for b in Example 3.3, we see that the only additional information we need to compute r^2 is Σy^2.

EXAMPLE 3.5 From the table prepared in Example 3.3, $\Sigma y^2 = 4{,}359$. Using the short-cut method for r^2,

$$r^2 = \frac{(1{,}818)^2}{(3{,}228)[(12)(4{,}359) - (225)^2]} = \frac{3{,}305{,}124}{(3{,}228)(52{,}308 - 50{,}625)} = \frac{3{,}305{,}124}{(3{,}228)(1{,}683)}$$
$$= \frac{3{,}305{,}124}{5{,}432{,}724} = 0.6084 = 60.84\%$$

This means that about 60.84 percent of the total variation in total factory overhead is explained by DLH and the remaining 39.16 percent is still unexplained. A relatively low r^2 indicates that there is a lot of room for improvement in our estimated cost–volume formula ($y' = \$10.5836 + \$0.5632x$). Machine hours or a combination of DLH and machine hours might improve r^2.

STANDARD ERROR OF THE ESTIMATE (s_e)

The standard error of the estimate, designated s_e, is defined as the standard deviation of the regression. It is computed as

$$s_e = \sqrt{\frac{\Sigma(y - y')^2}{n - 2}} = \sqrt{\frac{\Sigma y^2 - a\,\Sigma y - b\,\Sigma xy}{n - 2}}$$

The statistics can be used to gain some idea of the accuracy of our predictions.

EXAMPLE 3.6 Going back to our example data, s_e is calculated as

$$s_e = \sqrt{\frac{4{,}359 - (10.5836)(225) - (0.5632)(3{,}414)}{12 - 2}} = \sqrt{\frac{54.9252}{10}} = 2.3436$$

If a manager wants to be 95 percent confident of the prediction, the confidence interval is the *estimated cost* $\pm 2(2.3436)$.

STANDARD ERROR OF THE REGRESSION COEFFICIENT (s_b) AND THE t-STATISTIC

The standard error of the regression coefficient, designated s_b, and the t-statistic are closely related. s_b gives an estimate of the range in which the true coefficient will "actually" fall. The t-statistic shows the statistical significance of an independent variable x in explaining the dependent variable y. It is determined by dividing the estimated regression coefficient b by its standard error s_b. Thus the t-statistic measures how many standard errors the coefficient is away from zero. Generally, any t value greater than $+2$ or less than -2 is acceptable. The higher the t value, the greater the confidence we have in the coefficient as a predictor.

3.9 THE CONTRIBUTION APPROACH TO THE INCOME STATEMENT

The traditional approach to the income statement discussed in Chapter 2 shows the functional classification of costs, that is, manufacturing costs vs. nonmanufacturing expenses (or operating expenses). It is not organized according to cost behavior. The contribution approach, however, looks at cost behavior. That is, it shows the relationship of variable costs and fixed costs, regardless of the functions with which a given cost item is associated. The contribution approach to income determination provides data that are useful for managerial planning and decision making. It is not acceptable, however, for income tax or external reporting purposes. A contribution income statement highlights the concept of *contribution margin*, which is the difference between sales and variable costs. The traditional format, on the other hand, emphasizes the concept of *gross margin*, which is the difference between sales and cost of goods sold. These two concepts are independent and have nothing to do with each other. Gross margin is available to cover nonmanufacturing expenses, whereas contribution margin is available to cover fixed costs. The concept of contribution margin has numerous applications for internal management. Following is a comparison made between the traditional format and the contribution format.

TRADITIONAL FORMAT

Sales		$15,000
Less: Cost of Goods Sold		7,000
Gross Margin		$ 8,000
Less: Operating Expenses		
Selling	$2,100	
Administrative	1,500	3,600
Net Income		$ 4,400

CONTRIBUTION FORMAT

Sales		$15,000
Less: Variable Expenses		
Manufacturing	$4,000	
Selling	1,600	
Administrative	500	6,100
Contribution Margin		$ 8,900
Less: Fixed Expenses		
Manufacturing	$3,000	
Selling	500	
Administrative	1,000	4,500
Net Income		$ 4,400

Summary

(1) Direct materials and direct labor are both ____________. Factory overhead contains both ____________ and ____________ costs.

(2) Within the ____________ range of activity, the fixed costs do not change ____________ regardless of changes in volume or the level of activity.

(3) Fixed costs are subdivided into two types: ____________ and ____________.

(4) Several methods are available for separating a semivariable cost into its fixed and variable components. They include the ____________, the ____________, and the method of ____________.

(5) When there is more than one independent variable involved, the regression is called ____________.

(6) Simple regression takes the following mathematical form (assuming there exists a linear relationship between a cost and an activity): ____________.

(7) The coefficient of determination is a measure of the ____________ in a regression.

(8) The ____________ relies on two extreme data points in trying to break down a mixed cost into its variable and fixed elements.

(9) ____________ is available to cover selling and administrative expenses, whereas contribution margin is available to cover ____________.

(10) Factory overhead, taken as a whole, is ____________ in behavior.

(11) The ____________, designated s_e, is defined as the standard deviation of the regression.

(12) The higher the ____________, the greater the confidence in the value of the coefficient as a predictor.

(13) The contribution approach to income measurement emphasizes costs by ____________, whereas the ____________ approach to income measurement focuses on cost by ____________.

(14) An example of discretionary fixed costs would be: (*a*) executive salaries; (*b*) rent; (*c*) insurance; (*d*) none of these.

(15) Contribution margin and gross margin are synonymous: (*a*) true; (*b*) false.

Answers: (1) variable costs, variable, fixed; (2) relevant, in total; (3) discretionary, committed; (4) high–low method, scattergraph method, least squares; (5) multiple regression; (6) $y = a + bx$; (7) goodness of fit; (8) high–low method; (9) gross margin, fixed costs; (10) mixed; (11) standard error of the estimate; (12) *t*-statistic; (13) behavior, traditional, function; (14) (*d*); (15) (*b*).

Solved Problems

3.1 Some cost data for producing four different products are given below. Fill in the missing data in the blanks for each product.

Product	Total Variable Cost (TVC)	Total Fixed Cost (TFC)	Total Cost (TC)	Unit Variable Cost (UVC)	Unit Fixed Cost (UFC)	Volume in Units (V)
1	(*a*) ______	$ 50,000	$120,000	(*b*) ______	$5	(*c*) ______
2	$100,000	(*d*) ______	(*e*) ______	(*f*) ______	$5	50,000
3	$ 15,000	(*g*) ______	$165,000	$15	(*h*) ______	(*i*) ______
4	(*j*) ______	$100,000	$800,000	(*k*) ______	(*l*) ______	20,000

SOLUTION

(*a*) \$120,000 − \$50,000 = \$70,000 (TC − TFC = TVC)
(*b*) \$70,000 ÷ 10,000 units = \$7 (TVC ÷ V = UVC)
(*c*) \$50,000 ÷ \$5 = 10,000 units (TFC ÷ UFC = V)
(*d*) 50,000 units × \$4 = \$200,000 (UFC × V = TFC)
(*e*) \$100,000 + \$200,000 = \$300,000 (TVC + TFC = TC)
(*f*) \$100,000 ÷ 50,000 units = \$2 (TVC ÷ V = UVC)
(*g*) \$165,000 − \$15,000 = \$150,000 (TC − TVC = TFC)
(*h*) \$150,000 ÷ 1,000 units = \$150 (TFC ÷ V = UFC)
(*i*) \$15,000 ÷ \$15 = 1,000 units (TVC ÷ UVC = V)
(*j*) \$800,000 − \$100,000 = \$700,000 (TC − TFC = TVC)
(*k*) \$700,000 ÷ 20,000 units = \$35 (TVC ÷ V = UVC)
(*l*) \$100,000 ÷ 20,000 units = \$5 (TFC ÷ V = UFC)

3.2 Classify the following fixed costs as committed (C) or discretionary (D) costs.

(*a*) Patent amortization
(*b*) Advertising
(*c*) Depreciation
(*d*) Property taxes
(*e*) Research and development
(*f*) Training
(*g*) Insurance
(*h*) Public relations
(*i*) Rent
(*j*) Executive salaries

SOLUTION

(*a*) C; (*b*) D; (*c*) C; (*d*) C; (*e*) D; (*f*) D; (*g*) C; (*h*) D; (*i*) C; (*j*) C.

3.3 The cost–volume formula showing the relationship between repair costs y and machine hours x came out as follows: $y' = \$500 + \$0.50x$, where y' = estimated repair costs. Identify the amount or the symbol that represents each of the following: (*a*) the dependent variable, (*b*) the independent variable, (*c*) the slope of the regression line, (*d*) the fixed portion of repair costs, (*e*) the variable portion of repair costs per machine hour, and (*f*) the estimated repair cost if the planned machine hours used are 1,000 hours.

SOLUTION

(*a*) y'; (*b*) x; (*c*) \$0.50; (*d*) \$500; (*e*) \$0.50; (*f*) $y' = \$500 + (\$0.50)(1{,}000 \text{ hours}) = \$1{,}000$.

3.4 In an effort to control selling expenses, the Sell Big Corporation wants to develop a cost–volume formula for its selling expenses. An investigation of individual expense items shows

	Fixed	Variable
Sales commissions	—	30% of sales
Advertising	\$50,000	—
Travel and entertainment	30,000	5% of sales
Sales staff salaries	12,000	—
Depreciation, rent, and insurance—sales office	5,000	—

Determine the cost–volume formula in the form of $y' = a + bx$.

SOLUTION

Fixed costs = \$50,000 + \$30,000 + \$12,000 + \$5,000 = \$97,000. Thus, the formula is: $y' = \$97{,}000 + 0.35x$, where y' = estimated selling expenses and x = sales.

3.5 The XYZ Tool Manufacturing Co. shows the following factory overhead costs at various levels of direct labor hours for the last four months:

Month	Direct Labor Hours x	Factory Overhead y
July	2,500 hours	\$ 7,000
August	1,500	5,000
September	2,000	6,000
October	3,000	8,000
	9,000 hours	\$26,000

Determine the monthly fixed overhead and the variable overhead rate per direct labor hour (DLH) using (*a*) the scattergraph method and (*b*) the high–low method.

SOLUTION

(*a*) From the scattergraph illustrated in Fig. 3-4, we note that the regression line cuts the y axis at the \$2,000 fixed cost point. The variable portion is computed as

Factory overhead at the 3,000-hour level of activity	\$8,000
Less: Fixed portion	2,000
Variable portion	\$6,000

Therefore, the variable overhead rate per hour is \$6,000/3,000 hours = \$2 per DLH. The cost–volume formula is \$2,000 fixed, plus \$2 per hour of direct labor (or $y' = \$2{,}000 + \$2x$, where y' = estimated factory overhead and x = DLH).

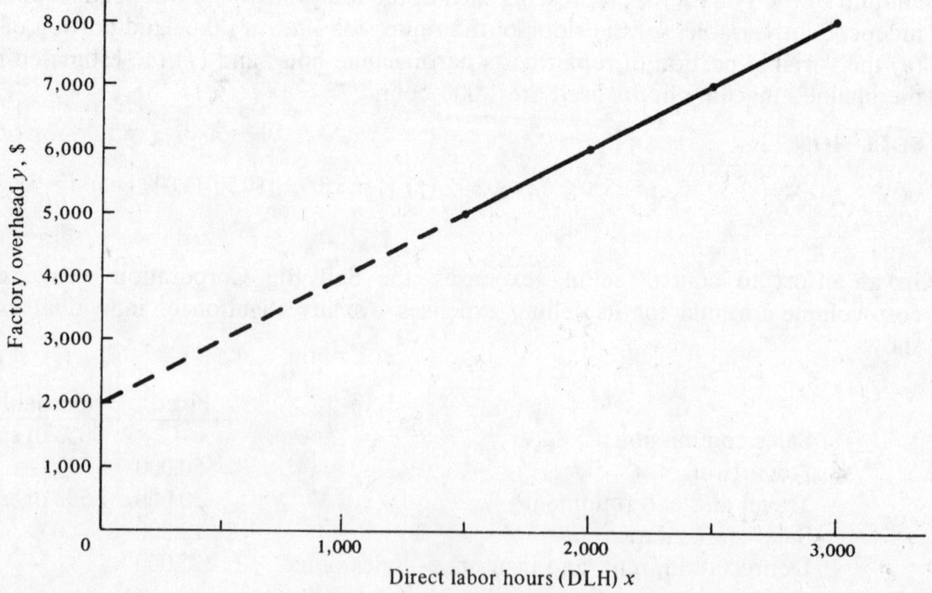

Fig. 3-4

(*b*) The high–low method goes as follows:

	DLH (x)	FO (y)
High	3,000 hours	$8,000
Low	1,500	5,000
Difference	1,500 hours	$3,000

Thus, the variable rate = $3,000/1,500 hours = $2 per DLH.

The fixed portion is computed as

	High	Low
FO	$8,000	$5,000
Variable cost ($2/DLH)	6,000	3,000
Fixed	$2,000	$2,000

Therefore, the cost–volume formula is $y' = \$2{,}000 + \$2x$.

3.6 Labor hours and production costs for the last four months of 19A, which you believe are representative for the year, were

Month	Labor Hours	Total Production Cost
September	2,500	$ 20,000
October	3,500	25,000
November	4,500	30,000
December	3,500	25,000
	14,000	$100,000

Based on the above information, select the best answer for questions 1 through 6.

Let a = fixed production costs per month
b = variable production costs per labor hour
n = number of months
x = labor hours per month
y = total monthly production costs
Σ = summation

1. The equation(s) required for applying the least-squares method of computation of fixed and variable production costs could be expressed as:

(*a*) $\Sigma xy = a\Sigma x + b\Sigma x^2$

(*b*) $\Sigma y = na + b\Sigma x$

(*c*) $y = a + bx^2$
$\Sigma y = na + b\Sigma x$

(*d*) $\Sigma xy = a\Sigma x + b\Sigma x^2$
$\Sigma y = na + b\Sigma x$

2. The cost function derived by the least-squares method:

(*a*) Is linear

(*b*) Must be tested for minima and maxima

(*c*) Is parabolic

(*d*) Indicates maximum costs at the point of the function's inflection

3. Monthly production costs are expressed as:

(*a*) $y = ax + b$ (*c*) $y = b + ax$

(*b*) $y = a + bx$ (*d*) $y = \Sigma a + bx$

4. The fixed monthly production cost in total is: (*a*) \$10,000; (*b*) \$9,500; (*c*) \$7,500; (*d*) \$5,000.
5. The variable production cost per labor hour is: (*a*) \$6; (*b*) \$5; (*c*) \$3; (*d*) \$2.
6. The least-squares method of cost analysis must be used in those situations where:
   (*a*) The mixed costs being analyzed consist of more than 50 percent fixed costs.
   (*b*) The variable portion of the mixed cost is constant per unit of activity.
   (*c*) The fixed costs being analyzed are discretionary rather than committed.
   (*d*) The variable portion of the mixed cost being analyzed must be determined in terms of some average amount per unit of activity.

(AICPA, adapted)

SOLUTION

1. (*d*); 2. (*a*); 3. (*b*); 4. (*c*); 5. (*b*).

Note on 4 and 5: Upon close examination, you will find that as labor hours go up by 1,000 hours, total production costs increase by \$5,000. Therefore, the slope, which is the variable portion per hour, comes out to be \$5,000/1,000 hours = \$5 per hour. From there, you can determine the fixed cost as

$$\$20{,}000 - (\$5)(2{,}500 \text{ hours}) = \$7{,}500$$

Note that in this particular problem you will end up with the same answer by using the high–low method, the scattergraph method, or the method of least squares.

6. (*d*).

3.7 Following are the direct labor hours and the repair costs of Jason Corporation over a seven-week period.

Direct Labor Hours (00 omitted)	Repair Costs (00 omitted)
40 hours	\$ 60
45	80
30	60
50	80
60	100
40	70
20	50
285 hours	\$500

1. Separate the repair costs into the fixed and variable components by using (*a*) the high–low method and (*b*) the method of least squares.
2. Compute the coefficient of determination.
3. Comment on the choice of direct labor hours in explaining the repair costs.

SOLUTION

1. (*a*) For the repair costs using the high–low method, we obtain

	DLH	Repair Costs
High	60 hours	\$100
Low	20	50
Difference	40 hours	\$ 50

Variable rate = \$50/40 hours = \$1.25 per DLH

	High	Low
Repair costs	\$100	\$50
Variable cost (\$1.25/hour)	75	25
Fixed portion	\$ 25	\$25

Therefore, the cost–volume formula is

\$25 + \$1.25 per DLH

(*b*) Based on the method of least squares, we obtain

Direct Labor Hours x	Repair Costs y	xy	x^2	y^2
40 hours	\$ 60	2,400	1,600	3,600
45	80	3,600	2,025	6,400
30	60	1,800	900	3,600
50	80	4,000	2,500	6,400
60	100	6,000	3,600	10,000
40	70	2,800	1,600	4,900
20	50	1,000	400	2,500
285 hours	\$500	21,600	12,625	37,400

From the table,

$$n = 7 \qquad \Sigma x = 285 \qquad \Sigma y = 500 \qquad \Sigma xy = 21{,}600 \qquad \Sigma x^2 = 12{,}625$$

Substituting these sum values into the b formula:

$$b = \frac{n\Sigma xy - (\Sigma x)(\Sigma y)}{n\Sigma x^2 - (\Sigma x)^2} = \frac{(7)(21{,}600) - (285)(500)}{(7)(12{,}625) - (285)^2}$$

$$= \frac{151{,}200 - 142{,}500}{88{,}375 - 81{,}225} = \frac{8{,}700}{7{,}150} = 1.22$$

$$a = \frac{\Sigma y}{n} - b\left(\frac{\Sigma x}{n}\right) = \frac{500}{7} - (1.22)\left(\frac{285}{7}\right) = 71.43 - 49.67 = 21.76$$

Thus, the formula is \$21.76 + \$1.22 per DLH

2. $$r^2 = \frac{[n\Sigma xy - (\Sigma x)(\Sigma y)]^2}{[n\Sigma x^2 - (\Sigma x)^2][n\Sigma y^2 - (\Sigma y)^2]} = \frac{(8{,}700)^2}{(7{,}150)[(7)(37{,}400) - (500)^2]} = \frac{75{,}690{,}000}{(7{,}150)(11{,}800)}$$

$$= \frac{75{,}690{,}000}{84{,}370{,}000} = 0.897 = 89.7\%$$

3. DLH was an excellent choice in explaining the behavior of repair costs, as the high r^2 indicated: 89.7 percent of the total change in repair costs was explained by DLH alone. Only 10.3 percent was due to chance.

3.8 Data for total power costs and machine hours are given below.

Power Costs (000 omitted)	Machine Hours (000 omitted)
\$ 7	9 hours
6	8
8	8
3	4
4	6
8	7
8	9
6	5
7	8
5	6
\$62	70 hours

1. Separate the power costs into the fixed and variable components using the method of least squares. Estimate the power costs when 6.5 machine hours are used.
2. Compute the coefficient of determination.
3. Does the regression equation need to be improved?

SOLUTION

1.

Power Costs y	Machine Hours x	xy	x^2	y^2
\$ 7	9	63	81	49
6	8	48	64	36
8	8	64	64	64
3	4	12	16	9
4	6	24	36	16
8	7	56	49	64
8	9	72	81	64
6	5	30	25	36
7	8	56	64	49
5	6	30	36	25
\$62	70	455	516	412

$$b = \frac{(10)(455) - (70)(62)}{(10)(516) - (70)^2} = \frac{210}{260} = 0.81$$

$$a = \frac{62}{10} - (0.81)\left(\frac{70}{10}\right) = 0.53$$

The estimated regression equation is

$$y' = \$0.53 + \$0.81x$$

where y' = estimated power costs and x = machine hours.

The estimated power cost for 6.5 machine hours is

$$y' = \$0.53 + \$0.81\,(6.5 \text{ hours}) = \$5.795$$

2. $$r^2 = \frac{(210)^2}{(260)[(10)(412) - (62)^2]} = \frac{(210)^2}{(260)(276)} = \frac{44{,}100}{71{,}760} = 0.6145 = 61.45\%$$

which means that the machine hours account for only 61.45 percent of the change in power costs.

3. The answer is yes. A low r^2 (61.45 percent) indicates that about 39 percent is unexplained by the estimated equation. It follows that the machine hour basis was not good enough to explain fully the behavior of power costs. Often factors such as weather may be responsible for part of the variation in such costs.

3.9 The GH Manufacturing Company makes a product called Z. Some of the manufacturing expenses are easily identified as fixed or variable directly with production. The cost accountant of the company is confronted with the problem of preparing a flexible budget for the coming year and wishes to determine the fixed and variable elements of the mixed factory overhead. The following details are provided for the first 10 months of the past year:

Month	Number of Units Produced x	Mixed Factory Overhead y
1	1,500	$ 800
2	2,000	1,000
3	3,000	1,350
4	2,500	1,250
5	3,000	1,300
6	2,500	1,200
7	3,500	1,400
8	3,000	1,250
9	2,500	1,150
10	1,500	800
	25,000	$11,500

Determine the fixed and variable elements of the mixed factory overhead using the high–low method.

(SMA, adapted)

SOLUTION

	x	y
High	3,500 units	$1,400
Low	1,500	800
Difference	2,000 units	$ 600

Variable rate: $600/2,000 units = $0.30/unit.

Fixed element:

	High	Low
Mixed overhead	$1,400	$800
Variable ($0.30/unit)	1,050	450
	$ 350	$350

Therefore, the formula is

$350 fixed + $0.30 per unit

3.10 Assume that six monthly observations of indirect manufacturing costs y and machine hours x are to be used as a basis for developing the cost–volume formula $y' = a + bx$. The sums are available as

$$\Sigma x = 570 \quad \Sigma y = 3{,}785 \quad \Sigma xy = 364{,}000 \quad \Sigma x^2 = 55{,}000 \quad \Sigma y^2 = 2{,}413{,}925$$

(*a*) Determine the fixed cost and the variable rate using the method of least squares.
(*b*) Compute the coefficient of determination.

SOLUTION

(*a*)
$$b = \frac{(6)(364{,}000) - (570)(3{,}785)}{(6)(55{,}000) - (570)^2} = \frac{26{,}550}{5{,}100} = \$5.21$$
$$a = \frac{3{,}785}{6} - (\$5.21)\left(\frac{570}{6}\right) = 630.83 - 494.95 = \$135.88$$

Therefore, the formula is

$$y' = \$135.88 + \$5.21x$$

where y' = estimated indirect manufacturing expenses and x = machine hours.

(*b*)
$$r^2 = \frac{(26{,}550)^2}{(5{,}100)[(6)(2{,}413{,}925) - (3{,}785)^2]} = \frac{(26{,}550)^2}{(5{,}100)(157{,}325)} = 0.8785$$

3.11 The Progressive Company Ltd. has recorded the following sales (000 omitted) since its inception in 19M2:

19M2	$10	19M8	$125
19M3	20	19M9	150
19M4	30	19N0	180
19M5	45	19N1	220
19M6	70	19N2	270
19M7	90		

1. Calculate 19N3 sales, using the method of least squares.
2. Compute the coefficient of determination and the standard error of the estimate.
3. Comment on the reliability of the estimated sales equation, together with the necessary assumptions if the estimated equation is to be used to predict sales. An interpretation of the standard error of the estimate and the coefficient of determination should be included.

(SMA, adapted)

SOLUTION

1. For regression purposes, a year can be given a number so that the $\Sigma x = 0$. Since the company has 11 years of data, which is an odd number, the year in the middle is assigned a value of zero.

Year	x	Sales y (000 omitted)	xy	x^2	y^2
19M2	−5	$ 10	−50	25	100
19M3	−4	20	−80	16	400
19M4	−3	30	−90	9	900
19M5	−2	45	−90	4	2,025
19M6	−1	70	−70	1	4,900
19M7	0	90	0	0	8,100
19M8	+1	125	125	1	15,625
19M9	+2	150	300	4	22,500
19N0	+3	180	540	9	32,400
19N1	+4	220	880	16	48,400
19N2	+5	270	1,350	25	72,900
	0	$1,210	2,815	110	208,250

$$b = \frac{(11)(2{,}815) - (0)(1{,}210)}{(11)(110) - (0)^2} = \frac{30{,}965}{1{,}210} = \$25.59$$

$$a = \frac{1{,}210}{11} - (25.59)\left(\frac{0}{11}\right) = \$110$$

Therefore, the estimated equation is

$$y' = \$110 + \$25.59x$$

where y' = estimated sales and x = year index value.

To calculate 19N3 sales, we assign +6 to the x value for the year 19N3. Thus, $y' = \$110 + \$25.59(+6) = \$263.54$.

2.
$$r^2 = \frac{(30{,}965)^2}{(1{,}210)[(11)(208{,}250) - (1{,}210)^2]} = \frac{(30{,}965)^2}{(1{,}210)(826{,}650)} = \frac{958{,}830{,}000}{1{,}000{,}246{,}500} = 0.958$$

$$s_e = \sqrt{\frac{\Sigma y^2 - a\Sigma y - b\Sigma xy}{n-2}} = \sqrt{\frac{(208{,}250) - (110)(1{,}210) - (25.59)(2{,}815)}{11-2}}$$

$$= \sqrt{\frac{3{,}114.15}{9}} = 18.60$$

3. The high r^2 (0.958) ensures that annual sales shows an increasing trend. We may use the normal distribution (assuming normality of the error term) and s_e to place a confidence interval on the y value for any of the original x values. For example, we can state that there is a 95 percent probability that the interval ($98.39 to $172.79) contains the true sales for 19M8 (assigned a value +1), where $y' = \$110 + \$25.59(+1) = \$135.59$ and the upper and lower limits are $\$135.59 \pm 2(18.60)$, or $98.39 to $172.79.

3.12 A government economist wishes to establish the relationship between annual family income x and savings y. A sample of 100 families has been randomly selected for various annual income levels between $5,000 and $30,000. A thorough investigation of these families has been made and the following calculations have been obtained (x and y are measured in thousands of dollars):

$$\Sigma x = \$1{,}239 \qquad \Sigma y = \$79 \qquad \Sigma xy = \$1{,}613 \qquad \Sigma x^2 = \$17{,}322 \qquad \Sigma y^2 = \$293$$

1. Determine the equation for the estimated regression line.
2. State the meaning of the slope b and the intercept value a.
3. Compute the coefficient of determination r^2.
4. Calculate the standard error of the estimate s_e.

SOLUTION

1.
$$b = \frac{(100)(1{,}613) - (1{,}239)(79)}{(100)(17{,}322) - (1{,}239)^2} = \frac{63{,}419}{197{,}079} = 0.3218$$

$$a = \frac{79}{100} - (0.3218)\left(\frac{1{,}239}{100}\right) = -3.1971$$

Therefore, the estimated relationship between annual income and savings is

$$-\$3.1971 + \$0.3218 \text{ per dollar of annual income}$$

2. The b value, $0.3218, means that an average family saves about $0.32 for every dollar they earn annually. The intercept value a (−3.1971) means that an average family has an annual debt of $3,197.10.

3. $$r^2 = \frac{(63{,}419)^2}{(197{,}079)[(100)(293) - (79)^2]} = \frac{(63{,}419)^2}{(197{,}079)(23{,}059)} = 0.885$$

4. $$s_e = \sqrt{\frac{293 - (-3.1971)(79) - (0.3218)(1{,}613)}{100 - 2}} = 0.520$$

3.13 The Ramon Company manufactures a wide range of products at several different plant locations. The Franklin plant, which manufactures electrical components, has been experiencing some difficulties with fluctuating monthly overhead costs. The fluctuations have made it difficult to estimate the level of overhead that will be incurred for any one month. Management wants to be better able to estimate overhead costs accurately in order to plan its operations and financial needs. A trade association publication to which Ramon Company subscribes indicates that for companies that manufacture electrical components, overhead tends to vary with direct labor hours. One member of the accounting staff proposes that the cost behavior pattern for overhead costs be determined. Then, overhead costs could be predicted from the budgeted direct labor hours. Another member of the accounting staff suggests that a good starting point for determining the cost behavior patterns of overhead costs would be an analysis of historical data. The historical cost behavior pattern would provide a basis for determining the cost behavior pattern. The methods proposed for this purpose are the high–low method and simple linear regression. Data on direct labor hours and the respective overhead costs incurred were collected for the past two years. The raw data follow:

19A	Direct Labor Hours x	Overhead Costs y
January	20,000 hours	$84,000
February	25,000	99,000
March	22,000	89,500
April	23,000	90,000
May	20,000	81,500
June	19,000	75,500
July	14,000	70,000
August	10,000	64,500
September	12,000	69,000
October	17,000	75,000
November	16,000	71,000
December	19,000	78,000

19B	Direct Labor Hours x	Overhead Costs y
January	21,000 hours	$86,000
February	24,000	93,000
March	23,000	93,000
April	22,000	87,000
May	20,000	80,000
June	18,000	76,500
July	12,000	67,500
August	13,000	71,000
September	15,000	73,500
October	17,000	72,500
November	15,000	71,000
December	18,000	75,000

Using linear regression, the following data were obtained:

Coefficient of determination (r^2)	0.9109
Coefficient of regression equation	
Constant	39,859
Independent variable	2.1549
Standard error of the estimate (s_e)	2,840
Standard error of the regression coefficient for the independent variable (s_b)	0.1437
Table t-statistic for a 95% confidence interval (when $n-2=24-2=22$)	2.074

(*a*) Using the high–low method, determine the cost behavior pattern of the overhead costs for the Franklin plant.

(*b*) Using the results of the regression analysis, calculate the estimate of overhead costs for 22,500 direct labor hours.

(*c*) Of the two proposed methods, which one should Ramon Company employ to determine the historical cost behavior pattern of the Franklin plant's overhead costs? Explain your answer completely, indicating the reasons why the other method should not be used.

(CMA, adapted)

SOLUTION

(*a*)

	DLH	Overhead Costs
High (Feb. 19A)	25,000 hours	$99,000
Low (Aug. 19A)	10,000	64,500
Difference	15,000 hours	$34,500

Variable rate = $34,500/15,000 hours = $2.30 per DLH

The fixed element is

Total overhead costs at 25,000 DLH	$99,000
Less: Variable costs (25,000 @ $2.30)	57,500
Fixed	41,500

Therefore, total overhead costs are $41,500 fixed + $2.30 DLH.

(*b*) The regression result says:

Total overhead costs = $39,859 + $2.1549 DLH

Therefore, the estimated cost for 22,500 hours used is

$39,859 + $2.1549(22,500 hours) = $88,344.25

(*c*) The data seem to indicate that the regression equation of $y' = \$39,859 + \$2.1549x$, where x = DLH, provides a good estimate of the behavior of overhead costs. The r^2 indicates that over 90 percent of the total variation in total overhead costs can be explained by the regression equation. The standard error of the estimate (s_e = $2,840) is reasonable for the level of costs involved. The standard error of the regression coefficient (0.1437) is small relative to the coefficient. This resulted in a t-value of 2.074, which is considered statistically significant. All in all, regression analysis seems to be adequate for determining the historical cost behavior pattern of overhead costs of the Franklin plant. The company should not employ the high–low method, because this method relies on only two pieces of the raw data and discards the rest. This method (by definition) uses the two extreme points, which in this case appear to be abnormal.

3.14 The controller of the Connecticut Electronics Company believes that the identification of the variable and fixed components of the firm's costs will enable the firm to make better planning and control decisions. Among the costs the controller is concerned about is the behavior of indirect supplies expense. He believes that there is some correlation between the machine hours worked and the amount of indirect supplies used. A member of the controller's staff has suggested that a simple linear regression model be used to determine the cost behavior of indirect supplies. The regression equation shown below was developed from 40 pairs of observations using the method of least squares. The regression equation and related measures are

$$S = \$200 + \$4H$$

where S = total monthly costs of indirect supplies
H = machine hours per month

Standard error of the estimate (s_e) = 100
Coefficient of determination (r^2) = 0.7569

1. When a simple linear regression model is used to make inferences about a population relationship from sample data, what assumptions must be made before the inferences can be accepted as valid?
2. Assume the assumptions identified in part 1 are satisfied for the indirect supplies expense of the company.
   (*a*) Explain the meaning of "200" and "4" in the equation $S = \$200 + \$4H$.
   (*b*) Calculate the estimated cost of indirect supplies if 900 machine hours are to be used during a month.
   (*c*) In addition to the estimate for the cost of indirect supplies, the controller would like the range of values for the estimate if a 95 percent confidence interval is specified. He would use this range to judge whether the estimated costs indicated by the regression analysis were good enough for planning purposes. Calculate, for 900 machine hours, the range of the estimate for the cost of indirect supplies with a 95 percent confidence interval.
3. Explain briefly what the value of the coefficient of determination (r^2) indicates in this case if the company wishes to predict the total cost of indirect supplies on the basis of estimated machine hours.

(CMA, adapted)

SOLUTION

1. The statistical assumptions which must be made are:
   - The relationship between the two variables (H, S) must be linear in the relevant range of observations.
   - The variance of the S values, given an H value, is the same (or constant) for each H value.
   - The deviations of actual values of S around the regression line are independent.
   - The population of S values is normally distributed around the regression line.
2. (*a*) The constant, \$200, is ordinarily considered to be an estimate of the fixed portion of the indirect supplies cost. However, it is a questionable estimate, since it corresponds to an observed value of $H = 0$, which usually is not a point observed in the sample data. Thus, it is not in the relevant range of observed points and the sample data do not really support an estimate of S when $H = 0$.

   The coefficient of H, \$4, represents an estimate of the variable costs associated with a unit change in machine hours per month. In this case, the coefficient 4 also could be considered the estimated marginal cost per machine hour per month.

(b) $S = \$200 + (\$4)(900 \text{ hours}) = \$3{,}800$.

(c) The problem does not provide enough data to calculate the most accurate range of the estimate for the cost of indirect supplies with a 95 percent confidence interval. The additional data needed are the t-distribution table value and the standard error of the regression coefficient. Note, however, that with 40 observations (and $40 - 2 = 38$ degrees of freedom), the t-distribution closely approximates the normal distribution. Thus, roughly a 95 percent confidence interval could be set as $\$3{,}800 + 1.96(100)$, or $\$3{,}604 \leqq S \leqq \$3{,}996$.

3. The machine hours account for about 75.69 percent of the total change in total monthly costs of indirect supplies. The remaining 24.31 percent is due to chance.

3.15 For the month of August 19A, Updike Co. presented the following income statement:

UPDIKE CO.
Income Statement
For the Month Ended August 31, 19A

Sales (1,000 units @ $50)	$50,000
Less: Cost of Goods Sold (60% variable)	20,000
Gross Margin	$30,000
Less: Operating Expenses	
Selling and Administrative (30% variable)	25,000
Net Income	$ 5,000

Recast the income statement in *contribution* format.

SOLUTION

UPDIKE CO.
Income Statement
(Contribution Format)
For the Month Ended August 31, 19A

Sales		$50,000
Less: Variable Expenses		
Manufacturing	$12,000	
Selling and Administrative	7,500	19,500
Contribution Margin		$30,500
Less: Fixed Expenses		
Manufacturing	$ 8,000	
Selling and Administrative	17,500	25,500
Net Income		$ 5,000

3.16 Assume the following data concerning the operation of the Mambo Company for the month of September:

Number of units sold	100 units
Selling price per unit	$20
Variable manufacturing costs/unit	$5
Fixed manufacturing costs	$300
Variable selling and administrative costs/unit	$4
Fixed selling and administrative costs	$110

Prepare an income statement for the month of September, using the traditional and contribution formats.

SOLUTION

THE MAMBO COMPANY
Income Statement
For the Month Ended September 30

TRADITIONAL FORMAT

Sales	$2,000
Less: Cost of Goods Sold	800*
Gross Margin	$1,200
Less: Operating Expenses	
Selling and Administrative	510†
Net Income	$ 690

CONTRIBUTION FORMAT

Sales		$2,000
Less: Variable Costs		
Manufacturing	$500	
Selling and Administrative	400	900
Contribution Margin		$1,100
Less: Fixed Costs		
Manufacturing	$300	
Selling and Administrative	110	410
Net Income		$ 690

*$800 = 100 units × $5 + $300
†$510 = $110 + 100 units × $4

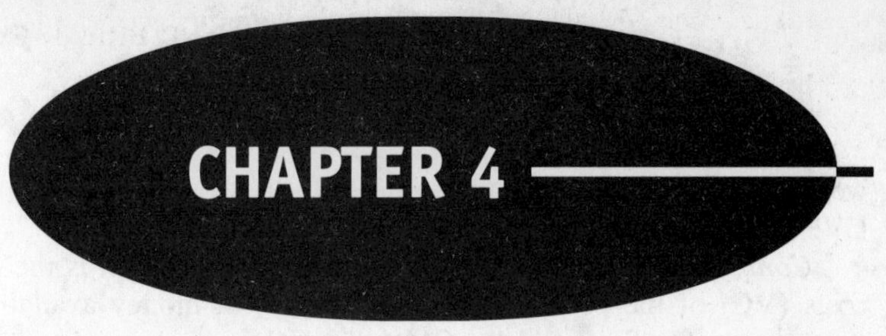

CHAPTER 4

Cost–Volume–Profit and Break-Even Analysis

4.1 COST–VOLUME–PROFIT AND BREAK-EVEN ANALYSIS DEFINED

Cost–volume–profit (CVP) analysis, together with cost behavior information, helps managers perform many useful analyses. CVP analysis deals with how profit and costs change with a change in volume. More specifically, it looks at the effects on profits of changes in such factors as variable costs, fixed costs, selling prices, volume, and mix of products sold. By studying the relationships among costs, sales, and net income, management is better able to cope with many planning decisions. *Break-even analysis*, a branch of CVP analysis, determines the break-even sales, which is the level of sales at which total costs equal total revenue.

4.2 QUESTIONS ANSWERED BY CVP ANALYSIS

CVP analysis tries to answer the following questions:

(*a*) What sales volume is required to break even?

(*b*) What sales volume is necessary in order to earn a desired profit?

(*c*) What profit can be expected on a given sales volume?

(*d*) How would changes in selling price, variable costs, fixed costs, and output affect profits?

(*e*) How would a change in the mix of products sold affect the break-even and target income volume and profit potential?

4.3 CONCEPTS OF CONTRIBUTION MARGIN

For accurate CVP analysis, a distinction must be made between costs as being either variable or fixed. Semivariable costs (or mixed costs) must be separated into their variable and fixed components, which were discussed in the previous chapter. In order to compute the break-even point and perform various CVP analyses, note the following important concepts.

Contribution margin (CM). The contribution margin is the excess of sales (S) over the variable costs (VC) of the product. It is the amount of money available to cover fixed costs (FC) and to generate profits. Symbolically, $CM = S - VC$.

Unit CM. The unit CM is the excess of the unit selling price (p) over the unit variable cost (v). Symbolically, unit CM $= p - v$.

CM ratio. The CM ratio is the contribution margin as a percentage of sales, i.e.,

$$\text{CM ratio} = \frac{CM}{S} = \frac{S - VC}{S} = 1 - \frac{VC}{S}$$

The CM ratio can also be computed using per-unit data as follows:

$$\text{CM ratio} = \frac{\text{Unit } CM}{p} = \frac{p - v}{p} = 1 - \frac{v}{p}$$

Note that the CM ratio is 1 minus the variable cost ratio. For example, if variable costs account for 70 percent of the price, the CM ratio is 30 percent.

EXAMPLE 4.1 To illustrate the various concepts of CM, consider the following data for Company Z:

	Per Unit	Total	Percentage
Sales (1,500 units)	$25	$37,500	100%
Less: Variable costs	10	15,000	40
Contribution margin	$15	$22,500	60%
Less: Fixed costs		15,000	
Net income		$ 7,500	

From the data listed above, CM, unit CM, and the CM ratio are computed as

$$CM = S - VC = \$37{,}500 - \$15{,}000 = \$22{,}500$$

$$\text{Unit CM} = p - v = \$25 - \$10 = \$15$$

$$\text{CM ratio} = \frac{CM}{S} = \frac{\$22{,}500}{\$37{,}500} = 60\% \quad \text{or} \quad 1 - \frac{VC}{S} = 1 - 0.4 = 0.6 = 60\%$$

4.4 BREAK-EVEN ANALYSIS

The break-even point, the point of no profit and no loss, provides managers with insights into profit planning. It can be computed in three different ways:

1. The equation approach
2. The contribution approach
3. The graphical approach

The *equation approach* is based on the cost–volume equation, which shows the relationships among sales, variable and fixed costs, and net income:

$$S = VC + FC + \text{Net income}$$

At the break-even volume, $S = VC + FC + 0$.

Defining x = volume in *units*, the above relationship can be rewritten in terms of x:

$$px = vx + FC$$

To find the break-even point in units, simply solve the equation for x.

EXAMPLE 4.2 In Example 4.1, $p = \$25$, $v = \$10$, and $FC = \$15{,}000$. Thus, the equation is

$$\begin{aligned} \$25x &= \$10x + \$15{,}000 \\ \$25x - \$10x &= \$15{,}000 \\ (\$25 - \$10)x &= \$15{,}000 \\ \$15x &= \$15{,}000 \\ x &= \frac{\$15{,}000}{\$15} = 1{,}000 \text{ units} \end{aligned}$$

Therefore, Company Z breaks even at a sales volume of 1,000 units.

The *contribution margin approach*, another technique for computing the break-even point, is based on solving the cost–volume equation. Solving the equation $px = vx + FC$ for x yields

$$x_{\mathrm{BE}} = \frac{FC}{p - v}$$

where $p - v$ is the unit CM by definition, and x_{BE} = break-even unit sales volume.

In words,

$$\text{Break-even point in } \textit{units} = \frac{\text{Fixed costs}}{\text{Unit CM}}$$

If the break-even point is desired in terms of dollars, then

$$\text{Break-even point in } \textit{dollars} = \text{Break-even point in units} \times \text{Unit sales price}$$

or, alternatively,

$$\text{Break-even point in } \textit{dollars} = \frac{\text{Fixed costs}}{\text{CM ratio}}$$

EXAMPLE 4.3 Using the same data given in Example 4.1, where unit CM = \$25 − \$10 = \$15 and the CM ratio = 60%, we get:

$$\text{Break-even point in units} = \frac{\$15{,}000}{\$15} = 1{,}000 \text{ units}$$

$$\text{Break-even point in dollars} = 1{,}000 \text{ units} \times \$25 = \$25{,}000$$

or, alternatively,

$$\frac{\$15{,}000}{0.6} = \$25{,}000$$

The *graphical approach* is based on the so-called *break-even chart* as shown in Fig. 4-1. Sales revenue, variable costs, and fixed costs are plotted on the vertical axis, while volume, x, is plotted on the horizontal axis. The break-even point is the point where the total sales revenue line intersects the total cost line. The chart can also effectively report profit potentials over a wide range of activity. The *profit–volume (P–V) chart*, as shown in Fig. 4-2, focuses more directly on how profits vary with changes in volume. Profits are plotted on the vertical axis, while units of output are shown on the horizontal axis. Note that the slope of the chart is the unit CM.

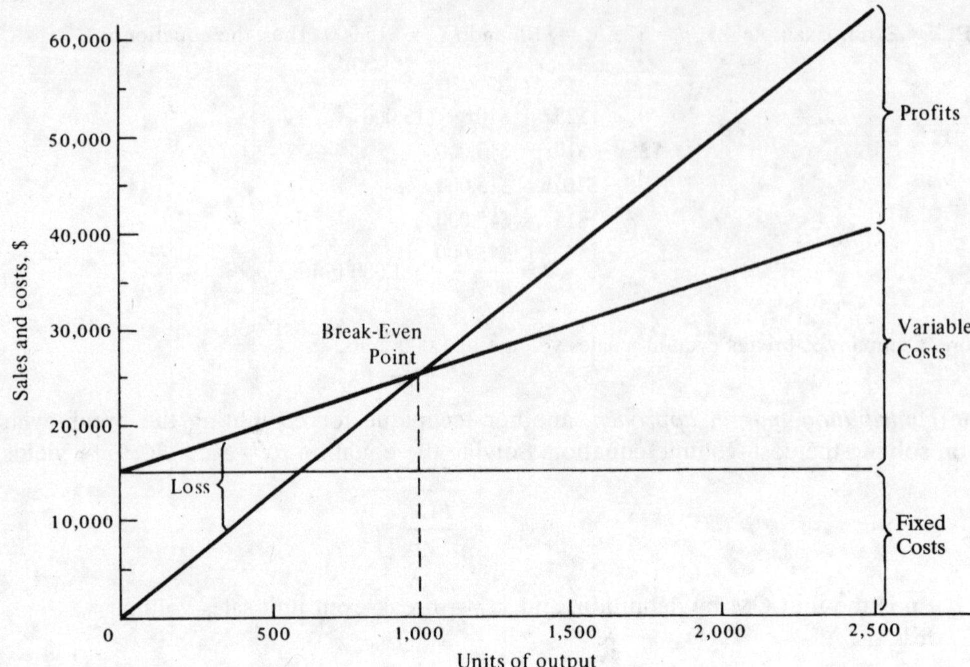

Fig. 4-1 Break-even chart.

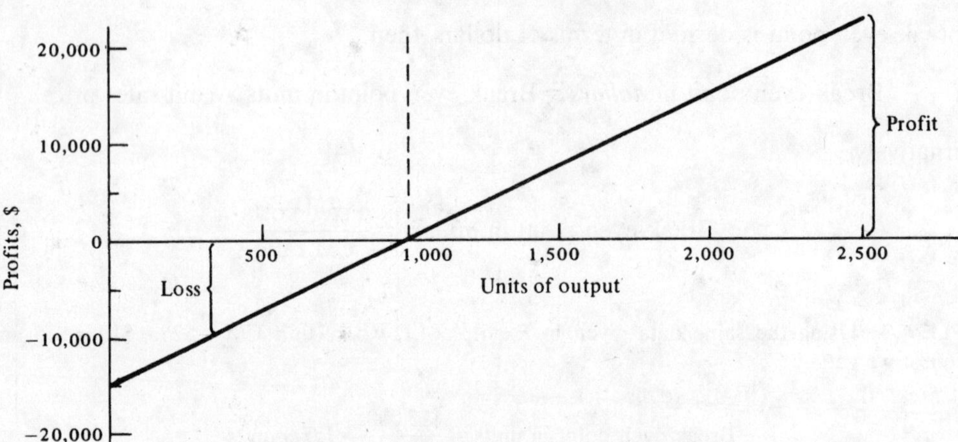

Fig. 4-2 Profit–volume (*P–V*) chart.

4.5 TARGET INCOME VOLUME AND MARGIN OF SAFETY

DETERMINATION OF TARGET INCOME VOLUME

Besides being able to determine the break-even point, CVP analysis determines the sales required to attain a particular income level or target net income. There are two ways in which target net income can be expressed:

Case 1. As a specific dollar amount *Case 2.* As a percentage of sales

Case 1 As a specific dollar amount, the cost–volume equation specifying target net income is

$$px = vx + FC + \text{Target income}$$

Solving the equation for x yields

$$x_{TI} = \frac{FC + \text{Target income}}{p - v}$$

where x_{TI} = sales volume required to achieve a given target income.

In words,

$$\text{Target income sales volume} = \frac{\text{Fixed costs} + \text{Target income}}{\text{Unit CM}}$$

Case 2 Specifying target income as a percentage of sales, the cost–volume equation is

$$px = vx + FC + \%(px)$$

Solving this for x yields:

$$x_{TI} = \frac{FC}{p - v - \%(p)}$$

In words,

$$\text{Target income sales volume} = \frac{\text{Fixed costs}}{\text{Unit CM} - \text{\% of unit sales price}}$$

EXAMPLE 4.4 Using the same data given in Example 4.1, assume that Company Z wishes to attain:

Case 1. A target income of $15,000 before tax

Case 2. A target income of 20% of sales

In Case 1, target income sales volume (in units) required is

$$x_{TI} = \frac{FC + \text{Target income}}{p - v} = \frac{\$15{,}000 + \$15{,}000}{\$25 - \$10} = 2{,}000 \text{ units}$$

To prove:

Sales (2,000 units)	$50,000
VC (2,000 units)	−20,000
CM	$30,000
FC	−15,000
Net income	$15,000

In Case 2, the target income volume required is

$$x_{TI} = \frac{FC}{p - v - \%(p)} = \frac{\$15{,}000}{\$15 - (20\%)(\$25)} = \frac{\$15{,}000}{\$15 - \$5} = 1{,}500 \text{ units}$$

To prove:

Sales (1,500 units)	$37,500 (100%)
VC (1,500 units)	−15,000
CM	$22,500 (60%)
FC	−15,000
Net income	$ 7,500 (20%)

IMPACT OF INCOME TAXES

If target income is given on an after-tax basis, the target income volume formula becomes

$$\text{Target income volume} = \frac{\text{Fixed costs} + [\text{Target after-tax income}/(1 - \text{tax rate})]}{\text{Unit CM}}$$

EXAMPLE 4.5 Assume in Example 4.1 that Company Z wants to achieve an after-tax income of \$6,000. An income tax is levied at 40 percent. Then,

$$\text{Target income volume} = \frac{\$15{,}000 + [\$6{,}000/(1 - 0.4)]}{\$15}$$

$$= \frac{\$15{,}000 + \$10{,}000}{\$15} = 1{,}667 \text{ units}$$

MARGIN OF SAFETY

The margin of safety is a measure of difference between the actual level of sales and the break-even sales. It is the amount by which sales revenue may drop before losses begin, and is expressed as a percentage of budgeted sales:

$$\text{Margin of safety} = \frac{\text{Budgeted sales} - \text{Break-even sales}}{\text{Budgeted sales}}$$

The margin of safety is often used as a measure of risk. The larger the ratio, the safer is the situation, since there is less risk of reaching the break-even point.

EXAMPLE 4.6 Assume that Company Z projects sales of \$30,000 with a break-even sales level of \$25,000. The expected margin of safety is

$$\frac{\$30{,}000 - \$25{,}000}{\$30{,}000} = 16.7\%$$

4.6 SOME APPLICATIONS OF CVP ANALYSIS

The concepts of contribution margin have many applications in profit planning and short-term decision making. Some applications are illustrated in Examples 4.7 to 4.11 using the same data as in Example 4.1.

EXAMPLE 4.7 Recall from Example 4.1 that Company Z has a CM of 60 percent and fixed costs of \$15,000 per period. Assume that the company expects sales to go up by \$10,000 for the next period. How much will income increase?

Using the CM concepts, we can quickly compute the impact of a change in sales on profits. The formula for computing the impact is

$$\text{Change in net income} = \text{Dollar change in sales} \times \text{CM ratio}$$

Thus, in this question,

$$\text{Increase in net income} = \$10{,}000 \times 60\% = \$6{,}000$$

Therefore, the income will go up by \$6,000, assuming there is no change in fixed costs.

If we are given the change in sales in *units* instead of dollars, then the formula becomes

$$\text{Change in net income} = \text{Change in unit sales} \times \text{Unit CM}$$

EXAMPLE 4.8 What before-tax income is expected on sales of \$47,500?

The answer is the difference between the CM and the fixed costs:

CM: \$47,500 × 60%	\$28,500
Less: Fixed costs	15,000
Net income	\$13,500

EXAMPLE 4.9 Company Z is considering increasing the advertising budget by $5,000, which would increase sales revenue by $8,000. Should the advertising budget be increased?

The answer is no, since the increase in the CM is less than the increased cost:

Increase in CM: $8,000 × 60%	$4,800
Increase in advertising	5,000
Decrease in net income	$ (200)

EXAMPLE 4.10 Company Z's sales manager is considering a $3,000 increase in sales salaries. What additional sales are required to cover the higher cost?

The increase in fixed cost must be matched by an equal increase in CM:

$$\text{Increase in CM} = \text{Increase in fixed cost}$$
$$0.60 \text{ sales} = \$3{,}000$$
$$\text{Sales} = \$5{,}000$$

EXAMPLE 4.11 Consider the original data. Assume again that Company Z is currently selling 1,500 units per period. In an effort to increase sales, management is considering cutting its unit price by $5 and increasing the advertising budget by $1,000. If these two steps are taken, management feels that unit sales will go up by 60 percent. Should the two steps be taken?

A $5 reduction in the selling price will cause the unit CM to decrease from $15 to $10. Thus,

Proposed CM: 2,400 units × $10	$24,000
Present CM: 1,500 units × $15	22,500
Increase in CM	$ 1,500
Increase in advertising outlay	1,000
Increase in net income	$ 500

The answer, therefore, is yes. Alternatively, the same answer can be obtained by developing comparative income statements in contribution margin format:

	Present (1,500 units)	Proposed (2,400 units)	Difference
Sales	$37,500 (@$25)	$48,000 (@$20)	$10,500
Less: Variable costs	15,000	24,000	9,000
CM	$22,500	$24,000	$ 1,500
Less: Fixed costs	15,000	16,000	1,000
Net income	$ 7,500	$ 8,000	$ 500

4.7 SALES MIX ANALYSIS

Break-even and cost–volume–profit analysis requires some additional computations and assumptions when a company produces and sells more than one product. Different selling prices and different variable costs result in different unit CM and CM ratios. As a result, break-even points vary with the relative proportions of the products sold, called the *sales mix*. In break-even and CVP analysis, it is necessary to predetermine the sales mix and then compute a *weighted-average CM*. It is also necessary to assume that the sales mix does not change for a specified period. The break-even formula for the company as a whole is

$$\text{Companywide break-even in units (or in dollars)} = \frac{\text{Fixed costs}}{\textit{Average}\text{ unit CM (or }\textit{average}\text{ CM ratio)}}$$

EXAMPLE 4.12 Assume that Company X has two products with the following CM data:

	A	B
Selling price	\$15	\$10
Variable cost	12	5
Unit CM	\$ 3	\$ 5
Sales mix	60%	40%
Fixed costs	\$76,000	

The weighted-average unit CM = (\$3)(0.6) + (\$5)(0.4) = \$3.80. Therefore the company's break-even point in units is

$$\frac{\$76{,}000}{\$3.80} = 20{,}000 \text{ units}$$

which is divided as follows:

A:	20,000 units × 60% =	12,000 units
B:	20,000 units × 40%	8,000
		20,000 units

EXAMPLE 4.13 Assume that Company Y produces and sells three products with the following data:

	A	B	C	Total
Sales	\$30,000	\$60,000	\$10,000	\$100,000
Sales mix	30%	60%	10%	100%
Less: VC	24,000	40,000	5,000	69,000
CM	\$ 6,000	\$20,000	\$ 5,000	\$ 31,000
CM ratio	20%	$33\frac{1}{3}$%	50%	31%

Total fixed costs are \$18,600.

The CM ratio for Company Y is \$31,000/\$100,000 = 31 percent. Therefore the break-even point *in dollars* is

$$\frac{\$18{,}600}{0.31} = \$60{,}000$$

which will be split in the mix ratio of 3:6:1 to give us the following break-even points for the individual products A, B, and C:

A:	\$60,000 × 30% =	\$18,000
B:	\$60,000 × 60% =	36,000
C:	\$60,000 × 10% =	6,000
		\$60,000

One of the most important assumptions underlying CVP analysis in a multiproduct firm is that the sales mix will not change during the planning period. If the sales mix changes, the break-even point will also change.

EXAMPLE 4.14 Assume that total sales from Example 4.13 remain unchanged at $100,000 but that a shift is expected in mix from product B to product C, as follows:

	A	B	C	Total
Sales	$30,000	$30,000	$40,000	$100,000
Sales mix	30%	30%	40%	100%
Less: VC	24,000	20,000*	20,000	64,000
CM	$ 6,000	$10,000	$20,000	$ 36,000
CM ratio	20%	$33\frac{1}{3}$%	50%	36%

*$20,000 = $30,000 × $66\frac{2}{3}$%.

Note that the shift in sales mix toward the more profitable line C has caused the CM ratio for the company as a whole to go up from 31 percent to 36 percent. The new break-even point is $18,600/0.36 = $51,667. The break-even dollar volume has decreased from $60,000 to $51,667.

4.8 BREAK-EVEN AND CVP ANALYSIS ASSUMPTIONS

The basic break-even and CVP models are subject to a number of limiting assumptions:

(*a*) The behavior of both sales revenue and expenses is *linear* throughout the entire *relevant* range of activity.

(*b*) All costs are classified as fixed or variable.

(*c*) There is only one product or a *constant* sales mix.

(*d*) Inventories do not change significantly from period to period.

(*e*) Volume is the only factor affecting variable costs.

4.9 ABSORPTION VS. DIRECT COSTING

Currently, the most commonly accepted theory of product costing holds that the cost of producing a product includes direct materials, direct labor, and an apportioned share of the factory overhead costs. This method of assigning costs to products, called *absorption (full) costing*, is the method generally required for tax purposes.

Because all costs, including fixed overhead, are applied to production under absorption costing, variations in unit-product cost may result solely from variations in production volume. If fixed costs are $200,000 and 20,000 units are produced, unit fixed cost is $10; if volume is 40,000, unit fixed cost is $5. Because these variations are not controllable at the production manager level and may obscure other significant variations in cost, they can be excluded from product cost through the use of a costing technique referred to as *direct (variable or marginal) costing*.

Under direct costing, all variable manufacturing costs are charged to the product, and all fixed costs (including fixed manufacturing costs) are charged to expense. Thus, all manufacturing costs must first be classified as fixed or variable. Direct materials and direct labor costs are usually completely variable, but factory overhead costs must be separated into variable and fixed portions. All variable costs (direct materials, direct labor, and variable overhead) are assigned to production and become part of the unit costs of the products produced. All fixed costs are assumed to be costs of the period and are charged to expenses.

In summary, the only difference between absorption costing and direct costing is in the treatment of fixed manufacturing costs. Under absorption costing they are treated as product costs, and under direct costing they are treated as period costs.

The differences between direct and absorption costing can be seen from an illustration comparing the income statement that would result from applying each technique to the same data. Assume the following information:

		Variable costs (per unit)	
Beginning inventory	0	Direct materials	$2.00
Production (units)	10,000	Direct labor	1.00
Sales (units)	9,000	Factory overhead	0.30
		Total	$3.30

Fixed factory overhead	$ 6,000		
Selling expenses	15,000	Variable selling expenses (per unit)	$0.20
Administrative expenses	12,000		
Total	$33,000	Selling price (per unit)	$8.00

INCOME STATEMENT UNDER DIRECT COSTING

Under direct costing, the year's income statement is as shown in Fig. 4-3. Note that all of the fixed manufacturing costs are considered costs of the period and are not included in inventories. The fixed factory overhead is treated as a period cost and is deducted, along with the selling and administrative expenses, in the period incurred. That is,

Direct materials	xx
Direct labor	xx
Variable factory overhead	xx
Product cost	$xx

Sales (9,000 units at $8)		$72,000
Cost of Goods Sold:		
Variable Production Costs Incurred (10,000 units at $3.30)	$33,000	
Less: Inventory (1,000 units at $3.30)	3,300	29,700
Manufacturing Margin		$42,300
Variable Selling Expenses (9,000 units at $0.20)		1,800
Contribution Margin		$40,500
Period Costs:		
Factory Overhead	$ 6,000	
Selling Expenses	15,000	
Administrative Expenses	12,000	33,000
Net Income		$ 7,500

Fig. 4-3 Income statement under direct costing.

INCOME STATEMENT UNDER ABSORPTION COSTING

Figure 4-4 shows the income statement that would be prepared under absorption costing. Note that the fixed manufacturing costs are included as part of the product cost and that some of these costs are included in the ending inventory. Under absorption costing, the cost to be inventoried includes all manufacturing costs, both variable and fixed. Nonmanufacturing (operating) expenses—i.e., selling

Sales (9,000 units at $8)		$72,000
Cost of Goods Sold:		
Variable Costs of Production (10,000 units at $3.30)	$33,000	
Fixed Overhead Costs	6,000	
Total Costs of Producing 10,000 Units	$39,000	
Less: Inventory (1,000 units at $3.90*)	3,900	35,100
Gross Margin		$36,900
Operating Expenses:		
Selling ($15,000 fixed plus 9,000 units at $0.20 each)	$16,800	
Administrative	12,000	28,800
Net Income		$ 8,100

*$3.90 = $3.30 + ($6,000/10,000 units) = $3.30 + $0.60.

Fig. 4-4 Income statement under absorption costing

and administrative expenses—are treated as period expenses and thus are charged against current revenue:

Direct materials	$xx
Direct labor	xx
Variable factory overhead	xx
Fixed factory overhead	xx
Product cost	$xx

The ending inventory is priced at so-called full cost; that is, the cost of ending inventory includes fixed factory overhead.

Two important facts should be noted:

1. Effects of the two costing methods on net income:
   (*a*) When production exceeds sales, a larger net income will be reported under absorption costing.
   (*b*) When sales exceeds production, a larger net income will be reported under direct costing.
   (*c*) When sales and production are equal, net income will be the same under both methods.
2. Reconciliation of the direct and absorption costing net income figures:
   (*a*) The difference in net income can be reconciled as

   Change in inventory × Fixed factory overhead rate = Difference in net income

   (*b*) The above formula works only if the fixed overhead rate per unit does not change between the periods.

We can prove:

1. Difference in net income: $8,100 − $7,500 = $600. Absorption costing shows a larger net income.
2. Reconciliation of difference in net income:

Change in inventory × Fixed factory overhead rate = Difference in net income

$$1{,}000 \quad \times \quad \$0.6\left(\frac{\$6{,}000}{10{,}000\text{ units}}\right) \quad = \quad \$600$$

MANAGERIAL USE OF DIRECT COSTING

It is important to realize that direct costing is used for internal purposes only. It highlights the concept of contribution margin and focuses on the costs by behavior rather than by function. Its managerial uses include: (1) relevant cost analysis; (2) break-even and cost–volume–profit (CVP) analyses; and (3) short-term decision making.

An understanding of cost behavior is extremely useful for managerial planning and decision-making purposes. It allows managerial accountants to perform short-term planning analysis, such as break-even analysis. Cost–volume–profit analysis is useful as a frame of reference, as a vehicle for expressing overall managerial performance, and as a planning device via break-even techniques and what-if scenarios. Breaking down the costs by behavior, which is reflected in a contribution (direct costing) income statement, facilitates the use of various short-term profit-planning tools on the part of managerial accountants.

Direct costing, however, is not acceptable for external reporting or for income tax reporting. Companies that use direct costing for internal reporting must convert to absorption costing for external reporting.

Summary

(1) ____________ is the difference between sales and variable expenses.

(2) The unit contribution margin is the difference between ____________ and ____________.

(3) The margin of safety is the ratio by which the current sales value exceeds the ____________.

(4) If the ____________ changes, it is necessary to recompute the break-even point for the company as a whole.

(5) The formula $(S - VC)/S$, or $1 - (VC/S)$, is known as the ____________.

(6) Break-even analysis and cost–volume–profit analysis are synonymous: (*a*) true; (*b*) false.

(7) The break-even point is reached when sales revenue equals total fixed costs: (*a*) true; (*b*) false.

(8) An increase in total fixed costs causes the break-even point to ____________.

(9) The break-even point in units can be calculated by dividing total fixed costs by the ____________, whereas the break-even point in ____________ can be computed by dividing total fixed costs by the ____________.

(10) In the usual break-even chart, the activity level is measured on the ____________ axis.

(11) A change in income can be quickly computed by multiplying a change in sales in dollars by the ____________.

(12) One of the key assumptions underlying break-even analysis is that the behavior of both sales revenue and expenses is ____________ throughout the entire ____________ range of activity.

(13) Cost–volume–profit analysis helps management investigate the effects of changes in costs, price, and volume on ____________.

(14) There are two ways of expressing target income: as a specific dollar amount and as a ____________.

(15) The *P–V* chart shows the relationship between ____________ and ____________, and the slope of the chart is in effect the ____________.

Answers: (1) contribution margin; (2) selling price; unit variable cost; (3) break-even sales; (4) sales mix; (5) contribution margin ratio; (6) (*b*); (7) (*b*); (8) increase; (9) unit contribution margin, dollars, contribution margin ratio; (10) horizontal; (11) contribution margin ratio; (12) linear, relevant; (13) profits; (14) percentage of sales; (15) profits, volume of activity, unit contribution margin.

Solved Problems

4.1 The following information pertains to the budget of Quality Products, Inc., for the next year:

Sales	$50,000,000
Variable expenses	45,000,000
Fixed costs	3,000,000

Calculate the expected net income for each of the following independent cases:

(*a*) 10 percent increase in sales volume

(*b*) 10 percent increase in fixed costs

(*c*) 10 percent decrease in sales volume

(*d*) 10 percent increase in variable expenses

(*e*) 15 percent increase in fixed costs and 15 percent decrease in variable expenses

SOLUTION

	Sales	Variable Costs	CM	Fixed Costs	Net Income
(*a*)	$55,000,000	$49,500,000	$ 5,500,000	$3,000,000	$ 2,500,000
(*b*)	50,000,000	45,000,000	5,000,000	3,300,000	1,700,000
(*c*)	45,000,000	40,500,000	4,500,000	3,000,000	1,500,000
(*d*)	50,000,000	49,500,000	500,000	3,000,000	(2,500,000)
(*e*)	50,000,000	38,250,000	11,750,000	3,450,000	8,300,000

4.2 For each of the following cases, find the missing amounts:

	Sales in Units	Sales in Dollars	Variable Expenses	Contribution Margin per Unit	Fixed Costs	Net Income
Case 1	5,000	$90,000	$40,000	$(*a*)	$15,000	$ (*b*)
Case 2	3,000	(*c*)	4,000	3	(*d*)	2,000
Case 3	10,000	50,000	(*e*)	(*f*)	20,000	5,000

SOLUTION

(*a*) $$\text{Unit CM} = \frac{\$90{,}000 - \$40{,}000}{5{,}000 \text{ units}} = \$10 \text{ per unit}$$

(*b*) $$\text{Net income} = \$90{,}000 - \$40{,}000 - \$15{,}000 = \$35{,}000$$

(*c*) $$\begin{aligned} CM &= 3{,}000 \text{ units} \times \$3 = \$9{,}000 \\ \text{Sales} - \$4{,}000 &= \$9{,}000 \\ \text{Sales} &= \$13{,}000 \end{aligned}$$

(*d*) $$\begin{aligned} \$13{,}000 - \$4{,}000 - \text{Fixed costs} &= \$2{,}000 \\ \text{Fixed costs} &= \$7{,}000 \end{aligned}$$

(*e*) $$\begin{aligned} \$50{,}000 - \text{Variable expenses} - \$20{,}000 &= \$5{,}000 \\ \text{Variable expenses} &= \$25{,}000 \end{aligned}$$

(*f*) $$\text{Unit CM} = \frac{\$50{,}000 - \$25{,}000}{10{,}000 \text{ units}} = \$2.50$$

4.3 For each of the following cases, find the missing amounts:

	Sales in Dollars	Variable Expenses	Contribution Margin Ratio	Fixed Costs	Net Income
Case 1	$100,000	$50,000	(*a*)%	$30,000	$ (*b*)
Case 2	200,000	(*c*)	30	(*d*)	5,000
Case 3	(*e*)	(*f*)	40	25,000	25,000

SOLUTION

(*a*) $$\text{CM ratio} = \frac{\$100{,}000 - \$50{,}000}{\$100{,}000} = 50\%$$

(*b*) $$\text{Net income} = \$100{,}000 - \$50{,}000 - \$30{,}000 = \$20{,}000$$

(*c*) $$\frac{\$200{,}000 - \text{Variable expenses}}{\$200{,}000} = 30\%$$

$$\text{Variable expenses} = \$140{,}000$$

(*d*) $$\begin{aligned} \$200{,}000 - \$140{,}000 - \text{Fixed costs} &= \$5{,}000 \\ \text{Fixed costs} &= \$55{,}000 \end{aligned}$$

(*e*) $$\begin{aligned} CM - \text{Fixed costs} &= \text{Net income} \\ CM - \$25{,}000 &= \$25{,}000 \\ CM &= \$50{,}000 \end{aligned}$$

By definition, the CM ratio equals *CM*/Sales. 40% = $50,000/Sales; therefore, Sales = $125,000.

(*f*) $$\begin{aligned} CM &= \text{Sales} - \text{Variable expenses} \\ \$50{,}000 &= \$125{,}000 - \text{Variable expenses} \\ \text{Variable expenses} &= \$75{,}000 \end{aligned}$$

4.4 The following information is given for Egele-Kamp, Inc.:

Unit sales price	$ 10
Variable cost per unit	6
Total fixed costs	50,000

Determine the following:

(*a*) Contribution margin per unit
(*b*) Contribution margin ratio
(*c*) Break-even sales in units
(*d*) Break-even sales in dollars
(*e*) Sales in units required to achieve a net income of $4,000
(*f*) Sales in units required to achieve a net income of 15 percent of sales

SOLUTION

(*a*)
$$\text{Contribution margin per unit} = \$10 - \$6 = \$4$$

(*b*)
$$\text{Contribution margin ratio} = \frac{\$4}{\$10} = 40\%$$

(*c*)
$$\text{Break-even sales in units} = \frac{\$50{,}000}{\$4} = 12{,}500 \text{ units}$$

(*d*)
$$\text{Break-even sales in dollars} = 12{,}500 \text{ units} \times \$10 = \$125{,}000$$

or, alternatively,
$$\frac{\$50{,}000}{0.4} = \$125{,}000$$

(*e*)
$$\text{Target income sales in units} = \frac{\$50{,}000 + \$4{,}000}{\$4} = 13{,}500 \text{ units}$$

(*f*)
$$\text{Target income sales in units} = \frac{\$50{,}000}{\$4 - 15\%(\$10)} = \frac{\$50{,}000}{\$2.5} = 20{,}000 \text{ units}$$

4.5 The following data are given for Miratel Design, Inc., which markets multiple products:

Sales	$65,000
Variable expenses	39,000
Total fixed costs	12,000

Compute (*a*) the contribution margin ratio and (*b*) break-even sales in dollars.

SOLUTION

(*a*)
$$\text{Contribution margin ratio} = \frac{\$65{,}000 - \$39{,}000}{\$65{,}000} = 40\%$$

(*b*)
$$\text{Break-even sales in dollars} = \frac{\$12{,}000}{0.4} = \$30{,}000$$

4.6 The following information is given for Quality Electronics, Inc.:

Unit selling price	$ 250
Variable cost per unit	130
Fixed costs	26,000
Tax rate	40%

Determine the number of units that should be produced to achieve an after-tax target income of $6,000.

SOLUTION

$$\text{Target income sales in units} = \frac{\$26{,}000 + [\$6{,}000/(1-0.4)]}{\$250 - \$130} = \frac{\$36{,}000}{\$120} = 300 \text{ units}$$

4.7 The Anderson Company has recently purchased a plant to manufacture a new product. The following data pertain to the new operation:

Estimated annual sales	3,500 units @$20
Estimated costs:	
Direct materials	\$6.00/unit
Direct labor	\$1.00/unit
Factory overhead (all fixed)	\$12,000 per year
Selling expenses	30% of sales
Administrative expenses (all fixed)	\$16,000 per year

Determine (*a*) the break-even point in units and in dollars and (*b*) the selling price if profit per unit is \$2.04.

SOLUTION

(*a*)

Variable Costs		Fixed Costs	
Direct materials	\$ 6.00	Factory overhead	\$12,000
Direct labor	1.00	Administrative	16,000
Selling expenses	6.00		\$28,000
	\$13.00 per unit		

$$\text{Break-even point in units} = \frac{\$28{,}000}{\$20 - \$13} = 4{,}000 \text{ units}$$

$$\text{Break-even point in dollars} = 4{,}000 \text{ units} \times \$20 = \$80{,}000$$

(*b*)

$$\text{Sales} = \text{Variable costs} + \text{Fixed costs} + \text{Net income}$$

Let P = the selling price. Then

$$3{,}500P = \$7(3{,}500) + 0.3P(3{,}500) + \$28{,}000 + \$2.04(3{,}500)$$
$$2{,}450P = \$59{,}640$$
$$P = \$24.34$$

4.8 The Canadian Zinc Company is one of several suppliers of part X to an automobile manufacturing firm. Orders are distributed to the various die-casting companies on a fairly even basis; however, the sales manager of the company believes that with a reduction in price he could secure a 30 percent increase in units sold. The general manager has asked you to analyze the sales manager's proposal and submit your recommendation. The following data are available:

	Present	Proposed
Unit price	\$2.50	\$2.00
Unit sales	200,000 units	Plus 30%
Variable costs	\$350,000	Same unit variable cost
Fixed costs	\$120,000	\$120,000
Net profit	\$ 30,000	?

Calculate (*a*) net profit or loss on the sales manager's proposal and (*b*) unit sales required under the proposed price to make the original \$30,000 profit.

(SMA, adapted)

SOLUTION

(*a*)

Sales (260,000 units @\$2.00)	\$520,000
Less: Variable costs (@\$1.75)	455,000
CM	\$ 65,000
Fixed costs	120,000
Net income	\$ (55,000)

(*b*)

$$\text{Number of unit sales required} = \frac{\$120{,}000 + \$30{,}000}{\$2.00 - \$1.75} = 600{,}000 \text{ units}$$

4.9 The following information is given for the Vendor Company:

Fixed costs	\$30,000 per period
Variable cost	\$5/unit
Selling price	\$8/unit

(*a*) Compute the break-even sales in units and in dollars.
(*b*) Calculate the margin of safety at the 12,000-unit level.
(*c*) Find the net income when sales are \$120,000.
(*d*) Compute the sales in units required to produce a net income of \$10,000.
(*e*) Calculate the sales in units required to produce a net income of 10% of sales.
(*f*) Find the break-even in units if variable costs are increased by \$1 per unit and if total fixed costs are decreased by \$5,000.

SOLUTION

(*a*)

$$\text{Break-even point in units} = \frac{\$30{,}000}{\$8 - \$5} = 10{,}000 \text{ units}$$

$$\text{Break-even point in dollars} = 10{,}000 \text{ units} \times \$8 = \$80{,}000$$

(*b*)

$$\text{Margin of safety} = \frac{12{,}000 \text{ units} - 10{,}000 \text{ units}}{12{,}000 \text{ units}} = 16.7\%$$

(*c*)

Sales	\$120,000	
Variable costs	75,000	(15,000 units @\$5)
CM	\$ 45,000	
Fixed costs	30,000	
Net income	\$ 15,000	

(*d*)

$$\text{Target income volume} = \frac{\$30{,}000 + \$10{,}000}{\$8 - \$5} = 13{,}333 \text{ units}$$

(*e*)

$$\text{Target income volume} = \frac{\$30{,}000}{\$8 - \$5 - (10\%)(\$8)} = \frac{\$30{,}000}{\$2.2} = 13{,}636 \text{ units}$$

(*f*)

$$\text{Break-even in units} = \frac{\$25{,}000}{\$8 - \$6} = 12{,}500 \text{ units}$$

4.10 The Carey Company sold 100,000 units of its product at \$20 per unit. Variable costs are \$14 per unit (manufacturing costs of \$11 and selling expenses of \$3). Fixed costs are incurred uniformly throughout the year and amount to $792,000 (manufacturing costs of $500,000 and selling expenses of $292,000).

Calculate the following: (*a*) the break-even point in units and in dollars, (*b*) the number of units that must be sold to earn an income of $60,000 before income tax, (*c*) the number of units that must be sold to earn an after-tax income of $90,000 if the income tax rate is 40 percent, and (*d*) the number of units required to break even if the labor cost is 50 percent of variable costs and 20 percent of fixed costs, and if there is a 10 percent increase in labor costs.

(AICPA, adapted)

SOLUTION

(*a*)
$$\text{Break-even point in units} = \frac{\$792{,}000}{\$20 - \$14} = 132{,}000 \text{ units}$$

$$\text{Break-even point in dollars} = 132{,}000 \text{ units} \times \$20 = \$2{,}640{,}000$$

(*b*)
$$\text{Units required to earn a \$60,000 income} = \frac{\$792{,}000 + \$60{,}000}{\$6} = 142{,}000 \text{ units}$$

(*c*)
$$\text{Units required to earn an after-tax income of \$90,000} = \frac{\$792{,}000 + [\$90{,}000/(1 - 0.4)]}{\$6} = 157{,}000 \text{ units}$$

(*d*)
$$\text{Units required to break even} = \frac{\$792{,}000 + [(\$792{,}000 \times 20\%) \times 10\%]}{\$20 - [\$14 + (\$14 \times 50\%) \times 10\%]} = \frac{\$792{,}000 + \$15{,}840}{\$20 - \$14.70} = \frac{\$807{,}840}{\$5.30} = 152{,}423 \text{ units}$$

4.11 The Lublock Specialty, Inc., manufactures a product which sells for $5. At present the company produces and sells 50,000 units per year. Unit variable manufacturing and selling expenses are $2.50 and $0.50, respectively. Fixed costs are $70,000 for factory overhead and $30,000 for selling and administrative activities. The sales manager has proposed that the price be increased to $6. To maintain the present sales volume, advertising must be increased. The company's profit objective is 10 percent of sales.

Calculate (*a*) the additional expenditure the company can afford for advertising and (*b*) the new break-even point in units and in dollars, using the $6 selling price and the additional advertising outlay from part (*a*).

(CGA, adapted)

SOLUTION

(*a*) Let x = additional advertising outlay.

Sales	$300,000
Less: Variable costs	150,000
CM	$150,000
Fixed costs	100,000
Additional	x
Net income	$ 30,000

Thus, $x = \$20{,}000$.

(*b*)
$$\text{Break-even sales in units} = \frac{\$100{,}000 + \$20{,}000}{\$6 - \$3} = 40{,}000 \text{ units}$$

$$\text{Break-even sales in dollars} = 40{,}000 \text{ units} \times \$6 = \$240{,}000$$

4.12 Ro Company, a manufacturer of quality handmade pipes, has experienced a steady growth in its sales for the past five years. Increased competition, however, has led the president, Mr. Ro, to believe that an aggressive advertising campaign will be necessary next year to maintain the company's present growth. To prepare for next year's advertising campaign, the company's accountant presents the following data for the current year, 19A:

Variable costs (per pipe):	
Direct labor	$ 8.00
Direct materials	3.25
Variable overhead	2.50
Total variable costs	$ 13.75
Fixed costs:	
Manufacturing	$ 25,000
Selling	40,000
Administrative	70,000
Total fixed costs	$135,000
Sales price per pipe	$ 25
Expected sales, 19A (20,000 pipes)	$500,000
Income tax rate	40%

Mr. Ro has set the 19B sales target at a level of $550,000, or 22,000 pipes. Determine the following: (*a*) The projected after-tax net income for 19A; (*b*) the break-even sales in units for 19A; (*c*) the after-tax net income for 19B if an additional fixed selling expense of $11,250 is spent for advertising in 19B in order to attain the 19B sales target; (*d*) the break-even sales in dollars for 19B if the additional $11,250 is spent for advertising; (*e*) the sales in dollars required to equal 19A's after-tax net income, if the additional $11,250 is spent for advertising in 19B; and (*f*) the maximum amount that can be spent on advertising at a sales level of 22,000 pipes, if an after-tax net income of $60,000 is desired.

(CMA, adapted)

SOLUTION

(*a*)

Sales	$500,000
Less: Variable costs	275,000
CM	$225,000
Less: Fixed costs	135,000
Net income	$ 90,000
Less: Income taxes	36,000
Projected 19A's after-tax income	$ 54,000

(*b*)

$$\text{Break-even sales in units} = \frac{\$135{,}000}{\$25 - \$13.75} = 12{,}000 \text{ units}$$

(*c*)

$$\begin{aligned}\text{After-tax net income for 19B} &= (\text{Sales} - \text{Variable costs} - \text{Fixed costs}) \times (1 - \text{Tax rate})\\ &= (\$550{,}000 - \$302{,}500 - \$146{,}250)(1 - 0.4) = \$60{,}750\end{aligned}$$

(*d*)

$$\text{Break-even sales in dollars} = \frac{\$146{,}250}{1 - (\$13.75/\$25.00)} = \frac{\$146{,}250}{0.45} = \$325{,}000$$

(*e*)

$$\text{Required 19B sales level} = \frac{\$146{,}250 + [\$54{,}000/(1 - 0.4)]}{0.45} = \frac{\$236{,}250}{0.45} = \$525{,}000$$

(*f*) Let x = maximum advertising. Then

Sales	$550,000 (22,000 @$25)
Less: Variable costs	302,500 (@$13.75)
CM	$247,500
Less: Fixed costs	135,000
Advertising	x
Net income before tax*	$100,000

*$100,000 = $60,000/(1 − 0.4).

x is calculated as $12,500.

4.13 The Manhasset Machine Tool Corporation manufactures a variety of machine tools. The following are taken from the budget for 19A:

Sales (10,000 units)	$200,000
Variable costs	120,000
Fixed costs	90,000

(*a*) What is the break-even point in units in 19A?

(*b*) What sales volume would be necessary to earn an after-tax net income of $16,000 if the income tax rate is 40 percent?

(*c*) What sales volume would be necessary to earn a profit before tax equal to 10 percent of sales?

(*d*) What effect would a 10 percent price increase have on the break-even point?

(*e*) What are the principal assumptions underlying the break-even and cost–volume–profit calculations made in the above?

SOLUTION

(*a*) Unit sales price = $20. Unit variable cost = $12. Therefore,

$$\text{Break-even point} = \frac{\$90{,}000}{\$20 - \$12} = 11{,}250 \text{ units}$$

(*b*)

$$\text{Target income sales volume} = \frac{\$90{,}000 + [\$16{,}000/(1 - 0.4)]}{\$20 - \$12}$$

$$= \frac{\$90{,}000 + \$26{,}667}{\$8} = 14{,}583 \text{ units}$$

(*c*)

$$\text{Target income sales volume} = \frac{\$90{,}000}{\$20 - \$12 - (10\%)(\$20)} = 15{,}000 \text{ units}$$

(*d*) The new break-even point in units = $90,000/($22 − $12) = 9,000 units. The increase in unit CM due to the increase in unit sales price will cause the break-even point to drop from 11,250 units to 9,000 units.

(*e*) The principal assumptions are:

- Both sales revenue and expenses behave in a linear fashion within the specified range of activity, known as the relevant range.
- The sales mix remains constant throughout the budgeting period.
- Changes in inventories are negligible in amount.

4.14 The Candy Company is a wholesale distributor of candy. The company serves grocery, convenience, and drug stores in a large metropolitan area. Small but steady growth in sales has been achieved by the company over the past few years, while candy prices have been increasing. The company is formulating its plans for the coming fiscal year. Presented below are the data used to project the current year's after-tax net income of $110,400.

Average sales price per box	$ 4.00
Average variable costs per box:	
Cost of candy	$ 2.00
Selling	0.40
Total	$ 2.40
Annual fixed costs:	
Selling	$ 160,000
Administrative	280,000
Total	$ 440,000
Expected annual sales volume (390,000 boxes)	$1,560,000
Tax rate	40%

Candy manufacturers have announced that they will increase prices of their products an average of 15 percent in the coming year due to increases in materials and labor costs. The Candy Company expects that all other costs will remain at the same rates or levels as the current year.

(*a*) Determine the break-even point in boxes of candy for the current year.

(*b*) Calculate the sales price per box that the company must charge to cover the 15 percent increase in the cost of candy and still maintain the current contribution margin ratio.

(*c*) Determine the volume of sales in dollars the company must achieve in the coming year to maintain the same net income as projected for the current year if the sales price of candy remains at $4 per box and the cost of candy increases 15 percent.

(CMA, adapted)

SOLUTION

(*a*)
$$\text{Break-even sales in boxes of candy} = \frac{\$440{,}000}{\$4 - \$2.4} = 275{,}000 \text{ boxes}$$

(*b*)
$$\text{CM ratio} = 1 - \frac{\text{Variable costs}}{\text{Unit sales price}}$$

$$\text{New variable costs} = \$2.40 + (0.15)(\$2.00) = \$2.70$$

$$40\% = 1 - \frac{\$2.70}{p}$$

where p = unit sales price. If we solve this equation for p, we get $4.50.

(*c*) Sales volume in dollars to maintain $110,400 after-tax income:

$$\frac{\$440{,}000 + [\$110{,}400/(1 - 0.4)]}{1 - (\$2.70/\$4.00)} = \frac{\$624{,}000}{0.325} = \$1{,}920{,}000$$

4.15 The Pace Company has the following budget for the coming year:

Fixed costs	$80,000
Subcontracting costs (variable)	$4/unit
Other variable costs	$2/unit
Sales price	$10
Budgeted production and sales	25,000 units

As an alternative to subcontracting, the company can lease a plant for the year for $122,400. Total variable costs under this arrangement would be $2.40 per unit.

(*a*) Determine the break-even point in units under the initial budget.

(*b*) Calculate the margin of safety at the 25,000-unit level.

(*c*) Determine the break-even point in units under the lease arrangement.

(*d*) Determine whether the lease should be taken.

(*e*) Calculate the point of indifference between the subcontracting plan and the lease plan, i.e., the volume level in units where the profit under each plan would be equal.

SOLUTION

(*a*)
$$\text{Break-even sales in units} = \frac{\$80{,}000}{\$10 - \$6} = 20{,}000 \text{ units}$$

(*b*)
$$\text{Margin of safety} = \frac{25{,}000 \text{ units} - 20{,}000 \text{ units}}{25{,}000 \text{ units}} = 20\%$$

(*c*)
$$\text{Break-even point in units} = \frac{\$122{,}400}{\$10 - \$2.40} = 16{,}105 \text{ units}$$

(*d*) Yes, because it takes less units to break even under the lease arrangement.

(*e*) Let x = the volume of indifference.

Profits	
Subcontracting	Lease
$10x - 6x - \$80{,}000$	$10x - 2.40x - \$122{,}400$

We let them be equal to each other as follows:

$$\begin{aligned} 10x - 6x - \$80{,}000 &= 10x - 2.4x - \$122{,}400 \\ 3.6x &= \$42{,}400 \\ x &= 11{,}778 \text{ units} \end{aligned}$$

4.16 John Jay Company is selling a hardware product with a contribution margin of 40 percent on sales of $500,000 per year (50,000 units at $10). The fixed costs are $80,000 per year.

(*a*) How much increase in net income is expected in the coming year if sales increase by 10,000 units?

(*b*) How much increase in net income is expected in the coming year if sales are increased by $70,000?

(*c*) The sales manager feels that a $20,000 increase in the yearly advertising budget would increase annual sales by $60,000. Should the advertising budget be increased?

(*d*) The sales manager suggests cutting the present selling price by 10 percent and increasing the advertising budget by $25,000. If these two decisions are made, it is projected that unit sales will go up by 40 percent. Should this policy be approved?

SOLUTION

(*a*) The unit contribution margin is $\$10 \times 40\% = \$4$ per unit. Therefore, the increase in net income is 10,000 units $\times$ \$4 per unit = \$40,000.

(*b*)
$$\text{Increase in net income} = \$70{,}000 \times 40\% = \$28{,}000$$

(*c*)

Increase in CM ($60,000 × 40%)	$24,000
Increase in advertising (a fixed cost)	20,000
Increase in net income	$ 4,000

Therefore, the advertising should be increased.

(*d*) A reduction of $1 in the unit selling price will cause unit CM to drop from $4 to $3.

Proposed CM (50,000 units × 140% × $3 per unit)	$210,000
Present CM (50,000 units × $4 per unit)	200,000
Increased CM	$ 10,000
Increase in advertising	25,000
Decrease in net income	$ (15,000)

Therefore, the proposal should not be approved.

Alternatively, we can obtain the same answer by setting up comparative income statements:

	Present (50,000 units)	Proposed (70,000 units)	Difference
Sales	$500,000 (@$10)	$630,000 (@$9)	$130,000
Less: VC	300,000 (@$6)	420,000 (@$6)	120,000
CM	$200,000	$210,000	$ 10,000
Less: FC	80,000	105,000	25,000
Net income	$120,000	$105,000	$ (15,000)

4.17 The Tape Red Company has three major products, whose contribution margins are shown below:

	Product		
	A	B	C
Sales price	$15	$10	$8
Variable cost per unit	10	6	5
CM/unit	$ 5	$ 4	$3

Total fixed costs are $100,000.

Compute (*a*) the break-even point in units in total and for each product if the three products are sold in the proportions of 30, 50, and 20 percent, and (*b*) the break-even point in total and for each product if the sales mix ratio changes to 50, 30, and 20 percent.

SOLUTION

(*a*) Average contribution margin per unit = ($5) (30%) + ($4) (50%) + ($3) (20%) = $4.10 per unit

$$\text{Company break-even point} = \frac{\$100{,}000}{\$4.10} = 24{,}390 \text{ units}$$

which will be broken up, per product, into:

A	30% × 24,390 units = 7,317 units
B	50% × 24,390 units = 12,195 units
C	20% × 24,390 units = 4,878 units

(*b*) Average contribution margin per unit = ($5) (50%) + ($4) (30%) + ($3) (20%) = $4.30 per unit

$$\text{Company break-even point} = \frac{\$100{,}000}{\$4.30} = 23{,}256 \text{ units}$$

Individually,

A	50% × 23,256 units = 11,628 units
B	30% × 23,256 units = 6,977 units
C	20% × 23,256 units = 4,651 units

4.18 The Double Day Products Company has the following sales mix:

	Sales	Proportion	Variable Costs
A	$1,200,000	60%	$ 600,000
B	600,000	30	300,000
C	200,000	10	300,000
	$2,000,000	100%	$1,200,000

Total fixed costs: $600,000.

Compute the company's break-even sales in dollars and the individual products' break-even point, assuming the product mix does not change.

SOLUTION

$$\text{CM ratio} = 1 - \frac{\$1{,}200{,}000}{\$2{,}000{,}000} = 40\%$$

$$\text{Company break-even point} = \frac{\$600{,}000}{0.4} = \$1{,}500{,}000$$

Individually,

A	$\$1{,}500{,}000 \times 60\%$ =	$900,000
B	$\$1{,}500{,}000 \times 30\%$ =	450,000
C	$\$1{,}500{,}000 \times 10\%$ =	150,000

4.19 Andrew Manufacturing, Inc., manufactures two products—Baubles and Trinkets. The following data are projected for the coming year:

	Baubles		Trinkets		Total
	Units	Amount	Units	Amount	Amount
Sales	10,000	$10,000	8,000	$10,000	$20,000
Fixed cost		$ 2,000		$ 5,600	$ 7,600
Variable cost		6,000		3,000	9,000
Total cost		$ 8,000		$ 8,600	$16,600
Operating income		$ 2,000		$ 1,400	$ 3,400

(*a*) Determine the break-even sales in units for Baubles, assuming that the facilities are not used jointly.

(*b*) Determine the break-even sales in dollars for Trinkets, assuming that the facilities are not used jointly.

(*c*) Calculate the composite unit contribution margin, assuming that consumers purchase composite units of six Baubles and four Trinkets.

(*d*) Determine the break-even units for both products, assuming that consumers purchase composite units of six Baubles and four Trinkets.

(*e*) Calculate the composite contribution margin ratio, assuming that a composite unit is defined as one Bauble and one Trinket.

(*f*) Determine the break-even sales in dollars, assuming that Baubles and Trinkets become one-to-one complements and that there is no change in the company's costs.

(AICPA, adapted)

SOLUTION

(*a*)

$$\text{Break-even sales in units} = \frac{\$2{,}000}{\$1 - \$0.6} = 5{,}000 \text{ units}$$

(*b*) $$\text{Break-even sales in dollars} = \frac{\$5{,}600}{0.7} = \$8{,}000$$

(*c*)

	Baubles	Trinkets	Total
Sales price	$1.00	$1.250	$2.250
Variable cost	0.60	0.375	0.975
Unit CM	$0.40	$0.875	$1.275
Sales mix	60%	40%	

Therefore,

$$\text{Composite (or weighted-average) unit CM} = (\$0.40)(0.6) + (\$0.875)(0.4) = \$0.59$$

(*d*) $$\text{Break-even point for both products} = \frac{\$7{,}600}{0.59} = 12{,}881 \text{ units}$$

Individually,
Baubles: 60% (12,881 units) = 7,728 units
Trinkets: 40% (12,881 units) = 5,152 units

(*e*) $$\text{Composite (or weighted-average) CM ratio} = \frac{\$1.275}{\$2.250} = 0.57$$

(*f*) $$\text{Break-even point in dollars} = \frac{\$7{,}600}{0.57} = \$13{,}333$$

4.20 Hewtex Electronics manufactures and markets two products—tape recorders and electronic calculators. The projected income statement for both products is given below.

HEWTEX ELECTRONICS
Projected Income Statement
For the Year Ended December 31, 19A

	Tape Recorders Total (000)	Tape Recorders Per Unit	Electronic Calculators Total (000)	Electronic Calculators Per Unit	Total (000)
Sales	$1,050	$15.00	$3,150	$22.50	$4,200.00
Production Costs:					
Materials	$ 280	$ 4.00	$ 630	$ 4.50	$ 910.00
Direct Labor	140	2.00	420	3.00	560.00
Variable Overhead	140	2.00	280	2.00	420.00
Fixed Overhead	70	1.00	210	1.50	280.00
Total	$ 630	$ 9.00	$1,540	$11.00	$2,170.00
Gross Margin	$ 420	$ 6.00	$1,610	$11.50	$2,030.00
Fixed Selling and Administrative					1,040.00
Net Income before Income Taxes					$ 990.00
Income Taxes (55%)					544.50
Net Income					$ 445.50

The tape recorder business has been fairly stable the last few years, and the company does not intend to change the tape recorder price. However, due to increased competition, management has decided to reduce the wholesale price of its calculators from $22.50 to $20.00 per unit effective January 1, 19B. At the same time the company plans to spend an additional $57,000 on advertising during fiscal year 19B. As a consequence of these actions, management estimates that 80 percent of its total revenue will be derived from calculator sales as compared to 75 percent of total revenue in 19A. As in prior years, the sales mix is assumed to be the same at all volume levels.

The total fixed overhead costs will not change in 19B, nor will the variable overhead cost rates (applied on a direct labor hour basis). However, the cost of materials and direct labor is expected to change. The cost of solid-state electronic components will be cheaper in 19B. Hewtex estimates that material costs will drop 10 percent for the tape recorders and 20 percent for the calculators in 19B. However, direct labor costs for both products will increase 10 percent in the coming year.

Compute (*a*) the break-even sales in units for tape recorders and electronic calculators, using 19A data; (*b*) sales dollars required to earn an after-tax income of 9 percent on sales, using 19B estimates; and (*c*) the break-even sales in units for tape recorders and electronic calculators, using 19B estimates.

(CMA, adapted)

SOLUTION

(*a*) Fixed costs:

Overhead	$ 280,000
Selling and administrative	1,040,000
Total	$1,320,000

	Tape Recorders	Calculators
Unit CM	$7.00	$13.00
Mix	1/3	2/3

Composite (or weighted-average) unit contribution margin is $\$7.00(\frac{1}{3}) + \$13.00(\frac{2}{3}) = \$11.00$

Thus, the company's break-even point in units is $1,320,000/$11.00 = 120,000 units, which will be split:

$$\text{Tape recorders:} \quad 120{,}000 \times \frac{1}{3} = 40{,}000 \text{ units}$$

$$\text{Calculators:} \quad 120{,}000 \times \frac{2}{3} = 80{,}000 \text{ units}$$

(*b*) 19B fixed costs:

Overhead	$ 280,000
Selling and administrative	1,040,000
Advertising	57,000
Total	$1,377,000

	Tape Recorders	Calculators
Sales price/unit	$15.00 (100%)	$20.00 (100%)
Variable costs/unit:		
Materials	$ 3.60	$ 3.60
Direct labor	2.20	3.30
Overhead	2.00	$ 2.00
Total	$ 7.80 (52%)	$ 8.90 (44.5%)
Contribution margin	$ 7.20 (48%)	$11.10 (55.5%)

Composite (or weighted-average) CM ratio = (0.48)(20%) + (0.555)(80%) = 0.54

Therefore, the sales volume in dollars necessary in 19B to earn an after-tax income of 9 percent of sales is calculated as follows:

Letting S = sales volume in dollars,

$$S = \frac{\$1{,}377{,}000 + [0.09S/(1-0.55)]}{0.54}$$

$$0.54S = \$1{,}377{,}000 + \frac{0.09S}{1-0.55} \rightarrow 0.54S = \$1{,}377{,}000 + 0.2S \rightarrow 0.34S = \$1{,}377{,}000$$

Solving for S yields S = \$4,050,000.

(*c*) From part (*b*),

	Tape Recorders	Calculators	Total
Unit CM	\$7.20	\$11.10	
Mix	25% (¼)	75% (¾)	(computed based on sales in units)

Note:

Tape Recorders	Calculators	Total
\$840,000 (20%)	\$3,360,000 (80%)	\$4,200,000
÷ \$15/unit	÷ \$20/unit	
56,000 units (25%)	168,000 units (75%)	224,000 units

Therefore, composite (or weighted-average) unit CM = \$7.20(0.25) + \$11.10(0.75) = \$10.125. Thus, the company's break-even point in units is

$$\frac{\$1{,}377{,}000}{\$10.125} = 136{,}000 \text{ units}$$

which will be split

Tape recorders:	136,000 × 25% = 34,000 units
Calculators:	136,000 × 75% = 102,000 units

4.21 Assume the following data concerning operation of the Ames Manufacturing Company for the month of September:

Number of units sold	100 units
Selling price per unit	\$ 20
Variable manufacturing cost/unit	\$ 5
Fixed manufacturing costs	\$300
Variable selling and administrative cost/unit	\$ 4
Fixed selling and administrative costs	\$110

Prepare an income statement for the month of September, using the absorption costing (traditional) and direct costing (contribution) formats.

SOLUTION

AMES MANUFACTURING COMPANY

Income Statement
For the Month Ended September 30

ABSORPTION COSTING		DIRECT COSTING		
Sales	$2,000	Sales		$2,000
Less: Cost of Goods Sold	800*	Less: Variable Costs		
Gross Margin	$1,200	Manufacturing	500	
		Selling and Administrative	400	900
		Contribution Margin		$1,100
Less: Operating Expenses				
Selling and Administrative	510†	Less: Fixed Costs		
		Manufacturing	$300	
		Selling and Administrative	110	410
Net Income	$ 690	Net Income		$ 690

*$800 = (100 units × $5) + $300.
†$510 = $110 + (100 units × $4).

4.22 The following data relate to Flores Company for the year ended December 31, 19X8:

Cost of production:	
Direct materials	$168,000
Direct labor	252,000
Factory overhead:	
Variable	90,000
Fixed	180,000
Sales commission (variable)	44,000
Sales salaries (fixed)	46,000
General and administrative expenses (fixed)	62,000
Units produced	75,000 units
Units sold (@$18)	60,000

(*a*) Compute the amount of income before income taxes and ending inventory under (1) absorption costing and (2) direct costing.

(*b*) Reconcile the difference in income before taxes between the two methods.

SOLUTION

(*a*)	DIRECT COSTING		ABSORPTION COSTING	
Sales ($18 × 60,000)		$1,080,000		$1,080,000
Cost of goods sold	$408,000*		$552,000†	
Fixed manufacturing overhead	180,000			
Selling and administrative expenses	152,000	740,000	152,000	704,000
Income before income taxes		$ 340,000		$ 376,000

*Cost of goods sold—direct costing:

Direct materials	$168,000
Direct labor	252,000
Variable overhead	90,000
Variable costs to produce 75,000 units ($6.80 per unit)	$510,000
Less: Ending inventory (15,000 × $6.80)	102,000
Cost of goods sold	$408,000

†Cost of goods sold—absorption costing:

Direct materials	$168,000
Direct labor	252,000
Variable manufacturing overhead	90,000
Fixed manufacturing overhead	180,000
Costs to produce 75,000 units ($9.20/unit)	$690,000
Less: Ending inventory (15,000 × $9.20)	138,000
Cost of goods sold	$552,000

(*b*) You should expect income before income taxes to be higher under absorption costing than under direct costing. Since absorption costing treats all costs to manufacture, whether fixed or variable, as product costs, a portion of fixed overhead will remain in ending inventory and be expensed when that inventory is sold. Direct costing, on the other hand, treats all fixed costs as period costs. Therefore, no portion of the fixed overhead remains in inventory, and total expenses for the current period are higher.

Examination I

Chapters 1–4

Part I Indicate whether the following statements are true (T) or false (F).

_____ **1.** Management accounting is based on a set of generally accepted accounting principles.

_____ **2.** Factory overhead is all costs other than direct labor and direct materials.

_____ **3.** The terms *total manufacturing costs* and *cost of goods manufactured* are used interchangeably.

_____ **4.** Fixed costs are costs that do not vary with volume.

_____ **5.** Gross margin and contribution margin are synonymous.

_____ **6.** An example of a variable cost is depreciation based on the straight-line method.

_____ **7.** Semivariable costs (or mixed costs) contain both variable and fixed elements.

_____ **8.** If the sales mix changes, the break-even volume that was valid in the past may no longer be valid in the future.

_____ **9.** The break-even point in units can be computed by dividing total fixed costs by the contribution margin ratio.

_____ **10.** The high–low method of breaking up a mixed cost into the variable and fixed components gives the most accurate estimates for these components.

_____ **11.** The coefficient of determination is a measure of "goodness of fit."

_____ **12.** The vertical *axis* on a profit–volume (P–V) chart measures volume of activity.

_____ **13.** Product costs include direct labor.

Part II Complete the following statements.

1. Prime cost is the sum of _____________ and _____________.

2. Cost of goods sold is beginning finished goods inventory plus _____________ minus ending finished goods inventory.

3. Cost of direct materials purchased is cost of direct materials used _____________ beginning inventory _____________ ending inventory.

4. The contribution income statement approach subtracts _____________ from _____________ to arrive at _____________.

5. ____________ stay the same per unit of activity, whereas ____________ decrease as volume increases.

6. ____________ is the excess of sales over cost of goods sold, whereas contribution margin is the excess of sales over ____________.

7. ____________ arise from annual decisions by management to spend in certain fixed-cost areas such as advertising and research.

8. The ____________ ensures that the regression line estimated is the line of best fit.

9. As compared to ____________ accounting, ____________ accounting draws heavily from other disciplines such as finance and quantitative analysis.

10. Fixed costs can be broken down into two categories: ____________ and ____________.

11. The higher the ____________, the less the volume required to break even.

12. One of the major assumptions underlying break-even analysis is that changes in ____________ are insignificant in amount from period to period.

Part III Solve the following problems.

1. The annual profit budget of the Parker Co. shows:

Sales (30,000 units @ $3)		$90,000
Variable costs:		
Manufacturing	$20,000	
Selling and administrative	7,000	
Fixed costs:		
Manufacturing	21,000	
Selling and administrative	12,000	60,000
Net income		$30,000

Answer each part below independently of all other parts.

(*a*) What is the company's break-even point in units and in dollars?

(*b*) The company proposes to buy equipment to replace workers. If this is done, fixed costs will increase $3,280 and variable costs will decrease $3,000 when sales are $90,000. What is the new break-even point in units?

(*c*) Assume that fixed costs are increased by $2,000 and variable costs by $1,500 at the $90,000 sales level. How much must sales (in units) be increased to make the same $30,000 profit? How much must sales (in units) be increased to yield a before-tax net income of 30 percent of sales?

(*d*) The sales manager proposes an increase in unit sales price of 10 percent, with an expected drop of 20 percent in sales volume. If this step is taken, what would be the expected profit? Would you approve this plan? What would be the new break-even point in units?

2. Given the following data:

Production Units x	Mixed Cost y
1	2
2	3
3	4
4	5
5	6

(*a*) Find the cost-volume formula, using:

(1) The high–low method

(2) The method of least squares

(*b*) Compute the coefficient of determination (r^2) and comment on it.

3. From the following data, prepare a schedule of cost of goods manufactured.

Selling expenses	$12,000
Direct materials used	25,000
Factory overhead	30,000
Direct labor	52,000
Administrative expenses	10,000

	Inventories	
	Beginning	Ending
Direct materials	$1,000	$ 500
Work-in-process	5,000	6,000
Finished goods	4,000	2,500

Answers to Examination I

Part I

1. F **2.** F **3.** F **4.** T **5.** F **6.** F **7.** T **8.** T **9.** F **10.** F **11.** T **12.** F **13.** T.

Part II

1. direct materials, direct labor; **2.** cost of goods manufactured; **3.** minus, plus; **4.** variable expenses, sales, contribution margin; **5.** variable costs, fixed costs; **6.** gross margin (profit), variable expenses; **7.** discretionary fixed costs; **8.** method of least squares; **9.** financial, managerial; **10.** committed fixed costs, discretionary fixed costs; **11.** contribution margin; **12.** inventories.

Part III

1. (*a*)

$$\text{Break-even point in units} = \frac{\$33{,}000}{\$3 - \$0.9} = 15{,}714 \text{ units}$$

$$\text{Break-even point in dollars} = 15{,}714 \text{ units} \times \$3 = \$47{,}142$$

(*b*)

$$\text{Break-even point in units} = \frac{\$33{,}000 + \$3{,}280}{\$3 - \$0.8} = \frac{\$36{,}280}{\$2.2} = 16{,}491 \text{ units}$$

(*c*) Target income volume required to make a $30,000 profit equals

$$\frac{\$33{,}000 + \$2{,}000 + \$30{,}000}{\$3 - \$0.95} = \frac{\$65{,}000}{\$2.05} = 31{,}707 \text{ units}$$

The increase is, therefore, 31,707 − 15,714 = 15,993 units.

Target income volume required to yield a net income of 30 percent of sales is computed as follows:

$$\frac{\$33{,}000 + \$2{,}000}{\$3 - \$0.95 - (30\%)(\$3)} = \frac{\$35{,}000}{\$1.15} = 30{,}435 \text{ units}$$

The increase is, therefore, 30,435 units − 15,714 units = 14,721 units.

(*d*) New unit sale price $3.30
New sales volume 24,000 units

Sales (24,000 units @ $3.30)	$79,200
Variable costs (24,000 units)	21,600
CM	$57,600
Fixed costs	33,000
Net income	$24,600

We would not approve this proposal, since net income will decrease by $5,400 ($30,000 − $24,600).

The new break-even point in units equals

$$\frac{\$33{,}000}{\$3.30 - \$0.9} = 13{,}750 \text{ units}$$

2. (*a*) (1)

	Production Volume x	Mixed Cost y
High	5 units	$6
Low	1	2
Difference	4 units	$4

Thus, $\text{Variable rate} = \frac{\$4}{4 \text{ units}} = \$1 \text{ per unit}$

$$\text{Fixed cost} = \$6 - \$1\ (5 \text{ units}) = \$1$$

Therefore, the cost formula is $1 plus $1 per unit of output.

(2)

x	y	xy	x^2	y^2
1	2	2	1	4
2	3	6	4	9
3	4	12	9	16
4	5	20	16	25
5	6	30	25	36
15	20	70	55	90

$$b = \frac{(5)(70) - (15)(20)}{(5)(55) - (15)^2} = \frac{350 - 300}{275 - 225} = \frac{50}{50} = \$1 \text{ per unit}$$

$$a = \frac{20}{5} - (1)\left(\frac{15}{5}\right) = \$1$$

Therefore, the cost formula is: $1 + $1 per unit of output, which is the same as the formula obtained in part (*a*).

(*b*)

$$r^2 = \frac{(50)^2}{(50)[(5)(90) - (20)^2]} = \frac{2{,}500}{(50)(50)} = 1$$

which means that production volume (x) explains 100 percent of the change in a given mixed cost (y). In other words, production volume is perfectly correlated with the mixed cost.

3.

Schedule of Costs of Goods Manufactured

Direct materials used	$ 25,000
Direct labor	52,000
Factory overhead	30,000
Total manufacturing costs	$107,000
Add: Beginning work-in-process	5,000
Less: Ending work-in-process	(6,000)
Cost of goods manufactured	$106,000

Note that: (1) we are already given the figure for direct materials used, (2) finished goods inventories are used to compute the cost of goods *sold*, and (3) selling and administrative expenses, which are nonmanufacturing costs, do appear on the income statement.

Relevant Costs in Nonroutine Decisions

5.1 TYPES OF NONROUTINE DECISIONS

When performing the manufacturing and selling functions, management is constantly faced with the problem of choosing between alternative courses of action. Typical questions to be answered include: What to make? How to make it? Where to sell the product?, and What price should be charged? In the short run, management is typically faced with the following nonroutine, nonrecurring types of decisions:

1. Acceptance or rejection of a special order
2. Pricing standard products
3. Make or buy
4. Sell or process further
5. Add or drop a certain product line
6. Utilization of scarce resources

5.2 RELEVANT COSTS DEFINED

In each of the above situations, the ultimate management decision rests on cost data analysis. Cost data are important in many decisions, since they are the basis for profit calculations. Cost data are classified by function, behavior patterns, and other criteria, as discussed in Chapter 2. However, not all costs are of equal importance in decision making, and managers must identify the costs that are relevant to a decision. Such costs are called *relevant costs*. The relevant costs are the expected future costs (and also revenues) which differ between the decision alternatives. Therefore, the *sunk costs* (past and historical costs) are not considered relevant in the decision at hand. What is relevant are the incremental or differential costs.

Under the concept of relevant costs, which may be appropriately titled the *incremental*, *differential*, or *relevant cost approach*, the decision involves the following steps:

1. Gather all costs associated with each alternative.
2. Drop the sunk costs.

3. Drop those costs which do not differ between alternatives.
4. Select the best alternative based on the remaining cost data.

EXAMPLE 5.1 To illustrate the irrelevance of sunk costs and the relevance of incremental costs, let us consider a replacement decision problem. A company owns a milling machine that was purchased three years ago for $25,000. Its present book value is $17,500. The company is contemplating replacing this machine with a new one which will cost $50,000 and have a five-year useful life. The new machine will generate the same amount of revenue as the old one but will cut down substantially on variable operating costs. Annual sales and operating costs of the present machine and the proposed replacement are based on normal sales volume of 20,000 units and are estimated as follows:

	Present Machine	New Machine
Sales	$60,000	$60,000
Variable costs	35,000	20,000
Fixed costs:		
Depreciation (straight-line)	2,500	10,000
Insurance, taxes, etc.	4,000	4,000
Net income	$18,500	$26,000

At first glance, it appears that the new machine provides an increase in net income of $7,500 per year. The book value of the present machine, however, is a sunk cost and is irrelevant to this decision. Furthermore, sales and fixed costs such as insurance, taxes, etc., also are irrelevant, since they do not differ between the two alternatives being considered. Eliminating all the irrelevant costs leaves us with only the incremental costs, as follows:

Savings in variable costs	$15,000	
Less: Increase in fixed costs	10,000	(exclusive of $2,500 sunk cost)
Net annual cash savings arising from the new machine	$ 5,000	

5.3 OTHER DECISION-MAKING APPROACHES—TOTAL PROJECT AND OPPORTUNITY COST APPROACHES

The same decision can be obtained by using the *total project approach* (or *comparative statement approach*), which looks at all the items of revenue and cost data (whether they are relevant or not) under the two alternatives and compares the net income results. Under this approach, however, comparative income statements are prepared in a *contribution* format.

EXAMPLE 5.2 The total project approach to Example 5.1 would be shown as follows:

	Present Machine	New Machine	Increment (or Difference)
Sales	$60,000	$60,000	—
Less: Variable costs	35,000	20,000	$(15,000)
Contribution margin	$25,000	$40,000	$ 15,000
Less: Fixed costs			
Depreciation	—	$10,000	$ 10,000
Other	4,000	4,000	—
Net income	$21,000	$26,000	$ 5,000

The total project approach's schedule shows an increase in net income of $5,000 with the purchase of the new milling machine. Notice that $2,500 was dropped. [This example is discussed only to show the irrelevance of certain items in a replacement decision problem. The real decision to be made is whether this increase in net income (or savings) is enough to justify an additional investment of $50,000 in new machinery. This question should be answered using the concepts of return on investment and the time value of money.]

Besides the incremental approach and the total project approach, the concept of opportunity costs can be applied to solve a short-term, nonroutine decision problem. The approach is hereafter called the *opportunity cost approach*. As was discussed in Chapter 2, an opportunity cost is the net revenue lost by rejecting some alternative course of action. Its significance in decision making is that the best decision is always sought, since it considers the cost of the best available alternative *not* taken. The opportunity cost does not appear on formal accounting statements.

EXAMPLE 5.3 In Example 5.1, using the opportunity cost approach, the new machine alternative can be analyzed as follows:

	New Machine
Net income expected	$26,000
Less: Opportunity cost of not keeping the old machine	21,000 ($60,000 − $35,000 − $4,000)
Difference in favor of buying the new machine	$ 5,000

The opportunity cost in this example is the $21,000 net income from the old machine given up.

The opportunity cost approach is most effective when there are excessive alternatives available that are too numerous to consider on the total project approach's schedule.

5.4 PRICING SPECIAL ORDERS

A company often receives a short-term, special order for its products at lower prices than usual. In normal times, the company may refuse such an order because it will not yield a satisfactory profit. If times are bad, however, such an order should be accepted if the incremental revenue obtained from it exceeds the incremental costs involved. The company is better off receiving some revenue, above its incremental costs, than receiving nothing at all. Such a price, one lower than the regular price, is called a *contribution price*. This approach to pricing is often called the *contribution approach to pricing* or the *variable pricing model*. This approach is most appropriate under the following conditions:

1. When operating in a distress situation
2. When there is idle capacity
3. When faced with sharp competition or in a competitive bidding situation

EXAMPLE 5.4 Assume that a company with 100,000-unit capacity is currently producing and selling only 90,000 units of product each year at a regular price of $2. If the variable cost per unit is $1 and the annual fixed cost is $45,000, the income statement looks as follows:

		Per Unit
Sales (90,000 units)	$180,000	$2.00
Less: Variable cost (90,000 units)	90,000	1.00
Contribution margin	$ 90,000	$1.00
Less: Fixed cost	45,000	0.50
Net income	$ 45,000	$0.50

The company has just received an order that calls for 10,000 units @ \$1.20, for a total of \$12,000. The acceptance of this order will not affect regular sales. The company president is reluctant to accept the order, however, because the \$1.20 price is below the \$1.50 factory unit cost (\$1.50 = \$1.00 + \$0.50). Should the company accept the order?

The answer is yes. The company can add to total profits by accepting this special order even though the price offered is below the unit factory cost. At a price of \$1.20, the order will contribut \$0.20 per unit (CM per unit = \$1.20 − \$1.00 = \$0.20) toward fixed cost, and profit will increase by \$2,000 (10,000 units × \$0.20). Using the contribution approach to pricing, the variable cost of \$1 will be a better guide than the full unit cost of \$1.50. Note that the fixed costs do not change because of the presence of idle capacity.

The same result can be seen using the total project approach:

	Per Unit	Without Special Order (90,000 units)	With Special Order (100,000 units)	Difference
Sales	\$2.00	\$180,000	\$192,000	\$12,000
Less: Variable costs	1.00	90,000	100,000	10,000
CM	\$1.00	\$ 90,000	\$ 92,000	\$ 2,000
Less: Fixed cost	0.50	45,000	45,000	—
Net income	\$0.50	\$ 45,000	\$ 47,000	\$ 2,000

5.5 THE MAKE-OR-BUY DECISION

The decision whether to produce a component part internally or to buy it externally from an outside supplier is called a "make-or-buy" decision. This decision involves both quantitative and qualitative factors. The qualitative factors include ensuring product quality and the necessity for long-run business relationships with the supplier. The quantitative factors deal with cost. The quantitative effects of the make-or-buy decision are best seen through the relevant cost approach.

EXAMPLE 5.5 Assume that a firm has prepared the following cost estimates for the manufacture of a subassembly component based on an annual production of 8,000 units:

	Per Unit	Total
Direct materials	\$ 5	\$ 40,000
Direct labor	4	32,000
Variable factory overhead applied	4	32,000
Fixed factory overhead applied (150% of direct labor cost)	6	48,000
Total cost	\$19	\$152,000

The supplier has offered to provide the subassembly at a price of \$16 each. Two-thirds of fixed factory overhead, which represents executive salaries, rent, depreciation, and taxes, continue regardless of the decision. Should the company buy or make the product?

The key to the decision lies in the investigation of those relevant costs that change between the make-or-buy alternatives. Assuming that the productive capacity will be idle if not used to produce the subassembly, the analysis takes the following form:

	Per Unit		Total of 8,000 Units	
	Make	Buy	Make	Buy
Purchase price		$16		$128,000
Direct materials	$ 5		$ 40,000	
Direct labor	4		32,000	
Variable overhead	4		32,000	
Fixed overhead that can be avoided by *not* making	2		16,000	
Total relevant costs	$15	$16	$120,000	$128,000
Difference in favor of making	$1		$8,000	

The make-or-buy decision must be investigated, along with the broader perspective of considering how best to utilize available facilities. The alternatives are:

1. Leaving facilities idle
2. Buying the parts and renting out idle facilities
3. Buying the parts and using idle facilities for other products

5.6 THE SELL-OR-PROCESS-FURTHER DECISION

When two or more products are produced simultaneously from the same input by a joint process, these products are called *joint products*. The term *joint costs* is used to describe all the manufacturing costs incurred prior to the point where the joint products are identified as individual products, referred to as the *split-off point*. At the split-off point some of the joint products are in final form and salable to the consumer, whereas others require additional processing. In many cases, however, the company might have an option: it can sell the goods at the split-off point or process them further in the hope of obtaining additional revenue. In connection with this type of decision, called the "sell-or-process-further" decision, joint costs are considered irrelevant, since the joint costs have already been incurred at the time of the decision, and therefore represent sunk costs. The decision will rely exclusively on additional revenue compared to the additional costs incurred due to further processing.

EXAMPLE 5.6 The Jin Company produces three products, A, B, and C, from a joint process. Joint production costs for the year were $120,000. Product A may be sold at the split-off point or processed further. The additional processing requires no special facilities, and all additional processing costs are variable. Sales values and cost needed to evaluate the company's production policy regarding product A follow:

		Additional Cost and Sales Value after Further Processing	
Units Produced	Sales Value at Split-Off	Sales	Cost
3,000	$60,000	$90,000	$25,000

Should product A be sold at the split-off point or processed further?

To answer this question, consider the three decision-making approaches discussed earlier in the chapter, that is, the total project approach, the incremental approach, and the opportunity cost approach.

The total project approach follows:

	Sell	Process	Difference
Sales	$60,000	$90,000	$30,000
Costs	—	25,000	25,000
Net revenue	$60,000	$65,000	$ 5,000

The difference column above is essentially the basis for the incremental approach, which compares incremental revenue with the incremental costs. In this case:

Incremental sales revenue	$30,000
Incremental costs, additional processing	25,000
Incremental gain	$ 5,000

Still another way to look at the same problem is to utilize the concept of opportunity cost:

Sales revenue after processing product A		$90,000
Less: Costs		
Added processing	$25,000	
Opportunity cost, net revenue forgone	60,000	85,000
Difference in favor of further processing		$ 5,000

In summary, product A should be processed, as evidenced by any of the three methods presented above. Keep in mind that the joint production cost of $120,000 is not included in the analysis, since it is a sunk cost and therefore irrelevant to the decision.

5.7 ADDING OR DROPPING A PRODUCT LINE

The decision whether to drop an old product line or add a new one must take into account both qualitative and quantitative factors. However, any final decision should be based primarily on the impact the decision will have on contribution margin or net income.

EXAMPLE 5.7 The ABC grocery store has three major product lines: produce, meats, and canned food. The store is considering dropping the meat line because the income statement shows that it is operating at a loss. Note the income statement for these product lines below:

	Produce	Meats	Canned Food	Total
Sales	$10,000	$15,000	$25,000	$50,000
Less: Variable costs	6,000	8,000	12,000	26,000
CM	$ 4,000	$ 7,000	$13,000	$24,000
Less: Fixed costs				
Direct	$ 2,000	$ 6,500	$ 4,000	$12,500
Allocated	1,000	1,500	2,500	5,000
Total	$ 3,000	$ 8,000	$ 6,500	$17,500
Net income	$ 1,000	$ (1,000)	$ 6,500	$ 6,500

In this example, direct fixed costs are those costs that are identified directly with each of the product lines, whereas allocated fixed costs are the amount of common fixed costs allocated to the product lines using some base such as space occupied. The amount of common fixed costs typically continues regardless of the decision and thus cannot be saved by dropping the product line to which it is distributed.

The total project approach showing the effects on the company as a whole with and without the meat line is shown below:

	Keep Meats	Drop Meats	Difference
Sales	$50,000	$35,000	$(15,000)
Less: Variable costs	26,000	18,000	(8,000)
CM	$24,000	$17,000	$ (7,000)
Less: Fixed costs			
Direct	$12,500	$ 6,000	$ (6,500)
Allocated	5,000	5,000	—
Total	$17,500	$11,000	$ (6,500)
Net income	$ 6,500	$ 6,000	$ (500)

Alternatively, the incremental approach would show the following:

If Meats Dropped		
Sales revenue lost		$15,000
Gains:		
Variable cost avoided	$8,000	
Direct fixed costs avoided	6,500	14,500
Increase (decrease) in net income		$ (500)

From either of the two methods, we see that by dropping meats, the store will lose an additional $500. Therefore, the meat product line should be kept. One of the great dangers in allocating common fixed costs is that such allocations can make a product line look less profitable than it really is. Because of such an allocation, the meat line showed a loss of $1,000, but it in effect contributes $500 ($7,000 – $6,500) to the recovery of the store's common fixed costs.

5.8 UTILIZATION OF SCARCE RESOURCES

In general, the emphasis on products with higher contribution margin maximizes a firm's total net income, even though total sales may decrease. This is not true, however, where there are constraining factors or scarce resources. The constraining factor is the factor that restricts or limits the production or sale of a given product. The constraining factor may be machine hours, labor hours, or cubic feet of warehouse space. In the presence of these constraining factors, maximizing total profits depends on getting the highest contribution margin *per unit* of the factor (rather than the highest contribution margin per unit of product output).

EXAMPLE 5.8 Assume that a company produces two products, A and B, with the following contribution margins per unit:

	A	B
Sales	$8	$24
Variable costs	6	20
CM	$2	$ 4
Annual fixed costs	$42,000	

As is indicated by CM per unit, B is more profitable than A since it contributes more to the company's total profits than A ($4 vs. $2). But let us assume that the firm has a limited capacity of 10,000 labor hours. Further, assume that A requires 2 labor hours to produce and B requires 5 labor hours. One way to express this limited capacity is to determine the contribution margin per labor hour:

	A	B
CM/unit	$2.00	$4.00
Labor hours required per unit	2	5
CM per labor hour	$1.00	$0.80

Since A returns the higher CM per labor hour, it should be produced and B should be dropped.

Another way to look at the problem is to calculate *total CM* for each product.

	A	B
Maximum possible production	5,000 units (10,000 hours ÷ 2 hours)	2,000 units (10,000 hours ÷ 5 hours)
CM per unit	$ 2	$ 4
Total CM	$10,000	$8,000

Again, product A should be produced, since it contributes more than B ($10,000 vs. $8,000).

Summary

(1) ____________ to income measurement is an extremely useful tool for selecting the best source of action in a nonroutine decision problem.

(2) There are three primary approaches to alternative-choice problems. They are the total project approach, ____________, and the opportunity cost approach.

(3) ____________ in a decision are ____________ that differ between the alternatives being considered.

(4) A sunk cost is ____________ in alternative-choice problems.

(5) Companies compute their regular selling prices on the basis of certain formulas, called ____________, which add a ____________ to some cost base to obtain a selling price that will generate a reasonable return on investment.

(6) The contribution approach to pricing or ____________ is a method of pricing special orders.

(7) Make-or-buy decisions depend on both ____________ and quantitative factors.

(8) ____________ is the stage of production at which the different joint products are individually recognized.

(9) ____________ are irrelevant in the sell-or-process-further decision.

(10) When there are two or more products with limited capacity, the way to maximize total contribution margin of a firm is to manufacture the product with the highest contribution margin ____________.

(11) It will always be profitable to process joint products beyond ____________ as long as ____________ from such processing exceeds ____________.

(12) The final decision as to whether to keep an old product line depends primarily on the impact the decision will have on the incremental revenue: (*a*) true; (*b*) false.

(13) The book value of old equipment is irrelevant for future replacement decisions: (*a*) true; (*b*) false.

(14) An avoidable cost is the same as a sunk cost: (*a*) true; (*b*) false.

(15) Fixed costs are always irrelevant, whereas variable costs are relevant: (*a*) true; (*b*) false.

Answers: (1) the contribution approach; (2) the incremental (differential) approach; (3) relevant costs, expected future costs; (4) irrelevant; (5) cost-plus pricing formulas, markup; (6) the variable pricing model; (7) qualitative; (8) the split-off point; (9) joint costs; (10) per unit of that limited capacity; (11) the split-off point; the incremental revenue; the incremental cost; (12) (*b*); (13) (*a*); (14) (*b*); (15) (*b*).

Solved Problems

5.1 The Alpha Omega Food Giant Company owns and operates a chain of 125 supermarkets. Budgeted data for the Cypress store are as follows:

Annual sales	$425,000
Annual cost of goods sold and other operating expenses	382,000
Annual building ownership costs (not included above)	20,000

The company can lease the building to a large flower shop for $4,000 per month. Decide whether to continue operating this store or to lease, using:

1. The total project (or comparative statement) approach
2. The incremental (or relevant cost) approach
3. The opportunity cost approach

SOLUTION

1. The total project (or comparative statement) approach is shown below:

	Continue Operation	Lease
Sales revenue	$425,000	$48,000 ($4,000 × 12 months)
Less: Costs		
Cost of goods sold and cash operating expenses	$382,000	–
Building ownership costs	20,000	$20,000
Total costs	$402,000	$20,000
Net income	$ 23,000	$28,000

The company should lease the building.

2. Note that building ownership costs are not relevant because they are the same for each alternative. The incremental (or relevant cost) approach gives the following:

Cash inflow from continuing operation ($425,000 − $382,000)	$43,000
Less: Income from leasing	48,000
Incremental loss from continuing operation	$ (5,000)

Therefore, the company should not continue the operation of the Cypress store.

3. The opportunity cost approach can be shown as follows:

Sales revenue	$425,000
Less: Costs	
Cost of goods sold and other operating expenses	$382,000
Opportunity cost of leasing	48,000
Total costs	$430,000
Difference in favor of leasing	$ 5,000

5.2 The Spartan Company has an annual plant capacity of 25,000 units. Predicted data on sales and costs are given below.

Sales (20,000 units @ $50)	$1,000,000
Manufacturing costs:	
Variable (materials, labor, and overhead)	$40 per unit
Fixed overhead	$30,000
Selling and administrative expenses:	
Variable (sales commission—$1 per unit)	$2 per unit
Fixed	$7,000

A special order has been received from outside for 4,000 units at a selling price of $45 each. This order will have no effect on regular sales. The usual sales commission on this order will be reduced by one-half.

Should the company accept the order? Show supporting computations.

SOLUTION

Incremental revenue (4,000 units @ $45)	$180,000
Less: Incremental costs	
Variable manufacturing (4,000 units @ $40)	160,000
Variable selling and administrative (4,000 @ $1.50)	6,000
Incremental gain in favor of accepting the order	$ 14,000

5.3 Although the Missouri Company has the capacity to produce 16,000 units per month, current plans call for monthly production and sales of only 10,000 units at $15 each. Costs per unit are as follows:

Direct materials	$ 5.00
Direct labor	3.00
Variable factory overhead	0.75
Fixed factory overhead	1.50
Variable selling expense	0.25
Fixed administrative expense	1.00
	$11.50

1. Should the company accept a special order for 4,000 units @ $10?
2. What is the maximum price the Missouri Company should be willing to pay an outside supplier who is interested in manufacturing this product?
3. What would be the effect on the monthly contribution margin if the sales price was reduced to $14, resulting in a 10 percent increase in sales volume?

SOLUTION

1. The company should accept the special order because the proposed $10 sales price covers all variable manufacturing costs, which are:

Direct materials	$5.00 per unit
Direct labor	3.00
Variable factory overhead	0.75
Total	$8.75 per unit

If variable selling expense is applied to this order, there would still be a unit contribution margin of $1, or $4,000 in total.

2. Assuming that fixed costs cannot be reduced, and that variable costs such as direct labor really are variable, the company would be willing to pay an outside supplier as much as the variable manufacturing costs, that is, $8.75.

3. The effect on the monthly contribution margin if the sales price was reduced to $14 would be:

Present contribution margin [10,000 units ($15 – $9)]	$60,000
Proposed contribution margin [(11,000 units ($14 – $9)]	55,000
Reduction in contribution margin	$ 5,000

5.4 George Jackson operates a small machine shop. He manufactures one standard product which is available from many other similar businesses and also manufactures custom-made products. His accountant prepared the annual income statement shown below.

	Custom Sales	Standard Sales	Total
Sales	$50,000	$25,000	$75,000
Material	$10,000	$ 8,000	$18,000
Labor	20,000	9,000	29,000
Depreciation	6,300	3,600	9,900
Power	700	400	1,100
Rent	6,000	1,000	7,000
Heat and light	600	100	700
Other	400	900	1,300
	$44,000	$23,000	$67,000
	$ 6,000	$ 2,000	$ 8,000

The depreciation charges are for machines used in the respective product lines. The power charge is apportioned on the estimate of power consumed. The rent is for the building space, which has been leased for 10 years at $7,000 per year. The rent and heat and light are apportioned to the product lines based on amount of floor space occupied. All other costs are current expenses and are identified with the product line causing them.

A valued custom-parts customer has asked Mr. Jackson if he would manufacture 5,000 special units for him. Mr. Jackson is working at capacity and would have to give up some other business in order to take this special order. Though he cannot renege on custom orders already agreed to, he could reduce the output of his standard product by about one-half for one year while producing the specially requested custom part. The customer is willing to pay $7 for each part. The material cost will be about $2 per unit and the labor will be $3.60 per unit. Mr. Jackson will have to spend $2,000 for a special device which will be discarded when the job is done.

1. Calculate and present the following costs related to the 5,000-unit custom order:
   (*a*) The incremental cost of the order
   (*b*) The full cost of the order
   (*c*) The opportunity costs of accepting the order
   (*d*) The sunk costs related to the order
2. Should Mr. Jackson accept the special order? Explain your answer.

(CMA, adapted)

SOLUTION

1. (*a*) The incremental cost of the order is calculated as follows:

Costs incurred to fill order:		
Material	$10,000	(5,000 units × $2.00)
Labor	18,000	(5,000 units × $3.60)
Special overhead	2,000	
Total	$30,000	
Costs reduced for standard products:		
Material	$ 4,000	
Labor	4,500	
Other	450	
	$ 8,950	
Total incremental costs	$21,050	

Depreciation, rent, and heat and light are not affected by the order, since they are committed fixed costs and thus continue regardless of the order. Power might be affected, depending on the particular requirements of the special units. It is assumed here that the same amount of power will be used in each case.

(*b*) The full cost of the order is

Costs incurred to fill order [from (*a*)]	$30,000
Depreciation	1,800
Power	200
Rent	500
Heat and light	50
	$32,550

(*c*) The opportunity cost of taking the order is the net cash flow given up:

Sales of standard product	$12,500
Less: Material	$ 4,000
Labor	4,500
Power	200
Other	450
	$ 9,150
Opportunity cost of special order	$ 3,350

(*d*) The sunk costs are the costs that do not change as a result of choosing one order or the other:

Depreciation	$1,800
Power	200
Rent	500
Heat and light	50
	$2,550

2. On the basis of the data in the question, it would pay Mr. Jackson to accept the order.

New sales	$35,000	
Less: Standard sales	12,500	
		$22,500
Incremental costs [from 1.(*a*)]		21,050
Cash advantage to special units		$ 1,450

Other factors must also be considered, such as the long-run consequences of failing to satisfy standard parts customers, the reliability of the cost estimates, and the importance of this valued customer.

5.5 E. Berg and Sons build custom-made pleasure boats that range in price from $10,000 to $250,000. For the past 30 years, Mr. Berg, Sr., has determined the selling price of each boat by estimating the cost of material, labor, and a pro-rated portion of overhead, and adding 20 percent to their estimated costs. For example, a recent price quotation was determined as follows:

Direct materials	$ 5,000
Direct labor	8,000
Overhead	2,000
	$15,000
Plus 20%	3,000
Selling price	$18,000

The overhead figure was determined by estimating total overhead costs for the year and allocating them at 25 percent of direct labor.

If a customer rejected the price and business was slack, Mr. Berg, Sr., would often be willing to reduce his markup to as little as 5 percent over estimated costs. Thus, average markup for the year is estimated at 15 percent.

Mr. Ed Berg, Jr., has just completed a course on pricing, and believes the firm could use some of the techniques discussed in the course. The course emphasized the contribution margin approach to pricing, and Mr. Berg, Jr., feels that such an approach would be helpful in determining the selling prices of their custom-made pleasure boats.

Total overhead, which includes selling and administrative expenses for the year, has been estimated at $150,000, of which $90,000 is fixed and the remainder is variable in direct proportion to direct labor.

1. Assume that the customer in the example rejected the $18,000 quotation and also rejected a $15,750 quotation (5 percent markup) during a slack period. The customer countered with a $15,000 offer.

   (*a*) What is the minimum selling price Mr. Berg, Jr., could have quoted without reducing or increasing company net income?

(b) What is the difference in company net income for the year between accepting and rejecting the customer's offer?

2. What advantages does the contribution margin approach to pricing have over the approach used by Mr. Berg, Sr.?
3. What pitfalls are there, if any, to contribution margin pricing?

(CMA, adapted)

SOLUTION

1. (a) The minimum price needed to have no effects is $13,800, which is computed as follows:

Variable cost of quoted boat:	
Direct material	$ 5,000
Direct labor	8,000
Variable overhead (10% × 8,000)*	800
	$13,800

*Total overhead was $150,000, which is 25% of direct labor. Therefore,

$$\text{Direct labor} = \frac{\$150{,}000}{0.25} = \$600{,}000$$

$$\text{Variable overhead rate} = \frac{\text{Variable overhead}}{\text{Direct labor}} = \frac{(\$150{,}000 - \$90{,}000)}{\$600{,}000}$$

$$= \$60{,}000 \div \$600{,}000 = 10\%$$

(b) An *increase* in income of $1,200 (before taxes) would result from accepting the $15,000 offer.

Customer's offer	$15,000
Variable costs	13,800
Contribution to profit	$ 1,200

2. The contribution margin approach focuses on the relationship between future costs incurred as a result of taking an order and the revenue the order will produce. The impact of a specific order on profits can be estimated and the lower limits on price can be observed.
3. The major pitfall to the contribution margin approach to pricing is its failure to recognize the fixed costs explicitly. Although they can be overlooked in the short run, the fixed costs must be covered in the long run if the business is to continue.

5.6 JFK Manufacturing Corp. is using 10,000 units of part no. 300 as a component to assemble one of its products. It costs the company $18 per unit to produce it internally, computed as follows:

Direct materials	$ 45,000
Direct labor	50,000
Variable overhead	40,000
Fixed overhead	45,000
Total cost	$180,000

An outside vendor has just offered to supply the part for $16 per unit. If the company stops producing this part, one-third of the fixed overhead would be avoided. Should the company make or buy?

SOLUTION

	10,000 Units		
	Make	Buy	
Outside purchase price		$160,000	($16 × 10,000 units)
Direct materials	$ 45,000		
Direct labor	50,000		
Variable overhead	40,000		
Fixed overhead avoided	15,000		
	$150,000	$160,000	

As indicated above, the company is better off making the part.

5.7 The Vernom Corporation, which produces and sells to wholesalers a highly successful line of summer lotions and insect repellents, has decided to diversify in order to stabilize sales throughout the year. A natural area for the company to consider is the production of winter lotions and creams to prevent dry and chapped skin.

After considerable research, a winter products line has been developed. However, because of the conservative nature of the company management, Vernom's president has decided to introduce only one of the new products for this coming winter. If the product is a success, further expansion in future years will be initiated.

The product selected (called "Chap-off") is a lip balm that will be sold in a lipstick-type tube. The product will be sold to wholesalers in boxes of 24 tubes for $8 per box. Because of available capacity, no additional fixed charges will be incurred to produce the product. However, a $100,000 fixed charge will be absorbed by the product to allocate a fair share of the company's present fixed costs to the new product.

Using the estimated sales and production of 100,000 boxes of Chap-off as the standard volume, the accounting department has developed the following costs:

Direct labor	$2.00 per box
Direct materials	3.00 per box
Total overhead	1.50 per box
Total	$6.50 per box

Vernom has approached a cosmetics manufacturer to discuss the possibility of purchasing the tubes for Chap-off. The purchase price of the empty tubes from the cosmetics manufacturer would be $0.90 per 24 tubes. If the Vernom Corporation accepts the purchase proposal, it is estimated that direct labor and variable overhead costs would be reduced by 10 percent and direct material costs would be reduced by 20 percent.

1. Should the Vernom Corporation make or buy the tubes? Show calculations to support your answer.
2. What would be the minimum purchase price acceptable to the Vernom Corporation for the tubes? Support your answer with an appropriate explanation.
3. Instead of sales of 100,000 boxes, revised estimates show sales volume at 125,000 boxes. At this new volume, additional equipment, at an annual rental of $10,000, must be acquired to manufacture the tubes. However, this incremental cost would be the only additional fixed cost required even if sales increased to 300,000 boxes. (The 300,000 level is the goal for the third year of production.) Under these circumstances, should the Vernom Corporation make or buy the tubes? Show calculations to support your answer.
4. The company has the option of making and buying at the same time. What would be your

answer to question 3 if this alternative was considered? Show calculations to support your answer.

5. What nonquantifiable factors should the Vernom Corporation consider in determining whether they should make or buy the lipstick tubes?

(CMA, adapted)

SOLUTION

1. Vernom Corporation should make the tubes:

Cost saved by purchasing tubes:	
Material (20% × \$3.00)	\$0.60
Labor (10% × \$2.00)	0.20
Overhead (10% × 0.50*)	0.05
Total	\$0.85
Cost to buy	\$0.90

*Total overhead \$1.50 per unit
Allocated overhead \$1.00 per unit (\$100,000 ÷ 100,000)
Variable overhead \$0.50 per unit.

2. The problem asks for the minimum purchase price. The context of the problem implies that the maximum purchase price is what was really required. Vernom Corporation would not pay more than \$0.85 each because that is the cost to make the product internally. Obviously, the company would be willing to pay any amount which was less than \$0.85.

3. At a volume of 125,000 units, Vernom should buy the tubes. The cost of buying 125,000 tubes is \$112,500 (125,000 × \$0.90). The cost of making 125,000 tubes is

125,000 × \$0.85	\$106,250
Added fixed cost	10,000
	\$116,250

Buying the tubes will save \$3,750.

4. Vernom Corporation needs 125,000 tubes. The cost to buy 125,000 tubes is \$112,500. The cost to make 125,000 tubes is \$116,250. The cost to make 100,000 (standard volume) and buy 25,000 is

\$ 85,000
22,500
\$107,500

Therefore, to supply its needs, Vernom should choose this latter course of action.

5. There are many nonquantifiable factors which Vernom should consider in addition to the economic factors calculated above. Among such factors are:

(*a*) The quality of the purchased tubes as compared to Vernom-produced tubes
(*b*) The reliability of delivery to meet production schedules
(*c*) The financial stability of the supplier
(*d*) Development of an alternate source of supply
(*e*) Alternate uses of tube-manufacturing capacity
(*f*) The long-run character and size of the market

5.8 Answer the following four multiple-choice questions:

1. Buck Company manufactures part no. 1700 for use in its production cycle. The costs per unit for a 5,000-unit quantity follows:

Direct materials	$ 2
Direct labor	12
Variable overhead	5
Fixed overhead applied	7
	$26

Hollow Company has offered to sell Buck 5,000 units of part no. 1700 for $27 per unit. If Buck accepts the offer, some of the facilities presently used to manufacture part no. 1700 could be used to help with the manufacture of part no. 1211. This would save $40,000 in relevant costs in the manufacture of part no. 1211, and $3 per unit of the fixed overhead applied to part no. 1700 would be totally eliminated. By what amount would net relevant costs be increased or decreased if Buck accepts Hollow's offer?

(*a*) $35,000 decrease
(*b*) $20,000 decrease
(*c*) $15,000 decrease
(*d*) $5,000 increase

2. Relay Corporation manufactures batons. Relay can manufacture 300,000 batons a year at a variable cost of $750,000 and a fixed cost of $450,000. Based on Relay's predictions, 240,000 batons will be sold at the regular price of $5 each. In addition, a special order was placed for 60,000 batons to be sold at a 40 percent discount off the regular price. By what amount would income be increased or decreased as a result of the special order?

(*a*) $60,000 decrease
(*b*) $30,000 increase
(*c*) $36,000 increase
(*d*) $180,000 increase

3. Cardinal Company needs 20,000 units of a certain part to use in its production cycle. The following information is available:

Cost to Cardinal to make the part:	
Direct materials	$ 4
Direct labor	16
Variable overhead	8
Fixed overhead applied	10
	$38
Cost to buy the part from the Oriole Company	$36

If Cardinal buys the part from Oriole instead of making it, Cardinal could not use the released facilities in another manufacturing activity. Sixty percent of the fixed overhead applied will continue, regardless of what decision is made.

In deciding whether to make or buy the part, the total relevant costs to make the part are

(*a*) $560,000
(*b*) $640,000
(*c*) $720,000
(*d*) $760,000

4. The Reno Company manufactures part no. 498 for use in its production cycle. The cost per unit for 20,000 units of part no. 498 is as follows:

Direct materials	$ 6
Direct labor	30
Variable overhead	12
Fixed overhead applied	16
	$64

The Tray Company has offered to sell 20,000 units of part no. 498 to Reno for $60 per unit. Reno will make the decision to buy the part from Tray if there is a savings of $25,000 for Reno. If Reno accepts Tray's offer, $9 per unit of the fixed overhead applied would be totally eliminated. Furthermore, Reno has determined that the released facilities could be used to save relevant costs in the manufacture of part no. 575. In order to have a savings of $25,000, the amount of relevant costs that would be saved by using the released facilities in the manufacture of part no. 575 would have to be

(*a*) $80,000
(*b*) $85,000
(*c*) $125,000
(*d*) $140,000

(AICPA, adapted)

SOLUTION

1. (*c*) Relevant unit costs = $26 − $7 + $3 = $22

Total relevant costs:	
Savings on part no. 1211	$ 40,000
Savings on part no. 1700: 5,000 × $22	110,000
Subtotal	$150,000
Cost to purchase: 5,000 × $27	135,000
Decrease in net relevant costs	$ 15,000

2. (*b*) Variable cost per unit = $750,000 ÷ 300,000 = $2.50

Contribution margin per unit on special order = $5.00 − (0.40)($5.00) − $2.50 = $0.50

Therefore, income will increase: 60,000 × $0.50 = $30,000.

3. (*b*) In any make-or-buy decision, the relevant costs are those present and future costs that will be either incurred or avoided. Based on the facts given, costs that could be avoided would be the relevant costs.

Avoidable costs per unit:	
Direct material	$ 4
Direct labor	16
Variable overhead	8
Fixed avoidable overhead (40% × $10)	4
	$32

Relevant costs: $32 × 20,000 = $640,000. Note also that only 40 percent of the fixed overhead is a relevant cost, since 60 percent would continue in any event.

4. (*b*) On a per-unit basis, the avoidable costs for part no. 498, as given, are:

Avoidable costs per unit:	
Direct material	$ 6
Direct labor	30
Variable overhead	12
Fixed avoidable overhead	9
Total	$57

Only $9 of fixed overhead is avoidable, because that is the amount which would be eliminated; the remainder would continue.

It appears that Reno would lose $3 per unit ($60 − $57) by purchasing the part from Tray. An additional factor, however, is that Reno may be able to compensate for this loss by saving enough relevant costs on the manufacture of part no. 575 to recoup the $3 loss per unit and still have a savings of $25,000 besides. Reno would have to save $60,000 ($3 × 20,000) and another $25,000 for a total of $85,000 in the manufacture of part no. 575.

5.9 Products A and B are produced jointly in Department Z. Each product can be sold as is at the split-off point or processed further. During January, Department Z recorded a joint cost of $150,000. The following data for January are available:

		Selling Prices per Unit		Costs after
Product	Quantity	At Split-Off	If Processed Further	Split-Off
A	10,000 units	$5	$8	$40,000
B	20,000	1.50	2	5,000

Analyze whether individual products should be processed beyond the split-off point, using:

(*a*) The total project approach (or comparative statement approach)

(*b*) The incremental (differential) approach

(*c*) The opportunity cost approach

SOLUTION

For product A:

	(*a*)		(*b*)
	At Split-Off	At Completion	Difference (Increment)
Sales	$50,000	$80,000	$ 30,000
Costs	—	40,000	40,000
Net revenue	$50,000	$40,000	$ (10,000)

	(*c*)
	If Processed
Sales	$ 80,000
Costs:	
Additional	40,000
Opportunity cost of not selling at split-off	50,000
Loss	$ (10,000)

Based on any one of the three methods, product A should be sold at the split-off point.

For product B:

	(*a*)		(*b*)
	At Split-Off	At Completion	Difference (Increment)
Sales	$30,000	$40,000	$10,000
Costs	—	5,000	5,000
Net revenue	$30,000	$35,000	$ 5,000

	(*c*)
	If Processed
Sales	$40,000
Costs:	
Additional	5,000
Opportunity costs of not selling at split-off	30,000
Gain	$ 5,000

Product B should be processed further.

5.10 From a particular joint process, Watkins Company produces three products, X, Y, and Z. Each product may be sold at the point of split-off or processed further. Additional processing requires no special facilities, and production costs of further processing are entirely variable and traceable to the products involved. In 19X1, all three products were processed beyond split-off. Joint production costs for the year were $60,000. Sales values and costs needed to evaluate Watkins's 19X1 production policy follow:

			Additional Costs and Sales Values If Processed Further	
Product	Units Produced	Sales Values at Split-Off	Sales Values	Added Costs
X	6,000	$25,000	$42,000	$9,000
Y	4,000	41,000	45,000	7,000
Z	2,000	24,000	32,000	8,000

Joint costs are allocated to the products in proportion to the relative physical volume of output. Which of the products X, Y, and Z should Watkins subject to additional processing in order to maximize profits?

(AICPA, adapted)

SOLUTION

Watkins Company should process only product X, since its added sales revenue of $17,000 ($42,000 – $25,000) exceeds the added cost of $9,000. The computations for products X, Y, and Z are as follows:

	Product X	Product Y	Product Z
Sales revenue if processed further	$42,000	$45,000	$32,000
Sales revenue at split-off	25,000	41,000	24,000
Incremental sales	$17,000	$ 4,000	$ 8,000
Incremental costs	$ 9,000	$ 7,000	$ 8,000

5.11 The Discount Drug Company has three major product lines: drugs, cosmetics, and housewares. The company provides the following sales and cost information for the month of May for the store in total and for each separate product line (000 omitted):

	Drugs	Cosmetics	Housewares	Total
Sales	$240	$300	$360	$900
Less: Variable expenses	160	180	200	540
CM	$ 80	$120	$160	$360
Less: Fixed costs				
Salaries	$ 34	$ 40	$ 46	$120
Advertising	30	50	40	120
Other fixed costs	40	20	40	100
Total	$104	$110	$126	$340
Net income	$(24)	$ 10	$ 34	$ 20

The salaries represent wages paid to employees engaged directly in each product line area. The advertising represents direct advertising of each product line, and is avoidable if the line is dropped. Other fixed costs, which are all committed costs, will continue and will split equally between cosmetics and housewares.

1. Prepare a combined income statement for cosmetics and housewares on the assumption that drugs are discontinued with no effects on sales of the other product lines.
2. On the basis of the analysis in question 1, would you advise dropping the drugs line?

SOLUTION

1.

	Cosmetics	Housewares	Total
Sales	$300	$360	$660
Less: Variable expenses	180	200	380
CM	$120	$160	$280
Less: Fixed costs			
Salaries	40	$ 46	$ 86
Advertising	50	40	90
Other fixed costs	40	60	100
Total	$130	$146	$276
Net income	$ (10)	$ 14	$ 4

2. The answer is no. If the drugs line is dropped, the store's net income will be reduced from $20,000 to $4,000.

5.12 The Usery Company is considering discontinuing Department B, one of the three departments it currently maintains. The following information has been gathered for the three departments:

	(000 omitted)		
	Dept. A	Dept. B	Dept. C
Sales	$60,000	$50,000	$80,000
Cost of goods sold	$40,000	$42,000	$60,000
Operating expenses:			
Salaries	8,000	6,400	12,000
Rent	2,000	2,000	3,000
Utilities	1,000	2,700	2,000
Total costs	$51,000	$53,100	$77,000
Net income	$ 9,000	$ (3,100)	$ 3,000

If Department B is eliminated, the space it occupies will be divided equally among Departments A and C. Utilities are allocated on the basis of floor space occupied. 70 percent of the salaries in Department B would be eliminated; the other 30 percent would be split equally between Departments A and C.

1. Prepare a combined income statement for Departments A and C on the assumption that Department B is dropped.
2. Based on your analysis in question 1, should Department B be eliminated?
3. What qualitative factors should the Usery Company consider in making the decision as to whether or not Department B should be discontinued?

SOLUTION

1.

	Dept. A	Dept. C	Total
Sales	$60,000	$80,000	$140,000
Cost of goods sold	$40,000	$60,000	$100,000
Operating expenses:			
Salaries	8,960	12,960	21,920
Rent	3,000	4,000	7,000
Utilities*	2,350	3,350	5,700
Total costs	$54,310	$80,310	$134,620
Net income	$ 5,690	$ (310)	$ 5,380

*Utilities of Dept. B are allocated equally to Depts. A and C because the space occupied by Dept. B was split equally between Depts. A and C.

2. No, Department B should not be eliminated. If eliminated, the combined net income would be $5,380; with Department B the combined net income would be $8,900 ($9,000 + $3,000 − $3,100).
3. Some of the nonquantifiable questions you might want to ask are:
   (*a*) Would sales of other departments be affected?
   (*b*) Would customer goodwill be lost?
   (*c*) Can employees in Department B be released without effects on company morale?

5.13 As a result of an expansion program, Whitworth Enterprises, Inc., has excess capacity of 20,000 machine hours, which is expected to be absorbed by the domestic market in a few years.

The company has received inquiries from two companies located in another country. One offers to buy 210,000 units of product F at $0.60 per unit; the second offers to buy 300,000 units of product D at $0.70 per unit. Whitworth Enterprises can accept only one of these two offers. The estimated costs for these products are as follows:

	F	D
Materials	$0.25	$0.35
Direct labor	0.10	0.12
Factory overhead	0.20	0.28
Total estimated cost	$0.55	$0.75

Factory overhead is applied on a machine hour basis at $5.60 per hour; 75 percent of the factory overhead is estimated to be fixed. No selling and administrative expenses would be applicable to either order; transportation charges are to be paid by the buyer.

Which order should the company accept?

(CGA, adapted)

SOLUTION

Whitworth Enterprises, Inc., should accept the order for D, because it will provide the greater contribution margin, determined as follows:

	F		D	
Sales price per unit		$0.60		$0.70
Variable production costs per unit:				
Materials	$0.25		$0.35	
Direct labor	0.10		0.12	
Factory overhead (25%)	0.05	0.40	0.07	0.54
Contribution margin per unit		$0.20		$0.16
Total contribution margin:				
210,000 units × $0.20		$42,000		
300,000 units × $0.16				$48,000

5.14 The Amalgam Products, Inc., has 6,400 hours of plant capacity available to produce two products, A and B. The following data are given:

	A	B
Selling price	$15	$10
Variable cost per unit	7	4
Number of hours required to produce one unit	2	1

Which product should Amalgam produce?

SOLUTION

	A	B
Selling price	$15	$10
Variable cost per unit	7	4
Contribution margin per unit	$ 8	$ 6
Contribution per hour	$ 4	$ 6

Product B should be produced, since it would result in the greater contribution per unit of the constraining factor (per hour of plant capacity). The entire 6,400 hours of capacity should be devoted to the production of product B.

5.15 Mifflin Products, Inc., has 3,200 machine hours of plant capacity available for manufacturing two products with the following characteristics:

	X	Y
Selling price	$200	$165
Costs:		
Direct materials	$ 80	$ 40
Direct labor	40	35
Variable overhead*	15	30
Fixed overhead*	10	20
Operating expenses (all variable)	40	20
	$185	$145
Net income	$ 15	$ 20

*Applied on the basis of machine hours.

Compute the number of available machine hours that Mifflin Products, Inc., should devote to the manufacture of each product.

SOLUTION

Note that it takes twice as long to produce product Y because the variable or fixed overhead applied to product Y is twice as large as the one applied to product X.

	X	Y
Selling price	$200	$165
Variable costs	175	125
Unit CM	$ 25	$ 40
Hours per unit	÷ 1	÷ 2
CM/hour	$ 25	$ 20

All 3,200 hours should be devoted to the manufacture of product X because it would result in the greater CM per unit of the limiting factor (machine hours of plant capacity). The maximum CM attained by producing product X alone is $25 per hour × 3,200 hours = $80,000; this is greater than producing any combination of products X and Y.

5.16 North Star Guns is a high-technology enterprise making sophisticated products for the armaments market. One of the two profit centers, North Star Engineering, manufactures two types of electronic guidance units: "Standard" and "Deluxe." These units require a high degree of skill in manufacturing. However, because of a shortage of trained engineers, North Star Engineering has only 100 skilled employees, whose total labor capacity (allowing for sickness, leaves, and so on) is expected to be 100,000 hours per year. The data for North Star Engineering follow.

	Standard	Deluxe
Materials (parts)	$1,000	$4,000
Labor	10 hours @ $20	100 hours @ $20
Variable overhead per labor hour	$10	$10
Market price	$1,500	$10,000
Fixed overhead	$1,000,000	

Standard has a potentially unlimited market, but Deluxe has only the Army as a customer. North Star Engineering has a standing order for 500 Deluxe units per year from the Army.

1. What is the total amount of labor hours used now for each product?
2. Which product should be produced in order to maximize total contribution margin of North Star Engineering?

(SMA, adapted)

SOLUTION

1. and 2.

	Standard	Deluxe
Market price per unit	$1,500	$10,000
Materials	$1,000	$ 4,000
Labor	200	2,000
Variable overhead	100	1,000
Total variable costs	$1,300	$ 7,000
Unit CM	$ 200	$ 3,000
Hours per unit	÷ 10	÷ 100
CM per hour	$ 20	$ 30
Total labor hours used now	50,000	50,000*

*500 units × 100 hours = 50,000 hours. The remaining 50,000 hours (100,000 hours − 50,000 hours) are currently used for Standard.

With the present product mix, North Star Engineering is making a total CM of $2,500,000 (50,000 hours × $20 + 50,000 hours × $30). By devoting the entire 100,000 hours to the manufacture of Deluxe, North Star Engineering should be able to make a total CM of $3,000,000 (100,000 hours × $30), assuming it can promote the order from the Army up to 1,000 units.

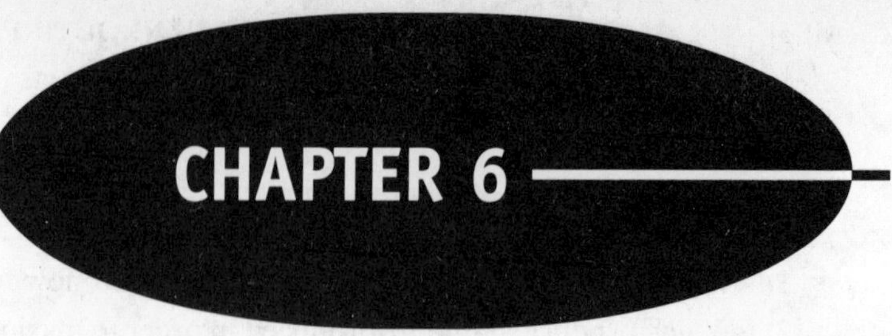

CHAPTER 6

Budgeting for Profit Planning

6.1 BUDGETING DEFINED

A *master* (comprehensive) *budget* is a formal statement of management's expectation regarding sales, costs, output, and other financial transactions of the firm for the coming period. Simply put, a *budget* is a set of projected or planned financial statements. It consists basically of a pro-forma income statement, a pro-forma balance sheet, and a cash budget. A budget is a tool used for both planning and control. At the beginning of the period, the budget is a plan or standard; at the end of the period, it serves as a control device to help management measure its performance against the plan so that future performance may be improved.

6.2 THE STRUCTURE OF THE MASTER BUDGET

The master budget is classified broadly into two categories: (1) the *operational budget*, reflecting the results of operating decisions; and (2) the *financial budget*, reflecting the financial decisions of the firm. The operating budget consists of:

- Sales budget, including a computation of expected cash receipts
- Production budget
- Direct material budget, including a computation of expected cash disbursements for materials
- Direct labor budget
- Factory overhead budget
- Ending inventory budget
- Selling and administrative expense budget
- Budgeted income statement, which can be prepared in a *traditional* or *contribution* format

The financial budget consists of:

- Cash budget
- Budgeted balance sheet

The major steps in preparing the master budget are:

1. Prepare a sales forecast.
2. Determine production volume.
3. Estimate manufacturing costs and operating expenses.
4. Determine cash flow and other financial effects.
5. Formulate projected financial statements.

6.3 ILLUSTRATION

To illustrate how all these budgets are put together, we will focus on a manufacturing company called the Johnson Company, which produces and markets a single product. We will assume that the company develops the master budget in *contribution format* for 19B on a *quarterly* basis. We will highlight the variable cost–fixed cost breakdown throughout the illustration.

THE SALES BUDGET

The sales budget is the starting point in preparing the master budget, since estimated sales volume influences nearly all other items appearing throughout the master budget. The sales budget ordinarily indicates the quantity of each product expected to be sold. Basically, there are three ways of making estimates for the sales budget:

1. Make a *statistical* forecast on the basis of an analysis of general business conditions, market conditions, and product growth curves.
2. Make an *internal* estimate by collecting the opinions of executives and salespersons.
3. Analyze the several factors that affect sales revenue and then predict the future behavior of each of these factors.

After sales volume has been estimated, the sales budget is constructed by multiplying the expected sales in units by the expected unit sales price. Generally, the sales budget includes a computation of expected cash collections from credit sales, which will be used later for cash budgeting.

EXAMPLE 6.1

THE JOHNSON COMPANY
Sales Budget
For the Year Ending December 31, 19B

	Quarter				
	1	2	3	4	Total
Expected sales in units	800	700	900	800	3,200
Unit sales price	×$80	×$80	×$80	×$80	×$80
Total sales	$64,000	$56,000	$72,000	$64,000	$256,000

SCHEDULE OF EXPECTED CASH COLLECTIONS

Accounts receivable, 12/31/19A	$ 9,500*				$ 9,500
1st quarter sales ($64,000)	44,800†	$17,920‡			62,720
2d quarter sales ($56,000)		39,200	$15,680		54,880
3d quarter sales ($72,000)			50,400	$20,160	70,560
4th quarter sales ($64,000)				44,800	44,800
Total cash collections	$54,300	$57,120	$66,080	$64,960	$242,460

*All $9,500 accounts receivable balance (see Example 6.10) is assumed to be collectible in the first quarter.
†70 percent of a quarter's sales are collected in the quarter of sale.
‡28 percent of a quarter's sales are collected in the quarter following, and the remaining 2 percent are uncollectible.

THE PRODUCTION BUDGET

After sales are budgeted, the production budget can be determined. The number of units expected to be manufactured to meet budgeted sales and inventory requirements is set forth in the production budget. The expected volume of production is determined by subtracting the estimated inventory at the beginning of the period from the sum of the units expected to be sold and the desired inventory at the end of the period. The production budget is illustrated as follows:

EXAMPLE 6.2

THE JOHNSON COMPANY
Production Budget
For the Year Ending December 31, 19B

	Quarter				
	1	2	3	4	Total
Planned sales (Example 6.1)	800	700	900	800	3,200
Desired ending inventory*	70	90	80	100†	100
Total needs	870	790	980	900	3,300
Less: Beginning inventory‡	80	70	90	80	80
Units to be produced	790	720	890	820	3,220

*10 percent of the next quarter's sales.
†Estimated.
‡The same as the previous quarter's ending inventory.

THE DIRECT MATERIAL BUDGET

When the level of production has been computed, a direct material budget should be constructed to show how much material will be required for production and how much material must be purchased to meet this production requirement. The purchase will depend on both expected usage of materials and inventory levels. The formula for computation of the purchase is:

Purchase in units = Usage + Desired ending material inventory units − Beginning inventory units

The direct material budget is usually accompanied by a computation of expected cash payments for materials.

EXAMPLE 6.3

THE JOHNSON COMPANY

Direct Material Budget

For the Year Ending December 31, 19B

	Quarter				
	1	2	3	4	Total
Units to be produced (Example 6.2)	790	720	890	820	3,220
Material needs per unit (pounds)	× 3	× 3	× 3	× 3	× 3
Material needs for production	2,370	2,160	2,670	2,460	9,660
Desired ending inventory of materials*	216	267	246	250†	250
Total needs	2,586	2,427	2,916	2,710	9,910
Less: Beginning inventory of materials‡	237	216	267	246	237
Materials to be purchased	2,349	2,211	2,649	2,464	9,673
Unit price	× $2	× $2	× $2	× $2	× $2
Purchase cost	$4,698	$4,422	$5,298	$4,928	$19,346

SCHEDULE OF EXPECTED CASH DISBURSEMENTS

	1	2	3	4	Total
Accounts payable, 12/31/19A§	$2,200				$ 2,200
1st quarter purchases ($4,698)	2,349	$2,349¶			4,698
2d quarter purchases ($4,422)		2,211	$2,211		4,422
3d quarter purchases ($5,298)			2,649	$2,649	5,298
4th quarter purchases ($4,928)				2,464	2,464
Total disbursements	$4,549	$4,560	$4,860	$5,113	$19,082

*10 percent of the next quarter's units needed for production.

†Estimated.

‡The same as the prior quarter's ending inventory.

§(Example 6.10).

¶Fifty percent of a quarter's purchases are paid for in the quarter of purchase; the remainder are paid for in the following quarter.

THE DIRECT LABOR BUDGET

The production requirements as set forth in the production budget also provide the starting point for the preparation of the direct labor budget. To compute direct labor requirements, expected production volume for each period is multiplied by the number of direct labor hours required to produce a single unit. The direct labor hours required to meet production requirements is then multiplied by the direct labor cost per hour to obtain budgeted total direct labor costs.

EXAMPLE 6.4

THE JOHNSON COMPANY

Direct Labor Budget

For the Year Ending December 31, 19B

	Quarter				
	1	2	3	4	Total
Units to be produced (Example 6.2)	790	720	890	820	3,220
Direct labor hours per unit	× 5	× 5	× 5	× 5	× 5
Total hours	3,950	3,600	4,450	4,100	16,100
Direct labor cost per hour	× $5	× $5	× $5	× $5	× $5
Total direct labor cost	$19,750	$18,000	$22,250	$20,500	$80,500

THE FACTORY OVERHEAD BUDGET

The factory overhead budget should provide a schedule of all manufacturing costs other than direct materials and direct labor. Using the contribution approach to budgeting requires the development of a predetermined overhead rate for the variable portion of the factory overhead. In developing the cash budget, we must remember that depreciation does not entail a cash outlay and therefore must be deducted from the total factory overhead in computing cash disbursements for factory overhead.

EXAMPLE 6.5 To illustrate the factory overhead budget, we will assume that:

- Total factory overhead budgeted = \$6,000 fixed (per quarter), plus \$2 per hour of direct labor.
- Depreciation expenses are \$3,250 each quarter.
- All overhead costs involving cash outlays are paid for in the quarter incurred.

THE JOHNSON COMPANY

Factory Overhead Budget

For the Year Ending December 31, 19B

	Quarter				
	1	2	3	4	Total
Budgeted direct labor hours (Example 6.4)	3,950	3,600	4,450	4,100	16,100
Variable overhead rate	× \$2	× \$2	× \$2	× \$2	× \$2
Variable overhead budgeted	\$ 7,900	\$ 7,200	\$ 8,900	\$ 8,200	\$32,200
Fixed overhead budgeted	6,000	6,000	6,000	6,000	24,000
Total budgeted overhead	\$13,900	\$13,200	\$14,900	\$14,200	\$56,200
Less: Depreciation	3,250	3,250	3,250	3,250	13,000
Cash disbursements for overhead	\$10,650	\$ 9,950	\$11,650	\$10,950	\$43,200

THE ENDING INVENTORY BUDGET

The desired ending inventory budget provides us with the information required for the construction of budgeted financial statements. Specifically, it will help compute the cost of goods sold on the budgeted income statement. Second, it will give the dollar value of the ending *materials* and *finished goods* inventory to appear on the budgeted balance sheet.

EXAMPLE 6.6

THE JOHNSON COMPANY

Ending Inventory Budget

For the Year Ending December 31, 19B

	Ending Inventory Units	Unit Cost	Total
Direct materials	250 pounds (Example 6.3)	\$ 2	\$ 500
Finished goods	100 units (Example 6.2)	\$41*	\$4,100

*The unit variable cost of \$41 is computed as follows:

	Unit Cost	Units	Total
Direct materials	\$2	3 pounds	\$ 6
Direct labor	5	5 hours	25
Variable overhead	2	5 hours	10
Total variable manufacturing cost			\$41

THE SELLING AND ADMINISTRATIVE EXPENSE BUDGET

The selling and administrative expense budget lists the operating expenses involved in selling the products and in managing the business. In order to complete the budgeted income statement in *contribution* format, variable selling and administrative expense per unit must be computed.

EXAMPLE 6.7

THE JOHNSON COMPANY
Selling and Administrative Expense Budget
For the Year Ending December 31, 19B

	Quarter				
	1	2	3	4	Total
Expected sales in units	800	700	900	800	3,200
Variable selling and administrative expense per unit*	× $4	× $4	× $4	× $4	× $4
Budgeted variable expense	$ 3,200	$ 2,800	$ 3,600	$ 3,200	$12,800
Fixed selling and administrative expenses:					
Advertising	1,100	1,100	1,100	1,100	4,400
Insurance	2,800				2,800
Office salaries	8,500	8,500	8,500	8,500	34,000
Rent	350	350	350	350	1,400
Taxes			1,200		1,200
Total budgeted selling and administrative expenses†	$15,950	$12,750	$14,750	$13,150	$56,600

*Includes sales agents' commissions, shipping, and supplies.
†Paid for in the quarter incurred.

THE CASH BUDGET

The cash budget is prepared for the purpose of cash planning and control. It presents the expected cash inflow and outflow for a designated time period. The cash budget helps management keep cash balances in reasonable relationship to its needs. It aids in avoiding unnecessary idle cash and possible cash shortages. The cash budget consists typically of four major sections:

1. The *receipts section*, which is the beginning cash balance, cash collections from customers, and other receipts
2. The *disbursements section*, which comprises all cash payments made by purpose
3. The *cash surplus* or *deficit section*, which simply shows the difference between the cash receipts section and the cash disbursements section
4. The *financing section*, which provides a detailed account of the borrowings and repayments expected during the budgeting period

EXAMPLE 6.8 To illustrate, we will make the following assumptions:

- The company desires to maintain a $5,000 minimum cash balance at the end of each quarter.
- All borrowing and repayment must be in multiples of $500 at an interest rate of 10 percent per annum. Interest is computed and paid as the principal is repaid. Borrowing takes place at the beginning of each quarter and repayment at the end of each quarter.

THE JOHNSON COMPANY
Cash Budget
For the Year Ending December 31, 19B

	Example	Quarter 1	2	3	4	Total
Cash balance, beginning	Given	$10,000	$ 9,401	$ 5,461	$ 9,106	$ 10,000
Add: Receipts:						
Collection from customers	6.1	54,300	57,120	66,080	64,960	242,460
Total cash available		$64,300	$66,521	$71,541	$74,066	$252,460
Less: Disbursements:						
Direct materials	6.3	$ 4,549	$ 4,560	$ 4,860	$ 5,113	$ 19,082
Direct labor	6.4	19,750	18,000	22,250	20,500	80,500
Factory overhead	6.5	10,650	9,950	11,650	10,950	43,200
Selling and administrative	6.7	15,950	12,750	14,750	13,150	56,600
Machinery purchase	Given	—	24,300	—	—	24,300
Income tax	Given	4,000	—	—	—	4,000
Total disbursements		$54,899	$69,560	$53,510	$49,713	$227,682
Cash surplus (deficit)		$ 9,401	$ (3,039)	$18,031	$24,353	$ 24,778
Financing:						
Borrowing		—	$ 8,500	—	—	$ 8,500
Repayment		—	—	$ (8,500)	—	(8,500)
Interest		—	—	(425)	—	(425)
Total financing		—	$ 8,500	$ (8,925)	—	$ (425)
Cash balance, ending		$ 9,401	$ 5,461	$ 9,106	$24,353	$ 24,353

THE BUDGETED INCOME STATEMENT

The budgeted income statement summarizes the various component projections of revenue and expenses for the budgeting period. However, for control purposes the budget can be divided into quarters or even months, depending on the need.

EXAMPLE 6.9

THE JOHNSON COMPANY
Budgeted Income Statement
For the Year Ending December 31, 19B

	Example No.		
Sales (3,200 units @ $80)	6.1		$256,000
Less: Variable expenses			
Variable cost of goods sold (3,200 units @ $41)	6.6	$131,200	
Variable selling and administrative	6.7	12,800	144,000
Contribution margin			$112,000
Less: Fixed expenses			
Factory overhead	6.5	$ 24,000	
Selling and administrative	6.7	43,800	67,800
Net operating income			$ 44,200
Less: Interest expense	6.8		425
Net income before taxes			$ 43,775
Less: Income taxes	20%		8,755
Net income			$ 35,020

THE BUDGETED BALANCE SHEET

The budgeted balance sheet is developed by beginning with the balance sheet for the year just ended and adjusting it, using all the activities that are expected to take place during the budgeting period. Some of the reasons why the budgeted balance sheet must be prepared are:

- It could disclose some unfavorable financial conditions that management might want to avoid.
- It serves as a final check on the mathematical accuracy of all the other budgets.
- It helps management perform a variety of ratio calculations.
- It highlights future resources and obligations.

EXAMPLE 6.10 To illustrate, we will use the following balance sheet for the year 19A.

THE JOHNSON COMPANY
Balance Sheet
For the Year Ended December 31, 19A

ASSETS		LIABILITIES AND STOCKHOLDERS' EQUITY	
Current Assets:		Current Liabilities:	
Cash	$ 10,000	Accounts Payable	$ 2,200
Accounts Receivable	9,500	Income Tax Payable	4,000
Materials Inventory	474	Total Current Liabilities	$ 6,200
Finished Goods Inventory	3,280	Stockholders' Equity:	
	$ 23,254	Common Stock, No-Par	$ 70,000
Fixed Assets:		Retained Earnings	37,054
Land	$ 50,000		
Building and Equipment	100,000		
Accumulated Depreciation	(60,000)		
	$ 90,000		
Total Assets	$113,254	Total Liabilities and Stockholders' Equity	$113,254

THE JOHNSON COMPANY
Budgeted Balance Sheet
For the Year Ended December 31, 19B

ASSETS			LIABILITIES AND STOCKHOLDERS' EQUITY		
Current Assets:			Current Liabilities:		
Cash	$ 24,353	(*a*)	Accounts Payable	$ 2,464	(*h*)
Accounts Receivable	23,040	(*b*)	Income Tax Payable	8,755	(*i*)
Materials Inventory	500	(*c*)	Total Current Liabilities	$ 11,219	
Finished Goods Inventory	4,100	(*d*)	Stockholders' Equity:		
	$ 51,993		Common Stock, No-Par	$ 70,000	(*j*)
Fixed Assets:			Retained Earnings	72,074	(*k*)
Land	$ 50,000	(*e*)			
Building and Equipment	124,300	(*f*)			
Accumulated Depreciation	(73,000)	(*g*)			
	$101,300				
Total Assets	$153,293		Total Liabilities and Stockholders' Equity	$153,293	

Computations:

(*a*) From Example 6.8 (cash budget).

(*b*) \$9,500 + \$256,000 sales − \$242,460 receipts = \$23,040.

(*c*) and (*d*) From Example 6.6 (ending inventory budget).

(*e*) No change.

(*f*) \$100,000 + \$24,300 (from Example 6.8) = \$124,300.

(*g*) \$60,000 + \$13,000 (from Example 6.5) = \$73,000.

(*h*) \$2,200 + \$19,346 − \$19,082 = \$2,464 (all accounts payable relate to material purchases), or 50% of 4th quarter purchase = 50% (\$4,928) = 2,464.

(*i*) From Example 6.9 (budgeted income statement).

(*j*) No change.

(*k*) \$37,054 + \$35,020 net income = \$72,074.

6.4 ZERO-BASE BUDGETING

Zero-base budgeting is a planning and budgeting tool that uses cost–benefit analysis of projects and functions to improve resource allocation in an organization. Traditional budgeting tends to concentrate on the incremental change from the previous year. It assumes that the previous year's activities are essential and must be continued. Under zero-base budgeting, however, cost estimates are built up from scratch, from the zero level, and must be justified.

The basic steps to effective zero-base budgeting are:

- Describe each organization's activity in a "decision" package.
- Analyze, evaluate, and rank all these packages in priority on the basis of cost–benefit analysis.
- Allocate resources accordingly.

Summary

(1) Budgeting is a tool for __________ and __________.

(2) The cash budget contains four major sections. They are the __________ section, the __________ section, the __________ section, and the __________ section.

(3) How much to produce is contingent on expected sales in units and the __________ and __________ inventories of finished goods.

(4) The __________ is prepared after the sales budget is completed. It is prepared in __________.

(5) The material purchase will depend on both __________ and __________.

(6) The __________ helps compute the __________ on the budgeted income statement. It also gives the dollar value of the materials and __________ to appear on the budgeted balance sheet.

(7) Cash budgets should include noncash charges such as depreciation: (*a*) true; (*b*) false.

(8) Cash budgets are prepared on a short-term basis such as on a monthly, quarterly, or even weekly basis: (*a*) true; (*b*) false.

(9) Operating budgets would include cash budgets: (*a*) true; (*b*) false.

(10) The ____________ shows the expected operating results for the budgeting year, while the ____________ shows the expected financial condition at the end of the budgeting period.

(11) The budgeted income statement can be prepared in a traditional or ____________ format.

(12) The idea behind preparing cash budgets is to avoid unnecessary cash ____________ and ____________.

(13) The budgeted balance sheet serves as a final check on the ____________ of all the other budgets. It could disclose some ____________ that management might wish to avoid.

(14) ____________ is so named because budgeting starts from scratch.

Answers: (1) planning, control; (2) cash receipts, cash disbursements, cash surplus (or deficit), financing; (3) beginning, ending; (4) production budget, physical units; (5) expected usage of materials for production, inventory levels; (6) desired ending inventory budget, cost of goods sold, finished goods; (7) (*b*); (8) (*a*); (9) (*b*); (10) budgeted income statement, budgeted balance sheet; (11) contribution; (12) surplus, deficit; (13) mathematical accuracy, unfavorable financial condition (or unfavorable financial ratios); (14) zero-base budgeting.

Solved Problems

6.1 The Barker Company manufactures two models of adding machines, A and B. The following production and sales data for the month of June are given for 19A:

	A	B
Estimated inventory (units) June 1	4,500	2,250
Desired inventory (units) June 30	4,000	2,500
Expected sales volume (units)	7,500	5,000
Unit sales price	$75	$120

Prepare a sales budget and a production budget for June 19A.

SOLUTION

BARKER COMPANY
Sales Budget
For June 19A

Product	Sales Volume	Unit Selling Price	Total Sales
A	7,500	$ 75	$ 562,500
B	5,000	120	600,000
			$1,162,500

BARKER COMPANY
Production Budget
For the Year 19A

	Product A	Product B
Expected sales	7,500	5,000
Ending inventory, desired	4,000	2,500
Total	11,500	7,500
Less: Beginning inventory	4,500	2,250
Total production (in units)	7,000	5,250

6.2 The following data pertain to the budget of K-Mart Industries, Inc.:

	Case 1	Case 2
Beginning inventory	30,000 units	10,000 units
Planned sales	100,000	50,000
Desired ending inventory	20,000	5,000

Compute the production volume required for each of the above two cases.

SOLUTION

	Case 1	Case 2
Planned sales	100,000 units	50,000 units
Add: Desired ending inventory	20,000	5,000
Total need	120,000	55,000
Less: Beginning inventory	30,000	10,000
Production required	90,000 units	45,000 units

6.3 The following data on production, materials required for products X and Y, and inventory pertain to the budget of LMN Company:

	Product X	Product Y
Production (units)	2,000	3,000
Materials (units)		
A	3.0	1.0
B	4.0	6.5

	Beginning	Desired Ending	Price/Unit
Materials inventory:			
A	2,000	3,000	$2
B	6,000	6,000	1.20

(*a*) Determine the number of material units needed to produce products X and Y.

(*b*) Calculate the cost of materials used for production.

(*c*) Determine the number of material units to be purchased.

(*d*) Calculate the cost of materials to be purchased.

SOLUTION

(*a*)

	Material A	Material B
Number of units of product X to be produced	2,000	2,000
Multiply by number of material units needed per product X	× 3	× 4
Total	6,000	8,000
Number of units of product Y to be produced	3,000	3,000
Multiply by number of material units needed for product Y	× 1.0	× 6.5
Total	3,000	19,500
Total number of material units needed for production of both products	9,000	27,500

(*b*)

	Material A	Material B
Total number of material units	9,000	27,500
Unit price	× $2	× $1.20
Cost of materials used for production	$18,000	$33,000

(*c*)

	Material A	Material B
Total number of units needed for production	9,000	27,500
Add: Desired ending inventory	3,000	6,000
Total material units needed	12,000	33,500
Less: Beginning inventory	2,000	6,000
Materials to be purchased	10,000	27,500

(*d*)

	Material A	Material B
Materials to be purchased	10,000	27,500
Unit price	× $2	× $1.20
Cost of materials to be purchased	$20,000	$33,000

6.4 A sales budget for the first five months of 19A is given for a particular product line manufactured by Kaehler Co. Ltd.:

	Sales Budget in Units
January	10,800
February	15,600
March	12,200
April	10,400
May	9,800

The inventory of finished products at the end of each month is to be equal to 25 percent of the sales estimate for the next month. On January 1, there were 2,700 units of product on hand. No work is in process at the end of any month.

Each unit of product requires two types of materials in the following quantities:

- Material A: 4 units
- Material B: 5 units

Materials equal to one-half of the next month's requirements are to be on hand at the end of each month. This requirement was met on January 1, 19A.

Prepare a budget showing the quantities of each type of material to be purchased each month for the first quarter of 19A.

(SMA, adapted)

SOLUTION

KAEHLER CO. LTD.

Production Budget
For the First Quarter and
For the Month of April, 19A

	January	February	March	April
Budgeted sales—units	10,800	15,600	12,200	10,400
+ Desired inventory, ending	3,900	3,050	2,600	2,450
	14,700	18,650	14,800	12,850
− Inventory on hand, beginning	2,700	3,900	3,050	2,600
Required monthly production	12,000	14,750	11,750	10,250

KAEHLER CO. LTD.

Direct Material Usage and Purchase Budget
For the First Quarter, 19A

MATERIAL A

	January	February	March
Production requirements—4 units of A for each unit of finished product	48,000	59,000	47,000
+ Desired inventory, ending	29,500	23,500	20,500
	77,500	82,500	67,500
− Inventory on hand, beginning	24,000	29,500	23,500
Budgeted purchases—units	53,500	53,000	44,000

MATERIAL B

	January	February	March
Production requirements—5 units of B for each unit of finished product	60,000	73,750	58,750
+ Desired inventory, ending	36,875	29,375	25,625
	96,875	103,125	84,375
− Inventory on hand, beginning	30,000	36,875	29,375
Budgeted purchases—units	66,875	66,250	55,000

6.5 Long Beach Tools Corporation has the following direct labor requirements for the production of a machine tool set:

Direct Labor	Required Time	Hourly Rate
Machining	6	10
Assembly	10	8

Forecasted sales for June, July, August, and September are 6,000, 5,000, 8,000, and 7,000 units, respectively. June 1 beginning inventory of the tool set was 1,500. The desired ending inventory each month is one-half of the forecasted sales for the following month.

1. Prepare a production budget for the months of June, July, and August.
2. Develop a direct labor budget for the months of June, July, and August and for each type of direct labor.

SOLUTION

1.

LONG BEACH TOOLS CORPORATION

Production Budget

	June	July	August
Forecasted sales	6,000 units	5,000	8,000
Add: Desired ending inventory	2,500	4,000	3,500
Total need	8,500	9,000	11,500
Less: Beginning inventory	1,500	2,500	4,000
Number of units to be produced	7,000	6,500	7,500

2.

LONG BEACH TOOLS CORPORATION

Direct Labor Budget

	June	July	August
Machining:			
Budgeted production	7,000	6,500	7,500
Direct labor hours per unit	× 6 hours	× 6	× 6
Total direct labor hours required	42,000 hours	39,000	45,000
	× $10	× $10	× $10
Direct labor cost	$420,000	$390,000	$450,000
Assembly:			
Budgeted production	7,000 units	6,500	7,500
Direct labor hours per unit	× 10 hours	× 10	× 10
Total direct labor hours required	70,000 hours	65,000	75,000
	× $8	× $8	× $8
Direct labor cost	$560,000	$520,000	$600,000

6.6 The following sales budget is given for Van Dyke Sales Company for the second quarter of 19X1:

	April	May	June	Total
Sales budget	$45,000	$50,000	$60,000	$155,000

Credit sales are collected as follows: 70 percent in month of sale, 20 percent in month following sale, 8 percent in second month following sale, and 2 percent uncollectible.

The accounts receivable balance at the beginning of the second quarter is $18,000, $3,600 of which represents uncollected February sales, and $14,400 uncollected March sales.

1. Calculate the total sales for February and March.
2. Compute the budgeted cash collections from sales for each month. (Without prejudice to

the answer to part 1, assume that February sales equal $40,000 and March sales equal $50,000.)

SOLUTION

1. $$\$3{,}600 = \text{February sales } (1 - 0.7 - 0.2)$$

$$\text{February sales} = \frac{\$3{,}600}{1 - 0.9} = \$36{,}000$$

$$\$14{,}400 = \text{March sales } (1 - 0.7)$$

$$\text{March sales} = \frac{\$14{,}400}{0.3} = \$48{,}000$$

2.

	April	May	June
Cash collections:			
February: $40,000 (8%)	$ 3,200		
March: $50,000 (20%)	10,000		
$50,000 (8%)		$ 4,000	
April: $45,000 (70%)	31,500		
$45,000 (20%)		9,000	
$45,000 (8%)			$ 3,600
May: $50,000 (70%)		35,000	
$50,000 (20%)			10,000
June: $60,000 (70%)			42,000
Total cash collections	$44,700	$48,000	$55,600

6.7 The following data are given for Erich From Stores:

	September Actual	October Actual	November Estimated	December Estimated
Cash sales	$ 7,000	$ 6,000	$ 8,000	$ 6,000
Credit sales	50,000	48,000	62,000	80,000
Total sales	57,000	54,000	70,000	86,000

Past experience indicates that net collections normally occur in the following pattern:

- No collections are made in the month of sale.
- Eighty percent of the sales of any month are collected in the following month.
- Nineteen percent of sales are collected in the second following month.
- One percent of sales are uncollectible.

1. Calculate the total cash receipts for November and December.
2. Compute the accounts receivable balance at November 30 if the October 31 balance is $50,000.

SOLUTION

1.

	November	December
Cash receipts:		
Cash sales	$ 8,000	$ 6,000
Cash collections:		
September sales: $50,000 (19%)	9,500	
October sales: $48,000 (80%)	38,400	
$48,000 (19%)		9,120
November sales: $62,000 (80%)		49,600
Total cash receipts	$55,900	$64,720

2. $\$50{,}000 + \$62{,}000 - \$9{,}500 - \$38{,}400 = \$64{,}100$

6.8 The treasurer of John Loyde Company plans for the company to have a cash balance of $91,000 on March 1. Sales during March are estimated at $900,000. February sales amounted to $600,000, and January sales amounted to $500,000. Cash payments for March have been budgeted at $580,000. Cash collections have been estimated as follows:

- Sixty percent of the sales for the month to be collected during the month.
- Thirty percent of the sales for the preceding month to be collected during the month.
- Eight percent of the sales for the second preceding month to be collected during the month.

The treasurer plans to accelerate collections by allowing a 2 percent discount for prompt payment. With the discount policy, she expects to collect 70 percent of the current sales and will permit the discount reduction on these collections. Sales of the preceding month will be collected to the extent of 15 percent with no discount allowed, and 10 percent of the sales of the second preceding month will be collected with no discount allowed. This pattern of collection can be expected in subsequent months. During the transitional month of March, collections may run somewhat higher. However, the treasurer prefers to estimate collections on the basis of the new pattern so that the estimates will be somewhat conservative.

1. Estimate cash collections for March and the cash balance at March 31 under the present policy and under the discount policy.
2. Is the discount policy desirable?

SOLUTION

1.

	Under the present policy		Under the discount policy	
Balance, March 1	$ 91,000		$ 91,000	
Collections:				
From March sales	540,000	($900,000 × 60%)	617,400*	
From Feb. sales	180,000	($600,000 × 30%)	90,000	($600,000 × 15%)
From Jan. sales	40,000	($500,000 × 8%)	50,000	($500,000 × 10%)
Total cash available	$851,000		$848,400	
Less: Disbursements	580,000		580,000	
Balance, March 31	$271,000		$268,400	

*$900,000 × 70% × 98% = $617,400.

2. No, because under the discount policy, the March 31 cash balance will be smaller.

6.9 Eastmark Stores wants to estimate cash disbursements for cash budgeting purposes for the first three months of 19B from the data given below.

(*a*) Cost of merchandise sold, estimated:

19A, December	$225,000
19B, January	250,000
February	280,000
March	210,000

Thirty-five percent of the cost of merchandise is to be paid for in the month of sale, and 65 percent of the cost is to be paid for in the month following the month of sale.

(*b*) Wages for each month are estimated as follows:

19A, December	$23,000
19B, January	26,000
February	31,000
March	25,000

Wages are all paid as incurred.

(*c*) Utilities are to be paid every other month at the amount of $320 per month. The first payment is to be made in February.

(*d*) Six months' rent and insurance amounting to a total of $9,700 is to be paid in January.

(*e*) An income tax of $12,500 is to be paid in March.

(*f*) Depreciation on office equipment has been estimated at $7,500 for the year.

(*g*) New equipment costing $50,000 is to be acquired in February with a down payment of $4,000 required at date of purchase.

(*h*) Other operating expenses have been estimated at $2,250 per month, which is to be paid each month.

Prepare a cash disbursement budget for each of the first three months of 19B.

SOLUTION

CASH DISBURSEMENTS BUDGET

For Three Months, 19B

	January	February	March	Total
Cost of merchandise sold:				
35% current	$ 87,500	$ 98,000	$ 73,500	$259,000
65% preceding month	146,250	162,500	182,000	490,750
Total	$233,750	$260,500	$255,500	$749,750
Wages	26,000	31,000	25,000	82,000
Utilities		320		320
Rent and insurance	9,700			9,700
Income tax			12,500	12,500
Equipment, down payment		4,000		4,000
Other operating expenses	2,250	2,250	2,250	6,750
Total disbursements	$271,700	$298,070	$295,250	$865,020

6.10 Kinsman, a retailer, provides the following data for 19A and 19B:

	December 31, 19A	December 31, 19B
Cash	$200,000	—
Trade accounts receivable	84,000	$ 78,000
Merchandise inventory	150,000	140,000
Accounts payable—merchandise	(95,000)	(98,000)

Budgeted sales for 19B are $1,200,000; sales for 19A were $1,100,000. Cash sales average 20 percent of total sales each year. Cost of goods sold for 19B is estimated to be $840,000. Budgeted 19B variable operating expenses are $120,000. They vary in proportion to sales and are paid 50 percent in the year incurred and 50 percent the following year. Unpaid variable expenses are not included in accounts payable above.

Fixed operating expenses, including $35,000 depreciation and $5,000 uncollectible accounts expense, total $100,000 per year. Such expenses involving cash payments are paid 80 percent in the year incurred and 20 percent the following year. Unpaid fixed expenses are not included in accounts payable above.

Prepare a cash budget for 19B with supporting computations on cash collections from credit sales and cash disbursements for purchases of merchandise and operating expenses.

(AICPA, adapted)

SOLUTION

CASH BUDGET

For the Year 19B

Beginning balance	$ 200,000
Collections (*a*)	1,201,000
Total	$1,401,000
Disbursements:	
Purchases of merchandise (*b*)	$ 827,000
Operating expenses (*c*)	175,000
Total disbursements	$1,002,000
Ending balance	$ 399,000

Supporting computations:

(*a*) Cash collections in 19B:

Trade accounts receivable, December 31, 19A, collected in 19B		$ 84,000
Budgeted 19B cash sales ($1,200,000 × 20%)		240,000
Budgeted 19B charge sales ($1,200,000 × 80%)		960,000
Less: Uncollectible accounts expense	$ (5,000)	
Trade accounts receivable, December 31, 19B	(78,000)	(83,000)
Cash collected in 19B		$1,201,000

(*b*) Cash disbursements for purchases of merchandise:

Cost of goods sold, 19B	$840,000
Inventory, December 31, 19B	140,000
Cost of goods available for sale	$980,000
Inventory, December 31, 19A	150,000
Purchases, 19B	$830,000
Increase in accounts payable—merchandise	3,000
Cash disbursed in 19B for purchases of merchandise	$827,000

(*c*) Cash disbursements for operating expenses:

Variable operating expenses:		
19B expenses of $120,000, 50% paid in 19B	$ 60,000	
19A expenses of $110,000 (10% of sales), 50% paid in 19B	55,000	
		$115,000
Fixed operating expenses:		
Total for each year	$100,000	
Less: Depreciation and uncollectible accounts expense	40,000	
Fixed operating expenses involving cash payments each year	$ 60,000	
19A paid in 19B ($60,000 × 20%)	$ 12,000	
19B paid in 19B ($60,000 × 80%)	48,000	60,000
Cash disbursed in 19B for variable and fixed operating expenses		$175,000

6.11 Some key figures from the budget of Moore Company for the first quarter of operations for 19B are shown below:

	January	February	March
Credit sales	$80,000	$70,000	$86,000
Credit purchases	34,000	32,000	40,000
Cash disbursements:			
Wages and salaries	4,000	3,500	4,200
Rent	1,500	1,500	1,500
Equipment purchases	25,000	—	2,000

The company estimates that 10 percent of its credit sales will never be collected. Of those that will be collected, one-half will be collected in the month of sale and the remainder will be collected in the following month. Purchases on account will all be paid for in the month following purchase. December 19B sales were $90,000.

Using the information given above, complete the cash budget given below.

	January	February	March
Beginning cash balance	$100,000		
Cash receipts:			
Cash collections from credit sales			
Total cash available			
Cash disbursements:			
Purchases			
Wages and salaries			
Rent			
Equipment purchases			
Total disbursements			
Ending cash balance			

SOLUTION

	January	February	March
Beginning cash balance	$100,000	$146,000	$174,500
Cash receipts:			
Cash collections from credit sales	76,500*	67,500†	70,200‡
Total cash available	$176,500	$213,500	$244,700
Cash disbursements:			
Purchases	—	$ 34,000	$ 32,000
Salaries	$ 4,000	3,500	4,200
Rent	1,500	1,500	1,500
Fixed assets	25,000	—	2,000
Total disbursements	$ 30,500	$ 39,000	$ 39,700
Ending cash balance	$146,000	$174,500	$205,000

---

*From December sales: $\frac{\$90{,}000 - (\$90{,}000 \times 0.1)}{2} = \$40{,}500$

January sales: $\frac{\$80{,}000 - (\$80{,}000 \times 0.1)}{2} = \$36{,}000$

Total = $76,500

†From January sales: $36,000

February sales: $\frac{\$70{,}000 - (\$70{,}000 \times 0.1)}{2} = \$31{,}500$

$67,500

‡From February sales: $31,500

March sales: $\frac{\$86{,}000 - (\$86{,}000 \times 0.1)}{2} = \$38{,}700$

$70,200

6.12 The Ray Company marks up all merchandise at 25 percent of gross purchase price. All purchases are made on account with terms of 1/10, net/60. Purchase discounts, which are recorded as miscellaneous income, are always taken. Normally, 60 percent of each month's purchases are paid for in the month of purchase, while the other 40 percent are paid during the first 10 days of the first month after purchase. Inventories of merchandise at the end of each month are kept at 30 percent of the next month's projected cost of goods sold.

Terms for sales on account are 2/10, net/30. Cash sales are not subject to discount. Fifty percent of each month's sales on account are collected during the month of sale, 45 percent are collected in the succeeding month, and the remainder are usually uncollectible. Seventy percent of the collections in the month of sale are subject to discount, while 10 percent of the collections in the succeeding month are subject to discount.

Projected sales data for selected months follow:

	Sales on Account—Gross	Cash Sales	Total Sales
December	$1,900,000	$400,000	$2,300,000
January	1,500,000	250,000	1,750,000
February	1,700,000	350,000	2,050,000
March	1,600,000	300,000	1,900,000

Select the best answer for each item.

1. Projected gross purchases for January are
   (*a*) $1,400,000 (*d*) $1,248,000
   (*b*) $1,470,000 (*e*) None of these
   (*c*) $1,472,000
2. Projected inventory at the end of December is
   (*a*) $420,000 (*d*) $393,750
   (*b*) $441,600 (*e*) None of these
   (*c*) $552,000
3. Projected payments to suppliers during February are
   (*a*) $1,551,200 (*d*) $1,509,552
   (*b*) $1,535,688 (*e*) None of these
   (*c*) $1,528,560
4. Projected sales discounts to be taken by customers making remittances during February are
   (*a*) $5,250 (*d*) $11,900
   (*b*) $15,925 (*e*) None of these
   (*c*) $30,500
5. Projected total collections from customers during February are
   (*a*) $1,875,000 (*d*) $1,188,100
   (*b*) $1,861,750 (*e*) None of these
   (*c*) $1,511,750

(AICPA, adapted)

SOLUTION

1. (*c*)

Ending inventory, January 31
+Planned sales at cost
−Ending inventory, December 31
Gross purchases for January

Ending inventory, January 31:	
30% (February cost of goods sold)	
= 30% (February sales ÷ 1.25)	
= 30% ($2,050,000 ÷ 1.25)	$ 492,000
Add: Planned sales at cost during January:	
$1,750,000 ÷ 1.25	1,400,000
Total needs	$1,892,000
Less: Ending inventory, December 31:	
30% (January cost of goods sold)	
= 30% ($1,400,000)	420,000
Gross purchases for January	$1,472,000

2. (*a*) (See part 1.)

3. (*b*)

Ending inventory, February 28:	
30% (March cost of goods sold)	
= 30% ($1,900,000 ÷ 1.25)	$ 456,000
Add planned sales at cost, February:	
$2,050,000 ÷ 1.25	1,640,000
Total needs	$2,096,000
Less: Ending inventory, January 31	
(from part 1)	492,000
Gross purchases for February	$1,604,000

Therefore, total February payments to suppliers:

From January purchases:	
99% × 40% × $1,472,000	$ 582,912
From February purchases:	
99% × 60% × $1,604,000	952,776
Total February payments	$1,535,688

4. (*e*)

January sales on account, $1,500,000:	
0.45 × $1,500,000 = $675,000 collected in February	
0.10 × $675,000 = $67,500 subject to discount	
0.02 × $67,500 = discounts taken in February	$ 1,350
February sales on account, $1,700,000:	
0.50 × $1,700,000 = $850,000 collected in February	
0.70 × $850,000 = $595,000 subject to discount	
0.02 × $595,000 = discounts taken in February	11,900
Total discounts taken in February	$13,250

5. (*b*)

February cash sales	$ 350,000
Collections on February sales on account:	
$850,000 − $11,900 discounts	838,100
Collections on January sales on account:	
$675,000 − $1,350 discounts	673,650
Total February cash collections	$1,861,750

6.13 The following information pertains to merchandise purchased by Westwood Plumbing Company for July, August, September, and October. During the month, 60 percent of the merchandise to be sold during the following month is purchased. The balance of the merchandise is purchased during the month. Gross margin averages 20 percent of sales.

	Purchases	
	For the Following Month	For the Current Month
July	$ 87,000	$ 92,000
August	96,000	100,000
September	120,000	89,000
October	110,000	92,000

Estimate the sales revenue for August, September, and October.

SOLUTION

Cost of sales:	August:	$87,000 ÷ 0.6 = $145,000
	September:	$96,000 ÷ 0.6 = $160,000
	October:	$120,000 ÷ 0.6 = $200,000

Since gross margin averages 20 percent of sales, cost of goods sold is equal to 80 percent of sales. Thus, sales are:

August:	$145,000 ÷ 0.8 = $181,250
September:	$160,000 ÷ 0.8 = $200,000
October:	$200,000 ÷ 0.8 = $250,000

6.14 Foster Company has gathered the following information for the month of July 19X1:

Sales: $200,000
Sales commissions: 10% of sales
Advertising expenses: $5,000 + 2% of sales
Miscellaneous selling expense: $1,000 + 1% of sales
Office salaries: $7,000
Office supplies: 0.5% of sales
Travel and entertainment: $4,000
Miscellaneous administrative expense: $1,750

Prepare a selling and administrative expense budget.

SOLUTION

FOSTER COMPANY

Selling and Administrative Expense Budget
For the Month of July, 19A

Selling expenses:	
Sales commissions	$20,000
Advertising expense	9,000
Miscellaneous selling expense	3,000
Total	$32,000
Administrative expenses:	
Office salaries	$ 7,000
Office supplies	1,000
Miscellaneous expense	1,750
Travel and entertainment	4,000
Total	$13,750
Total selling and administrative expenses	$45,750

6.15 In the fiscal quarter ended December 31, 19A, Eric Wills Lumber Company plans to sell 52,000 thousand board feet of lumber at a price of $125 per thousand board feet. There are to be 5,500 thousand board feet on hand October 1, with a cost of $65 per thousand board feet. The company plans to manufacture 53,000 thousand board feet of lumber during the quarter with the following manufacturing costs:

Direct materials	$971,500
Direct labor	$2,000,000
Factory overhead	25% of direct labor costs

The company uses the last-in, first-out (LIFO) method of inventory costing. Selling expenses are estimated at 25 percent of sales, and administrative expenses are expected to be 10 percent more than the previous quarter's $950,000. Prepare a budgeted income statement.

SOLUTION

ERIC WILLS LUMBER COMPANY

Budgeted Income Statement
For the Quarter Ended Dec. 31, 19A

Sales (52,000 @ $125)		$6,500,000
Less: Cost of Goods Sold		
Beginning Inventory (5,500 @ $65)	$ 357,500	
Direct Materials	971,500	
Direct Labor	2,000,000	
Factory Overhead (25% of $2,000,000)	500,000	
Cost of Goods Available for Sale	$3,829,000	
Less: Ending Inventory (6,500 units)*	423,000†	$3,406,000
Gross Profit		$3,094,000
Less: Operating Expenses		
Selling Expenses (25% of $6,500,000)	$1,625,000	
Administrative Expenses (110% of $950,000)	1,045,000	2,670,000
Net Income		$ 424,000

*5,500 units + 53,000 units − x = 52,000 units; x = 6,500 units.

†5,500 units @ $65	= $357,500
1,000 units @ $65.50 =	65,500
6,500 units	= $423,000

where the unit cost for the last quarter of 19A is computed as follows:

Cost of goods manufactured = $971,500 + $2,000,000 + $500,000
= $3,471,500

Unit cost = $3,471,500 ÷ 53,000 thousand board feet = $65.50

6.16 The Moore Distributor Company, Inc., has just received a franchise to distribute dishwashers. The company started business on January 1, 19A, with the following assets:

Cash	$45,000
Inventory	94,000
Warehouse, office, and delivery facilities and equipment	80,000

All facilities and equipment have a useful life of 20 years and no residual value. First-quarter sales are expected to be $360,000 and should be doubled in the second quarter. Third-quarter sales are expected to be $1,080,000. One percent of sales are considered to be uncollectible. The gross profit margin should be 30 percent. Variable selling expenses (except uncollectible accounts) are budgeted at 12 percent of sales and fixed selling expenses at $48,000 per quarter, exclusive of depreciation. Variable administrative expenses are expected to be 3 percent of sales, and fixed administrative expenses should total $34,200 per quarter, exclusive of depreciation. Prepare a budgeted income statement for the second quarter of 19A.

(CGA, adapted)

SOLUTION

THE MOORE DISTRIBUTOR COMPANY, INC.

Budgeted Income Statement

For the Second Quarter, 19A

Sales		$720,000
Cost of Goods Sold (70%)		504,000
Gross Profit (30%)		$216,000
Operating Expenses:		
Uncollectible Accounts (1%)	$ 7,200	
Depreciation	10,000*	
Selling:		
Variable (12%)	86,400	
Fixed	48,000	
Administrative:		
Variable (3%)	21,600	
Fixed	34,200	207,400
Income before Income Tax		$ 8,600

*1/4 ($800,000 ÷ 20 years).

6.17 A budget is being prepared for the first and second quarters of 19B for Aggarwal Retail Stores, Inc. The balance sheet as of December 31, 19A, is given below.

AGGARWAL RETAIL STORES, INC.

Balance Sheet

December 31, 19A

ASSETS		LIABILITIES AND EQUITIES	
Cash	$ 65,000	Accounts Payable	$ 83,000
Accounts Receivable	52,000	Income Tax Payable	20,000
Merchandise Inventory	75,000	Capital Stock	70,000
		Retained Earnings	19,000
Total Assets	$192,000	Total Liabilities and Equities	$192,000

Actual and projected sales are:

19A 3d quarter (actual)	$250,000
19A 4th quarter (actual)	300,000
19B 1st quarter (estimated)	200,000
19B 2d quarter (estimated)	230,000
19B 3d quarter (estimated)	220,000

Experience has shown that 60 percent of sales will be collected during the quarter of sales and 35 percent of sales will be collected in the following quarter. Gross profit averages 30 percent of sales. There is a basic inventory of $20,000. The policy is to purchase additional inventory each quarter in the amount necessary to provide for the following quarter's sales. Assume that payments are made in the quarter following the quarter of purchase. Selling and administrative expenses for each quarter are estimated at 4 percent of sales plus $15,000. They are paid as incurred. Income tax is equal to 40 percent of taxable income. The income tax liability as of December 31, 19A, is to be paid during the first quarter of 19B. Prepare a budgeted income statement for the first and second quarters of 19B and a budgeted balance sheet as of June 30, 19B.

SOLUTION

AGGARWAL RETAIL STORES, INC.

Budgeted Income Statement
For the Six Months Ending June 30, 19B

	First Quarter	Second Quarter	Total
Sales	$200,000	$230,000	$430,000
Less: Cost of Goods Sold (70%)	140,000	161,000	301,000
Gross Margin	$ 60,000	$ 69,000	$129,000
Less: Selling and Administrative Expenses			
($15,000 + 4% of sales)	23,000	24,200	47,200
Net Income before Tax	$ 37,000	$ 44,800	$ 81,800
Income Tax (40%)	14,800	17,920	32,720
Net Income	$ 22,200	$ 26,880	$ 49,080

AGGARWAL RETAIL STORES, INC.

Budgeted Balance Sheet
As of June 30, 19B

ASSETS		LIABILITIES AND EQUITIES	
Cash	$ 89,800 (*a*)	Accounts Payable	$ 97,000 (*d*)
Accounts Receivable	49,000 (*b*)	Income Tax Payable	32,720 (*e*)
Merchandise Inventory	129,000 (*c*)	Capital Stock	70,000
		Retained Earnings	68,080 (*f*)
Total Assets	$267,800	Total Liabilities and Equities	$267,800

Supporting computations:

Cash receipts:	First Quarter	Second Quarter	Total
60% of current sales	$120,000	$138,000	$258,000
35% of prior-quarter sales	105,000	70,000	175,000
Total receipts	$225,000	$208,000	$433,000

Cash disbursements:			
Merchandise purchases	$160,000	$181,000	$341,000
Selling and administrative expenses			
($15,000 + 4% of sales)	23,000	24,200	47,200
Income tax	20,000	—	20,000
Total disbursements	$203,000	$205,200	$408,200

Merchandise purchases:

	Fourth Quarter	First Quarter	Second Quarter	Total
\$20,000 basic + 70% of the following quarter's sales	\$160,000	\$181,000	\$174,000	\$515,000
Cash disbursements for merchandise purchases:		\$160,000	\$181,000	\$341,000

Account balances:

	Cash (*a*)	Accounts Receivable (*b*)	Merchandise Inventory (*c*)
Beginning balances	\$ 65,000	\$ 52,000	\$ 75,000
Receipts	433,000		
Sales		430,000	
Purchases (\$181,000 + \$174,000)			355,000
Total	\$498,000	\$482,000	\$430,000
Disbursements	408,200		
Collections		433,000	
Cost of sales (70% of \$430,000)			301,000
Ending balances	\$ 89,800	\$ 49,000	\$129,000

	Accounts Payable (*d*)	Income Tax Payable (*e*)	Retained Earnings (*f*)
Beginning balances	\$ 83,000	\$20,000	\$19,000
Purchases	355,000*		
Selling and administrative expenses	47,200		
Income tax		32,720	
Net income			49,080
Total	\$485,200	\$52,720	\$68,080
Disbursements	388,200†	20,000	
Ending balances	\$ 97,000	\$32,720	\$68,080

*\$181,000 + \$174,000 = \$355,000.
†Disbursements for merchandise purchases and selling and administrative expenses: \$341,000 + \$47,200 = \$388,200.

6.18 Over the past several years the Programme Corporation has encountered difficulties estimating its cash flows. The result has been a rather strained relationship with its banker.

Programme's controller would like to develop a means by which he can forecast the firm's monthly operating cash flows. The following data were gathered to facilitate the development of such a forecast.

1. Sales have been increased and are expected to increase at 0.5 percent each month.
2. Thirty percent of each month's sales are for cash; the other 70 percent are on open account.
3. Of the credit sales, 80 percent are collected in the first month following the sale and the remaining 20 percent are collected in the second month. There are no bad debts.
4. Gross margin on sales averages 25 percent.
5. Programme purchases enough inventory each month to cover the following month's sales.

6. All inventory purchases are paid for in the month of purchase at a 2 percent cash discount.
7. Monthly expenses are: payroll, \$1,500; rent, \$400; depreciation, \$120; other cash expenses, 1 percent of that month's sales. There are no accruals.
8. Ignore the effects of corporate income taxes, dividends, and equipment acquisitions.

Using the data above, develop a mathematical model the controller can use for his calculations. Your model should be capable of calculating the monthly operating cash inflows and outflows for any specified month.

(CMA, adapted)

SOLUTION

Let: S = current month's sales

t = number of months in the future the forecast is desired

Sales t months from now = $S(1.005)^t$

Collections t months from now $= 0.3S(1.005)^t + (0.8)(0.7)S(1.005)^{t-1} + (0.2)(0.7)S(1.005)^{t-2}$

$= 0.3S(1.005)^t + 0.56S(1.005)^{t-1} + 0.14S(1.005)^{t-2}$

Purchases t months from now $= 0.75S(1.005)^{t+1}$

Cash payments t months from now* $= (0.98)(0.75)S(1.005)^{t+1} + 0.015(1.005)^t + 1900$

$= 0.735S(1.005)^{t+1} + 0.01S(1.005)^t + 1900$

---

*If it is assumed that the discounts were included to arrive at the 25 percent gross margin, then the (0.98) in the first expression would not appear.

Standard Costs, Responsibility Accounting, and Cost Allocation

7.1 RESPONSIBILITY ACCOUNTING DEFINED

Responsibility accounting is the system for collecting and reporting revenue and cost information by areas of responsibility. It operates on the premise that managers should be held responsible for their performance, the performance of their subordinates, and all activities within their responsibility center. Responsibility accounting, also called *profitability accounting* and *activity accounting*, has the following advantages.

1. It facilitates delegation of decision making.
2. It helps management promote the concept of *management by objective*. In management by objective, managers agree on a set of goals. The manager's performance is then evaluated based on his or her attainment of these goals.
3. It provides a guide to the evaluation of performance and helps to establish standards of performance which are then used for comparison purposes.
4. It permits effective use of the concept of *management by exception*, which means that the manager's attention is concentrated on the important deviations from standards and budgets.

For an effective responsibility accounting system, the following three basic conditions are necessary.

(*a*) The organization structure must be well defined. Management responsibility and authority must go hand in hand at all levels and must be clearly established and understood.

(*b*) Standards of performance in revenues, costs, and investments must be properly determined and well defined.

(*c*) The responsibility accounting reports (or performance reports) should include only the items that are controllable by the manager of the responsibility center. Also, they should highlight items that call for managerial attention.

7.2 RESPONSIBILITY CENTERS AND THEIR PERFORMANCE EVALUATION

A well-designed responsibility accounting system establishes responsibility centers within the organization. A *responsibility center* is defined as a unit in the organization which has control over costs, revenues, and/or investment funds. Responsibility centers can be one of the following types.

Cost center. A cost center is the unit within the organization which is responsible only for costs. Examples include the production and maintenance departments of a manufacturing company, and the admissions department of a university.

Variance analysis based on *standard costs* and *flexible budgets* is a typical performance measure of a cost center.

Profit center. A profit center is the unit which is held responsible for the revenues earned and costs incurred in that center. Examples might include a sales office of a publishing company, an appliance department in a retail store, and an auto repair center in a department store. *The contribution approach to cost allocation* is widely used to measure the performance of a profit center.

Investment center. An investment center is the unit within the organization which is held responsible for the costs, revenues, and related investments made in that center. The corporate headquarters or division in a large decentralized organization is an example of an investment center. *Return on investment* and *residual income* are two key performance measures of an investment center.

Figure 7-1 illustrates the ways in which responsibility accounting can be used within an organization and highlights profit and cost centers. This chapter discusses in detail how the performance of both cost and profit centers is evaluated. Performance evaluation of the investment center is reserved until Chapter 9.

7.3 STANDARD COSTS AND VARIANCE ANALYSIS

One of the most important phases of responsibility accounting is establishing standard costs and evaluating performance by comparing actual costs with the standard costs. The difference between the actual costs and the standard costs, called the *variance*, is calculated for individual cost centers. The variance analysis is a key tool for measuring performance of a cost center.

The standard cost is based on physical and dollar measures; it is determined by multiplying the standard quantity of an input by its standard price. Two general types of variances can be calculated for most cost items: a *price variance* and a *quantity variance*. The price variance is calculated as follows:

$$\begin{aligned}\text{Price variance} &= \text{Actual quantity} \times (\text{Actual price} - \text{Standard price})\\ &= AQ \times (AP - SP)\\ &= \underset{(1)}{(AQ \times AP)} - \underset{(2)}{(AQ \times SP)}\end{aligned}$$

The quantity variance is calculated as follows:

$$\begin{aligned}\text{Quantity variance} &= (\text{Actual quantity} - \text{Standard quantity}) \times \text{Standard price}\\ &= (AQ - SQ) \times SP\\ &= \underset{(2)}{(AQ \times SP)} - \underset{(3)}{(SQ \times SP)}\end{aligned}$$

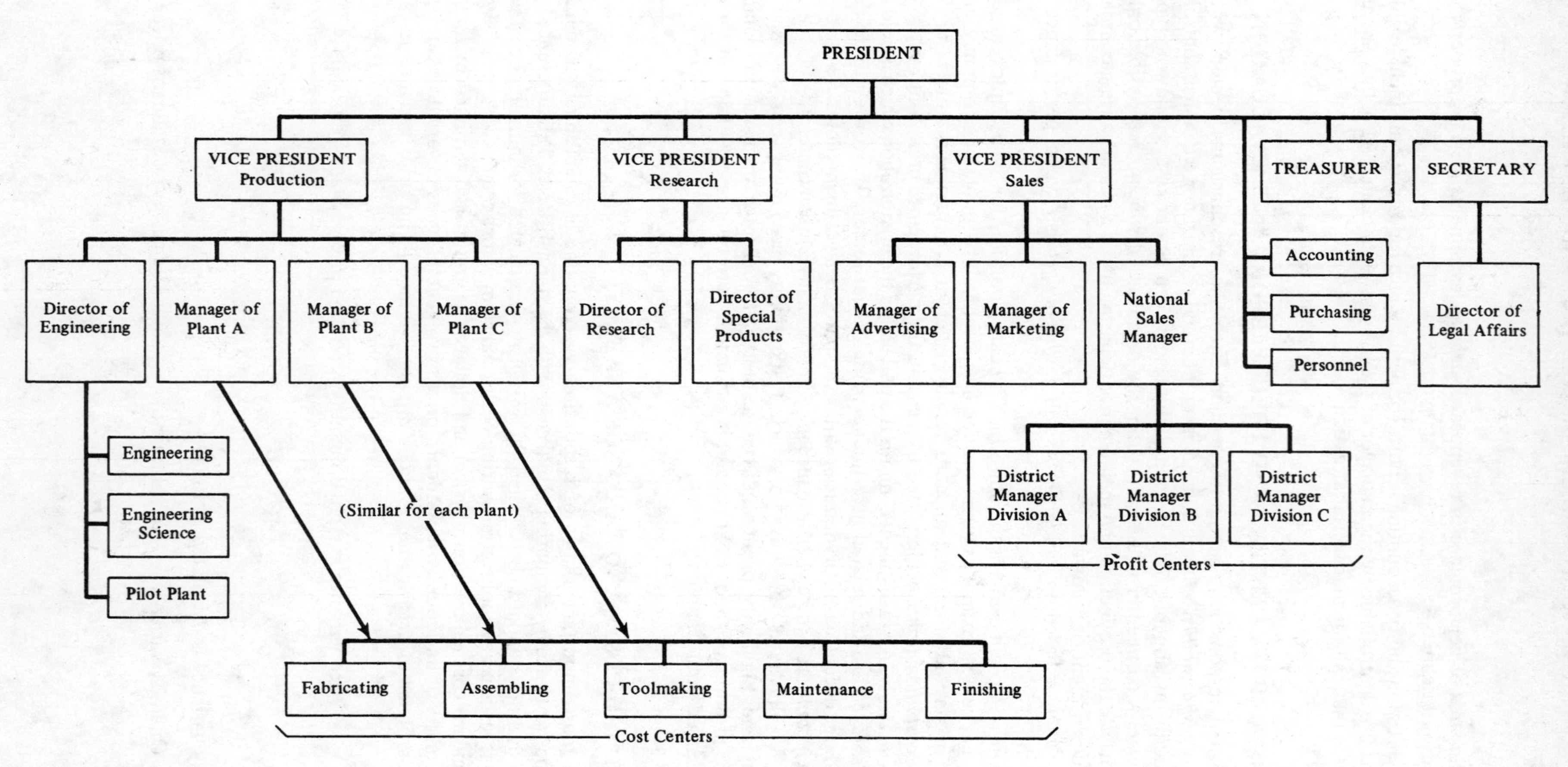

Fig. 7-1. Company XYZ.

Figure 7-2 shows a general model (three-column) for variance analysis that incorporates items (1), (2), and (3) from the above equations. It is important to note three things:

1. A price variance and a quantity variance can be calculated for all three variable cost items—direct materials, direct labor, and the variable portion of factory overhead. The variance is not called by the same name, however. For example, a price variance is called a *materials purchase price variance* in the case of direct materials, but a *labor rate variance* in the case of direct labor and a *variable overhead spending variance* in the case of variable factory overhead.

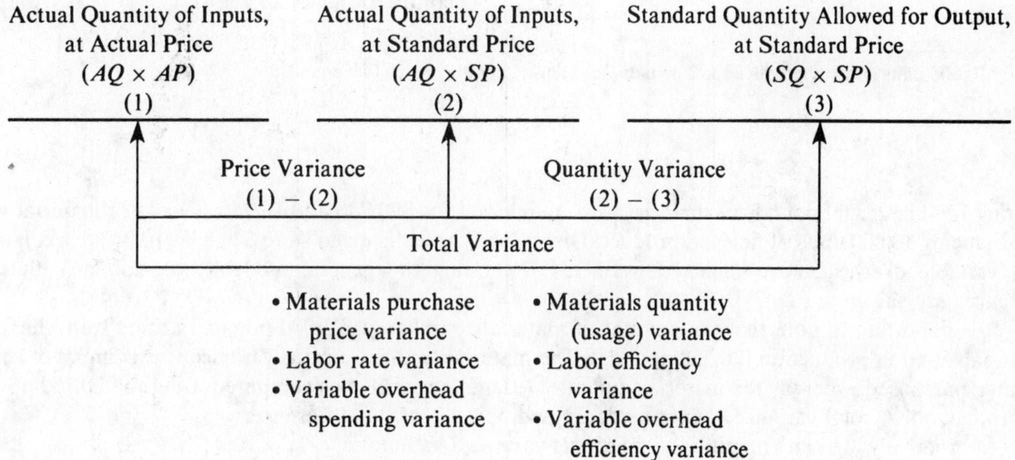

Fig. 7-2. A general model for variance analysis of variable manufacturing costs.

2. A variance is said to be *unfavorable* (U) if the actual price *AP* or actual quantity *AQ* exceeds the standard price *SP* or standard quantity *SQ*; a variance is said to be *favorable* (F) if the actual price or actual quantity is less than the standard price or standard quantity.
3. The standard quantity allowed for output—item (3)—is the key concept in variance analysis. This is the standard quantity that should have been used to produce actual output. It is computed by multiplying the output by the number of input units allowed.

We will now illustrate by an example the variance analysis for each of the variable manufacturing cost items.

MATERIALS VARIANCES

A materials purchase price variance is isolated at the time of purchase of the material. It is computed based on the actual quantity *purchased*. The purchasing department is responsible for any materials price variance that might occur. The materials quantity (usage) variance is computed based on the actual quantity used. The production department is responsible for any materials quantity variance that might occur. The possible causes for materials variances are given in Problems 7.4 and 7.5 at the end of this chapter.

EXAMPLE 7.1 Dallas Ewing Corporation uses a standard cost system. The standard variable costs for product J are as follows:

Materials: 2 pounds at $3 per pound
Labor: 1 hour at $5 per hour
Variable overhead: 1 hour at $3 per hour

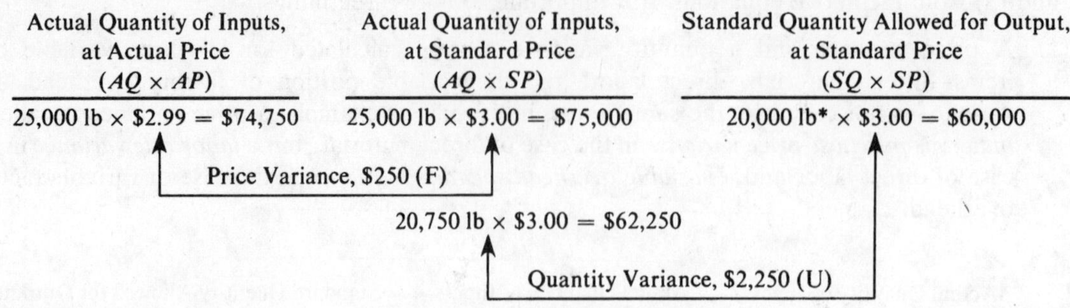

*10,000 units actually produced × 2 pounds (lb) allowed per unit = 20,000 pounds.

Fig. 7-3

During March, 25,000 pounds of material were purchased for $74,750 and 20,750 pounds of material were used in producing 10,000 units of finished product. Direct labor costs incurred were $49,896 (10,080 direct labor hours) and variable overhead costs incurred were $34,776. Using the general model (three-column), the materials variances are shown in Fig. 7-3.

It is important to note that the amount of materials purchased (25,000 pounds) differs from the amount of materials used in production (20,750 pounds). The materials purchase price variance was computed using 25,000 pounds purchased, whereas the materials quantity (usage) variance was computed using the 20,750 pounds used in production. A total variance cannot be computed because of the difference.

Alternatively, we can compute the materials variances as follows:

$$\begin{aligned}\text{Materials purchase price variance} &= AQ(AP - SP) = (AQ \times AP) - (AQ \times SP)\\ &= (25{,}000\text{ pounds})(\$2.99 - \$3.00)\\ &= \$74{,}750 - \$75{,}000 = \$250\ (\text{F})\end{aligned}$$

$$\begin{aligned}\text{Materials quantity (usage) variance} &= (AQ - SQ)\,SP\\ &= (20{,}750\text{ pounds} - 20{,}000\text{ pounds})(\$3.00)\\ &= \$62{,}250 - \$60{,}000 = \$2{,}250\ (\text{U})\end{aligned}$$

LABOR VARIANCES

Labor variances are both isolated when labor is used for production. They are computed in a manner similar to the materials variances, except that in the three-column model the terms *hours* and *rate* are used in place of the terms *quantity* and *price*. The production department is responsible for both the prices paid for labor services and the quantity of labor services used. Therefore, the production department must explain why any labor variances occur (see Problems 7.8 and 7.12).

EXAMPLE 7.2 Using the data given in Example 7.1, the labor variances can be calculated as shown in Fig. 7-4.

Alternatively, we can calculate the labor variances as follows:

$$\begin{aligned}\text{Labor rate variance} &= AH(AR - SR)\\ &= (AH \times AR) - (AH \times SR)\\ &= (10{,}080\text{ hours})(\$4.95 - \$5.00)\\ &= \$49{,}896 - \$50{,}400 = \$504\ (\text{F})\end{aligned}$$

$$\begin{aligned}\text{Labor efficiency variance} &= (AH - SH)SR\\ &= (10{,}080\text{ hours} - 10{,}000\text{ hours}) \times \$5.00\\ &= \$50{,}400 - \$50{,}000 = \$400\ (\text{U})\end{aligned}$$

Labor Variances

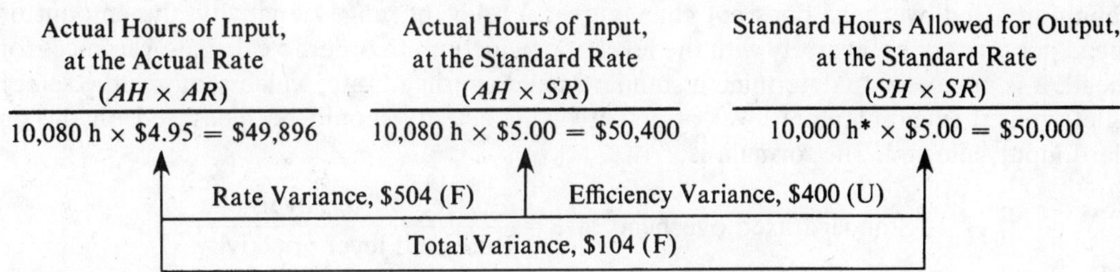

*10,000 units actually produced × 1 hours (h) allowed per unit = 10,000 hours.
Note: The symbols *AQ*, *SQ*, *AP*, and *SP* have been changed to *AH*, *SH*, *AR*, and *SR* to reflect the terms *hour* and *rate*.

Fig. 7-4

VARIABLE OVERHEAD VARIANCES

The variable overhead variances are computed in a way very similar to the labor variances. The production department is usually responsible for any variable overhead variance that might occur. Some of the possible causes for any overhead variance are given in Problems 7.10 and 7.12. Variances for fixed overhead are of questionable usefulness for control purposes, since these variances are usually beyond the control of the production department.

EXAMPLE 7.3 Using the data given in Example 7.1, the variable overhead variances can be computed as shown in Fig. 7-5.

Variable Overhead Variances

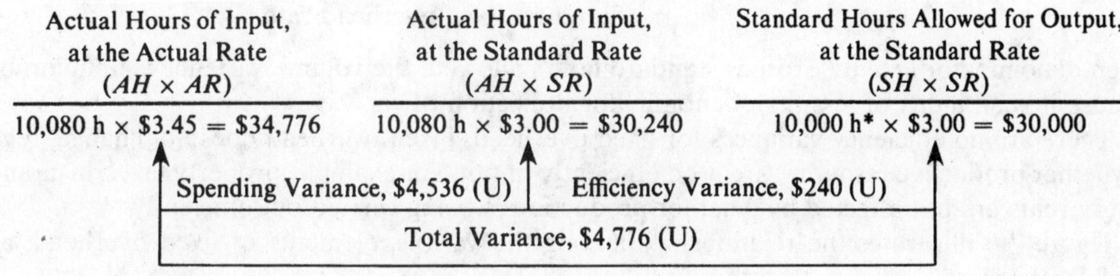

*10,000 units actually produced × 1 hour (h) allowed per unit = 10,000 hours.

Fig. 7-5

Alternatively, we can compute the variable overhead variances as follows:

$$\begin{aligned}\text{Variable overhead spending variance} &= AH(AR - SR) = (AH \times AR) - (AH \times SR)\\ &= (10{,}080\text{ hours})(\$3.45 - \$3.00)\\ &= \$34{,}776 - \$30{,}240 = \$4{,}536\text{ (U)}\end{aligned}$$

$$\begin{aligned}\text{Variable overhead efficiency variance} &= (AH - SH)SR\\ &= (10{,}080\text{ hours} - 10{,}000\text{ hours})(\$3.00)\\ &= \$30{,}240 - \$30{,}000 = \$240\text{ (U)}\end{aligned}$$

7.4 FIXED OVERHEAD VARIANCES

By definition, fixed overhead does not change over a relevant range of activity; the amount of fixed overhead per unit varies inversely with the level of production. In order to calculate variances for fixed overhead, it is necessary to determine a standard fixed overhead rate, which requires the selection of a predetermined (denominator) level of activity. This activity should be measured on the basis of standard inputs allowed. The formula is:

$$\text{Standard fixed overhead rate} = \frac{\text{Budgeted fixed overhead}}{\text{Budgeted level of activity}}$$

Total fixed overhead variance is simply under- or overapplied overhead. It is the difference between actual fixed overhead incurred and fixed overhead applied to production (generally, on the basis of standard direct labor hours allowed for actual production). Total fixed overhead variance combines fixed overhead spending (flexible budget) variance and fixed overhead volume (capacity) variance.

Fixed overhead spending (flexible budget) variance. This is the difference between actual fixed overhead incurred and budgeted fixed overhead. This variance is not affected by the level of production. Fixed overhead, by definition, does not change with the level of activity. The spending (flexible budget) variance is caused solely by events such as unexpected changes in prices and unforeseen repairs.

Fixed overhead volume (capacity) variance. This variance results when the actual level of activity differs from the denominator activity used in determining the standard fixed overhead rate. Note that the denominator used in the formula is the expected annual activity level. Fixed overhead volume variance is a measure of the cost of failure to operate at the denominator (budgeted) activity level, and may be caused by such factors as failure to meet sales targets, idleness due to poor scheduling, or machine breakdowns. The volume variance is calculated as follows:

$$\text{Fixed overhead volume variance} = (\text{Budgeted fixed overhead}) - (\text{Fixed overhead applied})$$

or

$$= (\text{Denominator activity} - \text{Standard hours allowed}) \times \text{Standard fixed overhead rate}$$

When denominator activity exceeds standard hours allowed, the volume variance is unfavorable (U), because it is an index of less-than-denominator utilization of capacity.

There are no efficiency variances for fixed overhead. Fixed overhead does not change, regardless of whether productive resources are used efficiently or not. For example, property taxes, insurance, and factory rents are not affected by whether production is being carried out efficiently.

Figure 7-6 illustrates the relationships among the various elements of fixed overhead, and the possible variances.

EXAMPLE 7.4 The Doubtfire Manufacturing Company has the following standard cost of factory overhead at a normal monthly production (denominator) volume of 1,300 direct labor hours:

Variable overhead (1 hour @ $2)
Fixed overhead (1 hour @ $5)

Fixed overhead budgeted is $6,500 per month. During the month of March, the following events occurred:

1. Actual overhead costs incurred (for 1,350 hours) were:

Variable	$2,853
Fixed	$6,725

2. Standard hours allowed were 1,250 hours (1 hour × 1,250 units of output).

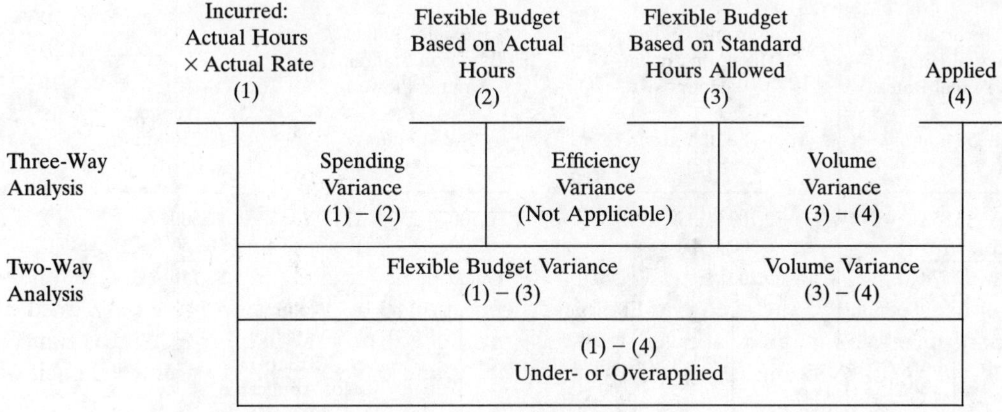

Fig. 7-6

Note the following:

Flexible budget formula:
Variable overhead rate, \$2 per direct labor hour
Fixed overhead budgeted, \$6,500
Standard overhead applied rates:
Variable, \$2 per direct labor hour
Fixed, \$5 per direct labor hour

Figure 7-7 shows all the variances for variable overhead as well as fixed overhead.

Alternatively, the fixed overhead volume variance can be calculated as follows:

$$\begin{aligned}\text{Fixed overhead volume variance} &= (\text{Denominator activity} - \text{Standard hours allowed}) \\ &\quad \times \text{Standard fixed overhead rate} \\ &= (1{,}300 \text{ hours} - 1{,}250 \text{ hours}) \times \$5 = 50 \text{ hours} \times \$5 = \$250 \text{ U}\end{aligned}$$

7.5 METHODS OF VARIANCE ANALYSIS FOR FACTORY OVERHEAD

Variance analysis for factory overhead consists of a two-, three-, or four-way method of computation, depending on the significance of the variance amounts compared to the cost of analysis. These methods are indicated in Figs 7-6 and 7-7.

The two-way analysis computes two variances: budget variance (sometimes called flexible budget or controllable variance) and volume variance, which means:

$$\begin{aligned}\text{Budget variance} &= \text{Variable spending variance} + \text{Fixed spending (budget) variance} \\ &\quad + \text{Variable efficiency variance} \\ \text{Volume variance} &= \text{Fixed volume variance}\end{aligned}$$

The three-way analysis computes three variances: spending, efficiency, and volume variances. Therefore,

$$\begin{aligned}\text{Spending variance} &= \text{Variable spending variance} + \text{Fixed spending (budget) variance} \\ \text{Efficiency variance} &= \text{Variable efficiency variance} \\ \text{Volume variance} &= \text{Fixed volume variance}\end{aligned}$$

Variance Analysis for Variable Overhead and Fixed Overhead

Incurred: Actual Hours × Actual Rate (1,350 hours) (1)	Flexible Budget Based on Actual Hours (1,350 hours) (2)	Flexible Budget Based on Standard Hours Allowed (1,250 hours) (3)	Applied (1,250 hours) (4)
V $2,853	$2,700 (1,350 × $2)	$2,500 (1,250 × $2)	$2,500
F 6,725	6,500	6,500	6,250
$9,578	$9,200	$9,000	$8,750

(Three-Way)	Spending Variance (1) − (2) V $153 (U) F 225 (U) $378 (U)	Efficiency Variance (Not Applicable) $200 (U) Not Applicable $200 (U)	Volume Variance (3) − (4) Not Applicable $250 (U) $250 (U)
(Two-Way)	Flexible Budget Variance (1) − (3) V $353 (U) F 225 (U) $578 (U)		Volume Variance (3) − (4) Not Applicable $250 (U) $250 (U)
	Under- or Overapplied (1) − (4) V $353 (U) F 475 (U) $828 (U)		

Fig. 7-7

The four-way analysis includes:

(*a*) Variable spending variance
(*b*) Fixed spending (budget) variance
(*c*) Variable efficiency variance
(*d*) Fixed volume variance

7.6 FLEXIBLE BUDGETS AND PERFORMANCE REPORTS

A flexible budget is a tool that is extremely useful in cost control. In contrast to the budget discussed in Chapter 6, the flexible budget is characterized as follows.

1. It is geared toward a range of activity rather than a single level of activity.
2. It is dynamic in nature rather than static. By using the cost–volume formula, a series of budgets can be easily developed for various levels of activity.

The primary use of the flexible budget is for accurate measure of performance by comparing actual costs for a given output with the budgeted costs for *the same level of output*. The key to formulating the flexible budget is the development of a *cost–volume formula* (also called the *flexible budget formula*), which was discussed in Chapter 3.

EXAMPLE 7.5 To illustrate the difference between the static budget and the flexible budget, assume that the fabricating department of Company XYZ is budgeted to produce 6,000 units during June. The budget for direct labor and variable overhead costs (or conversion costs) is set as shown below:

COMPANY XYZ
Direct Labor and Variable Overhead Budget
Fabricating Department
For the Month of June

Budgeted production	6,000 units	
Actual production:	5,800 units	
Direct labor		$39,000
Variable overhead costs:		
Indirect labor		6,000
Supplies		900
Repairs		300
		$46,200

Assume further that the company was able to produce only 5,800 units. If a static budget approach is used, the performance report will appear as follows.

COMPANY XYZ
Performance Report
Based on Static Budget
Fabricating Department
For the Month of June

	Budget	Actual	Variance (U) or (F)*
Production in units	6,000	5,800	200 (U)
Direct labor	$39,000	$38,500	$500 (F)
Variable overhead costs:			
Indirect labor	6,000	5,950	50 (F)
Supplies	900	870	30 (F)
Repairs	300	295	5 (F)
Total conversion costs	$46,200	$45,615	$585 (F)

*A variance represents the deviation of actual cost from the standard or budgeted cost.

Apparently, these cost variances are useless, since they have been derived by comparing the actual costs incurred at a 5,800-unit level of activity to the budgeted costs at a different level of activity (6,000-unit level of activity). From a control standpoint, it makes no sense to compare costs at one activity level to costs at a different activity level. It is like comparing oranges to apples, instead of comparing oranges that grow in Florida to oranges that grow in California.

Using the cost–volume formula and redeveloping the budget based on the 5,800 actual units of output gives the following performance report.

COMPANY XYZ
Performance Report
Fabricating Department
For the Month of June

Budgeted production 6,000 units
Actual production 5,800 units

	Cost–Volume Formula	Budget 5,800 Units	Actual 5,800 Units	Variance (U) or (F)
Direct labor	$6.50 per unit	$37,700	$38,500	$800 (U)
Variable overhead costs:				
Indirect labor	1.00	5,800	5,950	150 (U)
Supplies	0.15	870	870	0
Repairs	0.05	290	295	5 (U)
	$7.70	$44,660	$45,615	$955 (U)

Notice that all cost variances are unfavorable, as compared to the favorable cost variances on the performance report based on the static budget approach.

7.7 SEGMENTAL REPORTING AND THE CONTRIBUTION APPROACH TO COST ALLOCATION

Cost allocation is an important issue in managerial accounting for segmental reporting purposes. Segmental reporting is the process of reporting activities of various segments of an organization such as divisions, product lines, or sales territories. The contribution approach is valuable for segmental reporting because it emphasizes the cost behavior patterns and the controllability of costs that are generally useful for evaluating performance and making decisions. To be specific, the contribution approach to cost allocation is based on the theses that:

1. Fixed costs are much less controllable than variable.
2. *Direct* fixed costs and *common* fixed costs must be clearly distinguished. Direct fixed costs are those fixed costs which can be identified directly with a particular segment of an organization, whereas common fixed costs are those costs which cannot be identified directly with a particular segment.
3. Common fixed costs should be clearly identified as *unallocated* in the contribution income statement by segments. Any attempt to allocate these types of costs, on some arbitrary basis, to the segments of the organization would simply destroy the value of responsibility accounting. It would lead to unfair evaluation of performance and misleading managerial decisions.

EXAMPLE 7.6 The Putnam Company allocates national magazine advertising cost to territories on the basis of circulation, which is determined by an index that measures relative buying power in the territories. Top management wants to know if this method of allocation gives appropriate cost and benefit figures to make the following decisions:

(*a*) For deciding whether or not to close an unprofitable territory
(*b*) For deciding whether or not a territorial manager has obtained sufficient sales volume
(*c*) For determining how efficiently the territorial manager has operated the territory
(*d*) For determining whether or not advertising costs are satisfactorily controlled

(SMA, adapted)

The answers are as follows.

(*a*) It is not appropriate for deciding to close the territory. Closing the territory will not change the amount of national advertising expenses. For deciding what action to take with respect to the territory, the segment margin (sales less variable expenses less direct territorial fixed expenses) should be compared with the amount of cost that can be saved by closing that territory. This will show whether or not the territory is making a contribution to costs that will continue regardless of the decision.

(*b*) It may be appropriate for concluding that a territorial manager has obtained sufficient sales volume. National advertising is one of the general distribution costs to be allocated to territories if there is evidence of cause-and-effect relationships.

(*c*) The method is not appropriate. A territorial manager should be judged on the basis of expenses that he or she has to control. By its nature, national advertising must be centrally controlled.

(*d*) It is not appropriate to allocate national advertising costs to territories from a control standpoint. Control can be exercised only over the total expenditure for national advertising and at the source; control is not aided by allocating this total to territories.

The following concepts are highlighted in the contribution approach to cost allocation:

– *Contribution margin*—Sales less variable costs.

– *Contribution controllable by segment managers*—Contribution margin less direct fixed costs controllable by segment managers. Direct fixed costs include discretionary fixed costs such as certain advertising, research and development, sales promotion, and engineering.

– *Segment margin*—Contribution controllable by segment managers less fixed costs controllable by others. Fixed costs controllable by others include such traceable and committed fixed costs as depreciation, property taxes, insurance, and the segment managers' salaries.

– *Net income*—Segment margin less unallocated common fixed costs.

EXAMPLE 7.7 Figure 7-8 illustrates two levels of segmental income statements:

1. By segments defined as divisions
2. By segments defined as product lines of a division

The segment margin is viewed as being the best measure of the profitability of a segment. Unallocated fixed costs are common to the segments being evaluated and should be left unallocated in order not to distort performance results.

Summary

(1) ____________ is also called profitability accounting and activity accounting.

(2) There are three types of responsibility centers. They are cost centers, ____________, and ____________.

(3) ____________ based on ____________ is a typical measure of the performance of a cost center.

(4) The contribution approach to ____________ (or performance evaluation) is widely used for profitability analysis of various segments of an organization.

(5) Managerial performance should be evaluated only on the basis of those factors ____________ by the segment manager.

Segments Defined as Divisions

	Total Company	SEGMENTS Division 1	Division 2
Sales	$150,000	$90,000	$60,000
Variable Costs:			
Manufacturing	$ 40,000	$30,000	$10,000
Selling and Administrative	20,000	14,000	6,000
Total Variable Costs	$ 60,000	$44,000	$16,000
Contribution Margin	$ 90,000	$46,000	$44,000
Less: Direct Fixed Costs Controllable by Division Managers	55,000	33,000	22,000
Contribution Controllable by Division Managers	$ 35,000	$13,000	$22,000
Less: Fixed Costs Controllable by Others	15,000	10,000	5,000
Divisional Segment Margin	$ 20,000	$ 3,000	$17,000
Less: Unallocated Common Fixed Costs	10,000		
Net Income	$ 10,000		

Segments Defined as Product Lines of Division 2

	Division 2	SEGMENTS Deluxe Model	Regular Model
Sales	$60,000	$20,000	$40,000
Variable Costs:			
Manufacturing	$10,000	$ 5,000	$ 5,000
Selling and Administrative	6,000	2,000	4,000
Total Variable Costs	$16,000	$ 7,000	$ 9,000
Contribution Margin	$44,000	$13,000	$31,000
Less: Direct Fixed Costs Controllable by Product Line Managers	22,000	8,000	14,000
Contribution Controllable by Product Line Managers	$22,000	$ 5,000	$17,000
Less: Fixed Costs Controllable by Others	4,500	1,500	3,000
Product Line Segment Margin	$17,500	$ 3,500	$14,000
Less: Unallocated Common Fixed Costs	500		
Divisional Segment Margin	$17,000		

Fig. 7-8

(6) A flexible budget is geared toward __________ rather than a single level of activity.

(7) The key ingredient in flexible budgeting is __________.

(8) __________ is a system for reporting __________ and __________ information to the individual responsible for the revenue-causing and/or cost-incurring function.

(9) ____________ is most useful as a tool for measuring segment profitability.

(10) Costs that are shared jointly by several segments and therefore are not allocated to them are called joint or ____________ costs.

(11) The terms *contribution margin* and *segment margin* are synonymous: (*a*) true; (*b*) false.

(12) Discretionary fixed costs controllable by segment managers include rent and depreciation: (*a*) true; (*b*) false.

(13) Responsibility performance reports should include variances of actual amounts from the standard or budget: (*a*) true; (*b*) false.

(14) ____________ are those costs that are directly influenced by a manager within a given time span.

(15) A variance is said to be ____________ if the actual price or actual quantity exceeds the standard price or standard quantity.

(16) A ____________ variance and a ____________ variance are computed for all three ____________.

Answers: (1) responsibility accounting; (2) profit centers, investment centers; (3) variance analysis, flexible budgets; (4) cost allocation; (5) controllable; (6) a range of activity; (7) a cost–volume formula (or flexible budget formula); (8) responsibility accounting, revenue, cost; (9) segment margin; (10) common; (11) (*b*); (12) (*b*); (13) (*a*); (14) controllable costs; (15) unfavorable; (16) price, quantity, variable manufacturing cost items.

Solved Problems

7.1 What is the relationship between responsibility and authority?

SOLUTION

There should be a direct relationship between responsibility and authority. If an individual is answerable for his or her actions (responsible), that individual must have the authority to carry out actions and execute decisions. There is an undermining of a person's performance and incentive when authority is not given while the person is still held accountable.

7.2 Why is it necessary to have a clearly defined organizational structure before responsibility accounting can be effective?

SOLUTION

There must be a clear chain of command. Individuals must know to whom they are responsible and for what tasks or jobs they are responsible. Ideally, each individual in the organization should have only one boss. If an individual has more than one boss, the tasks for which the individual is responsible to each boss should be defined.

7.3 The standard cost sheet for Largo Corp. showed the following material cost related to one unit of product:

4 pieces at \$4 per piece = \$16 per unit

During February 19X1, 10,000 units were produced. The costs recorded showed the following:

Purchase of material	48,000 pieces at \$3.80
Issue of material	43,000 pieces

Determine the material purchase price variance and material quantity (usage) variance.

SOLUTION

See Fig. 7-9.

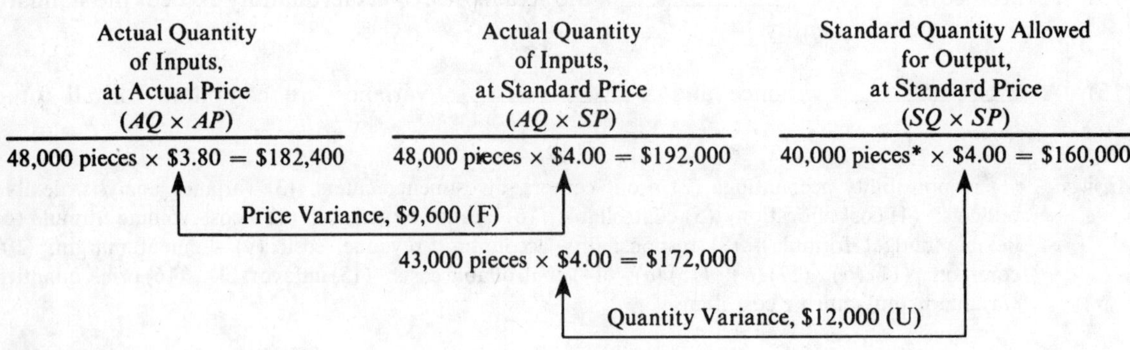

*10,000 units of output × 4 pieces = 40,000 pieces.

Fig. 7-9

Alternatively:

$$\text{Materials purchase price variance} = AQ(AP - SP) = (48{,}000 \text{ pieces})(\$3.80 - \$4.00) = \$9{,}600 \text{ (F)}$$

$$\text{Materials quantity (usage) variance} = (AQ - SQ)SP = (43{,}000 \text{ pieces} - 40{,}000 \text{ pieces})(\$4.00) = \$12{,}000 \text{ (U)}$$

7.4 Give the significance and possible explanation of each materials variance in Problem 7.3.

SOLUTION

Materials purchase price variance (Favorable). This variance shows the influence on cost of a reduction in prices. It may be explained by a purchase of standard-grade material at less-than-standard prices, or it may be explained by a purchase of a lower-grade material in order to economize on price.

Materials quantity (usage) variance (Unfavorable). This variance shows an increase in cost due to an increase in quantities used. It may be explained by poorly trained workers, by improperly adjusted machines, or by outright waste on the production line. In view of the favorable price variance, it is possible that the quality of the material was inferior, resulting in breakage in production.

7.5 What are some causes of unfavorable materials purchase price variances?

SOLUTION

Unfavorable materials price variances may be caused by: inaccurate standard prices, inflationary cost increases, scarcity in raw material supplies resulting in higher prices, and purchasing department inefficiencies.

7.6 The purchasing department of a large corporation using the responsibility accounting system delays placing an assembly department order for 10,000 parts at $2.00 each. By the time the order is placed, the price has risen to $2.20. Which department should be assigned the additional charges incurred? Why?

SOLUTION

The purchasing department should absorb the additional costs; it did not place the order when originally received. This will focus attention on cost efficiency as a function of time.

7.7 The standard cost sheet for York Corp. shows the following cost for a unit of product:

Direct labor: $2\frac{3}{4}$ hours at $7 an hour

During February 19X1, 10,000 units were completed. The actual cost incurred was:

28,000 hours at $8 per hour = $224,000

Determine the labor rate variance and labor efficiency variance.

SOLUTION

See Fig. 7-10.

Labor Variances

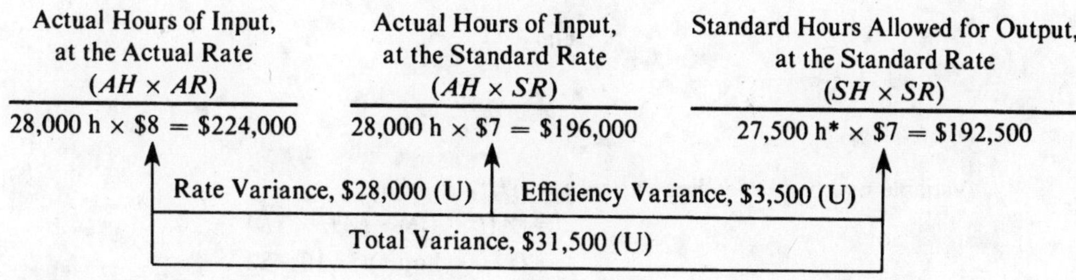

*10,000 units × 2.75 hours (h) = 27,500 hours.

Fig. 7-10

Alternatively:

$$\text{Labor rate variance} = AH(AR - SR)$$
$$= (28{,}000 \text{ hours})(\$8 - \$7)$$
$$= \$28{,}000 \text{ (U)}$$
$$\text{Labor efficiency variance} = (AH - SH)SR$$
$$= (28{,}000 \text{ hours} - 27{,}500 \text{ hours})(\$7) = \$3{,}500 \text{ (U)}$$

7.8 Give the significance and possible explanation of each labor variance in Problem 7.7.

SOLUTION

Labor rate variance (Unfavorable). This variance shows the effect on cost of an increase in the hourly rate, as compared to the standard rate. It may be explained by an increase in wages, poor scheduling of production resulting in overtime work, or the use of persons commanding higher hourly rates than contemplated in the standards.

Labor efficiency variance (Unfavorable). This variance shows the effect on cost of an increase in the number of hours worked, as compared to the standard time required to produce 10,000 units. It may be explained by poor supervision, poor quality of workers, improperly trained workers, poor quality of materials requiring more labor time in processing, or machine breakdowns.

7.9 Direct labor and variable overhead standards per finished unit for Century-Fox Metals Company are as follows: variable overhead, 10 hours at $2.00 per hour. During October, 5,000 units were produced. Direct labor hours used were 52,000 hours. Actual variable overhead costs were $109,200. Determine the spending variance and efficiency variance for variable overhead.

SOLUTION

See Fig. 7-11.

Variable Overhead Variances

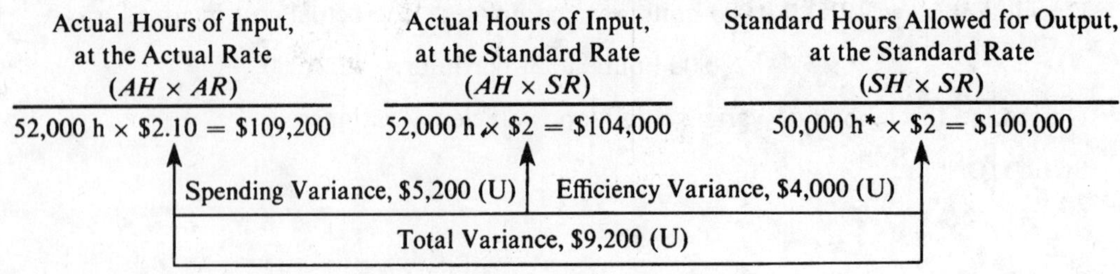

*5,000 units actually produced × 10 hours (h) allowed = 50,000 hours.

Fig. 7-11

Alternatively:

$$\text{Variable overhead spending variance} = AH(AR - SR)$$
$$= (AH \times AR) - (AH \times SR)$$
$$= (52{,}000 \text{ hours})(\$2.10 - \$2)$$
$$= \$109{,}200 - \$104{,}000 = \$5{,}200 \text{ (U)}$$

$$\text{Variable overhead efficiency variance} = (AH - SH)\,SR$$
$$= (52{,}000 \text{ hours} - 50{,}000 \text{ hours})(\$2) = \$4{,}000 \text{ (U)}$$

7.10 Give the significance and possible explanation of each variable overhead variance in Problem 7.9.

SOLUTION

Variable overhead spending variance (Unfavorable). This variance might be caused by a large number of factors: acquiring supplies for a price different from the standard, using more supplies than expected for the actual level of activity during the period, paying indirect laborers at a different rate than the standard rate, using more indirect labor than expected, waste, and theft of supplies.

Variable overhead efficiency variance (Unfavorable). This variance might be caused by such factors as: poorly trained workers, poor-quality materials, faulty equipment, work interruptions, poor production scheduling, poor supervision, employee unrest, etc.

7.11 E. T. Toys, Inc., produces toys for national distribution. The management has recently established a standard cost system to control costs. The standards on a particular toy are:

Materials:	12 pieces per toy at $0.56 per piece
Labor:	2 hours per toy at $3.75 per hour

During the month of February 19A, the company produced 1,000 toys. Production data for the month are as follows:

- Materials: 17,500 pieces were purchased for use in production, at a total cost of $8,925, of which 3,500 pieces were still in inventory at the end of the month.
- Labor: 2,500 hours were worked, at a cost of $10,500.

(*a*) Calculate the materials purchase price variance.
(*b*) Calculate the materials quantity (usage) variance.
(*c*) Calculate the labor rate variance.
(*d*) Calculate the labor efficiency variance.

(SMA, adapted)

SOLUTION

(*a*) and (*b*) See Fig. 7-12.

Materials Variances

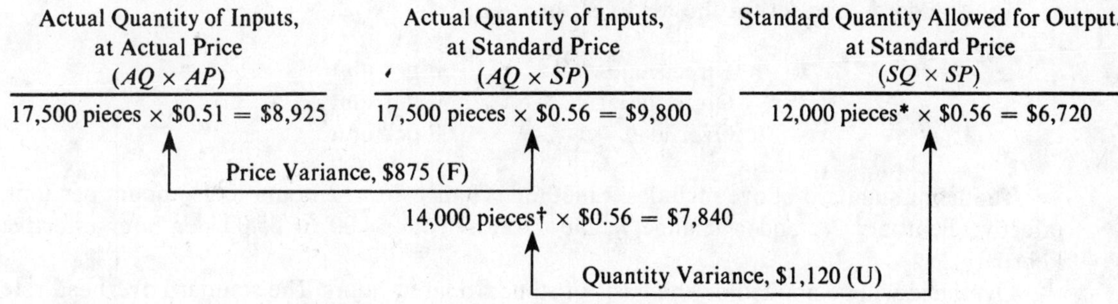

*1,000 toys × 12 pieces = 12,000 pieces.
†17,500 pieces − 3,500 pieces in inventory = 14,000 pieces used.

Fig. 7-12

Alternatively:

$$\text{Materials purchase price variance} = (17{,}500 \text{ pieces})(\$0.51 - \$0.56)$$
$$= \$8{,}925 - \$9{,}800$$
$$= \$875 \text{ (F)}$$
$$\text{Materials quantity (usage) variance} = (14{,}000 \text{ pieces} - 12{,}000 \text{ pieces})\ (\$0.56)$$
$$= \$1{,}120 \text{ (U)}$$

(*c*) and (*d*) See Fig. 7-13.

Labor Variances

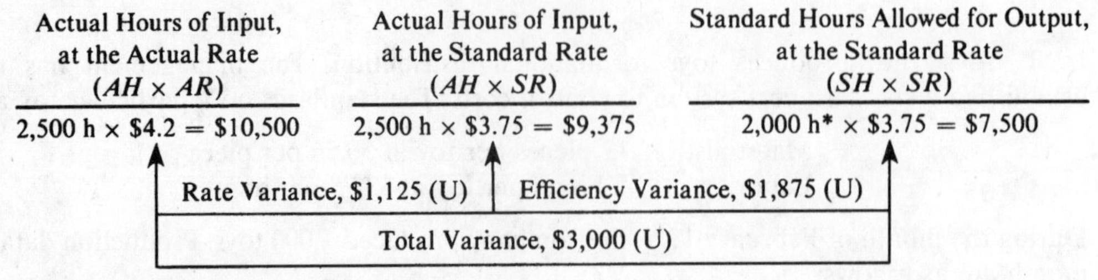

*1,000 toys × 2 hours (h) = 2,000 hours.

Fig. 7-13

Alternatively:

$$\text{Labor rate variance} = (2{,}500 \text{ hours})(\$4.2 - \$3.75)$$
$$= \$10{,}500 - \$9{,}375$$
$$= \$1{,}125 \text{ (U)}$$

$$\text{Labor efficiency variance} = (2{,}500 \text{ hours} - 2{,}000 \text{ hours})(\$3.75)$$
$$= \$1{,}875 \text{ (U)}$$

7.12 The Schock Manufacturing Company uses a standard cost system. The standards are set before January 1 each year and remain unchanged until December 31.

The standard costs set for the next year are:

Direct materials	$10.00 per unit
Direct labor	7.50 per unit
Overhead	6.00 per unit

The labor standard above includes a methods change from 2 hours to 1½ hours per unit, effective February 28, and a change in labor rates from $4.00 to $5.00 per hour effective February 28.

Overhead will be applied on the basis of standard labor hours. The standard overhead rate per hour is $4.00 (1½ hours × $4.00 = $6.00 per unit). The variable portion is $2.00 per hour. The original budgeted production volume for January was 5,000 units. The actual cost data for January are:

Units produced	6,000 units
Direct materials used	$62,000
Direct labor	11,000 hours costing $46,000
Actual overhead incurred:	
Variable	$23,000
Fixed	$14,000

1. Compute the variances for direct labor and variable overhead.
2. State the possible causes of each variance which you have computed.

SOLUTION

1. For the direct labor variances, see Fig. 7-14.

Labor Variances

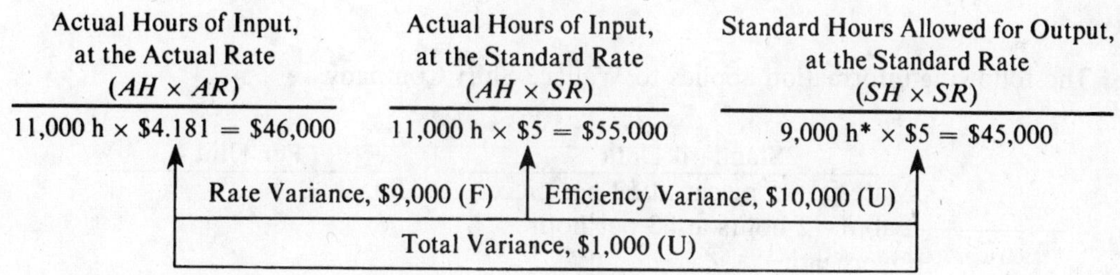

*6,000 units × 1½ hours (h) = 9,000 hours.

Fig. 7-14

Alternatively:

$$\text{Labor rate variance} = (11{,}000 \text{ hours})(\$4.181 - \$5) = \$9{,}000 \text{ (F)}$$
$$\text{Labor efficiency variance} = (11{,}000 \text{ hours} - 9{,}000 \text{ hours})(\$5) = \$10{,}000 \text{ (U)}$$

For the variable overhead variances, see Fig. 7-15.

Variable Overhead Variances

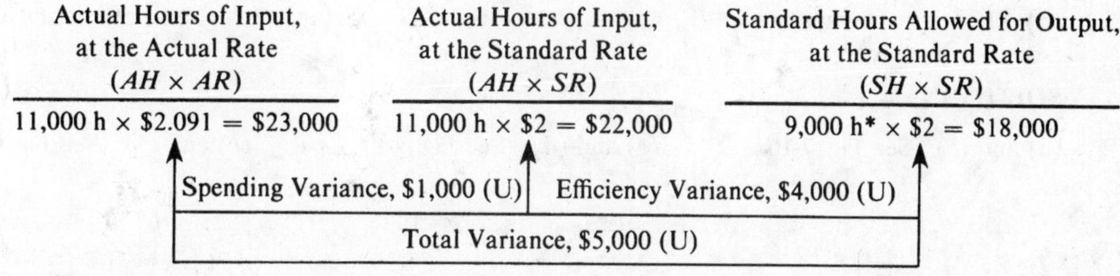

*6,000 units × 1½ hours (h) = 9,000 hours.

Fig. 7-15

Alternatively:

$$\text{Variable overhead spending variance} = (11{,}000 \text{ hours})(\$2.091 - \$2) = \$1{,}000 \text{ (U)}$$
$$\text{Variable overhead efficiency variance} = (11{,}000 \text{ hours} - 9{,}000 \text{ hours})(\$2) = \$4{,}000 \text{ (U)}$$

2. For labor:

   – *Favorable rate variance* may arise from: using unskilled workers paid lower rates, piecework, and inaccurate standards.

   – *Unfavorable efficiency variance* may arise from: production delays, using poor-quality machinery, employee unrest, power failure due to an energy shortage, poor production scheduling, using the wrong mixture of labor for a given job, and using poor-quality materials.

For variable overhead:

- *Unfavorable spending variance* may arise from: increase in supplier prices, inaccurate standards, waste, theft of supplies, etc.
- *Unfavorable efficiency variance* may arise from the same factors as unfavorable labor efficiency variance.

7.13 The following information applies to Wallace Shirt Company.

Standard Data	Per Unit
Material—3 pieces at $2 per piece	$6
Labor—2 hours at $3 per hour	6
Overhead:	
Fixed—2 hours at $2.50 per hour	5 ($50,000/10,000 units)
Variable—2 hours at $4 per hour	8 ($80,000/10,000 units)

Actual Data

Material—25,000 pieces of material were purchased at $2.10 per piece. Twenty-four thousand pieces of material were used.
Labor—17,000 hours at $2.50 per hour.
Overhead—Variable, $69,000; fixed, $43,000.
Actual units produced—9,000.

Compute the following:

(*a*) Materials purchase price variance
(*b*) Materials quantity (usage) variance
(*c*) Labor rate variance
(*d*) Labor efficiency variance
(*e*) Variable overhead spending variance
(*f*) Variable overhead efficiency variance

SOLUTION

(*a*) and (*b*) See Fig. 7-16. (*c*) and (*d*) See Fig. 7-17. (*e*) and (*f*) See Fig. 7-18.

Materials Variances

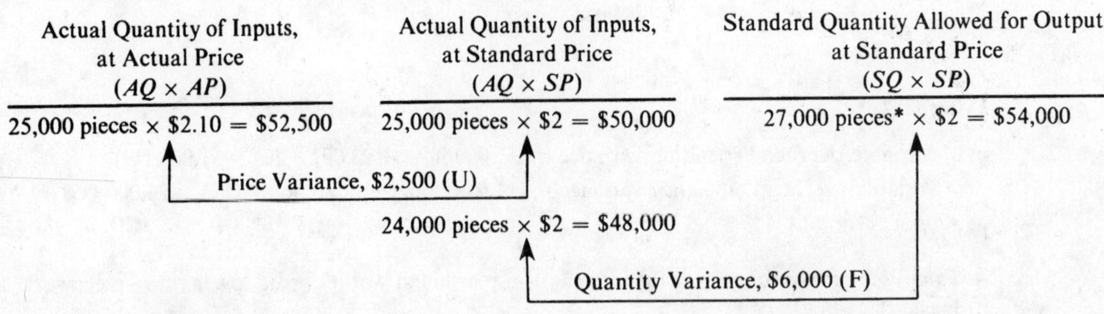

*9,000 units × 3 pieces = 27,000 pieces.

Fig. 7-16

Labor Variances

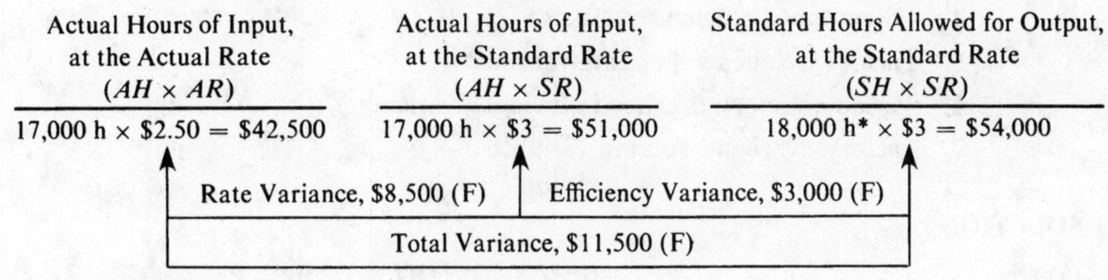

*9,000 units actually produced × 2 hours (h) = 18,000 hours.

Fig. 7-17

Variable Overhead Variances

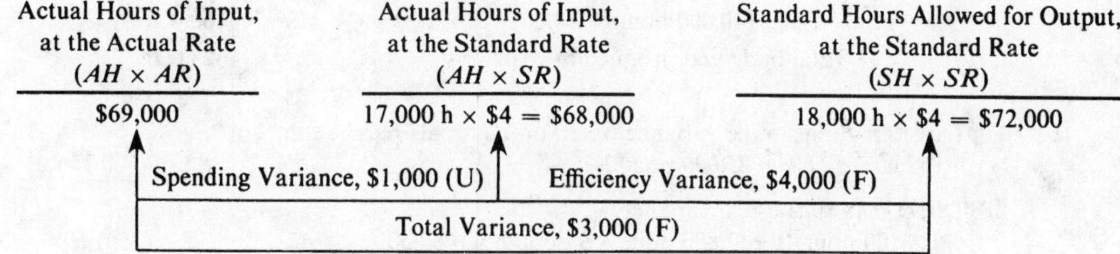

Fig. 7-18

7.14 At the beginning of 19X4, Beal Company adopted the following standards:

Direct material (3 pounds @ \$2.50 per pound)	\$ 7.50
Direct labor (5 hours @ \$7.50 per hour)	37.50
Factory overhead:	
Variable (\$3.00 per direct labor hour)	15.00
Fixed (\$4.00 per direct labor hour)	20.00
Standard cost per unit	\$80.00

Normal volume per month is 40,000 direct labor hours. Beal's January 19X4 budget was based on normal volume. During January, Beal produced 7,800 units, with records indicating the following:

Direct material purchased	25,000 pounds @ \$2.60
Direct material used	23,100 pounds
Direct labor	40,100 hours @ \$7.30
Factory overhead	\$300,000

(*a*) Prepare a flexible budget for January 19X4 production costs, based on actual production of 7,800 units.

(*b*) For the month of January 19X4, compute the following variances, indicating whether each is favorable or unfavorable:

1. Direct materials price variance, based on purchases
2. Direct materials usage variance

3. Direct labor rate variance
4. Direct labor efficiency variance
5. Factory overhead spending variance
6. Variable factory overhead efficiency variance
7. Factory overhead volume variance

(CPA, adapted)

SOLUTION

(*a*)

BEAL COMPANY
Flexible Budget
For the Month Ended January 31, 19X4

Direct materials (7,800 units × 3 pounds × $2.50)	$ 58,500
Direct labor (7,800 units × 5 hours × $7.50)	292,500
Factory overhead:	
Variable (7,800 units × 5 hours × $3.00)	117,000
Fixed (40,000 hours × $4.00)	160,000
Total budgeted production costs	$628,000

(*b*)

1. Direct materials price variance based on materials purchased:	
($2.60 − $2.50) × 25,000 pounds	$ 2,500 U
2. Direct materials usage variance:	
[23,100 pounds − (7,800 units × 3 pounds)] × $2.50	$ (750) F
3. Direct labor rate variance:	
($7.30 − $7.50) × 40,100 hours	$ (8,020) F
4. Direct labor efficiency variance:	
[40,100 hours − (7,800 units × 5 hours)] × $7.50	$ 8,250 U
5. Factory overhead spending variance:	
Actual total factory overhead	$300,000
Budgeted total factory overhead at actual hours:	
(40,100 × $3.00) + (40,000 × $4.00)	−$280,300
Factory overhead spending variance	$ 19,700 U
6. Variable factory overhead efficiency variance:	
Budgeted total factory overhead at actual hours	$280,300
Budgeted total factory overhead at standard hours:	
$117,000 + $160,000	−$277,000
Variable factory overhead efficiency variance	$ 3,300 U
7. Factory overhead volume variance:	
Budgeted total factory overhead at standard hours	$277,000
Applied total factory overhead:	
7,800 × 5 hours × ($3.00 + $4.00)	−$273,000
Factory overhead volume variance	$ 4,000 U

7.15 Eastern Company manufactures special electrical equipment and parts. Eastern uses standard costs, with separate standards established for each product. A special transformer is manufactured in the Transformer Department. Production volume is measured by direct labor hours in this department, and a flexible budget system is used to plan and control department overhead. Standard costs for the special transformer are determined annually in September for the coming year. The standard cost of a transformer for 19X7 was $67.00:

Direct materials:		
Iron	5 sheets @ \$2.00 =	\$10.00
Copper	3 spools @ \$3.00 =	9.00
Direct labor	4 hours @ \$7.00 =	28.00
Variable overhead	4 hours @ \$3.00 =	12.00
Fixed overhead	4 hours @ \$2.00 =	8.00
Total		\$67.00

Overhead rates were based on normal and expected monthly labor hours for 19X7, both of which were 4,000 direct labor hours. Practical capacity for this department is 5,000 direct labor hours per month. Variable overhead costs are expected to vary with the number of direct labor hours actually used.

During October 19X7, 800 transformers were produced. This was below expectations because a work stoppage occurred during contract negotiations with the labor force. Once the contract was settled, the department scheduled overtime in an attempt to catch up to expected production levels. Actual costs incurred in October 19X7 were as follows:

	Purchased	Used
Direct materials:		
Iron	5,000 sheets @ \$2.00 per sheet	3,900 sheets
Copper	2,200 spools @ \$3.10	2,600 spools
Direct labor:		
Regular time	2,000 hours @ \$7.00	
	1,400 hours @ \$7.20	
Overtime	600 of the 1,400 hours were subject to overtime premium. The total overtime premium of \$2,160 is included in variable overhead in accordance with corporate accounting practices.	
Variable overhead	\$10,000	
Fixed overhead	\$ 8,800	

Prepare a complete analysis of all production variances. Use a four-way analysis for overhead. Materials price variances are isolated at the time of purchase.

(CMA, adapted)

SOLUTION

Materials:	
Materials price variance: Iron = 5,000(\$2 − \$2)	\$ 0
Materials price variance: Copper = 2,200(\$3.10 − \$3)	\$ 220 U
Total	\$ 220 U
Materials quantity variance: Iron = \$2[3,900 − (800 × 5)]	\$ 200 F
Materials quantity variance: Copper = \$3[2,600 − (800 × 3)]	\$ 600 U
Total	\$ 400 U
Total materials variance: \$220 U + \$400 U	\$ 620 U
Labor:	
Labor rate variance: [(2,000 × \$7) + (1,400 × \$7.20) − (3,400 × \$7)]	\$ 280 U
Labor efficiency variance: [(3,400 × \$7) − (800 × 4 × \$7)]	\$1,400 U
Total labor variance: \$280 U + \$1,400 U	\$1,680 U
Variable overhead:	
Variable overhead spending variance: [\$10,000 − (3,400 × \$3)]	\$ 200 F
Variable overhead efficiency variance: [(3,400 × \$3) − (800 × 4 × \$3)]	\$ 600 U
Total variable overhead variance: \$200 F + \$600 U	\$ 400 U
Fixed overhead:	
Fixed overhead budget variance: [\$8,800 − (4,000 × \$2)]	\$ 800 U
Fixed overhead volume variance: \$2[4,000 − (800 × 4)]	\$1,600 U
Total fixed overhead variance: \$800 U + \$1,600 U	\$2,400 U

7.16 The following shows factory overhead budget information for Los Alamitos, Inc., for the year:

Indirect materials used	$0.50 per machine hour plus $6,000 fixed cost
Indirect labor	$92,000 fixed cost
Power	$0.95 per machine hour
Repairs and maintenance	$1.50 per machine hour plus $2,100 fixed cost
Depreciation	$9,500 fixed cost
Rent	$12,000 fixed cost

In 19A, the company operated at 11,000 machine hours and incurred the following overhead costs:

Indirect materials used	$11,700
Indirect labor	91,000
Power	10,650
Repairs and maintenance	19,200
Depreciation	9,500
Rent	12,500

Compare the flexible budget with the actual overhead, computing a variance for each item and for the total overhead. Indicate whether variances are favorable (F) or unfavorable (U).

SOLUTION

	Budget (11,000 hours)	Actual (11,000 hours)	Variance (U) or (F)
Indirect materials used	$ 11,500	$ 11,700	$ 200 (U)
Indirect labor	92,000	91,000	1,000 (F)
Power	10,450	10,650	200 (U)
Repairs and maintenance	18,600	19,200	600 (U)
Depreciation	9,500	9,500	—
Rent	12,000	12,500	500 (U)
Total	$154,050	$154,550	$ 500 (U)

7.17 Ina Machine Company's flexible budget is given below:

INA MACHINE COMPANY
Flexible Budget

Conversion Costs	Cost–Volume Formula	Number of Units 5,000	6,000	7,000
Direct labor	$7.00	$35,000	$42,000	$49,000
Variable overhead costs:				
Supplies	0.90	4,500	5,400	6,300
Utilities	0.15	750	900	1,050
Maintenance	1.25	6,250	7,500	8,750
Total	$9.30	$46,500	$55,800	$65,100

The production budgeted for September was 6,000 units. During the month, the company produced 6,200 units. The conversion costs incurred were:

Direct labor	$44,300
Supplies	6,120
Utilities	965
Maintenance	7,920

Prepare a performance report for September. Indicate whether variances are favorable (F) or unfavorable (U).

SOLUTION

INA MACHINE COMPANY
Flexible Budget

Budgeted production 6,000 units
Actual production 6,200 units

Conversion Costs	Cost–Volume Formula	Budget Based on 6,200 Units	Actual Costs 6,200 Units	Variance (F) or (U)
Direct labor	$7.00	$43,400	$44,300	$ 900 (U)
Variable overhead costs:				
Supplies	0.90	5,580	6,120	540 (U)
Utilities	0.15	930	965	35 (U)
Maintenance	1.25	7,750	7,920	170 (U)
Total	$9.30	$57,660	$59,305	$1,645 (U)

7.18 Charles Corporation has three divisions—marketing, production, and personnel. There is a manager in charge of each division. The flexible budgets for each division follow.

	Marketing Manager	Production Manager	Personnel Manager
Controllable costs:			
Direct material		$10,000	
Direct labor		25,000	
Salaries	$40,000		$35,000
Supplies	10,000	3,000	2,000
Maintenance	1,000	2,000	1,000
Total	$51,000	$40,000	$38,000

Actual costs by division were:

Controllable costs:			
Direct material		$12,000	
Direct labor		24,000	
Salaries	$51,000		$34,000
Supplies	800	2,000	1,500
Maintenance	200	1,500	500
Total	$52,000	$39,500	$36,000

1. Prepare and evaluate a performance report for the production manager.
2. Prepare and evaluate a performance report for the vice president. Other costs for the vice president are assumed to be: budgeted $35,000 and actual $34,400.

SOLUTION

1. ***Performance Report for Production Manager***

	Flexible Budget Cost	Actual Cost	Variance (U) or (F)
Controllable costs:			
Direct material	$10,000	$12,000	$2,000 (U)
Direct labor	25,000	24,000	1,000 (F)
Supplies	3,000	2,000	1,000 (F)
Maintenance	2,000	1,500	500 (F)
Total	$40,000	$39,500	$ 500 (F)

The cost of raw materials rose significantly, possibly because of deficient machinery due to the cutback in maintenance expenditures and/or to the lower labor cost, possibly because of the use of less skilled workers. Supplies decreased, indicating possible inadequacies for next period's production run.

2. ***Performance Report for Vice President***

Controllable costs:			
Marketing division	$ 51,000	$ 52,000	$1,000 (U)
Production division	40,000	39,500	500 (F)
Personnel division	38,000	36,000	2,000 (F)
Other costs	35,000	34,400	600 (F)
Total	$164,000	$161,900	$2,100 (F)

The marketing division is behind its cost allotment. The personnel division came in somewhat under its budgeted costs. Perhaps there has been a cutback in hiring, indicating a possible reduction in future production.

7.19 The University of Boyne offers an extensive continuing education program in many cities throughout the state. For the convenience of its faculty and administrative staff and also to save costs, the university operates a motor pool. Until February the motor pool operated with 20 vehicles. However, an additional automobile was acquired in February this year, increasing the total to 21 vehicles. The motor pool furnishes gasoline, oil, and other supplies for the cars, and hires one mechanic who does routine maintenance and minor repairs. Major repairs are done at a nearby commercial garage.

Each year a supervisor prepares an operating budget for the motor pool. The budget informs university management of the funds needed to operate the pool. Depreciation on the automobiles is recorded in the budget in order to determine the costs per mile.

The schedule below presents the annual budget approved by the university. The actual costs for March are compared to one-twelfth of the annual budget.

UNIVERSITY MOTOR POOL
Budget Report
For March 19A

	Annual Budget	One-Month Budget	March Actual	Variance (U) or (F)
Gasoline	$ 59,280	$ 4,940	$ 5,740	$800 (U)
Oil, minor repairs, parts, and supplies	3,600	300	380	80 (U)
Outside repairs	2,700	225	50	175 (F)
Insurance	6,000	500	525	25 (U)
Salaries and benefits	30,000	2,500	2,500	—
Depreciation	26,400	2,200	2,310	110 (U)
	$127,980	$10,665	$11,505	$840 (U)
Total miles	600,000	50,000	63,000	
Cost per mile	$0.2133	$0.2133	$0.1826	
Number of automobiles	20	20	21	

The annual budget was constructed upon the following assumptions:

(*a*) 20 automobiles in the pool
(*b*) 30,000 miles per year per automobile
(*c*) 15 miles per gallon per automobile
(*d*) $1.30 per gallon of gas
(*e*) $0.006 per mile for oil, minor repairs, parts, and supplies
(*f*) $135 per automobile in outside repairs

The supervisor is unhappy with the monthly report comparing budget and actual costs for March. He claims it presents unfairly his performance for March. His previous employer used flexible budgeting to compare actual costs to budgeted amounts.

1. Employing flexible budgeting techniques, prepare a report which shows budgeted amounts, actual costs, and monthly variation for March.
2. Explain briefly the basis of your budget figure for outside repairs.

(CMA, adapted)

SOLUTION

1.

UNIVERSITY MOTOR POOL
Monthly Budget Report
For March 19A

	Monthly Budget	March Actual	Variance (U) or (F)
Gasoline	$ 5,460	$ 5,740	$280 (U)
Oil, minor repairs, parts, and supplies	378	380	2 (U)
Outside repairs	236	50	186 (F)
Insurance	525	525	—
Salaries and benefits	2,500	2,500	—
Depreciation	2,310	2,310	—
Totals	$11,409	$11,505	$ 96 (U)
Number of automobiles	21	21	—
Actual miles	63,000	63,000	—
Cost per mile	$0.1811	$0.1826	$0.0015 (U)

Supporting calculations for monthly budget amounts:

Gasoline: $\dfrac{63{,}000 \text{ miles}}{15 \text{ miles/gallon}} \times \$1.30 \text{ per gallon} = \$5{,}460$

Oil, etc.: $63{,}000 \text{ miles} \times \$0.006 \text{ per mile} = \$378$

Outside repairs: $\dfrac{\$135 \text{ per auto} \times 21 \text{ autos}}{12 \text{ months}} = \$236.25$

Insurance: Annual cost for one auto $= \$6{,}000 \div 20$ autos $= \$300$ per auto

Annual cost for 21 autos $= 21 \times \$300 = \$6{,}300$

Monthly cost $= 6{,}300 \div 12 = \$525$

Salaries and benefits: No change

$\dfrac{\$30{,}000 \text{ annual cost}}{12 \text{ months}} = \$2{,}500\text{/month}$

Depreciation: Annual depreciation per auto $= \$26{,}400/20$ autos $= \$1{,}320$/auto

Annual depreciation for 21 autos $= \$1{,}320/\text{auto} \times 21 = 27{,}720$

Monthly depreciation $= \dfrac{27{,}720}{12} = \$2{,}310$

2. Outside automobile repairs are a function of the use of the automobile over its lifetime. These repairs, however, occur irregularly throughout the year and the life of the car. A monthly budget figure based on a per-mile charge becomes questionable. Therefore, the use of one-twelfth of the estimated annual outside repair costs adjusted for the number of cars in operation during a month appears to be more reasonable.

7.20 What is the relationship between responsibility accounting and cost control?

SOLUTION

There is a direct relationship between responsibility accounting and cost control. Costs are easier to control when a responsibility accounting system is in effect. Department heads know immediately when cost overruns occur and can work quickly to reduce them. Department heads are aware that their supervisors are receiving data on their performance and will make efforts to perform in a more cost-efficient manner.

7.21 List items that should be excluded from an assembly line foreman's responsibility accounting (or performance) report.

SOLUTION

Noncontrollable costs such as depreciation, insurance, property taxes, rent, and his own salary.

7.22 The printing department of a large corporation informs the marketing department that the price of printing 100,000 color flyers will be $60,000. The marketing department submits the material for the flyer two weeks later than originally planned and tells the printing department that the scheduled date of completion has been advanced two weeks. In order to achieve the new schedule, the printing department incurs an additional production cost of $15,000.

1. In an organization using responsibility accounting, where would the additional costs be assigned? Would these costs be considered controllable costs? What effect might this have on future printing orders from the marketing department?

2. In an organization that does not use responsibility accounting, where would the various costs be assigned? What effect might this have on future printing orders from the marketing department?

SOLUTION

1. In an organization using responsibility accounting, the originally quoted price of $60,000 plus the additional cost of $15,000 would be assigned to the marketing department. This would be considered a controllable cost. The long-range effect might be that the marketing department will become more cost-conscious and will plan activities better.
2. In an organization that does not employ responsibility accounting, the additional production costs most probably would be assigned to the printing department. There would be no motivation by the marketing department to adhere to scheduled dates or to plan printing needs in a better fashion.

7.23 You have a client who operates a large retail self-service grocery store that has a full range of departments. Management has encountered difficulty in using accounting data as a basis for making decisions concerning possible changes in departments operated, products, marketing methods, and so forth. List several overhead costs, or costs not applicable to a particular department, and explain how the existence of such costs (sometimes called *common costs* or *joint costs*) complicates and limits the use of accounting data in making decisions in such a store.

(AICPA, adapted)

SOLUTION

There are many examples of "common" costs to the sales department of a self-service grocery store. Some are rent, supervision, trucking, and advertising.

Common costs are usually apportioned on various arbitrary bases to the sales departments, but for numerous managerial decisions such apportionments produce misleading results. Decisions as to discounting a department, adding a department, enlarging a department, or decreasing a department cannot be made based on the data produced from the apportionments. For example, if a department is discontinued because it appears to be unprofitable, it may be determined that the costs of other departments will increase as a result of having to absorb more of the shared common costs. Thus, the overall operating results will be less favorable if the "unprofitable" department is discontinued. For decision-making purposes, the incremental approach discussed in Chapter 5 is more appropriate to arrive at the correct decision.

7.24 The monthly service charge a bank makes on a customer's checking account is based on the cost of handling each account. A customer disagrees with this policy because she cannot see how it is possible to determine the exact cost of handling her account. Do you agree with the customer? Discuss fully the problems involved in determining cost for such a service, including the limitations of the cost figures obtained.

(AICPA, adapted)

SOLUTION

This is a problem involving fixed and common costs. Within considerable limits, the cost of operating a bank would not change because of the addition of new accounts or the loss of old ones. The depreciation and other costs associated with the bank building, fixtures and equipment, salaries of officers, and other such items are fixed costs of operation within very wide limits. There would have to be a considerable change in the number of accounts before there would be any noticeable impact on those fixed costs. There is also a question of joint use of facilities among the various phases of bank operations. For example, the vault houses not only the files of commercial accounts, but also the savings account records, collateral on loans, coins and bills, and many other types of property and records. Unless the bank is large and the work highly specialized, a teller will handle a good many types of operations during a working day. A given official may make loans, open new accounts, advise customers as to investments, and so on. It would be extremely difficult to assign many of such operating expenses to any particular type of operation, let alone any account.

The problem of determining a reasonable and useful cost for handling an account involves obtaining data related to costs of functions and number of transactions handled, so that the direct or semidirect costs may be determined. The average labor cost per transaction for tellers and for transit, clearings, and bookkeeping functions can be obtained with considerable accuracy. Then it becomes necessary to allocate costs of all other necessary functions to these and other principal banking operations. Like all allocations of fixed or indirect overhead, the allocations will be arbitrary, but they can be made in a reasonable and logical manner by using appropriate bases.

While the costs obtained from such an accounting procedure may be useful for setting service charges, it must be recognized that they do have one important limitation. They are average costs and not "differential costs." Therefore, they have limited usefulness for certain types of management decisions relating to expansion or contraction of services or changes in operations.

7.25 From the following data, prepare a segmental income statement for the Christian Company for 19A.

		Division	
	Total	Alpha	Beta
Sales	$500,000	$200,000	$300,000
Fixed costs:			
Controllable by division managers	$125,000	$ 60,000	$ 65,000
Controllable by others	60,000	25,000	35,000
Variable costs:			
Manufacturing	210,000	100,000	110,000
Selling and administrative	70,000	35,000	35,000
Unallocated fixed costs:			
Manufacturing	20,000	—	—
Selling and administrative	10,000	—	—

SOLUTION

THE CHRISTIAN COMPANY
Income Statement by Segments

		Division	
	Total	Alpha	Beta
Sales	$500,000	$200,000	$300,000
Variable Costs:			
Manufacturing	$210,000	$100,000	$110,000
Selling and Administrative	70,000	35,000	35,000
Total Variable Costs	$280,000	$135,000	$145,000
Contribution Margin	$220,000	$ 65,000	$155,000
Less: Fixed Costs Controllable by Division Managers	125,000	60,000	65,000
Contribution Controllable by Division Managers	$ 95,000	$ 5,000	$ 90,000
Less: Fixed Costs Controllable by Others	60,000	25,000	35,000
Divisional Segment Margin	$ 35,000	$ (20,000)	$ 55,000
Less: Unallocated Common Costs:			
Manufacturing	20,000		
Selling and Administrative	10,000		
Total	$ 30,000		
Net Income	$ 5,000		

7.26 Compute the unknown amounts for the following segmented income statement (in thousands of dollars).

	Company Total	Division A	Division B
Sales	$5,000	$1,500	*(i)*
Unallocated fixed costs	*(a)*		
Fixed costs:			
Controllable by division managers	*(b)*	*(e)*	$ 500
Controllable by others	*(c)*	200	200
Contribution margin	2,200	*(f)*	*(j)*
Net income	400		
Variable costs:			
Manufacturing	*(d)*	*(g)*	1,000
Selling and administrative	1,200	400	*(k)*
Divisional segment margin	900	*(h)*	*(l)*

SOLUTION*

	Company Total	Division A	Division B
Sales	$5,000	$1,500	$3,500 *(i)*
Variable costs:			
Manufacturing	$1,600 *(d)*	$ 600 *(g)*	$1,000
Selling and administrative	1,200	400	800 *(k)*
Total variable costs	$2,800	$1,000	$1,800
Contribution margin	$2,200	$ 500 *(f)*	$1,700 *(j)*
Less: Fixed costs controllable by division managers	900 *(b)*	400 *(e)*	500
Contribution controllable by division managers	$1,300	$ 100	$1,200
Less: Fixed costs controllable by others	400 *(c)*	200	200
Divisional segment margin	$ 900	$ (100) *(h)*	$1,000 *(l)*
Less: Unallocated cost:	500 *(a)*		
Net income	$ 400		

*All amounts in thousands of dollars.

7.27 The Justa Corporation produces and sells three products. The three products, A, B, and C, are sold in a local market and in a regional market. At the end of the first quarter of the current year, the following income statement has been prepared:

	Total	Local	Regional
Sales	$1,300,000	$1,000,000	$300,000
Cost of goods sold	1,010,000	775,000	235,000
Gross margin	$ 290,000	$ 225,000	$ 65,000
Selling expenses	$ 105,000	$ 60,000	$ 45,000
Administrative expenses	52,000	40,000	12,000
Total	$ 157,000	$ 100,000	$ 57,000
Net income	$ 133,000	$ 125,000	$ 8,000

Management has expressed special concern with the regional market because of the extremely poor return on sales. This market was entered a year ago because of excess capacity. It was originally believed that the return on sales would improve with time, but after a year no noticeable improvement can be seen from the results as reported in the above quarterly statement.

In attempting to decide whether to eliminate the regional market, the following information has been gathered:

	Products		
	A	B	C
Sales	$500,000	$400,000	$400,000
Variable manufacturing expenses as a percentage of sales	60%	70%	60%
Variable selling expenses as a percentage of sales	3%	2%	2%

	Sales by Markets	
Product	Local	Regional
A	$400,000	$100,000
B	300,000	100,000
C	300,000	100,000

All administrative expenses and fixed manufacturing expenses are common to the three products and the two markets and are fixed for the period. Remaining selling expenses are fixed for the period and separable by market. All fixed expenses are based on a prorated yearly amount.

1. Prepare the quarterly income statement showing contribution margins by markets.
2. Assuming there are no alternative uses for the Justa Corporation's present capacity, would you recommend dropping the regional market? Why or why not?
3. Prepare the quarterly income statement showing contribution margins by products.
4. It is believed that a new product can be ready for sale next year if the Justa Corporation decides to go ahead with continued research. The new product can be produced by simply converting equipment presently used in producing product C. This conversion will increase fixed costs by $10,000 per quarter. What must be the minimum contribution margin per quarter for the new product to make the change-over financially feasible?

(CMA, adapted)

SOLUTION

1.

JUSTA CORPORATION
Quarterly Income Statement

	Total	Local	Regional
Sales	$1,300,000	$1,000,000	$300,000
Variable Expenses:			
Manufacturing (schedule A)	$ 820,000	$ 630,000	$190,000
Selling (schedule B)	31,000	24,000	7,000
Total Variable Expenses	$ 851,000	$ 654,000	$197,000
Contribution Margin	$ 449,000	$ 346,000	$103,000
Separable Fixed Selling Expenses	74,000	36,000	38,000
Net Market Contributions	$ 375,000	$ 310,000	$ 65,000
Common Fixed Expenses:			
Manufacturing	$ 190,000		
Administrative	52,000		
Total Common Fixed Expenses	$ 242,000		
Net Income	$ 133,000		

Schedule A—Variable Manufacturing Expenses

(1) Product	(2) %	(3) Local Sales	(4) Local Variable Expenses (2) × (3)	(5) Regional Sales	(6) Regional Variable Expenses (2) × (5)	(7) Total Variable Expenses (4) + (6)
A	60	$400,000	$240,000	$100,000	$ 60,000	$300,000
B	70	300,000	210,000	100,000	70,000	280,000
C	60	300,000	180,000	100,000	60,000	240,000
Totals			$630,000		$190,000	$820,000

Schedule B—Variable Selling Expenses

A	3	$400,000	$ 12,000	$100,000	$ 3,000	$ 15,000
B	2	300,000	6,000	100,000	2,000	8,000
C	2	300,000	6,000	100,000	2,000	8,000
Totals			$ 24,000		$ 7,000	$ 31,000

Separable fixed selling expenses computation:

	Local	Regional
Total selling expenses	$60,000	$45,000
Less: Variable (schedule B)	24,000	7,000
Fixed selling expenses	$36,000	$38,000

2. The answer is no; the regional market should not be dropped. The regional market sales are adequate to cover variable expenses and separable fixed expenses of the regional market and contribute $65,000 toward the recovery of the $242,000 common fixed expenses and net income.

If the regional market is dropped, the local market contribution margin must absorb its separable fixed selling expenses plus all common fixed expenses, as shown below:

Contribution margin	$346,000
Separable fixed selling expenses	36,000
Net market contribution	$310,000
Total common fixed expenses	242,000
Net income	$ 68,000

The corporation net income thus declines from $133,000 to $68,000. This $65,000 is the amount of the contribution loss from the regional market.

3.

JUSTA CORPORATION
Quarterly Income Statement

	Total	Product A	Product B	Product C
Sales	$1,300,000	$500,000	$400,000	$400,000
Variable Expenses:				
Manufacturing (schedule A)	$ 820,000	$300,000	$280,000	$240,000
Selling (schedule B)	31,000	15,000	8,000	8,000
Total Variable Expenses	$ 851,000	$315,000	$288,000	$248,000
Contribution Margin	$ 449,000	$185,000	$112,000	$152,000
Fixed Expenses:				
Manufacturing	$ 190,000			
Selling	74,000			
Administrative	52,000			
Total Fixed Expenses	$ 316,000			
Net Income	$ 133,000			

4. When the new product replaces product C, the minimum contribution margin per quarter must be at least $162,000 (the present contribution margin of product C + $10,000 of new fixed expenses) in order for Justa Corporation to be no worse off financially than it is currently. This contribution margin will still provide a net income of $133,000.

Examination II

Chapters 5–7

Part I Indicate whether the following statements are true (T) or false (F).

______ **1.** A responsibility center is a unit in which the manager is held accountable for the revenues earned.

______ **2.** In alternative-choice problems, both quantitative and qualitative factors should be carefully considered in reaching a decision.

______ **3.** The terms *differential costs* and *variable costs* may be used interchangeably.

______ **4.** Using the incremental approach, joint costs involving the decision to sell or process further are irrelevant.

______ **5.** A sunk cost is irrelevant to future decisions.

______ **6.** A flexible budget is one that excludes fixed costs and shows variable costs only.

______ **7.** A sales budget precedes a production budget.

______ **8.** Contribution margin and segment margin are synonymous terms.

______ **9.** A master budget is, simply put, a set of pro-forma financial statements.

______ **10.** The contribution approach to pricing is used primarily to price standard products.

Part II For each of the following multiple-choice statements, select the most appropriate answer.

1. Opportunity costs: (*a*) do not appear on formal accounting statements; (*b*) do not require dollar outlays; (*c*) both of the above; (*d*) neither of the above.

2. Assume that two products are manufactured from a joint process. Product B has additional sales revenue of $12,000 after additional processing costs of $9,000 and allocated joint costs of $25,000. It should be: (*a*) sold at the split-off point; (*b*) processed further.

3. The sales budget can be classified as: (*a*) a capital budget; (*b*) an operating budget; (*c*) a master budget; (*d*) a financial budget.

4. In preparing a merchandise purchase budget during a particular month, one must have information on: (*a*) the beginning inventory; (*b*) the desired ending inventory; (*c*) the amount of materials required for production; (*d*) all of the above.

5. If a cost cannot be allocated to certain segments of an organization, it should be: (*a*) excluded from the segmented income statement; (*b*) included in it; (*c*) included in it but not allocated.

6. Costs that can be eliminated if a particular division is discontinued are called: (*a*) opportunity costs; (*b*) incremental costs; (*c*) variable costs; (*d*) avoidable costs.

7. A cash budget consists of a: (*a*) cash receipts section; (*b*) cash disbursements section; (*c*) financing section; (*d*) all of the above.

8. The number of units to be produced is equal to planned sales in units: (*a*) + the desired ending inventory − the beginning inventory of finished goods; (*b*) + the beginning inventory − the desired ending inventory of finished goods; (*c*) neither of the above.

9. The Zinc Company has limited capacity in terms of the number of labor hours available. To maximize the profit of the company, it should concentrate on a product with the highest: (*a*) total sales; (*b*) contribution margin per machine hour; (*c*) contribution margin per unit of output; (*d*) none of the above.

10. In designing a responsibility accounting system, one should keep in mind a certain characteristic of each cost. This characteristic is: (*a*) the degree of cost controllability by the manager; (*b*) how the cost behaves with respect to volume; (*c*) the accuracy of cost allocation; (*d*) all of the above.

Part III Solve the following problems.

1. The Newport Store estimates its planned cash balance at $6,000 at September 1, 19A. Sales for September and the next three months have been projected as follows:

September	$31,500
October	31,000
November	32,500
December	33,000

Eighty percent of the sales are to be collected during the month of sales, and the remaining 20 percent are to be collected during the next month. Gross margin on sales averages 25 percent. Thirty percent of the merchandise is to be paid for during the month of sale, and the remaining 70 percent is to be paid for in the following month.

Expenses, which include depreciation of $750 each month, have been budgeted as follows:

October	$4,000
November	6,500
December	7,000

All the expenses are paid as incurred. Cash dividends of $3,250 are to be paid in November.

Prepare a cash budget for the months of October, November, and December.

2. Seal Beach Processing Company has 2,000 hours of available plant capacity to manufacture products V and W. Data on the two products are given below:

	V	W
Selling price per unit	$50	$75
Variable cost per unit	44	67
Contribution margin per unit	$ 6	$ 8
Time to produce each unit	⅓ hour	½ hour

(*a*) Which product should be produced?

(*b*) What would be the maximum contribution margin if the market will accept only 4,500 units of product V?

3. The following cost–volume formulas for factory overhead are given for the Cypress Tool Company for 19A:

Item	Cost–Volume Formula
Utilities	$800 per year, plus $0.40 per labor hour
Supplies	$1,100 per year, plus $0.90 per labor hour
Depreciation	$3,000 per year
Indirect labor	$2,700 per year, plus $0.60 per labor hour
Insurance	$600 per year

During the year, the following actual activity took place:

Budgeted labor hours	4,000 hours
Actual labor hours worked	4,200 hours
Actual overhead costs:	
Utilities ($800 fixed)	$2,600
Supplies ($1,100 fixed)	4,800
Depreciation	3,000
Indirect labor ($2,700 fixed)	5,350
Insurance	600

Prepare a performance report for 19A.

Answers to Examination II

Part I

1. F **2.** T **3.** F **4.** T **5.** T **6.** F **7.** T **8.** F **9.** T **10.** F.

Part II

1. (*c*) **2.** (*b*) **3.** (*b*) **4.** (*d*) **5.** (*c*) **6.** (*d*) **7.** (*d*) **8.** (*a*) **9.** (*b*) **10.** (*a*).

Part III

1.

NEWPORT STORE
Cash Budget
October–December 19A

	October	November	December	Total
Cash Balance, Beginning	$ 6,000	$10,337.50	$ 9,950	$ 6,000
Collection on Sales:				
80%, Current	24,800	26,000	26,400	77,200
20%, Preceding Month	6,300	6,200	6,500	19,000
Total Cash Available	$37,100	$42,537.50	$42,850	$102,200
Cash Disbursements:				
Cost of Goods Sold:				
30% of 75% of Current Sales	$ 6,975	$ 7,312.50	$ 7,425	$ 21,712.50
70% of 75% of Preceding Sales	16,537.50	16,275	17,062.50	49,875
Other Expenses Excluding Depreciation	3,250	5,750	6,250	15,250
Cash Dividends	—	3,250	—	3,250
Total Cash Needed	$26,762.50	$32,587.50	$30,737.50	$ 90,087.50
Cash Balance, Ending	$10,337.50	$ 9,950	$12,112.50	$ 12,112.50

2. (*a*) Contribution margin per hour:

$$\text{Product V} = (\$6 \text{ per unit})/\tfrac{1}{3} \text{ hour} = \$18 \text{ per hour}$$
$$\text{Product W} = (\$8 \text{ per unit})/\tfrac{1}{2} \text{ hour} = \$16 \text{ per hour}$$

Produce 6,000 units [(2,000 hours)/$\tfrac{1}{3}$ hour)] of product V. The maximum contribution margin obtained is as follows:

$$6{,}000 \text{ units} \times \$6 \text{ per unit} = \$36{,}000$$

or

$$2{,}000 \text{ hours} \times \$18 \text{ per hour} = \$36{,}000$$

(*b*) The limit of 4,500 units of product V means 1,500 hours of capacity, which leaves 500 hours for the production of product W. In other words:

	Units	Hours
Product V	4,500	1,500
Product W	1,000	500
		2,000

Therefore, the maximum contribution margin will be:

Product V:	4,500 units × $6 per unit = $27,000	(1,500 hours × $18 per hour)
Product W:	1,000 units × $8 per unit = 8,000	(500 hours × $16 per hour)
	$35,000	

3.

CYPRESS TOOL COMPANY
Performance Report
For the Year 19A

Budgeted Labor Hours 4,000
Actual Labor Hours 4,200

	Cost–Volume Formula	Budget Based on 4,200 Hours	Actual— 4,200 Hours	Variance (U) or (F)
Variable Overhead Costs:				
Utilities	$0.40 per hour	$ 1,680	$ 1,800	$120 (U)
Supplies	0.90	3,780	3,700	80 (F)
Indirect Labor	0.60	2,520	2,650	130 (U)
Total	$1.90	$ 7,980	$ 8,150	$170 (U)
Fixed Overhead Costs:				
Utilities		$ 800	$ 800	—
Supplies		1,100	1,100	—
Depreciation		3,000	3,000	—
Indirect Labor		2,700	2,700	—
Insurance		600	600	—
Total		$ 8,200	$ 8,200	—
Total Factory Overhead Costs		$16,180	$16,350	$170 (U)

Performance Evaluation, Transfer Pricing, and Decentralization

8.1 DECENTRALIZATION

As organizations grow, operations tend to increase in both volume and scope, and they are divided among a larger number of subunits such as divisions and centers. As a result, more of the freedom to make decisions is assigned to those subunits. *Decentralization* is the delegation of decision making to the subunits of an organization. It is a matter of degree. The lower the level where decisions are made, the greater is the decentralization. Decentralization is most effective in organizations where cost and profit measurement is necessary and is most successful in organizations where subunits are totally independent and autonomous. The benefits of decentralization include:

- Decisions are being made by those who have the most knowledge about local conditions.
- The burden of decision making is distributed. Top management is likely to have more time for the important strategic decisions.
- Greater managerial input of decision making has a desirable motivational effect.
- Managers have more control over results.

The costs of decentralization include:

- Managers have a tendency to look only at their division and lose sight of overall company goals.
- There can be costly duplication of services.
- Costs of obtaining sufficient information increase.

Two problems arise in a typical decentralized organization: *performance evaluation* and *transfer pricing*.

8.2 EVALUATION OF DIVISIONAL PERFORMANCE

The ability to measure performance is essential in developing management incentives and controlling the operation toward the achievement of organizational goals. A typical decentralized subunit is an *investment center*, which is responsible for an organization's invested capital (operating assets) and the related operating income. There are two widely used measurements of performance for the investment center: the *rate of return on investment (ROI)* and *residual income (RI)*.

8.3 RATE OF RETURN ON INVESTMENT (ROI)

ROI relates net income to invested capital. Specifically,

$$ROI = \frac{\text{Operating income}}{\text{Operating assets}}$$

ROI can be expressed as a product of the following two important factors:

$$ROI = \text{Margin} \times \text{Capital turnover}$$

$$= \frac{\text{Operating income}}{\text{Sales}} \times \frac{\text{Sales}}{\text{Operating assets}} = \frac{\text{Operating income}}{\text{Operating assets}}$$

Margin is a measure of profitability or operating efficiency, whereas turnover measures how well a division manages its assets.

EXAMPLE 8.1 Consider the following financial data for a division:

Operating assets	$100,000
Operating income	18,000
Sales	200,000

$$ROI = \frac{\text{Operating income}}{\text{Operating assets}} = \frac{\$18,000}{\$100,000} = 18\%$$

Alternatively,

$$\text{Margin} = \frac{\text{Operating income}}{\text{Sales}} = \frac{\$18,000}{\$200,000} = 9\%$$

$$\text{Turnover} = \frac{\text{Sales}}{\text{Operating assets}} = \frac{\$200,000}{\$100,000} = 2 \text{ times}$$

Therefore,

$$ROI = \text{Margin} \times \text{Turnover} = 9\% \times 2 \text{ times} = 18\%$$

The breakdown of ROI into margin and turnover (often called the *Du Pont formula*) has several advantages over the original formula in terms of profit planning. They are:

- The importance of turnover as a key to overall return on investment is emphasized in the breakdown. In fact, turnover is just as important as profit margin.
- The importance of sales is explicitly recognized, which is not reflected in the regular formula.
- The breakdown stresses the possibility of trading one off for the other in an attempt to improve the overall performance of a division.

EXAMPLE 8.2 The breakdown of ROI into its two components shows that a number of combinations of margin and turnover can yield the same rate of return, as shown below.

	Margin (%)	×	Turnover	=	ROI (%)
(1)	9	×	2 times	=	18
(2)	8	×	2.25	=	18
(3)	6	×	3	=	18
(4)	4	×	4.5	=	18
(5)	3	×	6	=	18
(6)	2	×	9	=	18

The turnover–margin relationship and its resulting ROI are depicted in Fig. 8-1. Figure 8-1 indicates that the turnover and margin factors complement each other. In other words, a weak margin can be complemented by a strong turnover, and vice versa. It also shows how important turnover is as a key to profit making. In fact, these two factors are equally important in overall profit performance.

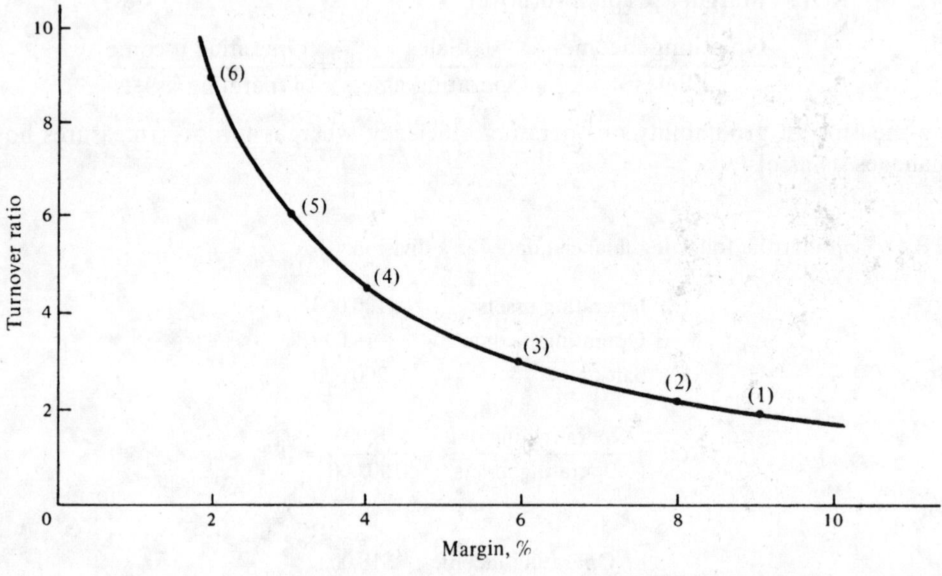

Fig. 8-1

8.4 ROI AND PROFIT PLANNING

The breakdown of ROI into turnover and margin gives management insight into planning for profit improvement. Generally speaking, management can:

1. Improve margin
2. Improve turnover
3. Improve both

Alternative 1 demonstrates a popular way of improving performance. Margins may be increased by reducing expenses, raising selling prices, or increasing sales faster than expenses. Alternative 2 may be achieved by increasing sales while holding the investment in assets relatively constant, or by reducing assets. Alternative 3 may be achieved by increasing sales revenue or by any combinations of alternatives 1 and 2.

EXAMPLE 8.3 Assume that management sets a 20 percent ROI as a profit target. It is currently making an 18 percent return on its investment.

$$ROI = \frac{\text{Operating income}}{\text{Sales}} \times \frac{\text{Sales}}{\text{Operating assets}}$$

Present:

$$18\% = \frac{18{,}000}{200{,}000} \times \frac{200{,}000}{100{,}000}$$

Alternative 1: Increase margin by reducing expenses.

$$20\% = \frac{20{,}000}{200{,}000} \times \frac{200{,}000}{100{,}000}$$

Alternative 2: Increase turnover by reducing investment in assets.

$$20\% = \frac{18{,}000}{200{,}000} \times \frac{200{,}000}{90{,}000}$$

Alternative 3: Increase both margin and turnover by disposing of obsolete and redundant inventories.

$$20\% = \frac{19{,}000}{200{,}000} \times \frac{200{,}000}{95{,}000}$$

Excessive investment in assets is just as much of a drag on profitability as excessive expenses. In this case, cutting unnecessary inventories also helps cut down expenses of carrying those inventories, so that both margin and turnover are improved at the same time. In practice, alternative 3 is much more common than alternative 1 or 2.

8.5 RESIDUAL INCOME (RI)

Another approach to measuring performance in an investment center is *residual income (RI)*. RI is the operating income which an investment center is able to earn above some minimum rate of return on its operating assets. RI, unlike ROI, is an absolute amount of income rather than a specific rate of return. When RI is used to evaluate divisional performance, the objective is to maximize the total amount of residual income, not to maximize the overall ROI figure.

$$RI = \text{Operating income} - (\text{Minimum required rate of return} \times \text{Operating assets})$$

EXAMPLE 8.4 In Example 8.1, assume the minimum required rate of return is 13 percent. Then the residual income of the division is

$$\$18{,}000 - (13\% \times \$100{,}000) = \$18{,}000 - \$13{,}000 = \$5{,}000$$

RI is regarded as a better measure of performance than ROI because it encourages investment in projects that would be rejected under ROI, which will be explained in the next section. A major disadvantage of RI, however, is that it cannot be used to compare divisions of different sizes. RI tends to favor larger divisions because of the larger amount of dollars involved.

8.6 INVESTMENT DECISIONS UNDER ROI AND RI

The decision whether to use ROI or RI as a measure of divisional performance affects managers' investment decisions. Under the ROI method, division managers tend to accept only the investments whose returns exceed the division's ROI; otherwise, the division's overall ROI would decrease. Under the RI method, on the other hand, division managers would accept an investment as long as it earns a rate in excess of the minimum required rate of return. The addition of such an investment will increase the division's overall RI.

EXAMPLE 8.5 Consider the same data given in Examples 8.1 and 8.4:

Operating assets	$100,000
Operating income	$ 18,000
Minimum required rate of return	13%
ROI = 18% and *RI* = $5,000	

Assume that the division is presented with a project that would yield 15 percent on a $10,000 investment. The division manager would not accept this project under the ROI approach, since the division is already earning 18 percent. Acquiring this project will bring down the present ROI to 17.73 percent, as shown below:

	Present	New Project	Overall
Operating assets (a)	$100,000	$10,000	$110,000
Operating income (b)	18,000	1,500*	19,500
ROI ($b \div a$)	18%	15%	17.73%

*$10,000 × 15% = $1,500.

Under the RI approach, the manager would accept the new project, since it provides a higher rate than the minimum required rate of return (15 percent vs. 13 percent). Accepting the new project will increase the overall residual income to $5,200, as shown below:

	Present	New Project	Overall
Operating assets (a)	$100,000	$10,000	$110,000
Operating income (b)	18,000	1,500	19,500
Minimum required income at 13% (c)	13,000	1,300*	14,300
$RI\,(b - c)$	$ 5,000	$ 200	$ 5,200

*$10,000 × 13% = $1,300.

8.7 TRANSFER PRICING

Goods and services are often exchanged between various divisions of a decentralized organization. The question then is: What monetary values should be assigned to these exchanges or transfers? Market price? Some kind of cost? Some version of either? Unfortunately, there is no single transfer price that will please everybody—that is, top management, the selling division, and the buying division—involved in the transfer.

The choice of a transfer pricing policy (i.e., which type of transfer price to use) is normally decided by top management. The decision typically includes consideration of the following:

- *Goal congruence.* Will the transfer price promote the goals of the company as a whole? Will it harmonize the divisional goals with organizational goals?
- *Performance evaluation.* Will the selling division receive enough credit for its transfer of goods and services to the buying division? Will the transfer price hurt the performance of the selling division?
- *Autonomy.* Will the transfer price preserve autonomy, the freedom of the selling and buying division managers to operate their divisions as decentralized entities?
- *Other factors* such as minimization of tariffs and income taxes and observance of legal restrictions.

8.8 ALTERNATIVE TRANSFER PRICING SCHEMES

Transfer prices can be based on:

- Market price
- Cost-based price—variable or full cost
- Negotiated price
- General formula, which is usually the sum of variable costs per unit and opportunity cost for the company as a whole (lost revenue per unit on outside sales).

MARKET PRICE

Market price is the best transfer price in the sense that it will maximize the profits of the company as a whole, if it meets the following two conditions:

- There exists a competitive market price.
- Divisions are independent of each other.

If either one of these conditions is violated, market price will not lead to an optimal economic decision for the company.

COST-BASED PRICE—VARIABLE OR FULL COST

Cost-based transfer price, another alternative transfer pricing scheme, is easy to understand and convenient to use. But there are some disadvantages, including:

- Inefficiencies of the selling divisions are passed on to the buying divisions with little incentive to control costs. The use of standard costs is recommended in such a case.
- The cost-based method treats the divisions as cost centers rather than profit or investment centers. Therefore, measures such as ROI and RI cannot be used for evaluation purposes.

The variable cost-based transfer price has an advantage over the full cost method because in the short run it may tend to ensure the best utilization of the overall company's resources. The reason is that, in the short run, fixed costs do not change. Any use of facilities without incurrence of additional fixed costs will increase the company's overall profits.

NEGOTIATED PRICE

A negotiated price is generally used when there is no clear outside market. A negotiated price is a price agreed upon between the buying and selling divisions that reflects unusual or mitigating circumstances. This method is widely used when no intermediate market price exists for the product transferred and the selling division is assured of a normal profit.

EXAMPLE 8.6 Company X has just purchased a small company that specializes in the manufacture of part no. 323. Company X is a decentralized organization, and will treat the newly acquired company as an autonomous division called Division B, with full profit responsibility. Division B's fixed costs total $30,000 per month, and variable costs per unit are $18. Division B's operating capacity is 5,000 units. The selling price per unit is $30. Division A of Company X is currently purchasing 2,500 units of part no. 323 per month from an outside supplier as $29 per unit, which represents the normal $30 price less a quantity discount. Top management of the company wishes to decide what transfer price should be used.

Top management may consider the following alternative prices:

(*a*) $30 market price

(*b*) $29, the price that Division A is currently paying to the outside supplier

(*c*) $23.50 negotiated price, which is $18 variable cost plus one-half of the benefits of an internal transfer [($29 − $18) × ½] (*d*) $24 full cost, which is $18 variable cost plus $6 ($30,000 ÷ 5,000 units) fixed cost per unit

(*e*) $18 variable cost

We will discuss each of these prices:

(*a*) $30 would not be an appropriate transfer price. Division B cannot charge a price more than the price that Division A is paying now ($29).

(*b*) $29 would be an appropriate transfer price if top management wishes to treat the divisions as autonomous investment centers. This price would cause all of the benefits of internal transfers to accrue to the selling division, with the buying division's position remaining unchanged.

(*c*) $23.50 would be an appropriate transfer price if top management wishes to treat the divisions as investment centers, but wishes to share the benefits of an internal transfer *equally* between them, as follows:

Variable costs of Division B	$18.00
One-half of the difference between the variable costs of Division B and the price Division A is paying ($29 − $18) × ½	5.50
Transfer price	$23.50

Note that $23.50 is just *one* example of a negotiated transfer price. The exact price depends on how they divide the benefits.

(*d*) $24 [$24 = $18 + ($30,000 ÷ 5,000 units)] would be an appropriate transfer price if top management treats the divisions like cost centers with no profit responsibility. All benefits from both divisions will accrue to the buying division. This will maximize the profits of the company as a whole, but affect the performance of the selling division adversely. Another disadvantage of this cost-based approach is that inefficiencies (if any) of the selling division are passed on to the buying division.

(*e*) $18 would be an appropriate transfer price for guiding top management in deciding whether transfers between the two divisions should take place. Since $18 is less than the outside purchase price of the buying division, and the selling division has excess capacity, the transfer should take place, because it will maximize the profits of the company as a whole. However, if $18 is used as a transfer price, then all of the benefits of the internal transfer accrue to the buying division, and it will hurt the performance of the selling division.

GENERAL FORMULA

It is not easy to find a cure-all answer to the transfer pricing problem, since the three problems of goal congruence, performance evaluation, and autonomy must all be considered simultaneously. It is generally agreed, however, that some form of competitive market price is the best approach to the transfer pricing problem. The following formula may be helpful in this effort:

Transfer price = Variable costs per unit + Opportunity costs per unit for the company as a whole

Opportunity costs are defined here as net revenue forgone by the company as a whole if the goods and services are transferred internally. The reasoning behind this formula is that the selling division should be allowed to recover its variable costs plus opportunity cost (i.e., revenue that it could have made by selling to an outsider) of the transfer. The selling department should not have to suffer lost income by selling within the company.

EXAMPLE 8.7 Company X has more than 50 divisions, including A, B, and K. Division A, the buying division, wants to buy a component for its final product and has an option to buy from Division B or from an outside supplier at the market price of $200. If Division A buys from the outside supplier, it will in turn buy selected raw materials from Division K for $40. This will increase its contribution to overall company profits by $30 ($40 revenue minus $10 variable costs). Division B, on the other hand, can sell its component to Division A or to an

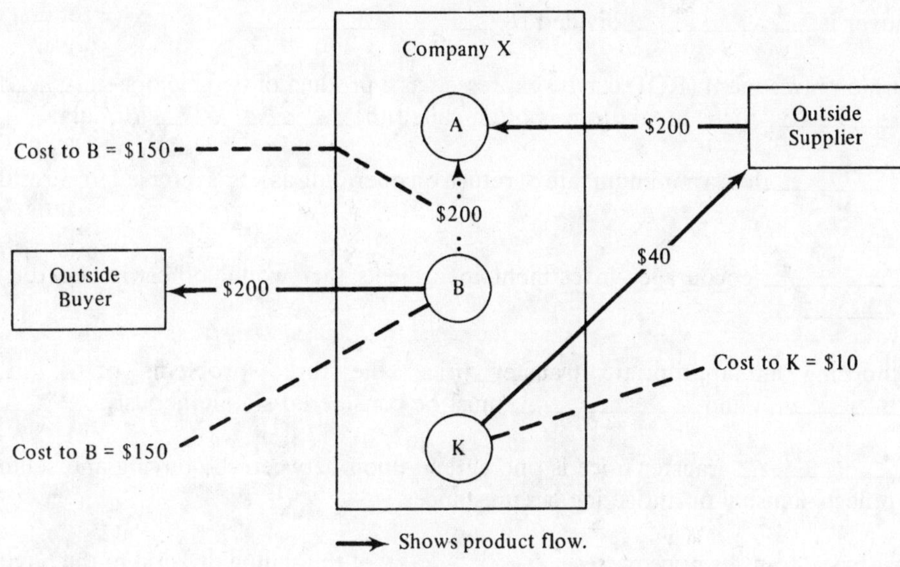

Fig. 8-2

outside buyer at the same price. Division B, working at full capacity, incurs variable costs of $150. Will the use of $200 as a transfer price lead to optimal decisions for the company as a whole? Figure 8-2 depicts the situation.

The optimal decision from the viewpoint of Company X as a whole can be looked at in terms of its net cash outflow, as follows:

	Division A's Action	
	Buy from B	Buy from Outsider
Outflow to the company as a whole	$(150)	$(200)
Cash inflows	—	to B: 50 ($200 − $150) to K: 30 ($40 − $10)
Net cash outflow to the company as a whole	$(150)	$(120)

To maximize the profits of Company X, Division A should buy from an outside supplier. The transfer price that would force Division A to buy outside should be the sum of variable costs and opportunity costs, that is,

$$\$150 + \$50 + \$30 = \$230 \text{ per unit}$$

If the outside supplier charges Division A $230 or more, then Division A will definitely transfer from Division B at any transfer price. Regardless of the transfer price, net cash outflow to the company does not change.

Summary

(1) A(n) ____________ has control over both profits and investment.

(2) Decentralization is the delegation of ____________ to individual divisions of an organization.

(3) Operating income divided by sales is referred to as ____________.

(4) Turnover is ____________ divided by ____________.

(5) Return on investment (ROI) can be expressed as a product of two factors: ____________ and ____________. This breakdown is often called the ____________ formula.

(6) ____________ less a minimum rate of return on operating assets is referred to as residual income (RI).

(7) ____________ encourages investment in projects that would otherwise be rejected under ____________.

(8) In choosing an appropriate transfer price, the three problems of ____________, ____________, and ____________ must be considered simultaneously.

(9) A ____________ transfer price is one agreed upon between the buying and selling divisions that reflects unusual or mitigating circumstances.

(10) A cost-based transfer price passes ____________ of the selling division to the buying division. The use of ____________ avoids this problem.

(11) The general formula for computing a transfer price is: Transfer price = ____________ + ____________.

(12) The harmonizing of a manager's goals with the organization goals is called ____________.

(13) A transfer price based on ____________ will lead to an optimal economic decision under the conditions of the existence of competitive market price and independence of divisions.

(14) When ____________ is used to measure divisional performance, the objective is to maximize the total amount of ____________, not to maximize the overall ____________ figure.

(15) Many firms base transfer prices on ____________, since they are easy to understand and convenient to use.

(16) Transfer prices based on full cost are appropriate if top management treats the divisions like ____________.

(17) If the selling division has ____________, a transfer price based on ____________ would be an appropriate transfer price, although it would hurt the performance of the selling division.

Answers: (1) investment center; (2) decision making; (3) margin; (4) sales, operating assets; (5) margin, turnover, Du Pont; (6) operating income; (7) residual income (RI), return on investment (ROI); (8) goal congruence, performance evaluation, autonomy; (9) negotiated; (10) inefficiencies, standard costs; (11) variable costs per unit, opportunity costs per unit for the company as a whole; (12) goal congruence; (13) market price; (14) RI, residual income, ROI; (15) cost; (16) cost centers; (17) excess capacity, variable cost.

Solved Problems

8.1 Acme, a division of Ace Manufacturing, has assets of $225,000 and an operating income of $55,000.

1. What is the division's ROI?
2. If the minimum rate of return is 12 percent, what is the division's residual income?

SOLUTION

1. $$\frac{\$55{,}000}{\$225{,}000} = 24.44\%\ \text{ROI}$$

2.

Operating income	$55,000
Minus minimum required rate (12% × $225,000)	27,000
Residual income	$28,000

8.2 Consider the following:

	(000s omitted) Division A	Division B
Operating assets	$5,000	$12,500
Operating income	$1,000	$ 2,250
ROI	20%	18%

1. Which is the more successful division in terms of ROI?
2. Using 16 percent as the minimum required rate of return, compute the residual income for each division. Which division is more successful under this rate?

SOLUTION

1. Division A is more successful since it returns $0.20 for each dollar invested (vs. $0.18 for division B).
2. The residual income at 16 percent for each division is computed as follows:

	Division A	Division B
Operating income	$1,000	$2,250
Minimum required income	800 (16% × $5,000)	2,000 (16% × $12,500)
RI	$ 200	$ 250

Division B is more successful.

8.3 The following data are given for the Key West division for 19A:

Return on investment (ROI)	25%
Sales	$1,200,000
Margin	10%
Minimum required rate of return	18%

1. Compute the division's operating assets.
2. Compute the division's residual income (RI).

SOLUTION

1. By definition,

$$ROI = \text{Margin} \times \text{Turnover}$$
$$25\% = 10\% \times \text{Turnover}$$

Therefore, the turnover must be 2.5 times.

Since the turnover is sales/operating assets,

$$2.5 \text{ times} = \$1{,}200{,}000 \div \text{Operating assets}$$

Therefore,

$$\text{Operating assets} = \$480{,}000$$

2. $$RI = \text{Operating income} - \text{Minimum required operating income}$$

$$\text{Margin} = 10\% = \frac{\text{Operating income}}{\text{Sales}} = \frac{\text{Operating income}}{\$1{,}200{,}000}$$

Therefore, the operating income must be \$120,000.

$$RI = \$120{,}000 - (18\% \times \$480{,}000) = \$120{,}000 - \$86{,}400 = \$33{,}600$$

8.4 XYZ Corporation has three divisions whose income statements and balance sheets are summarized below:

	Division X	Division Y	Division Z
Sales	\$500,000	(*d*)	(*g*)
Operating income	\$ 25,000	\$30,000	(*h*)
Operating assets	\$100,000	(*e*)	\$250,000
Turnover	(*a*)	(*f*)	0.4
Margin	(*b*)	0.4%	5%
Return on investment (ROI)	(*c*)	2%	(*i*)

1. Supply the missing data in the table above and summarize the results.
2. Comment on the relative performance of each division. What questions can be raised as a result of their performance?

SOLUTION

1. Return on investment (ROI) is

$$\frac{\text{Operating income}}{\text{Operating assets}} = \frac{\text{Operating income}}{\text{Sales}} \times \frac{\text{Sales}}{\text{Operating assets}}$$
$$= \text{Margin} \times \text{Turnover}$$

(*a*) $$\text{Turnover} = \frac{\$500{,}000}{\$100{,}000} = 5 \text{ times}$$

(*b*) $$\text{Margin} = \frac{\$25{,}000}{\$500{,}000} = 5\%$$

(*c*) $$ROI = \text{Turnover} \times \text{Margin}$$
$$= 5 \text{ times} \times 5\% = 25\%$$

(*d*)
$$\text{Margin} = 0.4\% = 0.004 = \frac{\text{Operating income}}{\text{Sales } d} = \frac{\$30{,}000}{\text{Sales } d}$$

$$d = \frac{\$30{,}000}{0.004} = \$7{,}500{,}000$$

(*e*)
$$ROI = 2\% = \frac{\text{Operating income}}{\text{Operating assets } e} = \frac{\$30{,}000}{\text{Operating assets } e}$$

$$e = \frac{\$30{,}000}{0.02} = \$1{,}500{,}000$$

(*f*)
$$\text{Turnover} = \frac{d}{e} = \frac{\$7{,}500{,}000}{1{,}500{,}000} = 5 \text{ times}$$

(*g*)
$$\text{Turnover} = 0.4 = \frac{\text{Sales } g}{\$250{,}000} \qquad g = 0.4 \times \$250{,}000 = \$100{,}000$$

(*h*)
$$\text{Margin} = 5\% = \frac{\text{Operating income } h}{\text{Sales } g} = \frac{h}{\$100{,}000}$$

$$h = \$100{,}000 \times 5\% = \$5{,}000$$

(*i*)
$$ROI = 0.4 \text{ times} \times 5\% = 2\% \quad \text{or} \quad \frac{\$5{,}000}{\$250{,}000} = 2\%$$

Summarizing the results gives:

	Division X	Division Y	Division Z
Turnover	5 times	5 times	0.4 times
Margin	5%	0.4%	5%
ROI	25%	2%	2%

2. Division X performed best. It appears that Divisions Y and Z are in trouble. Division Y turns over its assets as often as Division X, but Y's margin on sales is much lower. Thus, Division Y must work on improving its margin. The following questions are raised about Division Y: Is the low margin due to inefficiency? Is it due to excessive material, labor, and/or overhead costs? Division Z, on the other hand, does just as well as Division X in terms of profit margin—both divisions earn 5 percent on sales. But Division Z has a much lower turnover of capital than Division X. Therefore, Division Z should take a close look at its investment. Is too much tied up in inventories and receivables? Are there unused fixed assets? Is there idle cash sitting around?

8.5 Supply the missing data in the following table:

	Division A	Division B	Division C
Sales	$60,000	$75,000	$100,000
Operating income	(*a*)	$25,000	(*e*)
Operating assets	$30,000	(*c*)	$ 50,000
Return on investment (ROI)	15%	10%	20%
Minimum required rate of return	10%	(*d*)	(*f*)
Residual income (RI)	(*b*)	$ 5,000	0

SOLUTION

$$ROI = \frac{\text{Operating income}}{\text{Operating assets}}$$

$$RI = \text{Operating income} - \text{Minimum required income}$$

or
$$= \text{Operating income} - (\text{Minimum required rate of return} \times \text{Operating assets})$$

(a) $ROI = 15\% = \dfrac{\text{Operating income } a}{\$30{,}000} \qquad a = \$30{,}000 \times 15\% = \$4{,}500$

(b) $RI = \$4{,}500 - (10\% \times \$30{,}000) = \$4{,}500 - \$3{,}000 = \$1{,}500$

(c) $ROI = 10\% = \dfrac{\$25{,}000}{\text{Operating assets } c} \qquad c = \dfrac{\$25{,}000}{10\%} = \$250{,}000$

(d) $RI = \$25{,}000 - (\text{Minimum required rate of return } d \times \$250{,}000) = \$5{,}000 \qquad d = 8\%$

(e) $ROI = 20\% = \dfrac{\text{Operating income } e}{\$50{,}000} \qquad e = \$50{,}000 \times 20\% = \$10{,}000$

(f) $RI = \$0 = \$10{,}000 - (\text{Minimum required rate of return } f \times \$50{,}000) \qquad f = 20\%$

8.6 The Pip division has the following operating data:

Operating assets	$200,000
Operating income	$ 50,000
Minimum required rate of return	16%

1. Compute the ROI and RI for this division.
2. Assume that the Pip division is presented with an investment project yielding a 20 percent return on its investment requiring a cash outlay of $30,000. Would the manager of the Pip division accept this investment under the ROI approach? How about under the RI approach?

SOLUTION

1.

	ROI	RI
Operating assets	$200,000 (a)	$200,000
Operating income	$ 50,000 (b)	$ 50,000 (b)
ROI (b ÷ a)	25%	
Minimum required income (16% × $200,000)		32,000 (c)
RI (b − c)		$ 18,000

2. The manager of the Pip division would not accept this project under the ROI approach, since the division is already earning 25 percent. Accepting this project would reduce the present divisional performance, as shown below.

	Present	New Project	Overall
Operating assets (a)	$200,000	$30,000	$230,000
Operating income (b)	$ 50,000	$ 6,000*	$ 56,000
ROI (b ÷ a)	25%	20%	24.35%

*$30,000 × 20% = $6,000.

Under the RI approach, on the other hand, the manager would accept this project, since the new project provides a higher return than the minimum required rate of return (20 percent vs. 16 percent). The new project would increase the overall divisional residual income, as shown below.

	Present	New Project	Overall
Operating assets (*a*)	$200,000	$30,000	$230,000
Operating income (*b*)	$ 50,000	$ 6,000	$ 56,000
Minimum required return at 16% (*c*)	32,000	4,800*	36,800
RI ($b - c$)	$ 18,000	$ 1,200	$ 19,200

*$30,000 × 16% = $4,800.

8.7 Consider the following sales and operating data for the three divisions of a conglomerate:

	Division A	Division B	Division C
Sales	$140,000	$180,000	$250,000
Operating income	$ 5,000	$ 6,300	$ 14,400
Operating assets	$ 20,000	$ 35,000	$ 90,000
Minimum required rate of return	10%	19%	20%

(*a*) Compute the return on investment (ROI) for each division.

(*b*) Assume that each division is provided with an investment opportunity that could produce 20 percent return on investment. Which divisions would accept or reject it?

SOLUTION

(*a*)

	Division A	Division B	Division C
ROI	$\frac{\$5,000}{\$20,000} = 25\%$	$\frac{\$6,300}{\$35,000} = 18\%$	$\frac{\$14,400}{\$90,000} = 16\%$

(*b*) Division A would reject this investment opportunity, since the addition would lower the present divisional ROI. Divisions B and C would accept it because they would look better in terms of their divisional ROI.

8.8 Using the data from Problem 8.7, (*a*) compute the residual income (RI) for each division, and (*b*) assume that each division is provided with an investment opportunity that would produce an 18 percent return on investment. Which divisions will accept or reject it?

SOLUTION

(*a*)

	Division A	Division B	Division C
Operating income	$5,000	$6,300	$14,400
Minimum required income	10% × 20,000 = $2,000	19% × 35,000 = $6,650	20% × 90,000 = $18,000
RI	$3,000	$ (350)	$ (3,600)

(*b*) Division A would accept this investment project, since an 18 percent ROI is greater than 10 percent. Thus, it will increase the divisional residual income. Divisions B and C would reject it, since their minimum required rates of return are both greater than the 18 percent return that the new project earns.

8.9 The Texon Company is organized into autonomous divisions along regional market lines. Each division manager is responsible for sales, cost of operations, acquisition and financing of divisional assets, and working capital management.

The vice president of general operations for the company will retire in September 19X5, and a replacement is being sought. A review of the performance, attitudes, and skills of several management employees has been undertaken. Interviews have also been held with qualified outside candidates. The selection committee has narrowed the choice to the managers of divisions A and F.

Both candidates were appointed division managers in late 19X1. The manager of division A had been the assistant manager of that division for the preceding five years. The manager of division F had served as assistant division manager of division B before being appointed to his present post. He took over division F, a division newly formed in 19X0, when its first manager left to join a competitor. The financial results of their performance in the past three years are reported below.

1. Texon Company measures the performance of the divisions and the division managers on the basis of their return on investment (ROI). Is this an appropriate measurement for the division managers? Explain.
2. Many believe that a single measure, such as ROI, is inadequate to fully evaluate performance. What additional measure(s) could be used for performance evaluation? Give reasons for each measure listed.
3. On the basis of the information given, which manager would you recommend for vice president of general operations? Present reasons to support your answer.

	Division A			Division F		
	19X2	19X3	19X4	19X2	19X3	19X4
			(000 omitted)			
Estimated industry sales—market area	$10,000	$12,000	$13,000	$5,000	$6,000	$6,500
Division sales	$ 1,000	$ 1,100	$ 1,210	$ 450	$ 600	$ 750
Variable costs	$ 300	$ 320	$ 345	$ 135	$ 175	$ 210
Discretionary costs	400	405	420	170	200	230
Committed costs	275	325	350	140	200	250
Total costs	$ 975	$ 1,050	$ 1,115	$ 445	$ 575	$ 690
Net income	$ 25	$ 50	$ 95	$ 5	$ 25	$ 60
Assets employed	$ 330	$ 340	$ 360	$ 170	$ 240	$ 300
Liabilities	103	105	115	47	100	130
Net investment	227	235	245	123	140	170
Return on investment	11%	21%	39%	4%	18%	35%

(CMA, adapted)

SOLUTION

1. ROI can be an appropriate device to measure the performance of division managers, provided the limitations of the technique are clearly understood. However, ROI probably should not be employed as the only means of evaluating performance. In this case, ROI can be used as one of the measurements in evaluating division managers. The separate components of ROI (division net income and investment base) must be properly defined and valued for ROI to be a useful measure. The investment base should include only those assets that are under the control of division managers, and the division manager must exercise control over all revenues and expenses of the division. In this situation the investment base is defined as assets employed less division liabilities, which implies that corporate assets are not allocated to divisions. In addition, division managers evidently exercise control over the investment base because they are responsible for the acquisition of division assets.

Division managers apparently are responsible for all revenue and costs within the division because each division's sales are in a separate regional market. Therefore, the Texon ROI is an appropriate measure of division management performance because Texon has properly defined the components of ROI and division managers apparently can exercise control over the components of the ROI calculation.

2. A properly defined ROI may cause suboptimum behavior if it is used as the sole criterion of divisional performance. Emphasis on divisional ROI may result in the rejection of an investment project which has forecasted returns in excess of the firm's cost of capital if the project return is less than the division's present ROI; acceptance of such a project would reduce the division's actual ROI even though company profits would benefit. The suboptimum behavior which can result from ROI can be overcome by evaluating divisions on the basis of their residual income (division income less an amount representing the cost of capital employed by the division). When residual income is adopted for evaluation purposes, emphasis is placed on marginal profit dollars above the cost of capital rather than on the rate itself. Several other performance measures might be used in conjunction with ROI (and residual income) to identify components which contribute to divisional performance. Additional items management might examine include profit margin, profit growth, sales growth, market penetration, working capital management, new product development, and management personnel development. All of these would be compared with prior years' results and current budgets and projections to aid in the evaluation of divisional performance. While the net result of these items may be reflected in the ROI calculations, a closer examination of these items provides additional insight and a more comprehensive picture of performance.

3. An examination of the data provided indicates that the managers of divisions A and F both have good performance records. In addition to evaluating the furnished data, Texon would want to examine other factors regarding the managers of divisions A and F, such as personality, leadership traits, etc. A strong case could be made for either manager; however, *based on the facts as presented*, the manager of division F appears to be better qualified.

   The manager of division F was able to promote sales growth in excess of overall market growth, as shown below.

	Sales Growth	
	Division F	Overall
19X3	$\dfrac{\$600-\$450}{\$450}=33\%$	$\dfrac{\$6{,}000-\$5{,}000}{\$5{,}000}=20\%$
19X4	$\dfrac{\$750-\$600}{\$600}=25\%$	$\dfrac{\$6{,}500-\$6{,}000}{\$6{,}000}=8.3\%$

Thus, division F has increased its market share. During the same period division A, although experiencing sales growth (10 percent per year), lost some of its share of the market.

Both divisions have been able to reduce costs (relative to sales) during this period. For 19X4 each has costs of 92 percent of sales. The net income as a percent of sales has increased each year for both divisions.

Division F has had a greater income growth rate, 400 percent and 140 percent compared to 100 percent and 90 percent, than division A. This is the result of better sales growth and comparable cost management.

Division F is a newer division in a relatively early stage of its development. The manager of division F has been able to obtain sales and profit growth without encountering the disturbances which often confront the early years of new operations. The manager of division F also has a more diversified background because he has served with two divisions—divisions F and B.

The combination of excellent sales growth, good cost management, more diversified experience, and the demonstrated ability to manage a newly organized division effectively makes the manager of division F a better prospect for vice president of general operations.

8.10 Queens, Inc., is a producer and distributor of various motorized recreational scooter, bike, and motorcycle products. The Brooklyn division handles scooters and would like to earn a long-run rate of return of 20 percent. The Brooklyn division will change its unit selling price as necessary to provide this return. The following data are available on the division and its product:

Variable cost per scooter	$200
Total annual fixed costs	$1,220,000
Long-run normal demand	10,000 units each year
Average operating assets owned by the division	$1,400,000

1. Compute the per-unit selling price that will provide the desired rate of return.
2. Assume that actual sales fluctuate from 8,500 units to 11,500 units. Compute the margin, turnover, and ROI that would be realized on sales at the 8,500-, 10,000-, and 11,500-unit levels of activity. (Use the selling price computed in part 1 for your computations.)
3. Explain what your computations in part 2 suggest to you insofar as applying the rate-of-return formula to divisions subject to cyclical movement in the economy.

SOLUTION

1.
$$ROI = \frac{\text{Operating income}}{\text{Operating assets}}$$

$$0.20 = \frac{(10{,}000\text{ units} \times p) - [\overbrace{(10{,}000\text{ units} \times \$200)}^{\text{VC}} + \overbrace{\$1{,}220{,}000}^{\text{FC}}]}{\$1{,}400{,}000}$$

where p = selling price per unit.

$$0.20 = \frac{10{,}000p - \$2{,}000{,}000 - \$1{,}220{,}000}{\$1{,}400{,}000}$$

$$\$280{,}000 = 10{,}000p - \$3{,}220{,}000$$

$$\$280{,}000 + \$3{,}220{,}000 = 10{,}000p$$

$$\$3{,}500{,}000 = 10{,}000p$$

$$p = \frac{\$3{,}500{,}000}{10{,}000\text{ units}} = \$350\text{ per unit}$$

2.

Sales in Units	Margin $\left(\frac{\text{Operating Income}}{\text{Sales}}\right)$	Capital Turnover $\left(\frac{\text{Sales}}{\text{Operating Assets}}\right)$	ROI (Margin × Turnover)
8,500	1.85%	2.125	3.93%
10,000	8.00%	2.5	20.00%
11,500	12.55%	2.875	36.08%

Supporting computations are as follows.

At 8,500 units:

$$\begin{aligned}\text{Operating income} &= (8{,}500 \times \$350) - (8{,}500 \times \$200) - \$1{,}220{,}000\\ &= \$2{,}975{,}000 - \$1{,}700{,}000 - \$1{,}220{,}000\\ &= \$55{,}000\end{aligned}$$

$$\text{Margin} = \frac{\$55{,}000}{\$2{,}975{,}000} = 0.0185 = 1.85\%$$

$$\text{Turnover} = \frac{\$2{,}975{,}000}{\$1{,}400{,}000} = 2.125$$

$$ROI = 1.85\% \times 2.125 = 3.93\%$$

At 10,000 units:

$$\begin{aligned}\text{Operating income} &= (10{,}000 \times \$350) - (10{,}000 \times \$200) - \$1{,}220{,}000\\ &= \$3{,}500{,}000 - \$2{,}000{,}000 - \$1{,}220{,}000\\ &= \$280{,}000\end{aligned}$$

$$\text{Margin} = \frac{\$280{,}000}{\$3{,}500{,}000} = 0.08 = 8\%$$

$$\text{Turnover} = \frac{\$3{,}500{,}000}{\$1{,}400{,}000} = 2.5$$

$$ROI = 8\% \times 2.5 = 20\%$$

At 11,500 units:

$$\begin{aligned}\text{Operating income} &= (11{,}500 \times \$350) - (11{,}500 \times \$200) - \$1{,}220{,}000\\ &= \$4{,}025{,}000 - \$2{,}300{,}000 - \$1{,}220{,}000\\ &= \$505{,}000\end{aligned}$$

$$\text{Margin} = \frac{\$505{,}000}{\$4{,}025{,}000} = 0.1255 = 12.55\%$$

$$\text{Turnover} = \frac{\$4{,}025{,}000}{\$1{,}400{,}000} = 2.875$$

$$ROI = 12.55 \times 2.875 = 36.08\%$$

3. The computations in part 2 suggest the following with regard to divisions subject to cyclical movements in the economy.

   (*a*) ROI as a measurement of performance has some limitations. When unit sales were increased from 8,500 to 10,000 units (an increase of 17.6 percent), ROI increased more than 400 percent. When unit sales were 11,500 instead of 8,500 (an increase of 35.3 percent), ROI increased 818 percent! In other words, the ROI fluctuates greatly for changes in sales. This does not suggest that ROI should not be used for divisions that are subject to cyclical movements in the economy. Rather, management should be aware of how greatly ROI can fluctuate compared to changes in sales. For example, management can set target ROI to vary depending on the part of a cycle the economy is in, or perhaps set an ROI range rather than one ROI value.

   (*b*) The division manager has no (or very little) control over sales, which are affected greatly by outside economic forces. Therefore, top management should exercise caution in using ROI as a measure of divisional performance in this type of business.

8.11 From an organizational point of view, two approaches to transfer pricing are (*a*) to let the managers of profit centers bargain with one another and arrive at their own transfer prices (negotiated transfer pricing) and (*b*) to have the firm's top management set transfer prices for transactions between the investment centers. Identify the advantages and disadvantages of each approach.

(CGA, adapted)

SOLUTION

(*a*) Negotiated transfer pricing:

Advantages: The division managers have control over the transfer prices and can be held responsible for their resulting impact on profits.

Disadvantages: Individual managers, in their attempt to maximize profits of their own divisions, may make decisions detrimental to the overall profit of the firm as a whole.

(*b*) Ordinary transfer pricing:

Advantages: It is possible for top management to set transfer prices that will guide profit center managers to make decisions that will maximize the profits of the company as a whole.

Disadvantages: The managers do not have authority in an area affecting their own profit performance.

8.12 Division A normally purchases its parts from Division B of the same company. Division A has learned that Division B is increasing its price to $110 per unit. As a result, the Division A manager has decided to purchase the parts from an outside supplier at a unit cost of $100, $10 less than it would cost to purchase the same part from Division B. The Division B manager has explained that inflation is the cause of the price increase and that the loss of parts normally transferred to Division A will hurt the division as well as the company profits. The Division B manager feels that the company as a whole would benefit from the sale of parts to Division A. The following costs and unit purchases represent the normal annual transaction:

Units purchased	1,000
Division B's variable costs per unit	$95
Division B's fixed cost per unit	$10

1. Will the company as a whole benefit if Division A purchases the units from the outside supplier for $100 per unit? Assume that there are no alternative uses for Division B's facilities.
2. What would be the effect if the outside selling price decreases by $8.00 per unit, assuming that Division B remains idle?
3. If Division B's facilities could be put into production for other sales at an annual cost saving of $14,500, should Division A still purchase from the outside?

SOLUTION

There are two ways of solving this type of alternative-choice transfer pricing problem. One is to utilize the concept of opportunity cost. Using this approach, the questions can be analyzed as follows.

	1.	2.	3.
(*a*) Total purchase costs	$100,000	$92,000	$100,000
Total outlay costs if purchased inside	$ 95,000	$95,000	$ 95,000
Total opportunity costs if purchased inside	—	—	14,500
(*b*) Total relevant costs	$ 95,000	$95,000	$109,500
Net advantage (disadvantage) to company as a whole ($a - b$)	$ 5,000	$ (3,000)	$ (9,500)

Another approach is to use the straightforward comparative income statement approach without the need to discuss the concept of opportunity cost. The questions are analyzed individually as follows.

1.

	Division A's Action	
	Buy Outside	Buy Inside
Total purchase costs	$100,000	—
Total outlay costs	—	$95,000
Net cash outflow to the company as a whole	$100,000	$95,000

The company as a whole will benefit if Division A buys inside.

2.

	Buy Outside	Buy Inside
Total purchase costs	$92,000	—
Total outlay costs	—	$95,000
Net cash outflow to the company as a whole	$92,000	$95,000

The company as a whole will benefit if Division A buys from the outside supplier for $92 per unit.

3.

	Buy Outside	Buy Inside
Total purchase costs	$100,000	—
Total outlay costs	—	$95,000
Revenue (or cash savings) from using Division B's facilities	(14,500)	
Net cash outflow to the company as a whole	$ 85,000	$95,000

In this case, the company as a whole will be better off if Division A buys outside and Division B's facilities are utilized elsewhere.

8.13 The Domino Company has two decentralized divisions, A and B. Division A has always purchased certain units from Division B at $75 per unit. Because Division B plans to raise the price to $100 per unit, Division A desires to purchase these units from outside suppliers for $75 per unit. Division B's costs follow:

Division B's variable costs per unit	$70
Division B's annual fixed costs	$15,000
Division A's purchase	1,000 units

If Division A buys from an outside supplier, the facilities Division B uses to manufacture these units will remain idle. Would it be more profitable for the company to enforce the $100 transfer price than to allow Division A to buy from outside suppliers at $75 per unit?

(AICPA, adapted)

SOLUTION

Total purchase costs	$75,000
Total outlay costs if purchased inside	70,000
Net advantage to the company as a whole	$ 5,000

Therefore, it would be more profitable for the company to enforce the $100 transfer price.

Alternatively,

	Division A's Action	
	Buy Inside	Buy Outside
Total purchase costs	—	$75,000
Total outlay costs	$70,000	—
Net cash outflow to the company as a whole	$70,000	$75,000

8.14 The Caplow Company is a multidivisional company, and its managers have been delegated full profit responsibility and complex autonomy to accept or reject transfers from other divisions. Division A produces a subassembly with a ready competitive market. This subassembly is currently used by Division B for a final product that is sold outside at $1,200. Division A charges

Division B market price for the subassembly, which is $700 per unit. Variable costs are $520 and $600 for Divisions A and B, respectively.

The manager of Division B feels that Division A should transfer the subassembly at a lower price than market because at this price, Division B is unable to make a profit.

1. Compute Division B's profit contribution if transfers are made at the market price, and also the total contribution to profit for the company.
2. Assume that Division A can sell all its production in the open market. Should Division A transfer goods to Division B? If so, at what price?
3. Assume that Division A can sell in the open market only 500 units at $700 per unit out of the 1,000 units that it can produce every month, and that a 20 percent reduction in price is necessary to sell full capacity. Should transfers be made? If so, how many units should it transfer and at what price? Submit a schedule showing comparisons of contribution margins under three different alternatives to support your decision.

(SMA, adapted)

SOLUTION

1.

Selling price of final product		$1,200
Less: Division B's purchased cost	$700	
Division B's variable cost	600	1,300
Division B's loss		$ (100)
Selling price of final product		$1,200
Less: Division B's variable cost	$600	
Division A's variable cost	520	$1,120
Company contribution margin		$ 80

2.

Selling price of subassembly	$ 700
Less: Division A's variable cost	520
Company contribution margin	$ 180

The company contribution is $100 greater if the subassembly is sold on the intermediate market rather than to Division B. Thus it should be sold in the intermediate market. The market price would be the appropriate transfer price if transfers were made.

3. Alternative 1: Transfer 1,000 units to Division B.
Alternative 2: Sell 500 on the intermediate market and transfer 500 units to Division B.
Alternative 3: Sell 1,000 units on the intermediate market.

	Alternative 1	Alternative 2	Alternative 3
Company sales	$1,200,000[a]	$950,000[b]	$560,000[c]
Variable costs	1,120,000[d]	820,000[e]	520,000[f]
Contribution margin	$ 80,000	$130,000	$ 40,000

[a]1,000 @ $1,200
[b]500 @ $700 + 500 @ $1,200
[c]1,000 @ 80% of $700
[d]1,000 @ $520 + $1,000 @ $600
[e]1,000 @ $520 + 500 @ $600
[f]1,000 @ $520

Yes, transfers should be made. Five hundred units should be transferred to Division B. The transfer price should be set at a price greater than the variable cost of Division A ($520) and less than the marginal revenue to Division B ($600).

8.15 The shuttle division of the Tandem Corporation produces circuit boards which are sold to the transistor radio division of the company, as well as to outside buyers. The income statement (in contribution format) for the past year for the division is given below.

	To the Transistor Radio Divison	To Outside Buyers
Sales:		
20,000 units at $3.00	$60,000	
30,000 units at $4.00		$120,000
Variable expenses:		
$1.00	20,000	
$2.00		60,000
Contribution margin	$40,000	$ 60,000
Fixed costs	15,000	30,000
Net income	$25,000	$ 30,000

An outside supplier has just offered the manager of the transistor radio division to supply the circuit boards at $1.75 each. The manager of the shuttle division would not meet this price, arguing that it costs him $1.75 to manufacture and sell each unit of a circuit board. Assume that no additional sales can be made to outside buyers. Answer the following:

1. How did the shuttle division come up with the $1.75 unit cost figure?
2. Is the shuttle division required to meet the outside price of $1.75 for transistor radio sales?
3. Would you meet the $1.75 outside price if you were the manager of the shuttle division?

SOLUTION

1.

Unit variable cost	$1.00
Unit fixed cost ($15,000 ÷ 20,000 units)	0.75
Unit cost	$1.75

2. The answer is no. The manager of the shuttle division should be free to make his own decision, assuming that the shuttle division is an autonomous investment center in a decentralized firm.

3. The manager should still sell to the transistor radio division at the $1.75 price, since this would at least help the division recover the fixed costs of $15,000 allocated to it.

	Sales to the Transistor Radio Division	
	If the $1.75 Price Is Met	If No Sales Are Made
Sales (20,000 units @ $1.75)	$35,000	—
Variable costs @ $1.00	20,000	—
CM	$15,000	—
Fixed costs	15,000	$ 15,000
Net income	$ 0	$(15,000)

8.16 The Safeway division of Amco Products manufactures batteries that it sells primarily to the Alpha-Beta division for inclusion with that division's main product. In 19A, half of the batteries were sold to outside companies at a price of $2 each. The remaining batteries went to the Alpha-Beta division. Cost data for 19B for the Safeway division are given below.

Production	120,000 units
Variable manufacturing costs	$120,000
Fixed overhead	$60,000
Selling expenses (all variable)	$30,000
Administrative expenses (all fixed)	$20,000

1. What should be the transfer price for the batteries if the company uses:
   (*a*) Market price?
   (*b*) Variable cost?
   (*c*) A negotiated transfer price that will yield a markup of 20 percent on its product cost (absorption cost) for Safeway?
2. Prepare a schedule of Safeway division's contribution margin for each of the transfer pricing alternatives computed in part 1.

SOLUTION

1. (*a*) Market price: $2 per unit
   (*b*) Variable cost: ($120,000 + $30,000)/120,000 units = $1.25 per unit
   (*c*) Absorption cost: $120,000 + $60,000 = $180,000
   $180,000/120,000 units = $1.50 per unit

Thus, the negotiated transfer price is:

$1.50 + 20% ($1.50) = $1.50 + $0.30 = $1.80 per unit

2.

Safeway Division's Net Income

	Market Price		Variable Cost		Negotiated Transfer Price	
	Alpha-Beta	Outside Supplier	Alpha-Beta	Outside Supplier	Alpha-Beta	Outside Supplier
Sales:	(60,000 units)	(60,000 units)				
To outside supplier	—	$120,000	—	$120,000	—	$120,000
To Alpha-Beta	$120,000		$75,000		$108,000	
Variable costs:						
Manufacturing	60,000	60,000	60,000	60,000	60,000	60,000
Selling	15,000	15,000	15,000	15,000	15,000	15,000
Contribution margin	$ 45,000	$ 45,000	$ 0	$ 45,000	$ 33,000	$ 45,000
Total divisional CM	$90,000		$45,000		$78,000	

8.17 The Sattle Automobile Company has just acquired a battery division. The company's motor division is presently purchasing 100,000 batteries each year from Bendox Corporation at the price of $24 per battery. Through the acquisition of the battery division top management now feels that the company's motor division should begin to purchase its batteries from the newly acquired battery division. The battery division's cost per battery is as follows:

Direct materials	$12
Direct labor	4
Variable overhead	2
Fixed overhead	2*
Total unit cost	$20

*Based on 250,000 units of capacity of the battery division.

Top management wishes to decide on the transfer price to be charged on the intracompany transfers.

1. Explain why each of the following would or would not be an appropriate transfer price:
   (*a*) $24
   (*b*) $20
   (*c*) $21
   (*d*) $18
2. Assuming that the battery division is operating at full capacity, explain why each of the transfer prices given in parts 1(*a*) through 1(*d*) would or would not be an appropriate price.

SOLUTION

1. (*a*) $24 would not be an appropriate transfer price, since the price charged to the motor division should *not* exceed (or equal) the outside market price which the motor division is presently paying ($24).

   (*b*) $20 would be an appropriate price if top management treats the two divisions as simple cost centers with no profit responsibility. Note that $20 is the full absorption cost and all profits from both divisions will accrue to the motor division.

   (*c*) $21 would be an appropriate transfer price if top management wishes to treat the two divisions as profit or investment centers, but to share the benefits of the intracompany transfer *equally* between them. The $21 price is computed as follows:

Variable costs of the battery division	$18
One-half of the difference between the variable costs and the outside market price, that is, ½ × ($24 − $18) = $3	3
Transfer price	$21

   (*d*) $18 is an appropriate price that guides top management in making a decision as to whether transfers should take place. As long as the battery division has excess capacity, it can go as low as $18, which is the variable cost per unit. Anything above this price will result in a positive CM for the battery division.

2. None of these prices except for $24 is an appropriate transfer price if the battery division is selling all it can produce to outside customers. The reason is that the transfer price should not be lower than the battery division's (the selling division's) opportunity costs. In this problem, the opportunity cost is $24 per unit—the price that can be obtained from outside customers.

8.18 Company Q has three divisions, B, S, and L. It also deals with two other companies, X and Y. Division B can buy a widget from division S or from company X, which will meet S's market price of $200 per unit. If B buys from X, X in turn buys a component from division L for $40 per unit; the outlay costs to division L of supplying this component are $20 per unit. In filling B's order, S incurs outlay costs of $165 per unit. Assume that division S is working at full capacity and can provide the widget to an outside buyer (i.e., company Y) at the same market price of $200 per unit and with the same outlay costs of $165 per unit.

1. What alternative would be the best for company Q as a whole—B buying from company X or division S? Draw the boxes. Show supporting calculations.
2. What transfer price should be used to guide the managers of divisions B and S so as to maximize overall company net income (cash inflow)?
3. Suppose that division S has enough extra capacity to supply the widget to both division B and the outside buyer at the same time. How would this change your answers to parts 1 and 2? Show supporting calculations.

SOLUTION

1. See Fig. 8-3.

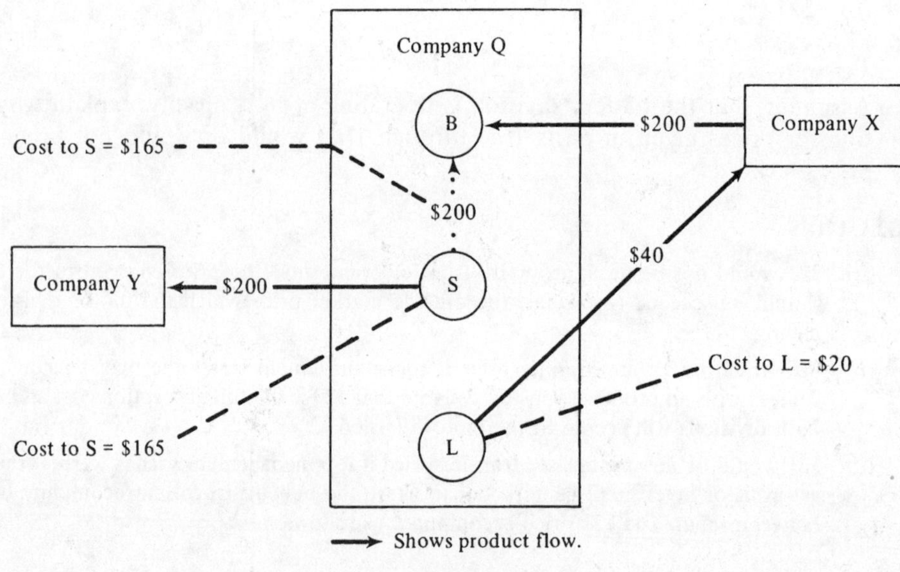

Fig. 8-3

The optimal action from the standpoint of company Q as a whole can be analyzed as follows:

	Division B's Action		
	Buy from Division S	Buy from Company X	
Outflow to the company as a whole	$(165)		$(200)
Cash inflows	—	To division L:	
		($40 – $20)	20
		To division S:	
		($200 – $165)	35
Net cash outflow to the company as a whole	$(165)		$(145)

Since a net outflow of \$145 is less than a net outflow of \$165, division B should buy from company X.

2.

$$\text{Transfer price } (TP) = \text{Variable costs } (VC) + \text{Opportunity costs } (OC)$$
$$= \$165 + \$20 + \$35 = \$220 \text{ per unit}$$

3. In part 1 it was assumed that division S could supply either division B or company Y, but not both. For this reason, an opportunity cost of \$35 (\$200 revenue from company Y − \$165 cost to division S) was included in the calculations. Since division S can now supply both division B and company Y, the \$35 appears on both alternatives as follows:

	Division B's Action		
	Buy from Division S	Buy from Company X	
Outflow to the company as a whole	\$(165)		\$(200)
Cash inflows	35	To division L: ($40 − $20)	20
		To division S: ($200 − $165)	35
Net cash outflow to the company as a whole	\$(130)		\$(145)

Now, since a net outflow of \$130 is less than a net outflow of \$145, division B should buy inside, from division S, to benefit company Q as a whole.

The transfer price will also not reflect the \$35.

$$TP = VC + OC = \$165 + \$20 = \$185$$

Since \$185 is less than the \$200 company X charges division B, division B will choose to buy from division S.

8.19 A. R. Oma, Inc., manufactures a line of men's perfumes and after-shave lotions. The manufacturing process is basically a series of mixing operations with the addition of certain aromatic and coloring ingredients. The finished product is packaged in a company-produced glass bottle and packed in cases containing six bottles.

A. R. Oma feels that the sale of its product is heavily influenced by the appearance and appeal of the bottle and has, therefore, devoted considerable managerial effort to the bottle production process. This has resulted in the development of certain unique bottle production processes in which management takes considerable pride.

The two areas (i.e., perfume production and bottle manufacture) have evolved over the years in an almost independent manner. In fact, a rivalry has developed between management personnel as to which division is more important to A. R. Oma. This attitude is probably intensified because the bottle manufacturing plant was purchased intact 10 years ago and no real interchange of management personnel or ideas (except at the top corporate level) has taken place.

Since the acquisition, all bottle production has been absorbed by the perfume manufacturing plant. Each area is considered a separate profit center and evaluated as such. As the new corporate controller, you are responsible for the definition of a proper transfer value to use in crediting the bottle production profit center and in debiting the packaging profit center.

At your request, the bottle division general manager has asked certain other bottle manufacturers to quote a price for the quantity and sizes (other suppliers) demanded by the perfume division. These competitive prices are:

Volume (Equivalent Cases*)	Total Price	Price per Case
2 million	$ 4 million	$2.00
4 million	$ 7 million	$1.75
6 million	$10 million	$1.67

*An "equivalent case" represents six bottles each.

A cost analysis of the internal bottle plant indicates that they can produce bottles at these costs:

Volume (Equivalent Cases)	Total Price	Price per Case
2 million	$3.2 million	$1.60
4 million	$5.2 million	$1.30
6 million	$7.2 million	$1.20

(Your cost analysts point out that these costs represent fixed costs of $1.2 million and variable costs of $1.00 per equivalent case.)

These figures have given rise to considerable corporate discussion as to the proper value to use in the transfer of bottles to the perfume division. This interest is heightened because a significant portion of a division manager's income is an incentive bonus based on profit center results.

The perfume production division has the following costs in addition to the bottle costs:

Volume (Cases)	Total Cost	Cost per Case
2 million	$16.4 million	$8.20
4 million	$32.4 million	$8.10
6 million	$48.4 million	$8.07

After considerable analysis, the marketing research department has furnished you with the following price–demand relationship for the finished product:

Sales Volume (Cases)	Total Sales Revenue	Price per Case
2 million	$25 million	$12.50
4 million	$45.6 million	$11.40
6 million	$63.9 million	$10.65

1. The A. R. Oma Company has used market price transfer prices in the past. Using the current market prices and costs, and assuming a volume of 6 million cases, calculate the income for
   (*a*) The bottle division
   (*b*) The perfume division
   (*c*) The corporation
2. Is this production and sales level the most profitable volume for
   (*a*) The bottle division?
   (*b*) The perfume division?
   (*c*) The corporation?

   Explain your answer.

3. The A. R. Oma Company uses the profit center concept for divisional operation.
   (*a*) What conditions should exist for a profit center to be established?
   (*b*) Should the two divisions of the A. R. Oma Company be organized as profit centers?

(CMA, adapted)

SOLUTION

(000 omitted in all calculations.)

1. (*a*) The bottle division profits:

Revenue	$10,000
Cost	7,200
Profit	$ 2,800

(*b*) The perfume division profits:

Revenue	$63,900
Cost	58,400 ($48,400 + $10,000)
Profit	$ 5,500

(*c*) The corporation profits:

Revenue	$63,900
Cost	55,600 ($48,400 + $7,200)
Profit	$ 8,300

2. (*a*) Yes.

	Volume		
Cases	2,000	4,000	6,000
Revenue	$4,000	$7,000	$10,000
Cost	3,200	5,200	7,200
Profit	$ 800	$1,800	$ 2,800*

(*b*) No.

	Volume		
Cases	2,000	4,000	6,000
Revenue	$25,000	$45,600	$63,900
Cost	20,400	39,400	58,400
Profit	$ 4,600	$ 6,200*	$ 5,500

(*c*) Yes.

	Volume		
Cases	2,000	4,000	6,000
Revenue	$25,000	$45,600	$63,900
Cost	19,600	37,600	55,600
Profit	$ 5,400	$ 8,000	$ 8,300*

*Highest profit.

This apparent inconsistency, where the bottle division and the corporation are the most profitable at

6 million volume and the perfume division is most profitable at 4 million volume, comes from the cost and revenues changing differently for the bottle division, perfume division, and the total corporation as volume changes. Based on market price transfer value, the divisions achieve maximum profit for themselves at different levels of sales based on the market price at the various levels relative to the division cost of these various levels. The corporation achieves maximum profit based on the selling price to outsiders relative to the total cost of making the product.

3. (*a*) Some of the conditions that should exist are:
   - Proper organization attitudes for decentralized operations.
   - The division level (or segment) must have freedom and independence so that it can buy outside the company when it is to its advantage to do so.
   - Other sources that are willing to quote a price for the quantity and sizes demanded.
   - Freedom to sell to outside parties.
   - Revenues and costs of the segment must be distinguishable from revenues and costs of other segments.

   (*b*) The bottle division should not be organized as a profit center. The bottle division makes special bottles for the perfume division and, therefore, it does not have an opportunity to sell to outside parties.

   The perfume division could be treated as a profit center. There are other manufacturers that are willing to quote a price for the quantity and sizes demanded by the perfume division and the perfume division sells to the outside.

8.20 The Ajax division of Gunnco Corporation, operating at capacity, has been asked by the Defco division of Gunnco to supply it with electrical fitting no. 1726. Ajax sells this part to its regular customers for \$7.50 each. Defco, which is operating at 50 percent capacity, is willing to pay \$5 each for the fitting. Defco will put the fitting into a brake unit that it is manufacturing on essentially a cost-plus basis for a commercial airplane manufacturer.

Ajax has a variable cost of producing fitting no. 1726 of \$4.25. The cost of the brake unit as being built by Defco follows:

Purchased parts (outside vendors)	\$22.50
Ajax fitting no. 1726	5.00
Other variable costs	14.00
Fixed overhead and administration	8.00
	\$49.50

Defco believes the price concession is necessary to get the job.

The company uses return on investment and dollar profits in the measurement of division and division manager performance.

1. Assume that you are the division controller of Ajax. Would you recommend that Ajax supply fitting no. 1726 to Defco? Why or why not? (Ignore any tax issues.)
2. Would it be to the short-run economic advantage of the Gunnco Corporation for the Ajax division to supply the Defco division with fitting no. 1726 at \$5 each? (Ignore any tax issues.)
3. Discuss the organizational and manager-behavior difficulties, if any, inherent in this situation.

As the Gunnco controller, what would you advise the Gunnco Corporation president do in this situation?

(CMA, adapted)

SOLUTION

1. The division controller should not recommend that Ajax supply Defco with fitting no. 1726 for the $5.00 per unit price. Ajax is operating at capacity and would lose $2.50 ($7.50 − $5.00) for each fitting sold to Defco. The management performance of Ajax is measured by return on investment and dollar profits; selling to Defco at $5.00 per unit would adversely affect those performance measures.
2. Gunnco would be $5.50 better off, in the short run, if Ajax supplied Defco the fitting for $5.00 and the brake unit was sold for $49.50. Assuming the $8.00 per unit for fixed overhead and administration represents an allocation of cost Defco incurs regardless of the brake unit order, Gunnco would lose $2.50 in cash flow for each fitting sold to Defco but gain $8.00 from each brake unit sold by Defco.
3. In the short run there is an advantage to the company as a whole of transferring the fitting at the $5.00 price and thus selling the brake unit for $49.50. In order to make this happen, Gunnco will have to overrule the decision of the Ajax management.

   This action would be counter to the purposes of decentralized decision making. If such action were necessary on a regular basis, the decentralized decision making inherent in the divisionalized organization would be a sham. Then the organization structure is inappropriate for the situation.

   On the other hand, if this is an occurrence of relative infrequency, the intervention of corporate management will not indicate inadequate organization structure. It may, however, create problems with division managements. In the case at hand, if Gunnco management requires that the fitting be transferred at $5.00, the result will be to enhance Defco's operating results at the expense of Ajax. This certainly is not in keeping with the concept that a manager's performance should be measured on the results achieved by the decisions he or she controls.

   In this case, it appears that Ajax and Defco serve different markets and do not represent closely related operating units. Ajax operates at capacity, Defco does not; no mention is made of any other interdivisional business. Therefore, the Gunnco controller should recommend that each division be free to act in accordance with its best interests. The company is better served in the long run if Ajax is permitted to continue dealing with its regular customers at the market price of $7.50. If Defco is having difficulties, the solution does not lie with temporary help at the expense of another division, but with a more substantive and long-term course of action.

Capital Budgeting

9.1 CAPITAL BUDGETING DECISIONS DEFINED

Capital budgeting is the process of making long-term planning decisions for investments. There are typically two types of investment decisions:

1. Selection decisions in terms of obtaining new facilities or expanding existing facilities. Examples include:
   (*a*) Investments in long-term assets such as property, plant, and equipment
   (*b*) Resource commitments in the form of new product development, market research, refunding of long-term debt, introduction of a computer, etc.
2. Replacement decisions in terms of replacing existing facilities with new facilities. Examples include replacing a manual bookkeeping system with a computerized system and replacing an inefficient lathe with one that is numerically controlled.

9.2 CAPITAL BUDGETING TECHNIQUES

There are several methods of evaluating investment projects. They are:

1. Payback period
2. Accounting rate of return (ARR) (also called *simple rate of return*)
3. Net present value (NPV)
4. Internal rate of return (IRR) (also called *time-adjusted rate of return*)
5. Profitability index (also called the *excess present value index*)

The NPV method and the IRR method are called *discounted cash flow* (*DCF*) methods, since they both recognize the time value of money and thus discount future cash flows. Each of the methods presented above is discussed below.

PAYBACK PERIOD

Payback period measures the length of time required to recover the amount of initial investment. The payback period is determined by dividing the amount of initial investment by the cash inflow through increased revenues or cost savings.

EXAMPLE 9.1 Assume:

Cost of investment	\$18,000
Annual cash savings	\$ 3,000

Then, the payback period is:

$$\frac{\$18{,}000}{\$3{,}000} = 6 \text{ years}$$

When cash inflows are not even, the payback period is determined by trial and error. When two or more projects are considered, the rule for making a selection decision is as follows:

Decision rule: Choose the project with the shorter payback period. The rationale behind this is: The shorter the payback period, the less risky the project, and the greater the liquidity.

EXAMPLE 9.2 Consider two projects whose cash inflows are not even. Assume that each project costs \$1,000.

Year	A	B
1	\$100	\$500
2	200	400
3	300	300
4	400	100
5	500	—
6	600	—

Based on trial and error, the payback period of project A is four years (\$100 + \$200 + \$300 + \$400 = \$1,000 in four years). The payback period of project B is

$$2 \text{ years} + \frac{\$100}{\$300} = 2\tfrac{1}{3} \text{ years}$$

Therefore, according to this method, choose project B over project A.

Advantages of the payback period method:

1. It is simple to compute and easy to understand.
2. It handles investment risk effectively.

Shortcomings of the payback period method:

1. It does not recognize the time value of money.
2. It ignores the impact of cash inflows after the payback period. It is essentially cash flows after the payback period which determine profitability of an investment.

ACCOUNTING (SIMPLE) RATE OF RETURN

Accounting rate of return (ARR) measures profitability from the conventional accounting standpoint by relating the required investment to the future annual net income. Sometimes the former is the average investment.

Decision rule: Under the ARR method, choose the project with the higher rate of return.

EXAMPLE 9.3 Consider the investment:

Initial investment	$6,500
Estimated life	20 years
Cash inflows per year	$1,000
Depreciation by straight line	$ 325

Then,

$$ARR = \frac{\$1,000 - \$325}{\$6,500} = 10.4\%$$

Using the *average* investment, which is usually assumed to be one-half of the original investment, the resulting rate of return will be doubled:

$$ARR = \frac{\$1,000 - \$325}{\frac{1}{2}(\$6,500)} = \frac{\$675}{\$3,250} = 20.8\%$$

The justification for using the average investment is that each year the investment amount is decreased by $325 through depreciation, and therefore the average is computed as one-half of the original cost.

Advantages: The method is easily understandable and simple to compute, and recognizes the profitability factor.

Shortcomings:

1. It fails to recognize the time value of money.
2. It uses accounting data instead of cash flow data.

NET PRESENT VALUE

Net present value (NPV) is the excess of the present value (PV) of cash inflows generated by the project over the amount of initial investment (I). Simply, $NPV = PV - I$. The present value of future cash flows is computed using the so-called cost of capital (or minimum required rate of return) as the discount rate.

Decision rule: If NPV is positive, accept the project. Otherwise, reject.

EXAMPLE 9.4

Initial investment	$12,950
Estimated life	10 years
Annual cash inflows	$ 3,000
Cost of capital (minimum required rate of return)	12%

Present value of cash inflows (PV):	
$3,000 × PV of annuity of $1 for 10 years and 12% [=$3,000 (5.65)]	$16,950
Initial investment (I)	12,950
Net present value ($NPV = PV - I$)	$ 4,000

Since the investment's NPV is positive, the investment should be accepted.

Advantages: The NPV method obviously recognizes the time value of money and is easy to compute whether the cash flows form an annuity or vary from period to period.

Disadvantage: It requires detailed long-term forecasts of incremental cash flow data.

For the purpose of computing present value of future cash flows, two tables are provided below.

Table 9-1—Present Value of $1

Table 9-2—Present Value of an Annuity of $1

INTERNAL RATE OF RETURN (OR TIME-ADJUSTED RATE OF RETURN)

Internal rate of return (IRR) is defined as the rate of interest that equates I with the PV of future cash inflows. In other words, at IRR, $I = PV$, or $NPV = 0$.

Decision rule: Accept if IRR exceeds the cost of capital; otherwise, reject.

EXAMPLE 9.5 Assume the same data given in Example 9.4. We will set up the following equality ($I = PV$):

$$\$12{,}950 = \$3{,}000 \times \text{PV factor}$$

$$\text{PV factor} = \frac{\$12{,}950}{\$3{,}000} = 4.317$$

which stands somewhere between 18 percent and 20 percent in the 10-year line of Table 9-2. Using the interpolation as follows:

	PV Factor	
18%	4.494	4.494
IRR		4.317
20%	4.192	
Difference	0.302	0.177

Therefore, $$IRR = 18\% + \frac{0.177}{0.302}(20\% - 18\%) = 18\% + 0.586(2\%) = 18\% + 1.17\% = 19.17\%$$

Since the investment's IRR is greater than the cost of capital (12 percent), the investment should be accepted.

Advantages: It does consider the time value of money and is therefore more exact and realistic than ARR.

Shortcomings:

1. It is difficult to compute, especially when the cash inflows are not even.
2. It fails to recognize the varying size of investment in competing projects and their respective dollar profitabilities.

The trial-and-error method for computing IRR when cash inflows are not even is summarized, step by step, as follows:

1. Compute NPV at the cost of capital, denoted here as r_1,
2. See if NPV is positive or negative.
3. If NPV is positive, then pick another rate (r_2) much higher than r_1. If NPV is negative, then pick another rate (r_2) much smaller than r_1. The true IRR at which $NPV = 0$ must be somewhere in between these two rates.
4. Compute NPV using r_2.
5. Use interpolation for the exact rate.

Table 9-1 Present Value of $1

Periods	4%	5%	6%	8%	10%	12%	14%	16%	18%	20%	22%	24%	26%	28%	30%	40%
1	0.962	0.952	0.943	0.926	0.909	0.893	0.877	0.862	0.847	0.833	0.820	0.806	0.794	0.781	0.769	0.714
2	0.925	0.907	0.890	0.857	0.826	0.797	0.769	0.743	0.718	0.694	0.672	0.650	0.630	0.610	0.592	0.510
3	0.889	0.864	0.840	0.794	0.751	0.712	0.675	0.641	0.609	0.579	0.551	0.524	0.500	0.477	0.455	0.364
4	0.855	0.823	0.792	0.735	0.683	0.636	0.592	0.552	0.516	0.482	0.451	0.423	0.397	0.373	0.350	0.260
5	0.822	0.784	0.747	0.681	0.621	0.567	0.519	0.476	0.437	0.402	0.370	0.341	0.315	0.291	0.269	0.186
6	0.790	0.746	0.705	0.630	0.564	0.507	0.456	0.410	0.370	0.335	0.303	0.275	0.250	0.227	0.207	0.133
7	0.760	0.711	0.665	0.583	0.513	0.452	0.400	0.354	0.314	0.279	0.249	0.222	0.198	0.178	0.159	0.095
8	0.731	0.677	0.627	0.540	0.467	0.404	0.351	0.305	0.266	0.233	0.204	0.179	0.157	0.139	0.123	0.068
9	0.703	0.645	0.592	0.500	0.424	0.361	0.308	0.263	0.225	0.194	0.167	0.144	0.125	0.108	0.094	0.048
10	0.676	0.614	0.558	0.463	0.386	0.322	0.270	0.227	0.191	0.162	0.137	0.116	0.099	0.085	0.073	0.035
11	0.650	0.585	0.527	0.429	0.350	0.287	0.237	0.195	0.162	0.135	0.112	0.094	0.079	0.066	0.056	0.025
12	0.625	0.557	0.497	0.397	0.319	0.257	0.208	0.168	0.137	0.112	0.092	0.076	0.062	0.052	0.043	0.018
13	0.601	0.530	0.469	0.368	0.290	0.229	0.182	0.145	0.116	0.093	0.075	0.061	0.050	0.040	0.033	0.013
14	0.577	0.505	0.442	0.340	0.263	0.205	0.160	0.125	0.099	0.078	0.062	0.049	0.039	0.032	0.025	0.009
15	0.555	0.481	0.417	0.315	0.239	0.183	0.140	0.108	0.084	0.065	0.051	0.040	0.031	0.025	0.020	0.006
16	0.534	0.458	0.394	0.292	0.218	0.163	0.123	0.093	0.071	0.054	0.042	0.032	0.025	0.019	0.015	0.005
17	0.513	0.436	0.371	0.270	0.198	0.146	0.108	0.080	0.060	0.045	0.034	0.026	0.020	0.015	0.012	0.003
18	0.494	0.416	0.350	0.250	0.180	0.130	0.095	0.069	0.051	0.038	0.028	0.021	0.016	0.012	0.009	0.002
19	0.475	0.396	0.331	0.232	0.164	0.116	0.083	0.060	0.043	0.031	0.023	0.017	0.012	0.009	0.007	0.002
20	0.456	0.377	0.312	0.215	0.149	0.104	0.073	0.051	0.037	0.026	0.019	0.014	0.010	0.007	0.005	0.001
21	0.439	0.359	0.294	0.199	0.135	0.093	0.064	0.044	0.031	0.022	0.015	0.011	0.008	0.006	0.004	0.001
22	0.422	0.342	0.278	0.184	0.123	0.083	0.056	0.038	0.026	0.018	0.013	0.009	0.006	0.004	0.003	0.001
23	0.406	0.326	0.262	0.170	0.112	0.074	0.049	0.033	0.022	0.015	0.010	0.007	0.005	0.003	0.002	
24	0.390	0.310	0.247	0.158	0.102	0.066	0.043	0.028	0.019	0.013	0.008	0.006	0.004	0.003	0.002	
25	0.375	0.295	0.233	0.146	0.092	0.059	0.038	0.024	0.016	0.010	0.007	0.005	0.003	0.002	0.001	
26	0.361	0.281	0.220	0.135	0.084	0.053	0.033	0.021	0.014	0.009	0.006	0.004	0.002	0.002	0.001	
27	0.347	0.268	0.207	0.125	0.076	0.047	0.029	0.018	0.011	0.007	0.005	0.003	0.002	0.001	0.001	
28	0.333	0.255	0.196	0.116	0.069	0.042	0.026	0.016	0.010	0.006	0.004	0.002	0.002	0.001	0.001	
29	0.321	0.243	0.185	0.107	0.063	0.037	0.022	0.014	0.008	0.005	0.003	0.002	0.001	0.001	0.001	
30	0.308	0.231	0.174	0.099	0.057	0.033	0.020	0.012	0.007	0.004	0.003	0.002	0.001	0.001		
40	0.208	0.142	0.097	0.046	0.022	0.011	0.005	0.003	0.001	0.001						

Table 9-2 Present Value of Annuity of $1

Periods	4%	5%	6%	8%	10%	12%	14%	16%	18%	20%	22%	24%	26%	28%	30%	40%
1	0.962	0.952	0.943	0.926	0.909	0.893	0.877	0.862	0.847	0.833	0.820	0.806	0.794	0.781	0.769	0.714
2	1.886	1.859	1.833	1.783	1.736	1.690	1.647	1.605	1.566	1.528	1.492	1.457	1.424	1.392	1.361	1.224
3	2.775	2.723	2.673	2.577	2.487	2.240	2.322	2.246	2.174	2.106	2.042	1.981	1.868	1.816	1.816	1.589
4	3.630	3.546	3.465	3.312	3.170	3.037	2.914	2.798	2.690	2.589	2.494	2.404	2.320	2.241	2.166	1.879
5	4.452	4.330	4.212	3.993	3.791	3.605	3.433	3.274	3.127	2.991	2.864	2.745	2.635	2.532	2.436	2.035
6	5.242	5.076	4.917	4.623	4.355	4.111	3.889	3.685	3.498	3.326	3.167	3.020	2.885	2.759	2.643	2.168
7	6.002	5.786	5.582	5.206	4.868	4.564	4.288	4.039	3.812	3.605	3.416	3.242	3.083	2.937	2.802	2.263
8	6.733	6.463	6.210	5.747	5.335	4.968	4.639	4.344	4.078	3.837	3.619	3.421	3.241	3.076	2.925	2.331
9	7.435	7.108	6.802	6.247	5.759	5.328	4.946	4.607	4.303	4.031	3.786	3.566	3.366	3.184	3.019	2.379
10	8.111	7.722	7.360	6.710	6.145	5.650	5.216	4.833	4.494	4.192	3.923	3.682	3.465	3.269	3.092	2.414
11	8.760	8.306	7.887	7.139	6.495	5.988	5.453	5.029	4.656	4.327	4.035	3.776	3.544	3.335	3.147	2.438
12	9.385	8.863	8.384	7.536	6.814	6.194	5.660	5.197	4.793	4.439	4.127	3.851	3.606	3.387	3.190	2.456
13	9.986	9.394	8.853	7.904	7.103	6.424	5.842	5.342	4.910	4.533	4.203	3.912	3.656	3.427	3.223	2.468
14	10.563	9.899	9.295	8.244	7.367	6.628	6.002	5.468	5.008	4.611	4.265	3.962	3.695	3.459	3.249	2.477
15	11.118	10.380	9.712	8.559	7.606	6.811	6.142	5.575	5.092	4.675	4.315	4.001	3.726	3.483	3.268	2.484
16	11.652	10.838	10.106	8.851	7.824	6.974	6.265	5.669	5.162	4.730	4.357	4.033	3.751	3.503	3.283	2.489
17	12.166	11.274	10.477	9.122	8.022	7.120	6.373	5.749	5.222	4.775	4.391	4.059	3.771	3.518	3.295	2.492
18	12.659	11.690	10.828	9.372	8.201	7.250	6.467	5.818	5.273	4.812	4.419	4.080	3.786	3.529	3.304	2.494
19	13.134	12.085	11.158	9.604	8.365	7.366	6.550	5.877	5.316	4.844	4.442	4.097	3.799	3.539	3.311	2.496
20	13.590	12.462	11.470	9.818	8.514	7.469	6.623	5.929	5.353	4.870	4.460	4.110	3.808	3.546	3.316	2.497
21	14.029	12.821	11.764	10.017	8.649	7.562	6.687	5.973	5.384	4.891	4.476	4.121	3.816	3.551	3.320	2.498
22	14.451	13.163	12.042	10.201	8.772	7.645	6.743	6.011	5.410	4.909	4.488	4.130	3.822	3.556	3.323	2.498
23	14.857	13.489	12.303	10.371	8.883	7.718	6.792	6.044	5.432	4.925	4.499	4.137	3.827	3.559	3.325	2.499
24	15.247	13.799	12.550	10.529	8.985	7.784	6.835	6.073	5.451	4.937	4.507	4.143	3.831	3.562	3.327	2.499
25	15.622	14.094	12.783	10.675	9.077	7.843	6.873	6.097	5.467	4.948	4.514	4.147	3.834	3.564	3.329	2.499
26	15.983	14.375	13.003	10.810	9.161	7.896	6.906	6.118	5.480	4.956	4.520	4.151	3.837	3.566	3.330	2.500
27	16.330	14.643	13.211	10.935	9.237	7.943	6.935	6.136	5.492	4.964	4.525	4.154	3.839	3.567	3.331	2.500
28	16.663	14.898	13.406	11.051	9.307	7.984	6.961	6.152	5.502	4.970	4.528	4.157	3.840	3.568	3.331	2.500
29	16.984	15.141	13.591	11.158	9.370	8.022	6.983	6.166	5.510	4.975	4.531	4.159	3.841	3.569	3.332	2.500
30	17.292	15.373	13.765	11.258	9.427	8.055	7.003	6.177	5.517	4.979	4.534	4.160	3.842	3.569	3.332	2.500
40	19.793	17.159	15.046	11.925	9.779	8.244	7.105	6.234	5.548	4.997	4.544	4.166	3.846	3.571	3.333	2.500

EXAMPLE 9.6 Consider the following investment whose cash flows are different from year to year:

Year	Cash Inflows
1	$1,000
2	2,500
3	1,500

Assume that the amount of initial investment is $3,000 and the cost of capital is 14 percent.

Step 1 NPV at 14 percent:

Year	Cash Inflows	PV Factor at 14%	Total PV
1	$1,000	0.877	$ 877
2	2,500	0.769	1,923
3	1,500	0.675	1,013
			$3,813

Thus, $NPV = \$3{,}813 - \$3{,}000 = \$813$

Step 2 We see that $NPV = \$813$ is positive at $r_1 = 14$ percent.

Step 3 Pick, say, 30 percent as r_2 to play safe.

Step 4 Computing NPV at $r_2 = 30$ percent:

Year	Cash Inflows	PV Factor at 30%	Total PV
1	$1,000	0.769	$ 769
2	2,500	0.592	1,480
3	1,500	0.455	683
			$2,932

Thus, $NPV = \$2{,}932 - \$3{,}000 = \$(68)$

Step 5 Interpolating:

	NPV	
14%	$813	$813
IRR		0
30%	−68	
Difference	$881	$813

Therefore, $IRR = 14\% + \frac{\$813}{\$881}(30\% - 14\%) = 14\% + 0.923(16\%) = 14\% + 14.76\% = 28.76\%$

SUMMARY OF DECISION RULES USING NPV AND IRR METHODS

Net present value (NPV):

1. Calculate the NPV, using the cost of capital as the discount rate.
2. If the NPV is positive, accept the project; otherwise, reject the project.

Internal rate of return (IRR):

1. Using present value tables, compute the IRR by trial-and-error interpolation.
2. If this rate of return exceeds the cost of capital, accept the project; if not, reject the project.

PROFITABILITY INDEX (OR EXCESS PRESENT VALUE INDEX)

The profitability index is the ratio of the total PV of future cash inflows to the initial investment, that is, *PV/I*. This index is used as a means of ranking projects in descending order of attractiveness. If the profitability index is greater than 1, then accept.

EXAMPLE 9.7 Using the data in Example 9.4, the profitability index *PV/I* is \$16,950/\$12,950 = 1.31. Since this project generates \$1.31 for each dollar invested (or its profitability index is greater than 1), the project should be accepted.

9.3 MUTUALLY EXCLUSIVE INVESTMENTS

Projects are said to be *mutually exclusive* if the acceptance of one project automatically excludes the acceptance of the other. In the case where one must choose between mutually exclusive investments, the NPV and IRR methods may give decision results that contradict each other. The conditions under which contradictory rankings can occur are:

1. Projects have different expected lives.
2. Projects have different size of investment.
3. The timing of the projects' cash flows differs. For example, the cash flows of one project increase over time, while those of the other decrease.

The contradiction results from different assumptions with respect to the reinvestment rate on cash flows released from the projects.

(*a*) The NPV method discounts all cash flows at the cost of capital, thus implicitly assuming that these cash flows can be reinvested at this rate.

(*b*) The IRR method implies a reinvestment rate at IRR. Thus, the implied reinvestment rate will differ from project to project.

The NPV method generally gives correct ranking, since the cost of capital is a more realistic reinvestment rate.

EXAMPLE 9.8 Assume the following:

	Cash Flows					
	0	1	2	3	4	5
A	$(100)	$120	—	—	—	—
B	(100)	—	—	—	—	$201.14

Computing IRR and NPV at 10 percent gives the different rankings as follows:

	IRR	NPV at 10%
A	*20%**	9.09
B	15%	*24.90**

*Highest profit.

The general rule is to go by NPV ranking. Thus project B would be chosen over project A.

9.4 CAPITAL RATIONING

Many firms specify a limit on the overall budget for capital spending. *Capital rationing* is concerned with the problem of selecting the mix of acceptable projects that provides the *highest overall NPV* in such a case. The profitability index is used widely in ranking projects competing for limited funds.

EXAMPLE 9.9

Projects	I	PV	Profitability Index	Ranking
A	\$ 70,000	\$112,000	1.6	1
B	100,000	145,000	1.45	2
C	110,000	126,500	1.15	5
D	60,000	79,000	1.32	3
E	40,000	38,000	0.95	6
F	80,000	95,000	1.19	4

Assume that the company's fixed budget is \$250,000. Using the profitability index, we select projects A, B, and D:

	I	PV
A	\$ 70,000	\$112,000
B	100,000	145,000
D	60,000	79,000
	\$230,000	\$336,000

where NPV = \$336,000 − \$230,000 = \$106,000.

9.5 INCOME TAX FACTORS

Income taxes make a difference in many capital budgeting decisions. In other words, the project which is attractive on a pretax basis may have to be rejected on an after-tax basis. Income taxes typically affect both the amount and the timing of cash flows. Since net income, not cash inflows, is subject to tax, after-tax cash inflows are not usually the same as after-tax net income.

Let us define:

S = Sales
E = Cash operating expenses
d = Depreciation
t = Tax rate

Then, before-tax cash inflows = $S - E$ and net income = $S - E - d$.

By definition,

$$\text{After-tax cash inflow} = \text{Before-tax cash inflow} - \text{Taxes}$$
$$\text{After-tax cash inflow} = (S - E) - (S - E - d)(t)$$

Rearranging gives the *short-cut formula*:

$$\text{After-tax cash inflow} = (S - E)(1 - t) + (d)(t)$$

As can be seen, the deductibility of depreciation from sales in arriving at net income subject to taxes *reduces* income tax payments and thus serves as a *tax shield*.

$$\text{Tax shield} = \text{Tax savings on depreciation} = (d)(t)$$

EXAMPLE 9.10 Assume:

$$S = \$12{,}000$$
$$E = \$10{,}000$$
$$d = \$500\text{/year by straight-line}$$
$$t = 40\%$$

Then,

$$\text{After-tax cash inflow} = (\$12{,}000 - \$10{,}000)(1 - 0.4) + (\$500)(0.4)$$
$$= \$1{,}200 + \$200 = \$1{,}400$$

Note that a Tax shield = Tax savings on depreciation = $(d)(t)$ = ($500) (0.4) = $200.

After-tax cash *outflow* would be similarly computed by simply dropping S in the previous formula. Therefore,

$$\text{After-tax cash } \textit{outflow} = (-E)(1-t) + (d)(t)$$

EXAMPLE 9.11 Assume:

$$E = \$6{,}000$$
$$d = \$800\text{/year by straight-line}$$
$$t = 40\%$$

Then,

$$\text{After-tax cash } \textit{outflow} = (-\$6{,}000)(1 - 0.4) + (\$800)(0.4) = -\$3{,}600 + \$320 = -\$3{,}280 = \$3{,}280$$

Since the tax shield is $d \times t$, the higher the depreciation deduction, the higher the tax savings on depreciation. Therefore, the accelerated depreciation methods such as the double-declining-balance method and the sum-of-the-years'-digits methods produce higher tax savings than the straight-line method. They will produce higher present values for the tax savings, which greatly affect investment decisions.

EXAMPLE 9.12 We will now look at the present values of tax shield effects of alternative depreciation methods. Assume:

Initial investment	$100,000
Estimated life	4 years
Salvage value	0
Cost of capital after taxes	15%
Tax rate	40%

(*a*) *Straight-line depreciation:*

		15% PV Factor	PV of Tax Savings
Annual depreciation ($100,000 ÷ 4 = $25,000):			
Depreciation deduction	$25,000		
Multiply by 40%	× 40%		
Income tax savings, years 1–4	$10,000	2.855	$28,550

(*b*) *Sum-of-the-years'-digits depreciation:*

Year	Multiplier*	Depreciation Deduction	Tax Shield: Income Tax Savings at 40%	15% PV Factor	PV of Tax Savings
1	4/10	$40,000	$16,000	0.870	$13,920
2	3/10	30,000	12,000	0.756	9,072
3	2/10	20,000	8,000	0.658	5,264
4	1/10	10,000	4,000	0.572	2,288
					$30,544

*The denominator for the sum-of-the-years'-digits method is $1+2+3+4=10$ or

$$S=\frac{n(n+1)}{2}=\frac{4(4+1)}{2}=10$$

where:

S = sum of the years
n = life of the asset

(*c*) *Double-declining-balance depreciation:*

Year	Book Value	Rate* (%)	Depreciation Deduction	Tax Shield: Income Tax Savings at 40%	15% PV Factor	PV of Tax Savings
1	$100,000	50	$50,000	$20,000	0.870	$17,400
2	50,000	50	25,000	10,000	0.756	7,560
3	25,000	50	12,500	5,000	0.658	3,290
4	12,500	50	12,500†	5,000	0.572	2,860
						$31,110

*The percentage rate for the double-declining-balance method is 2 × straight-line rate = 2 × 25% = 50%.
†The asset is depreciated to zero salvage value in the fourth year.

9.6 CAPITAL BUDGETING DECISIONS AND THE MODIFIED ACCELERATED COST RECOVERY SYSTEM (MACRS)

Although the traditional depreciation methods still can be used for computing depreciation for book purposes, 1981 saw a new way of computing depreciation deductions for tax purposes. The current rule is called the *Modified Accelerated Cost Recovery System* (MACRS) rule, as enacted by Congress in 1981 and then modified somewhat in 1986 under the Tax Reform Act of 1986. This rule is characterized as follows:

1. It abandons the concept of useful life and accelerates depreciation deductions by placing all depreciable assets into one of eight property age classes. It calculates deductions based on an allowable percentage of the asset's original cost (see Tables 9-3 and 9-4).

   With a shorter asset tax life than useful life, the company can deduct depreciation more quickly and save more in income taxes in the earlier years, thereby making an investment more attractive. The rationale behind the system is that this way the government encourages companies to invest in facilities and increase productive capacity and efficiency. [Remember that the higher d is, the larger the tax shield $(d)(t)$ is.]

Table 9-3 Modified Accelerated Cost Recovery System Classification of Assets

	Property class					
Year	3-year	5-year	7-year	10-year	15-year	20-year
1	33.3%	20.0%	14.3%	10.0%	5.0%	3.8%
2	44.5	32.0	24.5	18.0	9.5	7.2
3	14.8*	19.2	17.5	14.4	8.6	6.7
4	7.4	11.5*	12.5	11.5	7.7	6.2
5		11.5	8.9*	9.2	6.9	5.7
6		5.8	8.9	7.4	6.2	5.3
7			8.9	6.6*	5.9*	4.9
8			4.5	6.6	5.9	4.5*
9				6.5	5.9	4.5
10				6.5	5.9	4.5
11				3.3	5.9	4.5
12					5.9	4.5
13					5.9	4.5
14					5.9	4.5
15					5.9	4.5
16					3.0	4.4
17						4.4
18						4.4
19						4.4
20						4.4
21						2.2
Total	100%	100%	100%	100%	100%	100%

*Denotes the year of changeover to straight-line depreciation.

2. Since the allowable percentages in Table 9-3 add up to 100%, there is no need to consider the salvage value of an asset in computing depreciation.
3. A company may elect to use the straight-line method. The straight-line convention must follow what is called the *half-year convention*. This means that the company can deduct only half of the regular straight-line depreciation amount in the first year. The reason for electing to use the MACRS optional straight-line method is that some firms may prefer to stretch out depreciation deductions using the straight-line method rather than to accelerate them. Those firms are usually ones that are just starting out or have little or no income and wish to show more income on their income statements.

EXAMPLE 9.13 Assume that a machine falls under a 3-year property class and costs $3,000 initially. The straight-line option under MACRS differs from the traditional straight-line method in that under this method the company can deduct only $500 depreciation in the first year and the fourth year ($3,000/3 years = $1,000; $1,000/2 = $500). The following table compares the straight line with half-year convention with the MACRS.

Table 9-4 MACRS by Property Class

MACRS Property Class and Depreciation Method	Useful Life (ADR Midpoint Life)*	Examples of Assets
3-year property, 200% declining balance	4 years or less	Most small tools are included; the law specifically excludes autos and light trucks from this property class.
5-year property, 200% declining balance	More than 4 years to less than 10 years	Autos and light trucks, computers, typewriters, copiers, duplicating equipment, heavy general-purpose trucks, and research and experimentation equipment are included.
7-year property, 200% declining balance	10 years or more to less than 16 years	Office furniture and fixtures and most items of machinery and equipment used in production are included.
10-year property, 200% declining balance	16 years or more to less than 20 years	Various machinery and equipment, such as that used in petroleum distilling and refining and in the milling of grain, are included.
15-year property, 150% declining balance	20 years or more to less than 25 years	Sewage treatment plants, telephone and electrical distribution facilities, and land improvements are included.
20-year property, 150% declining balance	25 years or more	Service stations and other real property with an ADR midpoint life of less than 27.5 years are included.
27.5-year property, straight-line	Not applicable	All residential rental property is included.
31.5-year property, straight-line	Not applicable	All nonresidential real property is included.

*"ADR midpoint life" means the "useful life" of an asset in a business sense; the appropriate ADR midpoint lives for assets are designated in the Internal Revenue Service Code.

Year	Straight-Line (Half-Year) Depreciation	Cost		MACRS %	MACRS Deduction
1	$ 500	$3,000	×	33.3%	$ 999
2	1,000	3,000	×	44.5	1,335
3	1,000	3,000	×	14.8	444
4	500	3,000	×	7.4	222
	$3,000				$3,000

EXAMPLE 9.14 A machine costs $10,000. Annual cash inflows are expected to be $5,000. The machine will be depreciated using the MACRS rule and will fall into the 3-year property class. The cost of capital after taxes is 10 percent. The estimated life of the machine is four years. The salvage value of the machine at the end of the fourth year is expected to be $1,200. The tax rate is 30 percent.

The formula for computation of after-tax cash inflows $(S-E)(1-t)+(d)(t)$ needs to be computed separately. The NPV analysis can be performed as follows.

					Present Value Factor @ 10%	Present Value
Initial investment: $10,000					1.000	$(10,000.00)
$(S-E)(1-t)$:						
$5,000(1 − 0.3) = $3,500 for 4 years					3.170*	$ 11,095.00
$(d)(t)$:						
Year	Cost	MACRS %	d	$(d)(t)$		
1	$10,000 ×	33.3%	$3,330	$ 999	0.909†	908.09
2	$10,000 ×	44.5	4,450	1,335	0.826†	1,102.71
3	$10,000 ×	14.8	1,480	444	0.751†	333.44
4	$10,000 ×	7.4	740	222	0.683†	151.63
Salvage value:						
$1,200 in year 4: $1,200 (1 − 0.3) = 840‡†					0.683†	573.72
Net present value (NPV)						$4,164.59

*From Table 9-4.
†From Table 9-3.
‡Any salvage value received under the MACRS rules is a *taxable gain* (the excess of the selling price over book value, $1,200 in this example), since the book value will be zero at the end of the life of the machine.

Since $NPV = PV - I =$ $4,164.59 is positive, the machine should be bought.

Summary

(1) The NPV method and the IRR method are called ____________ methods.

(2) ____________ is the process of making ____________ decisions.

(3) ____________ divides ____________ by the cash inflow through increased revenues or cash savings in operating expenses.

(4) The shorter the ____________, the less risky the project and the greater the ____________.

(5) Accounting rate of return does not recognize the ____________.

(6) Internal rate of return is the rate at which ____________ equals ____________.

(7) Accept the investment if its IRR exceeds ____________.

(8) IRR is especially difficult to compute when the cash flows are ____________.

(9) In ____________, the NPV and the IRR methods may produce ____________.

(10) ____________ is used widely in ranking the investments competing for limited funds.

(11) The ____________ method discounts all cash flows at the ____________, thus implicitly assuming that these cash flows can be reinvested at this rate.

(12) Income taxes affect both ____________ and ____________ of cash flow.

(13) ____________ is obtained by multiplying the depreciation deduction by the income tax rate.

(14) The traditional accelerated depreciation methods such as ____________ and ____________ produce higher tax savings on depreciation than the straight-line method does.

(15) MACRS rules abandon the concept of ____________.

(16) The straight-line method with ____________ allows the company to deduct only the half of the regular straight-line deduction amount in the ____________ year.

(17) Immediate disposal of the old machine usually results in ____________ that is fully deductible from current income for tax purposes.

Answers: (1) discounted cash flow (DCF); (2) capital budgeting, long-term investment; (3) payback period, the initial amount of investment; (4) payback period, liquidity; (5) time value of money; (6) present value of cash inflows, the initial investment; (7) the cost of capital; (8) not even; (9) mutually exclusive investments, conflicting rankings; (10) profitability index (or excess present value index); (11) NPV, cost of capital; (12) the amount, the timing; (13) tax shield; (14) the double-declining-balance method, the sum-of-the-years'-digits method; (15) useful life; (16) the half-year convention, first; (17) a loss.

Solved Problems

9.1 The following data are given for Alright Aluminum Company:

Initial cost of proposed equipment	$75,000
Estimated useful life	7 years
Estimated annual savings in cash operating expenses	$18,000
Predicted residual value at the end of the useful life	$ 3,000
Cost of capital	12%

Compute the following:

(*a*) Payback period

(*b*) Present value of estimated annual savings

(*c*) Present value of estimated residual value

(*d*) Total present value of estimated cash inflows

(*e*) Net present value (NPV)

(*f*) Internal rate of return (IRR)

SOLUTION

(*a*) $$\text{Payback period} = \frac{\text{Initial investment}}{\text{Annual savings}} = \frac{\$75{,}000}{\$18{,}000} = 4.167 \text{ years}$$

(*b*) $12,000 × PV factor of an annuity of $1 at 12% for 7 years = $18,000 × 4.564 = $82,152

(*c*) $3,000 × PV factor of $1 = $3,000 × 0.452 = $1,356

(*d*) Total PV = $82,152 + $1,356 = $83,508

(*e*) $$NPV = PV - I = \$83{,}508 - \$75{,}000 = \$8{,}508$$

(*f*) At IRR, $I = PV$. Thus,

$$\$75{,}000 = \$18{,}000 \times \text{PV factor}$$

$$\text{PV factor} = \frac{\$75{,}000}{\$18{,}000} = 4.167$$

which is, in the seven-year line, somewhere between 14 percent and 16 percent.

Using the interpolation,

	PV factor	
14%	4.288	4.288
True rate		4.167
16%	4.039	
Difference	0.249	0.121

$$IRR = 14\% + \frac{4.288 - 4.167}{4.288 - 4.039}(16\% - 14\%)$$

$$= 14\% + \frac{0.121}{0.249}(2\%) = 14\% + 0.97\% = 14.97\%$$

9.2 The John-in-the-Box Store is a fast-food restaurant chain. Potential franchisees are given the following revenue and cost information:

Building and equipment	$490,000
Annual revenue	520,000
Annual cash operating costs	380,000

The building and equipment have a useful life of 20 years. The straight-line method for depreciation is used. Ignore income taxes.

(*a*) What is the payback period?

(*b*) What is the accounting (simple) rate of return?

SOLUTION

(*a*) $$\text{Payback period} = \frac{\$490{,}000}{\$520{,}000 - \$380{,}000} = \frac{\$490{,}000}{\$140{,}000} = 3.5 \text{ years}$$

(*b*) $$\text{Annual depreciation} = \frac{\$490{,}000}{20 \text{ years}} = \$24{,}500$$

$$\text{Accounting (simple) rate of return} = \frac{\$140{,}000 - \$24{,}500}{\$490{,}000} = 23.57\%$$

9.3 The Rango Company is considering a capital investment for which the initial outlay is $20,000. Net annual cash inflows (before taxes) are predicted to be $4,000 for 10 years. Straight-line depreciation is to be used, with an estimated salvage value of zero. Ignoring income taxes, compute the items listed below.

1. Payback period
2. Accounting rate of return (ARR)
3. Net present value (NPV), assuming a cost of capital (before tax) of 12 percent
4. Internal rate of return (IRR)

SOLUTION

1.
$$\text{Payback period} = \frac{\text{Initial investment}}{\text{Annual cash flow}} = \frac{\$20{,}000}{\$4{,}000/\text{year}} = 5 \text{ years}$$

2.
$$\text{Accounting rate of return (ARR)} = \frac{\text{Average annual net income}}{\text{Initial investment}}$$

$$\text{Depreciation} = \frac{\$20{,}000}{10 \text{ years}} = \$2{,}000/\text{year}$$

$$\text{Accounting rate of return} = \frac{(\$4{,}000 - \$2{,}000)/\text{year}}{\$20{,}000} = 0.10 = 10\%$$

3. Net present value (NPV) = PV of cash inflows [discounted at the cost of capital (12%)] − Initial investment

$$= \$4{,}000 \times (\text{PV Factor}) - \$20{,}000 = \$4{,}000(5.650) - \$20{,}000 = \$2{,}600$$

4. Internal rate of return (IRR) = Rate which equates the amount invested with the present value of cash inflows generated by the project

Therefore, we set the following equation:

$$\$20{,}000 = \$4{,}000 \text{ (PV Factor)}$$

$$\text{PV Factor} = \frac{\$20{,}000}{\$4{,}000} = 5$$

which stands between 14 percent and 16 percent.

	Table Value	
14%	5.216	5.216
True rate		5.000
16%	4.833	
Differcncc	0.383	0.216

Using interpolation,

$$IRR = 14\% + \left(\frac{5.216 - 5.000}{5.216 - 4.833}\right)(16\% - 14\%) = 14\% + \frac{0.216}{0.383}(2\%)$$

$$= 14\% + (0.564)(2\%) = 14\% + 1.13\% = 15.13\%$$

9.4 Consider an investment which has the following cash flows:

Year	Cash Flows
0	$(31,000)
1	10,000
2	20,000
3	10,000
4	10,000
5	5,000

1. Compute the following:
   (*a*) Payback period
   (*b*) Net present value (NPV) at 14 percent cost of capital
   (*c*) Internal rate of return (IRR)
2. Based on (*b*) and (*c*) in part 1, make a decision.

SOLUTION

1. (*a*) Payback period:

		Recovery of Initial Outlay		
Year	Cash Flow	Needed	Balance	Payback Period in Years
1	$10,000	$31,000	$21,000	1.00
2	20,000	21,000	1,000	1.00
3	10,000	1,000	—	0.10
				2.1

(*b*) NPV:

Year	Cash Flow	PV Factor at 14%	PV
0	$(31,000)	1.000	$(31,000)
1	10,000	0.877	8,770
2	20,000	0.769	15,380
3	10,000	0.675	6,750
4	10,000	0.592	5,920
5	5,000	0.519	2,595
	Net present value (NPV)		$ 8,415

(*c*) By definition, IRR is the rate at which $PV = I$ or $NPV = 0$. We know from part (*b*) that *NPV* at 14 percent = $8,415. We will try 30 percent and see what happens to NPV.

Year	Cash Flow	PV Factor at 30%	PV
0	$(31,000)	1.000	$(31,000)
1	10,000	0.769	7,690
2	20,000	0.592	11,840
3	10,000	0.455	4,550
4	10,000	0.350	3,500
5	5,000	0.269	1,345
			$ (2,075)

Now we are sure that the true IRR is somewhere between 14 percent and 30 percent.
Using interpolation:

	NPV	
14%	$ 8,415	$8,415
True rate		0
30%	−2,075	
Difference	$10,490	$8,415

Therefore, $IRR = 14\% + \dfrac{\$8{,}415}{\$8{,}415 - (-\$2{,}075)}(30\% - 14\%)$

$$= 14\% + \frac{\$8{,}415}{\$10{,}490}(16\%) = 14\% + 12.835\% = 26.835\%$$

2. Under the NPV method, accept, since the NPV is a positive $8,415. Under the IRR method, accept, since the IRR of 26.835 percent exceeds the cost of capital of 14 percent.

9.5 Fill in the blanks for each of the following independent cases. Assume in all cases that the investment has a useful life of 10 years.

	Annual Cash Inflow	Investment	Cost of Capital	IRR	NPV
1.	$100,000	$449,400	14%	(*a*)	(*b*)
2.	$ 70,000	(*c*)	14%	20%	(*d*)
3.	(*e*)	$200,000	(*f*)	14%	$35,624
4.	(*g*)	$300,000	12%	(*h*)	$39,000

SOLUTION

1. (*a*) 18%; ($449,400/$100,000 = 4.494, the present value factor for 18% and 10 years)
   (*b*) $72,200; ($100,000 × 5.216 = $521,600, so NPV = $521,600 − $449,400 = $72,200)
2. (*c*) $293,440; ($70,000 × 4.192, the present value factor for 20% and 10 years; at IRR, $PV = I$)
   (*d*) $71,680; ($70,000 × 5.216 = $365,120, so NPV = $365,120 − $293,440 = $71,680)
3. (*e*) $38,344; ($200,000/5.216 factor for 14% and 10 years)
   (*f*) 10%; ($NPV = PV - I$; $PV = NPV + I$; Total PV = $35,624 + $200,000; $235,624/$38,344 = 6.145, the present value factor for 10%)
4. (*g*) $60,000; (Total PV = $39,000 + $300,000; $339,000/5.650 factor for 12% = $60,000)
   (*h*) About 15%; ($300,000/$60,000 = 5, which stands halfway between 14% and 16%)

9.6 Horn Corp. invested in a four-year project. Horn's cost of capital is 8 percent. Additional information on the project is as follows:

Year	Cash Inflow from Operations, Net of Income Taxes	Present Value of $1 at 8%
1	$2,000	0.926
2	2,200	0.857
3	2,400	0.794
4	2,600	0.735

Assuming a positive net present value of $500, what was the amount of the original investment?

(AICPA, adapted)

SOLUTION

Since $NPV = PV - I$, $I = PV - NPV$:

Year	Cash Inflow	Present Value of $1	Total PV
1	$2,000	0.926	$1,852
2	2,200	0.857	1,885
3	2,400	0.794	1,906
4	2,600	0.735	1,911
Present value of future *inflows* (PV)			$7,554
Net present value (NPV)			500
Initial outlay (I)			$7,054

9.7 Gene, Inc., invested in a machine with a useful life of six years and no salvage value. The machine was depreciated using the straight-line method and it was expected to produce annual cash inflow from operations, net of income taxes, of $2,000. The present value of an ordinary annuity of $1 for six periods at 10 percent is 4.355. The present value of $1 for six periods at 10 percent is 0.564. Assuming that Gene used an internal rate of return of 10 percent, what was the amount of the original investment?

(AICPA, adapted)

SOLUTION

By definition, at IRR, $PV = I$ or $NPV = 0$. To obtain the amount of initial investment, all you have to do is to find the present value of $2,000 a year for six periods.

$$PV = \$2,000 \times 4.355 = \$8,710$$

9.8 Mercury Transit, Inc., has decided to inaugurate express bus service between its headquarters city and a nearby suburb (one-way fare, $0.50), and is considering the purchase of either 32- or 52-passenger buses, on which pertinent estimates are as follows:

	32-Passenger Bus	52-Passenger Bus
Number of each to be purchased	6	4
Useful life	8 years	8 years
Purchase price of each bus (paid on delivery)	$80,000	$110,000
Mileage per gallon	10	7½
Salvage value per bus	$ 6,000	$ 7,000
Drivers' hourly wage	$ 3.50	$ 4.20
Price per gallon of gasoline	$ 0.60	$ 0.60
Other annual cash expenses	$ 4,000	$ 3,000

During the four daily rush hours, all buses will be in service and are expected to operate at full capacity (state law prohibits standees) in both directions of the route, each bus covering the route 12 times (six round trips) during the four-hour period. During the remainder of the 16-hour day, 500 passengers would be carried and Mercury Transit would operate only four buses on the route. Part-time drivers would be employed to drive the extra hours during the rush hours. A bus traveling the route all day would go 480 miles, and one traveling only during rush hours would go 120 miles a day during the 260-day year.

Ignoring income taxes, answer the following:

1. Prepare a schedule showing the computation of the estimated annual gross revenues from the new route for each alternative.
2. Prepare a schedule showing the computation of the estimated annual drivers' wages for each alternative.
3. Prepare a schedule showing the computation of the estimated annual cost of gasoline for each alternative.
4. Assume that your computations in 1, 2, and 3 are as follows:

	32-Passenger Bus	52-Passenger Bus
Estimated annual revenues	$365,000	$390,000
Estimated annual drivers' wages	67,000	68,000
Estimated annual cost of gasoline	32,000	36,000

Assuming that a minimum rate of return of 12 percent before income taxes is desired and that all annual cash flows occur at the end of the year, determine whether the 32- or the 52-passenger buses should be purchased. Use the NPV method.

(AICPA, adapted)

SOLUTION

1.

	32-Passenger Bus	52-Passenger Bus
Capacity per trip	32	52
Trips by each bus during rush hours	× 12	× 12
Rush-hour passengers carried by each bus	384	624
Number of buses	× 6	× 4
Total rush-hour passengers carried daily	2,304	2,496
Total other passengers daily	500	500
Total daily passengers	2,804	2,996
Days per year	× 260	× 260
Total passengers carried annually	729,040	778,960
Fare per passenger	× $0.50	× $0.50
Total annual revenue	$364,520	$389,480

Note that the 500 passengers represent 500 one-way fares.

2. Estimated annual drivers' wages:

	32-Passenger Bus	52-Passenger Bus
Buses operating daily during rush hours	6	4
Rush hours	× 4	× 4
Rush-hour time for all drivers	24	16
Buses operating remainder of day	4	4
Remaining hours	× 12	× 12
Regular driving time, excluding rush hours	48	48
Total daily driver hours	72	64
Days per year	× 260	× 260
Total annual driver hours	18,720	16,640
Hourly wage rate	× $3.50	× $4.20
Total annual drivers' wages	$65,520	$69,888

3. Estimated annual cost of gasoline:

	32-Passenger Bus	52-Passenger Bus
Buses operating during rush hours	6	4
Rush-hour mileage per bus	× 120	× 120
Total rush-hour mileage	720	480
Buses operating during remainder of day	4	4
Mileage per bus, remainder of day	× 360	× 360
Total mileage for remainder of day	1,440	1,440
Total daily mileage	2,160	1,920
Days per year	× 260	× 260
Total annual mileage	561,600	499,200
Miles per gallon	÷ 10	÷ 7½
Annual gallons of gasoline consumption	56,160	66,560
Price per gallon	× \$0.60	× \$0.60
Total annual cost of gasoline	\$33,696	\$39,936

4. Computations of net annual cash inflows:

	32-Passenger Bus	52-Passenger Bus
Annual revenues	\$365,000	\$390,000
Less: Cash disbursements		
Drivers' wages	\$ 67,000	\$ 68,000
Gasoline	32,000	36,000
Other expenses	4,000	3,000
Total	\$103,000	\$107,000
Net annual cash inflow	\$262,000	\$283,000

Item	Year(s) Having Cash Flows	Amount of Cash Flows	12 Percent Factor	Present Value of Cash Flows
Purchase 32-passenger buses:				
Cost of the buses	Now	\$(480,000)	1.000	\$ (480,000)
Net annual cash inflows	1–8	262,000	4.968	1,301,616
Salvage value	8	36,000	0.404	14,544
Net present value				\$ 836,160
Purchase 52-passenger buses:				
Cost of the buses	Now	\$(440,000)	1.000	\$ (440,000)
Net annual cash inflows	1–8	283,000	4.968	1,405,944
Salvage value	8	28,000	0.404	11,312
Net present value				\$ 977,256
Net present value in favor of purchasing the 52-passenger buses				\$ 141,096

9.9 Data relating to three investments are given below:

	A	B	C
Investment (I)	$30,000	$20,000	$50,000
Useful life	10	4	20
Annual cash savings	$ 6,207	$ 7,725	$ 9,341

Rank the projects according to their attractiveness using the following:

(*a*) Payback period

(*b*) IRR

(*c*) NPV at 14 percent cost of capital

SOLUTION

(*a*) Payback period:

Project	Payback Period	Rank
A	$30,000/$6,207 = 4.833 years	2
B	$20,000/$7,725 = 2.588 years	1
C	$50,000/$9,341 = 5.353 years	3

(*b*) IRR ranking:

Project	Closest Rate	Rank
A	16%	3
B	20%	1
C	18%	2

(*c*) NPV at 14%:

Project	Annual Savings	PV Factor	Total PV	I	*NPV*	Rank
A	$6,207	5.216	$32,376	$30,000	$ 2,376	3
B	7,725	2.914	22,511	20,000	2,511	2
C	9,341	6.623	61,865	50,000	11,865	1

9.10 Rand Corporation is considering five different investment opportunities. The company's cost of capital is 12 percent. Data on these opportunities under consideration are given below.

Project	Investment	PV at 12%	NPV	IRR	Profitability Index (rounded)
(*a*)	$35,000	$39,325	$4,325	16%	1.12
(*b*)	20,000	22,930	2,930	15	1.15
(*c*)	25,000	27,453	2,453	14	1.10
(*d*)	10,000	10,854	854	18	1.09
(*e*)	9,000	8,749	(251)	11	0.97

1. Rank these five projects in descending order of preference, according to
   - NPV
   - IRR
   - Profitability index

2. Which ranking would you prefer?
3. Based on your answer in part 2, which projects would you select if $55,000 is the limit to be spent?

SOLUTION

1.

	Order of Preference		
	NPV	IRR	Profitability Index
(*a*)	1	2	2
(*b*)	2	3	1
(*c*)	3	4	3
(*d*)	4	1	4
(*e*)	5	5	5

2. The profitability index approach is generally considered the most dependable method of ranking projects competing for limited funds. It is an index of relative attractiveness, measured in terms of how much you get out for each dollar invested.
3. Based on the answer in part 2, projects (*a*) and (*b*) should be selected, where combined NPV would be $7,255 ($2,930 + $4,325) with the limited budget of $55,000.

9.11 A medium-sized manufacturing company is considering the purchase of a small computer in order to reduce the cost of its data processing operations. At the present time, the manual bookkeeping system in use involves the following direct cash expenses per month:

Salaries	$7,500
Payroll taxes and fringe benefits	1,700
Forms and supplies	600
	$9,800

Existing furniture and equipment are fully depreciated in the accounts and have no salvage value. The cost of the computer, including alterations, installation, and accessory equipment, is $100,000. This entire amount is depreciable for income tax purposes on a double-declining basis at the rate of 20 percent per annum.

Estimated annual costs of computerized data processing are as follows:

Supervisory salaries	$15,000
Other salaries	24,000
Payroll taxes and fringe benefits	7,400
Forms and supplies	7,200
	$53,600

The computer is expected to be obsolete in three years, at which time its salvage value is expected to be $20,000. The company follows the practice of treating salvage value as inflow at the time that it is likely to be received.

1. Compute the savings in annual cash expenses after taxes. Assume a 50 percent tax rate.
2. Decide whether or not to purchase the computer, using the net present value method. Assume a minimum rate of return of 10 percent after taxes.

(SMA, adapted)

SOLUTION

1.

Annual cash expenses of the manual bookkeeping machine system, $9,800 × 12	$117,600
Annual cash expenses of computerized data processing	53,600
Annual cash savings	$ 64,000

	Year 1	Year 2	Year 3
Annual cash savings (*a*)	$64,000	$64,000	$ 64,000
Depreciation	20,000	16,000	12,800
Inflow before tax	$44,000	$48,000	$ 51,000
Income tax (50%) (*b*)	22,000	24,000	25,600
Cash inflow after tax ($a - b$)	$42,000	$40,000	$ 38,400

2.

	After-Tax Cash Inflow		PV Factor	PV
Year 1	$42,000	×	0.909	$ 38,178
Year 2	40,000	×	0.826	33,040
Year 3	38,400	×	0.750	28,800
Year 3 Salvage	20,000	×	0.750	15,000
Year 3 Tax loss	15,600*	×	0.750	11,700
				$126,718
Investment (I)				100,000
Net present value (NPV)				$ 26,718

*The $15,600 tax benefit of the loss on the disposal of the computer at the end of year 3 is computed as follows:

Estimated salvage value		$ 20,000
Estimated book value:		
Historical cost	$100,000	
Accumulated depreciation	48,800	51,200
Estimated loss		$(31,200)
Tax rate		50%
Tax effect of estimated loss		$(15,600)

Since the net present value is positive, the computer should be purchased to replace the manual bookkeeping system.

9.12 The Michener Company purchased a special machine one year ago at a cost of $12,500. At that time, the machine was estimated to have a useful life of six years and a $500 disposal value. The annual cash operating cost is approximately $20,000.

A new machine that has just come on the market will do the same job but with an annual cash operating cost of only $17,000. This new machine costs $16,000 and has an estimated life of five years with a $1,000 disposal value. The old machine could be used as a trade-in at an allowance of $5,000. Straight-line depreciation is used, and the company's income tax rate is 50 percent. Compute the internal rate of return on the new investment.

(CGA, adapted)

SOLUTION

Cash outflow:			
Cost of new machine		$16,000	
Trade-in allowance for old machine		5,000	
Net cash outflow (I)		$11,000	
Cash savings (annual):			
Cash operating costs:			
Old machine	$20,000		
New machine	17,000	$ 3,000	$3,000
Depreciation expense (annual):			
Old machine [($12,500 − $500) ÷ 6 years]	$ 2,000		
New machine [($11,000 cash outflow + $10,500 old machine's book value); ($21,500 − $1,000) ÷ 5 years]	4,100		
Additional annual depreciation		2,100	
Taxable savings		$ 900	
Income tax on savings ($900 × 0.50)			450
Annual cash savings after income tax			$2,550

Internal rate of return factor: $11,000 ÷ $2,550 = 4.314

By interpolation:

	Present Value Factor		Present Value Factor
4%	4.452	4%	4.452
6%	4.212	IRR	4.314
	0.240		0.138

$$IRR = \left(\frac{0.138}{0.240} \times 2\%\right) + 4\% = 1.15\% + 4\% = 5.15\%$$

9.13 Two new machines are being evaluated for possible purchase. Forecasts relating to the two machines are:

	Machine 1	Machine 2
Purchase price	$50,000	$60,000
Estimated life (straight-line depreciation)	4 years	4 years
Estimated scrap value	None	None
Annual cash benefits before income tax:		
Year 1	$25,000	$45,000
Year 2	25,000	19,000
Year 3	25,000	25,000
Year 4	25,000	25,000
Income tax rate	40%	40%

Compute the net present value of each machine.

(CGA, adapted)

SOLUTION

After-tax cash benefit:

Year	Cash Benefit (*a*)	Depreciation	Taxable Income	Income Tax (*b*)	Net After-Tax Cash Inflow (*a*) − (*b*)
			Machine 1		
1	$25,000	$12,500	$12,500	$5,000	$20,000
2	25,000	12,500	12,500	5,000	20,000
3	25,000	12,500	12,500	5,000	20,000
4	25,000	12,500	12,500	5,000	20,000
			Machine 2		
1	$45,000	$15,000	$30,000	$12,000	$33,000
2	19,000	15,000	4,000	1,600	17,400
3	25,000	15,000	10,000	4,000	21,000
4	25,000	15,000	10,000	4,000	21,000

Net present value:

Year	Cash (Outflow) Inflow	Present Value of $1 8 Percent	Net Present Value of Cash Flow
		Machine 1	
0	$(50,000)	1.000	$(50,000)
1–4	20,000	3.312	66,240
		Net present value	$ 16,240
		Machine 2	
0	$(60,000)	1.000	$(60,000)
1	33,000	0.926	30.558
2	17,400	0.857	14,912
3	21,000	0.794	16,674
4	21,000	0.735	15,435
		Net present value	$ 17,579

9.14 The Lon-Ki Manufacturing Company must decide between two investments, A and B, which are mutually exclusive. The data on these projects are as follows (in thousands of dollars):

	Year				
Project	0	1	2	3	4
A	$(100)	$120.00	—	—	—
B	(100)	—	—	—	$193.80

1. For each project, compute:
   (*a*) NPV at 12 percent cost of capital
   (*b*) IRR
2. Why the conflicting ranking? Make a recommendation on which project should be chosen.

SOLUTION

1. (*a*) NPV at 12 percent:

Project	Cash Inflow	PV at $1	PV	NPV
A	$120.00	0.893	$107.16	$ 7.16
B	$193.80	0.636	123.26	23.26

(*b*) IRR:

Project		IRR
A	$100/$120 = 0.833	20%
B	$100/$193.80 = 0.516	18%

2. The conflicting ranking results from different assumptions regarding the reinvestment rate on the cash inflows released by the project. The NPV method assumes the cost of capital (12 percent in this problem) as the rate for reinvestment, whereas the IRR method assumes that the cash inflows are reinvested at their own internal rate of return (20 percent in the case of project A). We recommend the use of NPV for ranking mutually exclusive investments, because we think the cost of capital is a more realistic reinvestment rate.

9.15 After-tax cash flows for two mutually exclusive projects (with economic lives of four years each) are:

Year	Project X	Project Y
0	$(12,000)	$(12,000)
1	5,000	0
2	5,000	0
3	5,000	0
4	5,000	25,000

The company's cost of capital is 10 percent. Compute the following:

1. The internal rate of return for each project.
2. The net present value for each project.
3. Which project should be selected? Why?

(CGA, adapted)

SOLUTION

1. Project X:

$$\text{IRR factor} = \frac{\$12,000}{\$5,000} = 2.4$$

	Present Value Factor		Present Value Factor
24%	2.404	24%	2.404
25%	2.362	IRR factor	2.400
	0.042		0.004

$$\text{Internal rate of return} = 24\% + \left(\frac{0.004}{0.042} \times 1\%\right) = 24\% + 0.1\% = 24.1\%$$

Project Y:

Year	Cash (Outflow) Inflow	Present Value of $1 20%	Net Present Value of Cash Flow	Present Value of $1 22%	Net Present Value of Cash Flow
0	$(12,000)	1.000	$(12,000)	1.000	$(12,000)
4	25,000	0.482	12,050	0.451	11,275
			$ 50		$ (725)

$$\text{Internal rate of return} = 20\% + \left(2\% \times \frac{\$50}{\$775}\right) = 20\% + 0.13\% = 20.13\%$$

2. Project X:

Year	Cash (Outflow) Inflow	Present Value of $1 10%	Net Present Value of Cash Flow
0	$(12,000)	1.000	$(12,000)
1–4	5,000	3.170	15,850
		Net present value	$ 3,850

Project Y:

Year	Cash (Outflow) Inflow	Present Value of $1 10%	Net Present Value of Cash Flow
0	$(12,000)	1.000	$(12,000)
4	25,000	0.683	17,075
		Net present value	$ 5,075

In summary,

Project	IRR	NPV
X	24.1%	$3,850
Y	20.13%	5,075

3. Using the IRR method, project X is superior to project Y; using the NPV method, project Y is more attractive than X. The decision hinges on the assumption made about reinvestment of cash inflow. Theory suggests resorting to the NPV method because the cost of capital reinvestment assumption implicit in this method is considered to be a more realistic assumption than the IRR, where a reinvestment at the IRR is assumed.

9.16 A machine costs $1,000 initially. Annual cash inflows are expected to be $300. The machine will be depreciated using the MACRS rule and will fall into the three-year property class. No salvage value is anticipated. The cost of capital is 16 percent. The estimated life of the machine is five years. The tax rate is 40 percent. Make a decision using NPV.

SOLUTION

	Year(s) Having Cash Flows	Amount of Cash Flows	16% PV Factor	PV
Initial investment	Now	$1,000	1.000	$(1,000)
Annual cash inflows:				
$300				
×60%				
$180	1–5	180	3.274	589

Depreciation deductions:

Year	Cost	MACRS %	Depreciation	Tax Shield				
1	$1,000	33.3%	$333	$133.20	1	$133.20	0.862	$114.82
2	1,000	44.5	445	178.00	2	178.00	0.743	132.25
3	1,000	14.8	148	59.20	3	59.20	0.641	37.95
4	1,000	7.4	74	29.60	4	29.60	0.552	16.34
Net present value								$ (109.32)

The machine should not be bought, because the NPV of −$109.32 is negative.

9.17 A firm is considering the purchase of an automatic machine for $6,200. The machine has an installation cost of $800 and zero salvage value at the end of its expected life of five years. Depreciation is by the straight-line method with the *half-year convention*. The machine is considered a five-year property. Expected cash savings before tax is $1,800 per year over the five years. The firm is in the 40 percent tax bracket. The firm has determined the cost of capital (or minimum required rate of return) as 10 percent after taxes. Should the firm purchase the machine? Use the NPV method.

SOLUTION

	Year(s) Having Cash Flows	Amount of Cash Flows	10% PV Factor	PV
Initial investment	Now	$(7,000)	1.000	$(7,000)
Annual cash inflows:				
$1,800				
×60%				
$1,080	1–5	1,080	3.791	4,094

Depreciation deductions:

Year	Depreciation	Tax shield at 40%				
1	$ 700	$280	1	$ 280	0.909	$ 255
2	1,400	560	2	560	0.826	463
3	1,400	560	3	560	0.751	421
4	1,400	560	4	560	0.683	382
5	1,400	560	5	560	0.621	348
6	700	280	6	280	0.564	158
Net present value						$ (879)

The firm should not buy the automatic machine, since its NPV is negative.

9.18 The Wessels Corporation is considering installing a new conveyor for materials handling in a warehouse. The conveyor will have an initial cost of $75,000 and an installation cost of $5,000. Expected benefits of the conveyor are: (*a*) Annual labor cost will be reduced by $16,500, and (*b*) breakage and other damages from handling will be reduced by $400 per month. Some of the firm's costs are expected to increase as follows: (*a*) Electricity cost will rise by $100 per month, and (*b*) annual repair and maintenance of the conveyor will amount to $900.

Assume that the firm uses the MACRS rules for depreciation in the five-year property class. No salvage value will be recognized for tax purposes. The conveyor has an expected useful life of eight years and a projected salvage value of $5,000. The tax rate is 40 percent.

1. Estimate future cash inflows for the proposed project.
2. Determine the project's NPV at 10 percent. Should the firm buy the conveyor?

SOLUTION

1. Annual cash inflow:

$16,500	Reduction in labor cost
4,800	Reduction in breakage
−1,200	Increase in electricity costs
−900	Increase in repair and maintenance cost
$19,200	

2. Initial amount of investment is:

$$\$75{,}000 + \$5{,}000 = \$80{,}000$$

					Year(s) Having Cash Flows	Amount of Cash Flows	10% PV Factor	PV
Initial investment					Now	$(80,000)	1.000	$(80,000)
Annual cash inflow:	$19,200							
	×60%							
After-tax cash inflow:	$11,520				1–8	11,520	5.335	61,459.20
Depreciation deduction:								
Year	Cost	MACRS	Depreciation	Tax Shield				
1	$80,000	20%	$16,000	$ 6,400	1	$ 6,400	0.909	$ 5,817.60
2	80,000	32	25,600	10,240	2	10,240	0.826	8,458.24
3	80,000	19.2	15,360	6,144	3	6,144	0.751	4,614.14
4	80,000	11.5	9,200	3,680	4	3,680	0.683	2,513.44
5	80,000	11.5	9,200	3,680	5	3,680	0.621	2,285.28
6	80,000	5.8	4,640	1,856	6	1,856	0.564	1,046.78
Salvage value, fully taxable since book value will be zero:								$ 24,735.48
	$5,000							
	×60%							
	$3,000				8	$ 3,000	0.467	$ 1,401.00
								$ 7,595.68

The Wessels Corporation should buy and install the conveyor, since it brings a positive NPV.

9.19 Wisconsin Products Company manufactures several different products. One of the firm's principal products sells for $20 per unit. The sales manager of Wisconsin Products has stated repeatedly that he could sell more units of this product if they were available. In an attempt to substantiate his claim, the sales manager conducted a market research study last year at a cost of $44,000 to determine potential demand for this product. The study indicated that Wisconsin Products could sell 18,000 units of this product annually for the next five years.

The equipment currently in use has the capacity to produce 11,000 units annually. The variable production costs are $9 per unit. The equipment has a book value of $60,000 and a remaining useful life of five years. The salvage value of the equipment is negligible now and will be zero in five years.

A maximum of 20,000 units could be produced annually on the new machinery which can be purchased. The new equipment costs $300,000 and has an estimated useful life of five years with no salvage value at the end of five years. Wisconsin Products' production manager has estimated that the new equipment would provide increased production efficiencies that would reduce the variable production costs to $7 per unit.

Wisconsin Products Company uses straight-line depreciation on all of its equipment for tax purposes. The firm is subject to a 40 percent tax rate, and its after-tax cost of capital is 15 percent.

The sales manager felt so strongly about the need for additional capacity that he attempted to prepare an economic justification for the equipment, although this was not one of his responsibilities. His analysis, presented below, disappointed him because it did not justify acquiring the equipment.

Required Investment		
Purchase price of new equipment		$300,000
Disposal of existing equipment:		
Loss of disposal	$60,000	
Less: Tax benefit (40%)	24,000	36,000
Cost of market research study		44,000
Total investment		$380,000

Annual Returns	
Contribution margin from product:	
Using the new equipment [18,000 × ($20 − $7)]	$234,000
Using the existing equipment [11,000 × ($20 − $9)]	121,000
Increase in contribution margin	$113,000
Less: Depreciation	60,000
Increase in before-tax income	$ 53,000
Income tax (40%)	21,200
Increase in income	$ 31,800
Less: 15% cost of capital on the additional investment required (0.15 × $380,000)	57,000
Net annual return of proposed investment in new equipment	$ (25,200)

1. The controller of Wisconsin Products Company plans to prepare a discounted cash flow analysis for this investment proposal. The controller has asked you to prepare corrected calculations of

   (*a*) The required investment in the new equipment

   (*b*) The recurring annual cash flows

Explain the treatment of each item of your corrected calculations that is treated differently from the original analysis prepared by the sales manager.

2. Calculate the net present value of the proposed investment in the new equipment.

SOLUTION

1. (*a*)

Purchase price of new equipment		$(300,000)
Disposal of existing equipment:		
Selling price	$ 0	
Book value	60,000	
Loss on disposal	$60,000	
Tax rate	0.4	
Tax benefit of loss on disposal		24,000
Required investment (I)		$(276,000)

(*b*)

Increased cash flows resulting from change in contribution margin:		
Using new equipment [18,000 ($20 − $7)]*		$ 234,000
Using existing equipment [11,000 ($20 − $9)]		121,000
Increased cash flows		$ 113,000
Less: Taxes (0.40 × $113,000)		45,200
Increased cash flows after taxes		$ 67,800
Depreciation tax shield:		
Depreciation on new equipment ($300,000 ÷ 5)	$60,000	
Depreciation on existing equipment ($60,000 ÷ 5)	12,000	
Increased depreciation charge	$48,000	
Tax rate	0.4	
Depreciation tax shield		19,200
Recurring annual cash flows		$ 87,000

*The new equipment is capable of producing 20,000 units, but Wisconsin Products can sell only 18,000 units annually.

The sales manager made several errors in his calculations of required investment and annual cash flows. The errors are as follows:

Required investment:

- The cost of the market research study ($44,000) is a sunk cost because it was incurred last year and will not change regardless of whether the investment is made or not.
- The loss on the disposal of the existing equipment does not result in an actual cash cost as shown by the sales manager. The loss on disposal results in a reduction of taxes, which reduces the cost of the new equipment.

Annual cash flows:

- The sales manager considered only the depreciation on the new equipment rather than just the additional depreciation which would result from the acquisition of the new equipment.
- The sales manager also failed to consider that the depreciation is a noncash expenditure which provides a tax shield.
- The sales manager's use of the discount rate (i.e., cost of capital) was incorrect. The discount rate should be used to reduce the value of future cash flows to their current equivalent at time period zero.

2.

Present value of future cash flows ($87,000 × 3.36)	$292,320
Required investment (I)	276,000
Net present value	$ 16,320

9.20 The Baxter Company manufactures toys and other short-lived-fad–type items. The research and development department came up with an item that would make a good promotional gift for office equipment dealers. Aggressive and effective effort by Baxter's sales personnel has resulted in almost firm commitments for this product for the next three years. It is expected that the product's value will be exhausted by that time.

In order to produce the quantity demanded, Baxter will need to buy additional machinery and rent some additional space. It appears that about 25,000 square feet will be needed; 12,500 square feet of presently unused, but leased, space is available now. (Baxter's present lease with 10 years to run costs $3.00 a foot.) There is another 12,500 square feet adjoining the Baxter facility which Baxter will rent for three years at $4.00 per square foot per year if it decides to make this product.

The equipment will be purchased for about $900,000. It will require $30,000 in modifications, $60,000 for installation, and $90,000 for testing; all of these activities will be done by a firm of engineers hired by Baxter. All of the expenditures will be paid for on January 1, 19X1.

The equipment should have a salvage value of about $180,000 at the end of the third year. No additional general overhead costs are expected to be incurred.

The following estimates of revenues and expenses for this product for the three years have been developed.

	19X1	19X2	19X3
Sales	$1,000,000	$1,600,000	$800,000
Material, labor, and incurred overhead	$ 400,000	$ 750,000	$350,000
Assigned general overhead	40,000	75,000	35,000
Rent	87,500	87,500	87,500
Depreciation	450,000	300,000	150,000
	$ 977,500	$1,212,500	$622,500
Income before tax	$ 22,500	$ 387,500	$177,500
Income tax (40%)	9,000	155,000	71,000
	$ 13,500	$ 232,500	$106,500

1. Prepare a schedule which shows the incremental after-tax cash flows for this project.

2. If the company requires a two-year payback period for its investment, would it undertake this project? Show your supporting calculations clearly.

3. Calculate the after-tax accounting rate of return for the project.

4. A newly hired business-school graduate recommends that the company consider the use of net present value analysis to study this project. If the company sets a required rate of return of 20 percent after taxes, will this project be accepted? Show your supporting calculations clearly. (Assume all operating revenues and expenses occur at the end of the year.)

(CMA, adapted)

SOLUTION

1\.

Incremental After-Tax Cash Flow (000 omitted)

	19X1	19X2	19X3
Sales	$1,000	$1,600	$800
Material, labor, overhead	$ 400	$ 750	$350
Added rent	50	50	50
Depreciation	450	300	150
Incremental costs	$ 900	$1,100	$550
Incremental income	$ 100	$ 500	$250
Incremental taxes	40	200	100
Incremental income after taxes	$ 60	$ 300	$150
Add back depreciation	450	300	150
Incremental operation cash flow	$ 510	$ 600	$300
Salvage value			180
Net incremental after-tax cash flow	$ 510	$ 600	$480

Initial investment for project:

Purchase price	$ 900
Modification	30
Installation	60
Testing	90
Total	$1,080

2\. The project should be undertaken if the criterion is a two-year payback.

19X1	$ 510,000
19X2	600,000
	$1,110,000

Payback is in two years, which is greater than cost of $1,080,000.

The payback period is:

$$\frac{510}{510} + \frac{570}{600} = 1.95 \text{ years}$$

3\.

19X1 income	$ 13,500
19X2 income	232,500
19X3 income	106,500
	$352,500

Average income: $117,500 ($352,500/3)

$$\text{Accounting rate of return} = \frac{\$117{,}500}{\$1{,}080{,}000} = 10.88\%$$

4\. The project should be adopted if a 20 percent after-tax rate of return is required.

Present Value of Cash Flows at 20%

19X1	0.83 × 510,000 =	$ 423,300
19X2	0.69 × 600,000 =	414,000
19X3	0.58 × 480,000 =	278,400
Present value		$1,115,700

The present value of $1,115,700 is greater than the initial outlay of $1,080,000; therefore, the project more than satisfies the 20 percent requirement.

9.21 R. Oliver and J. Rand have formed a corporation to franchise a quick food system for shopping malls. They have just completed experiments with the prototype machine which will serve as the basis of the operation. Because the system is new and untried, they have decided to conduct a pilot operation in a nearby mall. If it proves successful, they will aggressively market the franchises.

The income statements below represent Oliver and Rand's best estimates of income from the mall operation for the next four years. At the end of the four-year period they intend to sell the operation and concentrate on the sale of and supervision of franchises. Based on the income stream projected, they believe the operation can be sold for $190,000; the income tax liability from the sale will be $40,000.

1. Calculate the cash flow for the mall operation for the four-year period beginning January 1, 19X6, ignoring income tax implications.

2. Adjust the cash flows for the tax consequences as appropriate.

Projected Income
For Years Ending December 31

	19X6	19X7	19X8	19X9
Sales	$120,000	$150,000	$200,000	$230,000
Less: Cost of goods sold	$ 60,000	$ 75,000	$100,000	$110,000
Wages	24,000	30,000	40,000	44,000
Supplies	2,000	2,300	2,400	3,200
Personal property taxes	1,000	1,200	1,600	1,800
Annual rental charge*	12,000	12,000	12,000	12,000
Depreciation†	11,000	11,000	11,000	11,000
Development costs‡	20,000	20,000	20,000	20,000
Total expenses	$130,000	$151,500	$187,000	$202,000
Net income before taxes	$(10,000)	$ (1,500)	$ 13,000	$ 28,000
Less: Income taxes @ 40%	—§	—§	600§	11,200
Net income after taxes	$(10,000)	$ (1,500)	$ 12,400	$ 16,800

*The shopping mall requires tenants to sign a 10-year lease. Three years' rental is payable at the beginning of the lease period, with annual payments at the end of each of the next seven years.

†Construction of an operational machine is estimated to be completed on January 1, 19X7. The $130,000 purchase price will be paid at that time. The salvage value at the end of its 10-year life is estimated at $20,000. Straight-line depreciation is to be used for statement purposes and sum-of-the-years'-digits for tax purposes.

‡The prototype machine cost $200,000 to develop and build in 19X6. It is not suitable for commercial use. However, since it was the basis of the system, it is to be amortized at $20,000 per year. The same amount will be deducted for tax purposes.

§The losses of the first two years are offset against the $13,000 income in 19X8 before income tax charges are calculated.

(CMA, adapted)

SOLUTION

1.

	19X6	19X7	19X8	19X9
Recurring cash flows:				
Sales	$ 120,000	$150,000	$200,000	$230,000
Less: Cash expenditures				
Cost of goods sold	$ 60,000	$ 75,000	$100,000	$110,000
Wages	24,000	30,000	40,000	44,000
Supplies	2,000	2,300	2,400	3,200
Personal property taxes	1,000	1,200	1,600	1,800
Annual rental charges	12,000	12,000	12,000	12,000
Total cash expenditures	$ 99,000	$120,500	$156,000	$171,000
Total recurring cash flows before taxes	$ 21,000	$ 29,500	$ 44,000	$ 59,000
Nonrecurring cash flows:				
Cash flows at inception:				
Rental charges	$ (36,000)			
Purchase of new machine	(130,000)			
Cash flows at conclusion of mall operation:				
Sale of mall operation	—	—	—	$190,000
Total nonrecurring cash flows	$(166,000)	—	—	$190,000
Total cash flows before taxes	$(145,000)	$ 29,500	$ 44,000	$249,000

2.

	Calculation of Income Taxes			
	19X6	19X7	19X8	19X9
Income from operations:				
Net income (loss) before taxes as stated	$ (10,000)	$ (1,500)	$ 13,000	$ 28,000
Add: Amount for straight-line depreciation	11,000	11,000	11,000	11,000
Deduct: Amount for S-Y-D depreciation*	(20,000)	(18,000)	(16,000)	(14,000)
Taxable income (loss) before carryforward of operating loss	$ (19,000)	$ (8,500)	$ 8,000	$ 25,000
Operating loss carryforward	—	—	(8,000)	(19,500)
Taxable income	$ 0	$ 0	$ 0	$ 5,500
Income tax on income from operations (40%)	$ 0	$ 0	$ 0	$ 2,200
Income tax from sale of mall operation				40,000
Total income taxes				$ 42,200
Total cash flows before taxes (part 1)	$(145,000)	$ 29,500	$ 44,000	$249,000
Less: Income taxes	—	—	—	42,200
Total cash flows after taxes	$(145,500)	$ 29,500	$ 44,000	$206,800

---

*S-Y-D depreciation calculation:

Purchase price of equipment	$130,000
Salvage value	20,000
Depreciable base	$110,000

Year	Rate	Depreciation
19X6	10/55	$20,000
19X7	9/55	18,000
19X8	8/55	16,000
19X9	7/55	14,000

CHAPTER 10

Quantitative Approaches to Managerial Accounting

10.1 INTRODUCTION

In recent years much attention has been given to using a variety of quantitative methods in the decision-making process. Especially with the rapid development of computers, managers and accountants find it increasingly necessary to acquire knowledge about the use of quantitative (mathematical and statistical) methods.

The term *quantitative methods* (or *models*), also known as *operations research* and *management science*, describes sophisticated mathematical and statistical techniques in the solution of managerial planning and decision-making problems. Numerous techniques are available under these headings. We will explore four of the most important of these techniques: *linear programming models*, *learning curve theory*, and *inventory planning models*.

10.2 LINEAR PROGRAMMING AND SHADOW PRICES

Linear programming (LP) is concerned with the problem of allocating limited resources among competing activities in an optimal manner. Specifically, it is a technique used to maximize a revenue, contribution margin, or profit function, or to minimize a cost function subject to constraints. Linear programming consists of two important ingredients:

1. Objective function
2. Constraints (including *non-negativity* constraints), which are typically inequalities

EXAMPLE 10.1 A firm wishes to find an optimal product mix so as to maximize its total contribution without violating restrictions imposed upon the availability of resources. Or it may want to determine a least-cost combination of input materials while satisfying production requirements, maintaining required inventory levels, staying within production capacities, and using available employees. The objective function is to minimize production cost, and the constraints are production requirements, inventory levels, production capacity, and available employees.

APPLICATIONS

Other managerial applications include:

(*a*) Selecting an investment mix
(*b*) Blending chemical products
(*c*) Scheduling flight crews
(*d*) Assigning jobs to machines
(*e*) Determining transportation routes
(*f*) Determining distribution or allocation pattern

FORMULATION OF LP PROBLEMS

To formulate the LP problem, the first step is to define *decision variables* which one is trying to solve for. The next step is to express the objective function and constraints in terms of these decision variables. Notice, however, that, as in the name of *linear* programming, all the expressions must be of *linear* form.

EXAMPLE 10.2 A firm produces two products, A and B. Both products require time in two processing departments, the assembly department and the finishing department. Data on the two products are as follows:

	Products		
Processing	A	B	Available Hours
Assembly	2 hours	4	100
Finishing	3	2	90
CM/unit	$25	$40	

The firm wants to find the most profitable mix of these two products. First, define the decision variables as follows:

A = number of units of product A to be produced
B = number of units of product B to be produced

Then, the objective function which is to maximize total contribution margin CM is expressed as:

$$\text{Total } CM = \$25A + \$40B$$

Then, formulate the constraints as inequalities:

$$2A + 4B \leqq 100 \quad \text{(Assembly constraint)}$$
$$3A + 2B \leqq 90 \quad \text{(Finishing constraint)}$$

and do not forget to add the non-negativity constraints:

$$A, B \geqq 0$$

The LP model is:

Maximize: Total $CM = \$25A + \$40B$

Subject to: $2A + 4B \leqq \$100$
$3A + 2B \leqq \$90$
$A, B \geqq 0$

COMPUTATIONAL METHODS OF LP

Several solution methods are available to solve LP problems. They include:

1. The simplex method
2. The graphical method

The *simplex* method is the technique that is most commonly used to solve LP problems. It is an *algorithm*, which is an iteration method of computation used to move from one solution to another until the best solution is reached. The graphical solution is easier to use but limited to LP problems involving two (or at most three) decision variables. The graphical method follows the steps:

1. Change inequalities to equalities.
2. Graph the equalities.
3. Identify the correct side for the original inequalities.
4. After all this, identify the feasible region, the area of feasible solutions. *Feasible solutions* are values of decision variables that satisfy all the restrictions simultaneously.
5. Determine the contribution margin at all of the corners in the feasible region.

EXAMPLE 10.3 In Example 10.2, after having gone through steps 1 through 4, we obtain the feasible region (shaded area) shown in Fig. 10-1. Then we evaluate all of the corner points in the feasible region in terms of their CM, as follows:

	Corner Points		Contribution Margin CM
	A	B	$\$25A + \$40B$
ⓐ	30	0	(\$25)(30) + (\$40)(0) = \$750
ⓑ	20	15	(\$25)(20) + (\$40)(15) = \$1,100
ⓒ	0	25	(\$25)(0) + (\$40)(25) = \$1,000
ⓓ	0	0	(\$25)(0) + (\$40)(0) = \$0

The corner $(15B, 20A)$ produces the most profitable solution.

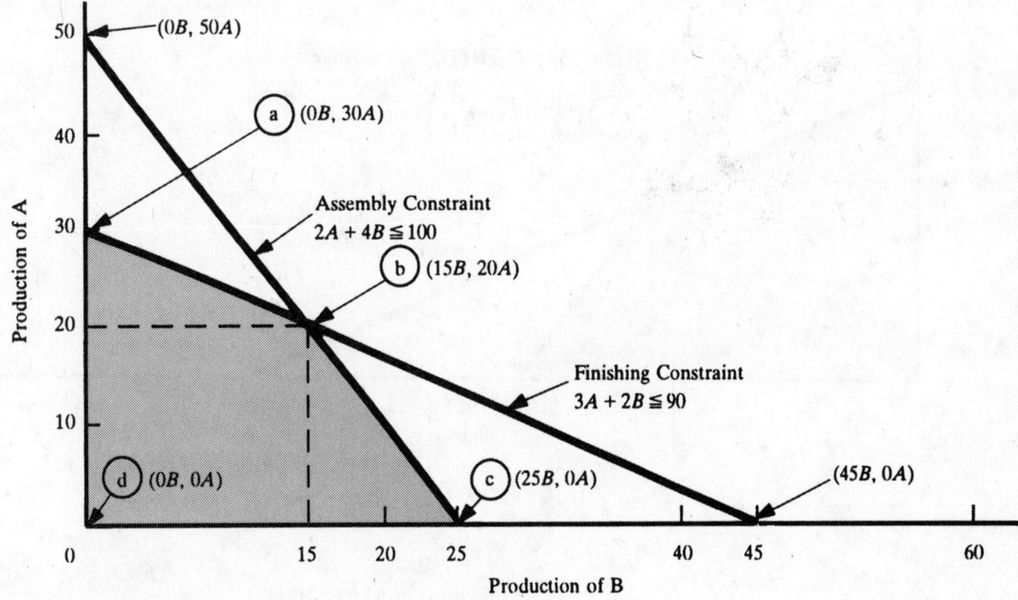

Fig. 10-1

SHADOW PRICES (OPPORTUNITY COST)

A decision maker who has solved an LP problem might wish to know whether it pays to add capacity in hours in a particular department. He or she would be interested in the monetary value to the firm of adding, say, an hour per week of assembly time. This monetary value is the additional contribution margin that could be earned. This amount is called the *shadow price* of the given resource. A shadow price is in a way an opportunity cost, the contribution margin that would be lost by *not* adding an additional hour of capacity. To justify a decision in favor of a short-term capacity expansion, the decision maker must be sure that the shadow price (or opportunity cost) exceeds the actual price of that expansion. Shadow prices are computed, step by step, as follows:

1. Add one hour (preferably, more than an hour, to make it easier to show graphically) to the constraint under consideration.
2. Resolve the problem and find the maximum CM.
3. Compute the difference between the CM of the original LP problem and the CM determined in step 2, which is the shadow price.

Other methods, such as using the *dual* problem, are also available to compute shadow prices.

EXAMPLE 10.4 Using the data in Example 10.3, we shall compute the shadow price of the assembly capacity. To make it easier to show graphically, we shall add eight hours of capacity to the assembly department, rather than one hour. The new assembly constraint is shown in Fig. 10-2 (shaded area = new feasible region).

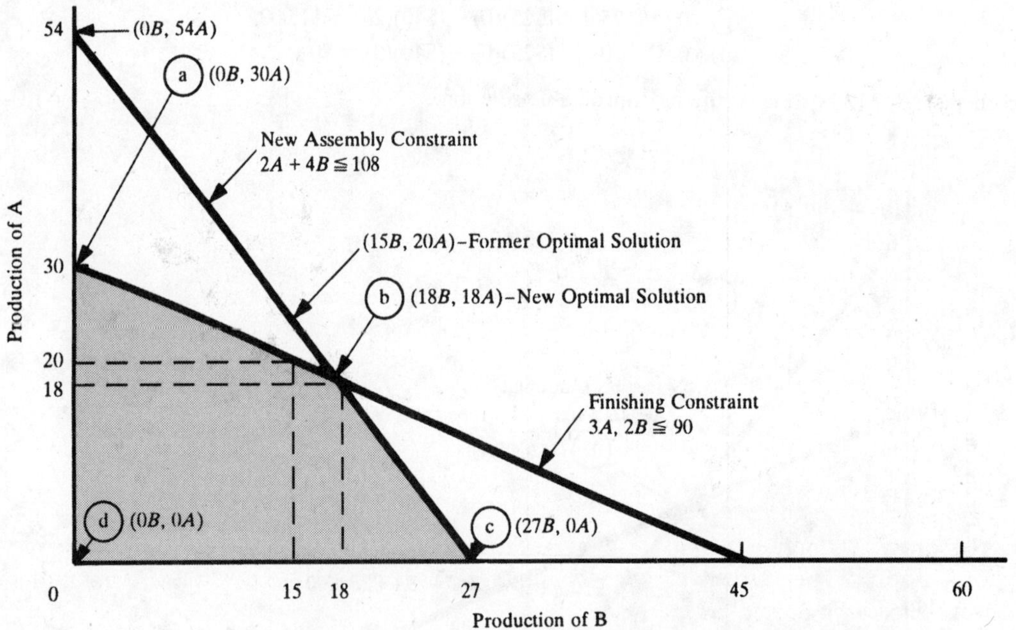

Fig. 10-2

Corner Points		Contribution Margin CM
A	B	$25A + $40B
ⓐ 30	0	($25)(30) + ($40)(0) = $750
ⓑ 18	18	($25)(18) + ($40)(18) = $1,170
ⓒ 0	27	($25)(0) + ($40)(27) = $1,080
ⓓ 0	0	($25)(0) + ($40)(0) = $0

As can be seen in the above table, the new optimal solution of 18*B*, 18*A* has total CM of $1,170 per week. Therefore, the shadow price of the assembly capacity is $70 ($1,170 − $1,100 = $70). The firm would be willing to pay up to $70 to obtain an additional eight hours per week, or $8.75 *per hour* per week.

10.3 THE LEARNING CURVE

The *learning curve* is based on the proposition that labor hours decrease in a definite pattern as labor operations are repeated. More specifically, it is based on the statistical findings that as the cumulative output doubles, the cumulative average labor input time required per unit will be reduced by some constraint percentage, ranging between 10 and 40 percent. The curve is usually designated by its complement. If the rate of reduction is 20 percent, the curve is referred to as an *80 percent learning curve.*

EXAMPLE 10.5 The following data illustrate the 80 percent learning curve relationship:

Quantity (in Units)		Time (in Hours)	
Per Lot	Cumulative	Total (Cumulative)	Average Time per Unit
15	15	600	40.0
15	30	960	32.0 (40.0 × 0.8)
30	60	1,536	25.6 (32.0 × 0.8)
60	120	2,460	20.5 (25.6 × 0.8)
120	240	3,936	16.4 (20.5 × 0.8)

As can be seen, as production quantities double, the average time per unit it takes goes down by 20 percent of its immediate previous time.

Applications of the learning curve theory include:

1. Pricing decisions based on the estimates of expected costs
2. Scheduling labor requirements
3. Capital budgeting decisions
4. Setting incentive wage rates

10.4 INVENTORY PLANNING AND CONTROL

Inventories provide a buffer to smooth out the differences in the time and location of demand and supply for a product. The purpose of inventory planning and control is to determine the optimum level of inventory necessary to minimize costs.

Inventory costs fall into three categories:

1. Order costs include all costs associated with preparing a purchase order.
2. Carrying costs include storage costs for inventory items plus opportunity cost (i.e., the cost incurred by investing in inventory).
3. Shortage (stockout) costs include those costs incurred when an item is out of stock. These include the lost contribution margin on sales plus lost customer goodwill.

Many inventory planning and control models are available, which basically try to answer the following questions:

1. How much to order?
2. When to order?

They include the basic economic order quantity (EOQ) model, the reorder point, and the determination of safety stock.

ECONOMIC ORDER QUANTITY (EOQ)

The EOQ model determines the order size that minimizes the sum of carrying and ordering costs.

Demand is assumed to be known and constant throughout the year. Order cost is assumed to be a fixed amount, and unit carrying costs are assumed to be constant. Since demand and lead time are assumed to be deterministic, there are no shortage costs. EOQ is computed as

$$EOQ = \sqrt{\frac{2(\text{Annual demand})\ (\text{Ordering cost})}{\text{Carrying cost per unit}}}$$

EXAMPLE 10.6 Oakman Sporting Goods Store buys baseballs at $25 per dozen from its wholesaler. Oakman will sell 35,000 dozen baseballs evenly throughout the year. Oakman desires a 12 percent return on investment (cost of capital) on its inventory investment. In addition, rent, insurance, taxes, etc., for each dozen baseballs in inventory is $0.50. The order cost is $10. Then the carrying cost per dozen is $0.50 + 12% ($25) = $3.50. Therefore,

$$EOQ = \sqrt{\frac{2(35{,}000)\ (\$10)}{\$3.50}} = \sqrt{200{,}000} = 447 \text{ dozen}$$

$$\text{Total inventory costs} = \text{Carrying cost per unit} \times \frac{EOQ}{2} + \text{Order cost} \times \frac{\text{Annual demand}}{EOQ}$$

$$= (\$3.50)\left(\frac{447}{2}\right) + (\$10)\left(\frac{35{,}000}{447}\right) = \$783 + \$783 = \$1{,}566$$

$$\text{Total number of orders per year} = \frac{\text{Annual demand}}{EOQ} = \frac{35{,}000}{447} = 78 \text{ orders}$$

REORDER POINT

Reorder point, which answers *when* to place an order, requires a knowledge about the *lead time*, which is the time interval between placing an order and receiving delivery. Reorder point can be computed as:

$$\text{Reorder point} = \text{Lead time} \times \text{Average usage per unit of time}$$

This gives the level of inventory at which the new order should be placed. If there is need for safety stock, then it should be added in the reorder point formula.

EXAMPLE 10.7 Assume that lead time is constant at two weeks and there are 50 working weeks in a year. Then the reorder time is

$$2 \text{ weeks} \times \frac{35{,}000 \text{ dozen}}{50 \text{ weeks}} = 2 \text{ weeks} \times 700 \text{ dozen used per week} = 1{,}400 \text{ dozen}$$

Therefore, when the inventory level drops to 1,400 dozen, the new order should be placed.

SAFETY STOCK

When lead time and demand are not certain, the firm must carry extra units of inventory, called *safety stock*, as protection against possible stockouts. To decide on the optimal level of safety stock, one must take into account costs of not having enough inventory, known as *stockout (shortage) costs*. Two methods of computing safety stock size are presented, using numerical examples. The first method does not recognize stockout costs, whereas the second method does.

EXAMPLE 10.8 (METHOD 1) Suppose that the store in Example 10.7 is faced with variable usage for its baseballs. Then it would compute safety stock as follows:

Maximum expected usage per week (assumed)	850 dozen
Average usage per week	700
Excess	150
Lead time	×2 weeks
Safety stock	300 dozen

The reorder point is then determined by adding this to the average usage during the lead time (the original formula):

$$\text{Reorder point} = \left(2 \text{ weeks} \times \frac{35{,}000}{50 \text{ weeks}}\right) + 300 \text{ dozen} = 1{,}400 \text{ dozen} + 300 \text{ dozen} = 1{,}700 \text{ dozen}$$

EXAMPLE 10.9 (METHOD 2) Suppose for Example 10.7 that the total usage over a two-week period is expected to be:

Total Usage	Probability
600	0.2
700	0.4
800	0.2
900	0.1
1,000	0.1
	1.00

Suppose further that stockout cost is estimated at $3.00 per dozen. Recall that the carrying cost is $3.50 per dozen.

Computation of Safety Stock

Safety Stock Levels in Units	Stockout and Probability	Average Stockout in Units	Average Stockout Costs	No. of Orders	Total Annual Stockout Costs	Carrying Costs	Total
0	100 with 0.2 200 with 0.1 300 with 0.1	70*	$210†	78	$16,380‡	$ 0	$16,380
100	100 with 0.1 200 with 0.1	30	90	78	7,020	350	7,370
200	100 with 0.1	10	30	78	2,340	700	3,040
300	0	0	0	78	0	1,050	1,050

*100(0.2) + 200(0.1) + 300(0.1) = 20 + 20 + 30 = 70 units.
†70 units × $3.00 = $210.
‡$210 × 78 times = $16,380.

The computation shows that the total costs are minimized at $1,050, when a safety stock of 300 dozen is maintained. Therefore, the reorder point is

$$1{,}400 \text{ dozen} + 300 = 1{,}700 \text{ dozen}$$

Summary

(1) LP consists of ____________ and ____________ including ____________ constraints.

(2) ____________ are values of decision variables that satisfy all the restrictions simultaneously.

(3) A shadow price is a(n) ____________. It is the ____________ the firm is willing to pay to obtain an additional unit of the resource.

(4) The ____________ is based on the statistical findings that as ____________ doubles, average labor time per unit is reduced by some constant percentage.

(5) Inventory planning models attempt to answer two basic questions: ____________ and ____________.

(6) The reorder point must add the size of safety stock when ____________ and ____________ are variable.

(7) The time interval between placing an order and ____________ is called ____________.

(8) One way of computing the safety stock size is to multiply the difference between ____________ and average usage by lead time.

(9) In computing the safety stock, the decision maker tries to balance off the costs of ____________ and the costs of carrying inventory.

(10) The solution to an LP problem is found on ____________ of the feasible region.

Answers: (1) an objective function, constraints, non-negative; (2) feasible solutions; (3) opportunity cost, maximum price; (4) learning curve, cumulative production; (5) how much to order, when to order; (6) demand (or usage), lead time; (7) receiving the delivery, lead time; (8) maximum usage; (9) stockouts (or shortage); (10) a corner.

Solved Problems

10.1 The following information relates to the Henry Company:

Units required per year	30,000
Cost of placing an order	$400
Unit carrying cost per year	$600

Assuming that the units will be required evenly throughout the year, what is the economic order quantity?

SOLUTION

$$EOQ = \sqrt{\frac{2(\text{Order cost})(\text{Annual demand})}{\text{Carrying cost}}} = \sqrt{\frac{2 \times \$400 \times 30{,}000}{\$600}} = \sqrt{\frac{\$24{,}000{,}000}{\$600}} = \sqrt{40{,}000} = 200$$

10.2 Pierce Incorporated has to manufacture 10,000 blades for its electric lawnmower division. The blades will be used evenly throughout the year. The setup cost every time a production run is made is \$80, and the cost to carry a blade in inventory for the year is \$0.40. Pierce's objective is to produce the blades at the lowest cost possible. Assuming that each production run will be for the same number of blades, how many production runs should Pierce make?

(AICPA, adapted)

SOLUTION

$$\text{Economic run size} = \sqrt{\frac{2 \times \text{Setup cost} \times \text{Demand per period}}{\text{Cost to hold one unit for one period}}}$$

By substituting the given information into this formula, the resulting run size is 2,000 units, as follows:

$$\sqrt{\frac{2 \times \$80 \times 10{,}000}{\$0.40}} = \sqrt{4{,}000{,}000} = 2{,}000$$

If each production run is to be 2,000 units and a total of 10,000 units are needed, there will have to be 5 runs (10,000 ÷ 2,000).

10.3 Politan Company manufactures bookcases. Setup costs are \$2.00. Politan manufactures 4,000 bookcases evenly throughout the year. Using the economic order quantity approach, find the cost of carrying one bookcase in inventory for one year when the optimal production run is 200.

(AICPA, adapted)

SOLUTION

$$200 = \sqrt{\frac{2 \times \$2 \times 4{,}000}{\text{Cost of carrying one unit for one period}}}$$

$$200 \times 200 = 40{,}000 = \frac{\$16{,}000}{\text{Cost of carrying one unit for one period}}$$

$$\text{Cost of carrying one unit for one period} = \$0.40$$

10.4 The Robney Company is a restaurant supplier which sells a number of products to various restaurants in the area. One of their products is a special meat cutter with a disposable blade.

The blades are sold in packages of 12 blades for \$20.00 per package. After a number of years, it has been determined that the demand for the replacement blades is at a constant rate of 2,000 packages per month. The packages cost the Robney Company \$10.00 each from the manufacturer and require a three-day lead time from date of order to date of delivery. The ordering cost is \$1.20 per order and the carrying cost is 10 percent per annum.

1. Calculate:

   (*a*) The economic order quantity

   (*b*) The number of orders needed per year

   (*c*) The total cost of buying and carrying blades for the year

2. Assuming that there is no safety stock and that the present inventory level is 200 packages, when should the next order be placed? (Use 360 days equals one year.)
3. Discuss the problems that most firms would have in attempting to apply this formula to their inventory problems.

(CMA, adapted)

SOLUTION

1. (*a*) The economic order quantity (EOQ) is

$$EOQ = \sqrt{\frac{2(24{,}000)(\$1.20)}{(\$10)(10\%)}} = \sqrt{57{,}600} = 240 \text{ units per order}$$

(*b*) The number of orders needed per year is

$$\frac{\text{Annual requirements}}{EOQ} = \frac{24{,}000}{240} = 100 \text{ orders per year}$$

(*c*) The total cost of buying and carrying blades for the year is

$$\frac{EOQ}{2}(\text{Holding cost per unit}) + \frac{\text{Annual requirements}}{EOQ}(\text{Ordering cost per order})$$

$$= \frac{240}{2}(\$10.00 \times 10\%) + \frac{24{,}000}{240}(\$1.20) = \$240$$

2. The optimal reorder point is lead time × average daily usage:

$$3 \text{ days} \times \frac{24{,}000 \text{ packages}}{360} = 200 \text{ packages}$$

Since the company has 200 packages now, it should place the next order immediately.

3. Some of the problems of applying the EOQ formula to inventory problems are:
   (*a*) Inventory is not always used at a constant rate, and the constant usage assumption is implicit in the EOQ formula.
   (*b*) The EOQ formula requires estimates of (1) annual sales, (2) ordering costs, (3) purchase price per unit, and (4) cost of carrying inventories. These estimates may be extremely difficult to obtain.

10.5 The Orphane Company buys raw materials from an outside supplier at $40 per unit; total annual needs are 6,400 units. The material is used evenly throughout the year. Order costs are $100 per order, and carrying costs for the year are $8 per unit in stock. The firm carries a safety stock of 50 units, has a lead time of one week, and works 50 weeks per year. Determine the economic order quantity (EOQ) and the reorder point.

SOLUTION

$$\text{Economic order quantity} = \sqrt{\frac{2 \times \$100 \times 6{,}400}{\$8.00}} = \sqrt{160{,}000} = 400 \text{ units}$$

$$\text{Reorder point} = \text{Average usage during lead time} + \text{Safety stock}$$

$$= 1 \text{ week} \times \frac{6{,}400}{50 \text{ weeks}} + 50 \text{ units}$$

$$= 128 \text{ units} + 50 \text{ units} = 178 \text{ units}$$

10.6 The purchasing agent responsible for ordering cotton underwear for Ace Retail Stores has come up with the following information:

Maximum daily usage	100 packages
Average daily usage	80 packages
Lead time	9 days
Economic order quantity	3,500 packages

1. Compute the safety stock.
2. Calculate the reorder point.

SOLUTION

1. The safety stock is computed as follows:

Maximum daily usage	100 packages
Average daily usage	80
Excess	20
Lead time	×9 days
Safety stock	180 packages

2. Reorder point = Average usage during lead time + Safety stock
   = 80 packages × 9 days + 180 packages = 720 + 180 = 900 packages

10.7 The Bolger Company has obtained the following costs and other data pertaining to one of its materials:

Working days per year	250
Average use per day	500 units
Maximum use per day	600 units
Lead time	5 days
Cost of placing one order	$36
Carrying cost per unit per year	$1

1. Calculate the economic order quantity.
2. Determine the safety stock.
3. Compute the reorder point.

(CGA, adapted)

SOLUTION

1. $$EOQ = \sqrt{\frac{2 \times 125{,}000 \times \$36}{\$1}} = \sqrt{9{,}000{,}000} = 3{,}000 \text{ units}$$

2.

Maximum use per day	600 units
Average use per day	500
Safety stock	100 units × 5 days of lead time = 500 units

3.

Average use per day (500) × Days of lead time (5)	2,500 units
Safety stock	500
Reorder point	3,000 units

10.8 Harrington & Sons, Inc., would like to determine the safety stock to maintain for a product so that the lowest combination of stockout cost and carrying cost will result. Each stockout will cost $75; the carrying cost for each safety stock unit will be $1; the product will be ordered five times a year. The following probabilities of running out of stock during an order period are associated with various safety stock levels:

Safety Stock Level	Probability of Stockout
10 units	40%
20	20
40	10
80	5

Using the expected value approach, determine the safety stock level.

(AICPA, adapted)

SOLUTION

Annual Number of Orders	×	Probability of Stockout	=	Expected Annual Stockouts	×	Cost per Stockout	=	Annual Stockout Cost	+	Annual Safety Stock Carrying Cost ($1 per unit)	=	Total Cost
5		0.4		2		$75		$150.00		$10		$160.00
5		0.2		1		75		75.00		20		95.00
5		0.1		0.5		75		37.50		40		77.50
5		0.05		0.25		75		18.75		80		98.75

The recommended level of safety stock is 40 units.

10.9 The Polly Company wishes to determine the amount of safety stock that it should maintain for product D that will result in the lowest cost. The following information is available:

Stockout cost	$80 per occurrence
Carrying cost of safety stock	$2 per unit
Number of purchase orders	5 per year

The available options open to Polly are as follows:

Units of Safety Stock	Probability of Running Out of Safety Stock
1. 20	40%
2. 40	20
3. 50	10
4. 55	5

What is the optimal amount of safety stock?

(AICPA, adapted)

SOLUTION

	Alternative			
	1.	2.	3.	4.
Stockout cost (given)	$ 80.00	$ 80.00	$ 80.00	$ 80.00
Multiplied by the probability of running out of stock for each alternative	40%	20%	10%	5%
Expected cost of a stockout	$ 32.00	$ 16.00	$ 8.00	$ 4.00
Weighted by the number of possible stockouts	5	5	5	5
	$160.00	$ 80.00	$ 40.00	$ 20.00
Carrying costs:				
Cost of carrying one unit	$ 2.00	$ 2.00	$ 2.00	$ 2.00
Multiplied by the number of units of stock per each alternative	20	40	50	55
	$ 40.00	$ 80.00	$100.00	$110.00
Total cost	$200.00	$160.00	$140.00	$130.00

10.10 The Starr Company manufactures several products. One of its main products requires an electric motor. The management of Starr Company uses the economic order quantity formula (EOQ) to determine the optimum number of motors to order. Management now wants to determine how much safety stock to order.

Starr Company uses 30,000 electric motors annually (300 working days). Using the EOQ formula, the company orders 3,000 motors at a time. The lead time for an order is five days. The annual cost of carrying one motor in safety stock is $10. Management has also estimated that the cost of being out of stock is $20 for each motor they are short.

Starr Company has analyzed the usage during past reorder periods by examining the inventory records. The records indicate the following usage patterns during the past reorder periods:

Usage During Lead Time	Number of Times Quantity Was Used
440	6
460	12
480	16
500	130
520	20
540	10
560	6
	200

1. Using an expected value approach, determine the level of safety stock for electric motors that Starr Company should maintain in order to minimize costs.
2. What would be Starr Company's new reorder point?
3. What factors should Starr Company have considered to estimate the out-of-stock costs?

(CMA, adapted)

SOLUTION

1. Starr Company is searching for the safety stock level which will minimize the expected total of the costs of carrying additional inventory and the costs associated with insufficient inventories (stockout

cost). The present reorder point, alternative safety stock levels, and probability of usage during lead time have to be computed before this level can be determined.

The present reorder point is calculated as follows:

$$\text{Average daily usage} = \frac{\text{Annual demand}}{\text{Number of working days}} = \frac{30{,}000 \text{ units}}{300 \text{ days}} = 100 \text{ units per day}$$

$$\text{Reorder point} = \text{Average daily usage} \times \text{Lead time} = (100 \text{ units/day}) \times 5 \text{ days} = 500 \text{ units}$$

Alternative safety stock levels would be the number of units needed to cover possible demand levels during lead time. These safety stock levels can be determined as follows:

$$\text{Possible safety stock levels} = \text{Possible demand} - \text{Reorder point}$$

The alternative safety stock levels are 0, 20, 40, and 60 units.

The probability of demand during lead time is:

Usage during Lead Time	Number of Times Quantity Was Used	Probability
440	6	0.03
460	12	0.06
480	16	0.08
500	130	0.65
520	20	0.10
540	10	0.05
560	6	0.03
	200	1.00

The safety stock level which will minimize costs for Starr Company is computed as follows:

Safety Stock Level	Number of Units Short	Probability		Average Number of Units Short	Total Annual Stockout Cost* (10 times × $20)	Annual Carrying Cost† ($10)	Total
0	20	0.10	2.0				
	40	0.05	2.0				
	60	0.03	1.8	5.8	$1,160	$ 0	$1,160
20	20	0.05	1.0				
	40	0.03	1.2	2.2	440	200	640
40	20	0.03	0.6	0.6	120	400	520
60	0	0	0	0	0	600	600

*Total annual stockout cost = Average number of units short × Number of orders × Stockout cost per unit.
†Annual carrying cost = Safety stock level × Carrying cost per unit.

A safety stock of 40 units will minimize Starr Company's annual stockout and carrying costs.

2. Present reorder point (demand during lead time—100 × 5) 500 units
Safety stock 40 units
New reorder point 540 units

3. The factors Starr Company should have considered when estimating the out-of-stock costs are:
   1. Possible lost contribution margin on motors not produced and sold.
   2. Costs associated with disrupted or idle production, such as wages of workers who could not be assigned to other production, cost of production rescheduling, extra cost of special purchases, etc.
   3. Possible loss of customers and customer goodwill.
   4. Additional clerical costs involved in keeping records of back orders.

10.11 McCormick Company, a regional supermarket chain, orders 480,000 cans of frozen orange juice per year from a California distributor. A two-dozen-can case of frozen juice delivered to McCormick's central warehouse costs \$4.80, including freight charges. The company borrows funds at a 10 percent interest rate to finance its inventories. The McCormick Company's purchasing agent has calculated that it costs \$15 to place an order for frozen juice and that the annual carrying expense (electricity, insurance, handling) is \$0.08 for each can of juice.

1. What is the EOQ?
2. How would you change your answer in part 1 if the California distributor offered a 10 percent discount off the delivery price for minimum orders of 72,000 cases?

(CGA, adapted)

SOLUTION

1.

$$EOQ = \sqrt{\frac{2 \times 480{,}000 \times \$15}{[(\$4.80 \div 24)(0.10)] + \$0.08}}$$

$$= \sqrt{\frac{14{,}400{,}000}{0.10}}$$

$$= \sqrt{144{,}000{,}000} = 12{,}000 \text{ cans}$$

or $12{,}000 \div 24 = 500$ cases

2. McCormick should decide to order in quantities of 72,000 cans, based on the following computations:

Order size	12,000 cans	72,000 cans
Number of orders per year	40	$6\frac{2}{3}$
Average inventory	6,000 cans	36,000 cans
Cost of placing orders at \$15	\$ 600	\$ 100
Cost of carrying inventory:		
$\$0.08 \times 6{,}000$	480	
$\$0.08 \times 36{,}000$		2,880
$[6{,}000 \times (\$4.80 \div 24)] \times 0.10$	120	
$[36{,}000 \times (\$4.80 \div 24)] \times 0.10$		720
Product cost:		
$(\$4.8 \div 24) \times 480{,}000$ cases	96,000	
$(\$4.32 \div 24) \times 480{,}000$ cases		86,400
Total cost including product cost	\$97,200	\$90,100

10.12 Stanley Electronics Products, Inc., finds that new-product production is affected by an 80 percent learning effect. The company has just produced 50 units of output at 100 hours per unit. Costs were as follows:

Materials @ \$20	\$1,000
Labor and labor-related costs:	
Direct labor—100 hours @ \$8	800
Variable overhead—100 hours @ \$2	200
	\$2,000

The company has just received a contract calling for another 50 units of production. It wants to add a 50 percent markup to the cost of materials and labor and labor-related costs. Determine the price for this job.

SOLUTION

Quantity	Total Time	Average Time per Unit
50 units	100 hours	2 hours
100	160	1.6 (80% × 2 hours)

Thus, for the new 50-unit job, it takes 60 hours total (160 hours − 100 hours).

Materials @ $20	$1,000
Labor and labor-related costs:	
Direct labor—60 hours @ $8	480
Variable overhead—60 hours @ $2	120
	$1,600
50 percent markup	800
Contract price	$2,400

10.13 Carson, Inc., uses a learning curve of 80 percent for all new products it develops. A trial run of 500 units of a new product shows total labor-related costs (direct, indirect labor, and fringe benefits) of $120,000. Management plans to produce 1,500 units of the new product during the next year.

1. Compute the expected labor-related costs for the year to produce the 1,500 units.
2. Find the unit cost of production for next year for labor-related costs.

SOLUTION

The 80 percent learning theory says that as cumulative quantities double, average time per unit falls to only 80 percent of the previous time. Therefore, the following data can be constructed:

Quantity	Time Cost	Average Cost per Unit
500 units	$120,000	$240 per unit
1,000	192,000	192 (80% × $240)
2,000	308,000	154 (80% × $192)

Thus,

Quantity	Total Cost
2,000	$308,000
500	120,000
1,500 units	$188,000

The expected labor-related costs for the 1,500 units of output is $188,000 and $125⅓ per unit ($188,000/1,500 units).

10.14 The Carson Company makes two products, X and Y. Their contribution margins are $50 and $90, respectively. Each product goes through three processes: cutting, finishing, and painting. The number of hours required by each process for each product and capacities available are given below:

	Hours Required in Each Process		
Product	Cutting	Finishing	Painting
X	2	4	3
Y	1	6	2
Capacities in hours	300	500	250

Formulate the objective function and constraints to determine the optimal product mix.

SOLUTION

Let X = Number of units of product X to be produced
Y = Number of units of product Y to be produced

Then, the LP formulation is as follows:

$$\begin{aligned} \text{Maximize:} \quad & TCM = \$50X + \$90Y \\ \text{Subject to:} \quad & 2X + 1Y \leqq 300 \\ & 4X + 6Y \leqq 500 \\ & 3X + 2Y \leqq 250 \\ & X, Y \geqq 0 \end{aligned}$$

10.15 The Oriental Quality Company produces either of two products as follows:

Product	Daily Capacity in Units Dept. X	Daily Capacity in Units Dept. Y	Unit Contribution Margin
A	400	150	$12
	or	or	
B	200	450	21

There is a maximum demand of 175 units per day for product A.

Develop the objective function and constraints:

(*a*) Maximum total contribution margin ____________.
(*b*) Dept. X constraint ____________.
(*c*) Dept. Y constraint ____________.
(*d*) Market demand constraint ____________.
(*e*) Non-negative constraint ____________.

SOLUTION

(*a*) $TCM = \$12A + \$21B$
(*b*) $1A + 2B \leqq 400$ *or* $2A + B \leqq 200$
(*c*) $1A + \frac{1}{3}B \leqq 150$ *or* $3A + B \leqq 450$
(*d*) $A \leqq 175$
(*e*) $A, B \geqq 0$

10.16 The Tripco Company produces and sells three products hereafter referred to as products A, B, and C. The company is currently changing its short-range planning approach in an attempt to incorporate some newer planning techniques. The controller and some of her staff have been conferring with a consultant on the feasibility of using a linear programming model for determining the optimum product mix.

Information for short-range planning has been developed in the same format as in prior years. This information includes expected sales prices and expected direct labor and material costs for each product. In addition, variable and fixed overhead costs were assumed to be the same for each product because approximately equal quantities of the products were produced and sold.

Price and Cost Information (per Unit)

	A	B	C
Selling price	$25.00	$30.00	$40.00
Direct labor	7.50	10.00	12.50
Direct materials	9.00	6.00	10.50
Variable overhead	6.00	6.00	6.00
Fixed overhead	6.00	6.00	6.00

All three products use the same type of direct material, which costs $1.50 per pound of material. Direct labor is paid at the rate of $5.00 per direct labor hour. There are 2,000 direct labor hours and 20,000 pounds of direct materials available in a month.

1. Formulate and label the linear programming objective function and constraints necessary to maximize Tripro's contribution margin. Use Q_A, Q_B, and Q_C to represent units of the three products.
2. What underlying assumptions must be satisfied to justify the use of linear programming?

(CMA, adapted)

SOLUTION

1. Objective function: Maximize: $Z = 2.50Q_A + 8.00Q_B + 11.00Q_C$

Constraints:

$$1.5Q_A + 2.0Q_B + 2.5Q_C \leqq 2{,}000 \text{ hours}$$
$$6.0Q_A + 4.0Q_B + 7.0Q_C \leqq 20{,}000 \text{ pounds}$$
$$Q_A,\ Q_B,\ Q_C \geqq 0$$

Supporting calculations:

Contribution margin:	A	B	C
Selling price	$25.00	$30.00	$40.00
Variable costs:			
Direct labor	$ 7.50	$10.00	$12.50
Direct material	9.00	6.00	10.50
Variable overhead	6.00	6.00	6.00
Total variable costs	$22.50	$22.00	$29.00
Contribution margin	$ 2.50	$ 8.00	$11.00
Labor hours:			
Direct labor in dollars	$ 7.50	$10.00	$123.50
Hours (Rate $5.00/hour)	$7.50/$5 = 1.5	$10/$5 = 2	$12.50/$5 = 2.5
Direct material in pounds:			
Direct material in dollars	$ 9.00	$ 6.00	$10.50
Pounds ($1.50 per pound)	$9/$1.50 = 6	$6/$1.50 = 4	$10.50/$1.50 = 7

2. The following assumptions must be satisfied to justify the use of linear programming:

(*a*) All functions (costs, prices, technological requirements) must be linear in nature.

(*b*) All parameters are assumed to be known with certainty.

(*c*) The decision variables are continuous.

10.17 Toy Corporation manufactures two products, Trinkets and Gadgets. The information regarding these products is as follows:

	Daily Capacities in Units			
Product	Cutting Department	Finishing Department	Sales Price per Unit	Variable Cost per Unit
Trinkets	400	240	\$50	\$30
	or	or		
Gadgets	200	320	70	40

The daily capacities of each department represent the maximum production for either Trinkets or Gadgets. However, any combination of Trinkets and Gadgets can be produced as long as the maximum capacity of the department is not exceeded; i.e., two Trinkets can be produced in the cutting department for each Gadget not produced, and three Trinkets can be produced in the finishing department for every four Gadgets not produced. Materials shortages prohibit the production of more than 180 Gadgets per day.

1. Set up the problem as a contribution margin maximization.
2. Solve the problem graphically.
3. Compute the shadow prices of cutting time.

(AICPA, adapted)

SOLUTION

1. Define t = Number of Trinkets to be produced
   g = Number of Gadgets to be produced

Then the formulation is:

$$\begin{aligned} \text{Maximize:} \quad & TCM = \$20t + \$30g \\ \text{Subject to:} \quad & (1)\ 1t + 2g \leqq 400 \\ & (2)\ 4t + 3g \leqq 960 \\ & (3)\ g \leqq 180 \\ & t, g \geqq 0 \end{aligned}$$

2. See Fig. 10-3.

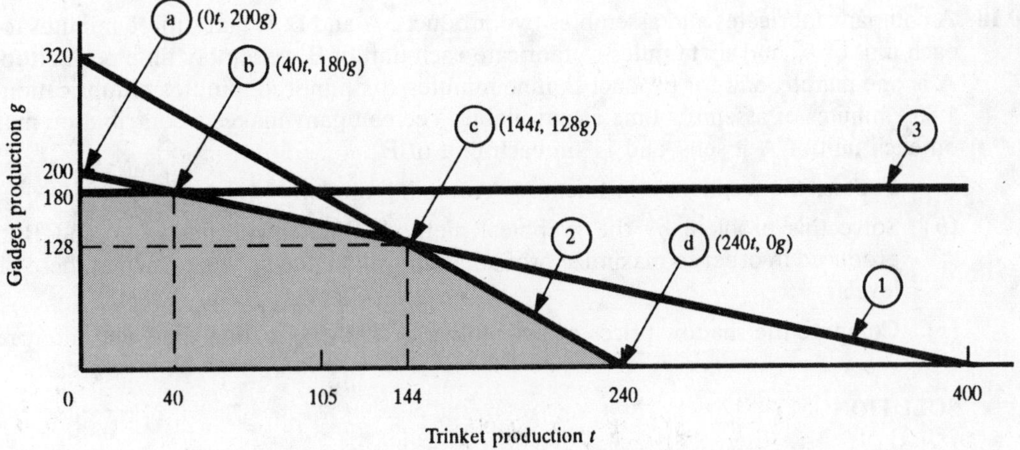

Fig. 10-3

Basic Feasible Solutions	Total Contribution Margin = $\$20t + \$30g$	TCM
ⓐ $t = 0$, $g = 200$	(\$20)(0) + (\$30)(200)	\$6,000
ⓑ $t = 40$, $g = 180$	(\$20)(40) + (\$30)(180)	6,200
ⓒ $t = 144$, $g = 128$	(\$20)(144) + (\$30)(128)	6,720
ⓓ $t = 240$, $g = 0$	(\$20)(240) + (\$30)(0)	4,800

By producing 144 Trinkets and 128 Gadgets, the corporation will maximize its total contribution margin when its scarce resource is productive capacity. Therefore, this production alternative is best.

3. The shadow price of cutting time is \$12, which is computed as follows: By increasing cutting department capacity by one unit, we get

$$t + 2g = 401$$

Solving the two equations:

$$t + 2g = 401$$
$$4t + 3g = 960$$

Multiplying the first equation by 4 and subtracting the second equation from it:

$$4t + 8g = 1{,}604$$
$$4t + 3g = 960$$
$$5g = 644$$
$$g = 128.8 \text{ Gadgets}$$

Substituting the value of g into the first equation:

$$t + 2g = 401$$
$$t + 257.6 = 401$$
$$t = 143.4 \text{ Trinkets}$$

The new contribution margin is then:

$$\$20\,(143.4) + \$30\,(128.8) = \$6{,}732$$

This means that increasing the cutting capacity by one unit yields an increase in contribution margin of \$12 (\$6,732 − \$6,720). Therefore, the shadow price of cutting capacity is \$12.

10.18 A company fabricates and assembles two products, A and B. It takes three minutes to fabricate each unit of A, and six minutes to fabricate each unit of B. Assembly time per unit for product A is one minute, and for product B, nine minutes. Six hundred minutes of fabrication time and 1,800 minutes of assembly time are available. The company makes a contribution margin of \$2 on each unit of A it sells, and \$1 on each unit of B.

(*a*) Express the problem as a linear programming model.

(*b*) Solve this problem by the graphical method. What quantities of A and B should be produced in order to maximize profits? What will be the profits earned at these production levels?

(*c*) Compute the shadow prices of assembly time and fabrication time, and interpret them.

SOLUTION

(*a*) Let A = Number of units of product A to produce
B = Number of units of product B to produce

Then

$$\begin{aligned} \text{Maximize:} \quad & TCM = \$2A + \$1B \\ \text{Subject to:} \quad & 3A + 6B \leqq 600 \quad \text{(fabrication)} \\ & 1A + 9B \leqq 1{,}800 \quad \text{(assembly)} \\ & A, B \geqq 0 \end{aligned}$$

(*b*) As shown in Fig. 10-4 (dark area = "feasible region"), the basic feasible solutions occur at the corner points 1 and 2 where

① $A = 0$	$B = 100$	$TCM = \$100$
② $A = 200$	$B = 0$	$TCM = \$400$

Thus, 200 units of A should be produced and no units of B. Profit will be \$400 at this level.

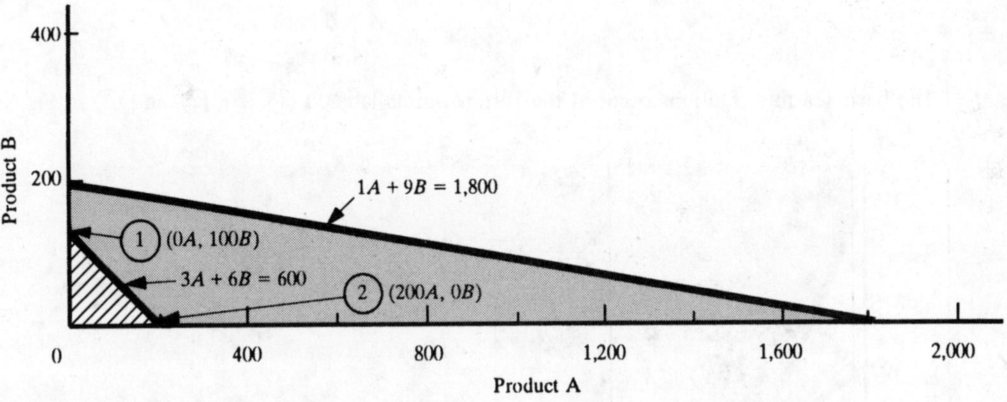

Fig. 10-4

(*c*) Before computing the shadow price, it is important to check to see if a constraint is binding with the optimal solution obtained in part (*b*).

$$3(200) + 6(0) = 600$$

The fabrication time constraint is binding, so there will be a positive shadow price for this resource. The procedure is to increase the right-hand side value by one minute and then to solve the problem again:

$$3A + 6B \leqq 601$$

Resolving the problem yields the optimal solution ($A = 200.33$, $B = 0$) and the corresponding maximum $CM = \$400.66$. Thus, the shadow price of the fabrication time is \$400.66 − \$400 = \$0.66. This \$0.66 is the maximum price the company would be willing to pay for an additional minute of fabrication time. This is also an *opportunity cost* in the sense that by not increasing the capacity for fabrication by one minute, the company will lose the opportunity to make \$0.66. In the case of assembly time, however, the shadow price would be zero, since the constraint is *not* binding, i.e.,

$$1(200) + 9(0) < 1{,}800$$

Since there is an unused amount of capacity for assembly, there is no shadow price and no opportunity cost involved. Therefore, no computation is necessary.

10.19 The United Refuse Chemical Company produces an industrial cleaner for carpets. This chemical is made from a mixture of two other chemicals, which both contain cleaning agent

ZIM and cleaning agent ZOOM. Their product must contain 175 units of agent ZIM and 150 units of agent ZOOM, and must weigh at least 100 pounds. Chemical A costs $8 per pound, while chemical B costs $6 per pound. Chemical A contains one unit of agent ZIM and three units of agent ZOOM. Chemical B contains seven units of agent ZIM and one unit of agent ZOOM. Set up the problem in the linear programming format and solve it graphically.

SOLUTION

Define A = Number of pounds of chemical A to be produced

B = Number of pounds of chemical B to be produced

Then, the LP formulation of this cost minimization problem is

$$\begin{aligned} \text{Minimize:} \quad & \$8A + \$6B \\ \text{Subject to:} \quad & A + 7B \geqq 175 \\ & 3A + B \geqq 150 \\ & A + B \geqq 100 \\ & A, B \geqq 0 \end{aligned}$$

The basic feasible solutions occur at the corner points labeled ⓐ, ⓑ, ⓒ, and ⓓ in Fig. 10-5.

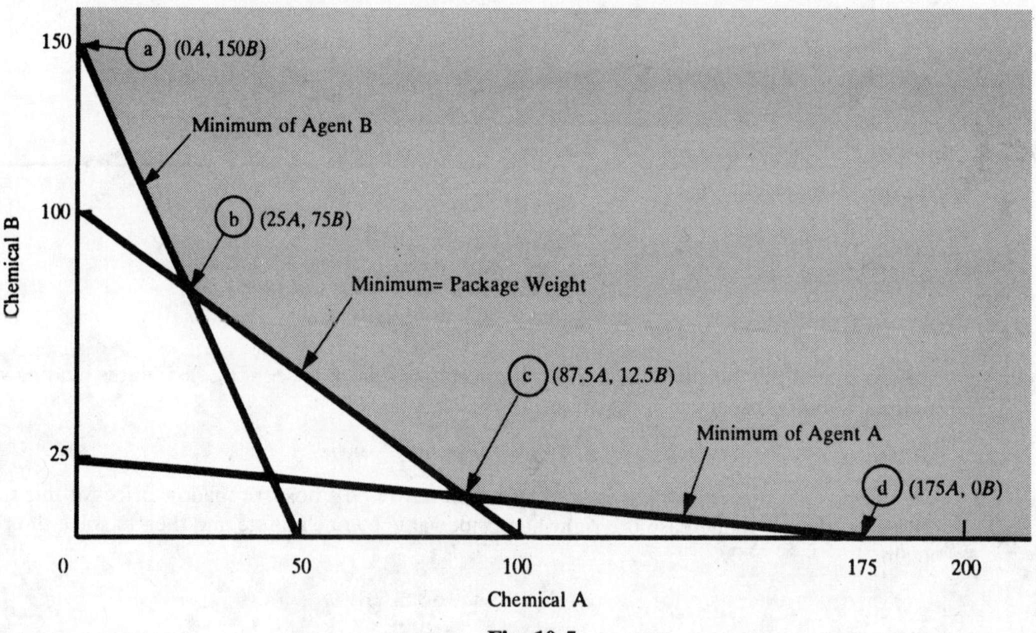

Fig. 10-5

Basic Feasible Solutions	Cost = $8A + $6B
ⓐA = 0, B = 150	($8)(0) + ($6)(150) = $900
ⓑA = 25, B = 75	($8)(25) + ($6)(75) = $650
ⓒA = 87.5, B = 12.5	($8)(87.5) + ($6)(12.5) = $775
ⓓA = 175, B = 0	($8)(175) + ($6)(0) = $1,400

Therefore, the least-cost mixture of the two chemicals A and B is: A = 25 pounds, B = 75 pounds.

10.20 The Frey Company manufactures and sells two products—a toddler bike and a toy high chair. Linear programming is employed to determine the best production and sales mix of bikes and chairs. This approach also allows Frey to speculate on economic changes. For example, management is often interested in knowing how variations in selling prices, resource costs, resource availabilities, and marketing strategies would affect the company's performance.

The demand for bikes and chairs is relatively constant throughout the year. The following economic data pertain to the two products:

	Bike (B)	Chair (C)
Selling price for unit	\$12	\$10
Variable cost per unit	8	7
Contribution margin per unit	\$ 4	\$ 3
Raw materials required		
Wood	1 board foot	2 board feet
Plastic	2 pounds	1 pound
Direct labor required	2 hours	2 hours

Estimates of the resource quantities available in a nonvacation month during the year are:

Wood	10,000 board feet
Plastic	10,000 pounds
Direct labor	12,000 hours

1. Formulate the problem for the nonvacation months in a linear programming format.
2. Solve the problem graphically. Determine the optimal product mix and the corresponding maximum contribution.
3. During the months of June, July, and August, the total direct labor hours available are reduced from 12,000 to 10,000 hours per month due to vacations.
   (*a*) What would be the best product mix and maximum total contribution margin when only 10,000 direct labor hours are available during a month?
   (*b*) The "shadow price" of a resource is defined as the marginal contribution of a resource or the rate at which profit would increase (decrease) if the amount of resource were increased (decreased). Based on your solution for part 2, what is the shadow price on direct labor hours in the original model for a nonvacation month?
4. Competition in the toy market is very strong. Consequently, the prices of the two products tend to fluctuate. Can analysis of data from the linear programming model provide information to management which will indicate when price changes made to meet market conditions will alter the optimum product mix? Explain your answer.

(CMA, adapted)

SOLUTION

1. The LP model is as follows.

Objective function: Maximize: $Z = \$4B + \$3C$

Constraints:

① $B + 2C \leqq 10{,}000$ board feet

② $2B + C \leqq 10{,}000$ pounds

③ $2B + 2C \leqq 12{,}000$ direct labor hours

$B, C \geqq 0$

2. From Fig. 10-6 we see that the basic feasible solutions occur at four corner points (not counting the origin). Evaluating them yields:

Basic Feasible Solutions	$Z = \$4B + \$3C$	Contribution Margin
ⓐ $B = 5{,}000$, $C = 0$	$\$4(5{,}000) + \$3(0)$	\$20,000
ⓑ $B = 4{,}000$, $C = 2{,}000$	$\$4(4{,}000) + \$3(2{,}000)$	22,000
ⓒ $B = 2{,}000$, $C = 4{,}000$	$\$4(2{,}000) + \$3(4{,}000)$	20,000
ⓓ $B = 0$, $C = 5{,}000$	$\$4(0) + \$3(5{,}000)$	15,000

Thus, the company can maximize its contribution margin for a nonvacation month by producing and selling 4,000 bikes and 2,000 chairs. This mix will yield a total contribution margin of \$22,000 in a month.

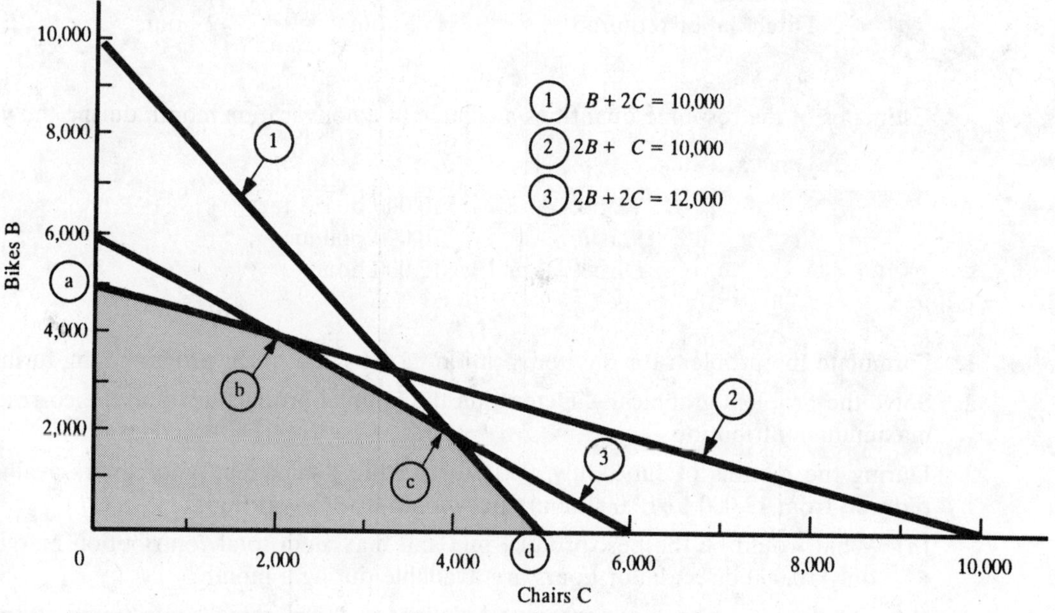

Fig. 10-6

3. (*a*) With the decrease in available direct labor hours from 12,000 to 10,000, the direct labor constraint (constraint ③) becomes $2B + 2C = 10{,}000$. This new labor constraint intersects the B axis at 5,000 units and the C axis at 5,000 units. In fact, this new constraint redefines the feasible solution region and makes the first two constraints—board feet of wood and pounds of plastic—superfluous. Consequently, any solution which satisfies constraint ③ automatically satisfies constraints ① and ②. Therefore, the problem has been reduced to a linear programming model with one constraint.

The solution to this problem is to produce and sell as many bikes as we can, because bikes and chairs require the same amount of scarce resource (two direct labor hours each) and bikes have a larger contribution margin than chairs (\$4 versus \$3). The solution, then, is to produce 5,000 bikes ($B = 10{,}000/2$) and no chairs ($C = 0$), for a maximum contribution margin of \$20,000 ($\$4 \times 5{,}000$).

(*b*) Based on the calculation in part 1, the shadow price on the decrease in direct labor hours for a nonvacation month is as follows:

$$\text{Shadow price} = \frac{\text{Change in total contribution margin}}{\text{Change in direct labor hours (DLH)}}$$

$$= \frac{\$22{,}000 - \$20{,}000}{12{,}000 \text{ DLH} - 10{,}000 \text{ DLH}}$$

$$= \frac{\$2{,}000}{2{,}000 \text{ DLH}}$$

$$= \$1 \text{ per DLH}$$

Thus, there is a \$1 reduction in contribution margin for every hour reduction in direct labor hours.

4. Yes, data from the linear programming model can be used to determine when the optimum product mix will change due to a change in product prices. Numerical solution of a linear programming application by using the simplex technique or by some computerized version of the simplex will provide data that can be used to calculate ranges for the contribution margins of the individual products. The range calculated for each product indicates the degree the individual contribution can vary before the optimum product mix will be affected and assumes that all other parameters are held constant. Consequently, as long as a price change does not cause the contribution margin of an individual product to fall outside of the calculated range, the price change will not affect the optimum product mix.

Financial Statement Analysis and Statement of Cash Flows

11.1 FINANCIAL STATEMENT ANALYSIS

The financial statements of an enterprise present the raw data of its assets, liabilities, and equities in the balance sheet and its revenue and expenses in the income statement. Without these data being subjected to analysis, many fallacious conclusions might be drawn concerning the financial condition of the enterprise.

Financial statement analysis is undertaken by creditors, investors, and other financial statement users in order to determine the creditworthiness and earning potential of an entity. This chapter explores ratio analysis that can be used to evaluate the financial health of a business.

It is important for the analyst to examine trends in accounts and ratios over the years, and to make comparisons with other firms in the industry. The analyst must be reasonably sure that the data given in different years within an enterprise, or within the industry, are comparable. Conclusions drawn from comparing the inventory of a company using LIFO (last-in, first-out) valuation with the inventory of a company using FIFO (first-in, first-out) valuation might have little validity. Also when two companies use different methods of depreciation, it will be difficult to compare their relative profitability and fixed assets balances.

11.2 RATIO ANALYSIS

Financial statement analysis uses as a primary tool a ratio which relates two figures applicable to different categories.

There are many ratios that the analyst can use, depending on what he or she considers important relationships. There is no point in computing ratios of unrelated items. For example, there is no interest in the ratio of sales returns and allowances to income taxes. We will illustrate a variety of ratios using the Ratio Company's financial statements, which follow.

THE RATIO COMPANY

Comparative Balance Sheet
(in Thousands of Dollars)
December 31, 19X3 and 19X2

ASSETS	19X3	19X2
Current Assets		
Cash	$ 30.0	$ 35
Accounts Receivable	20.0	15
Marketable Securities	20.0	15
Inventory	50.0	45
Total Current Assets	$120.0	$110
Plant Assets	100.0	90
Total Assets	$220.0	$200
LIABILITIES		
Current Liabilities	$ 55.4	$ 50
Long-Term Liabilities	80.0	75
Total Liabilities	$135.4	$125
STOCKHOLDERS' EQUITY		
Common Stock, 4,500 shares, $10 par value	$ 45.0	$ 45
Retained Earnings	39.6	30
Total Stockholders' Equity	$ 84.6	$ 75
Total Liabilities and Stockholders' Equity	$220.0	$200

THE RATIO COMPANY

Comparative Income Statement
(in Thousands of Dollars)
For the Years Ended December 31, 19X3 and 19X2

	19X3	19X2
Sales	$100.0	$110
Sales Returns and Allowances	20.0	8
Net Sales	$ 80.0	$102
Cost of Goods Sold	50.0	60
Gross Profit	$ 30.0	$ 42
Operating Expenses		
Selling Expenses	$ 11.0	$ 13
General Expenses	4.0	7
Total Operating Expenses	$ 15.0	$ 20
Income from Operations	$ 15.0	$ 22
Nonoperating Income	3.0	0
Income before Interest Expense and Taxes	$ 18.0	$ 22
Interest Expense	2.0	2
Income before Taxes	$ 16.0	$ 20
Income Taxes (40% rate)	6.4	8
Net Income	$ 9.6	$ 12

11.3 LIQUIDITY RATIOS

Liquidity is the company's ability to convert noncash assets into cash or to obtain cash in order to meet current liabilities. Liquidity applies to the short term, which is typically viewed as a time span of one year or less. A description of various liquidity measures follows.

WORKING CAPITAL

Working capital is equal to current assets less current liabilities. It is a safety cushion to creditors. A greater balance is required when the activity has difficulty borrowing on short notice.

The Ratio Company had a working capital of $64,600 in 19X3 ($120,000 – $55,400) and $60,000 in 19X2. The increase in working capital is a favorable sign.

CURRENT RATIO

The current ratio is equal to current assets divided by current liabilities. It is used to measure the ability of an enterprise to meet its current liabilities out of current assets. The limitation of the ratio is that it may rise just prior to financial distress because of a company's desire to improve its cash position by, for example, selling fixed assets. Such dispositions, while resulting in a more favorable current ratio, will have a detrimental effect upon production capacity. Another limitation of the current ratio is that it will be excessively high when inventory is carried on the LIFO basis.

The Ratio Company's current ratio for 19X3 was 2.17 ($120,000/$55,400; see Section 11.2) and for 19X2 it was 2.2. The ratio has remained fairly constant over the years.

QUICK (ACID-TEST) RATIO

The quick ratio is a stringent test of liquidity. It is found by dividing the most liquid current assets (cash, marketable securities, and accounts receivable) by current liabilities. Inventory is not included in this ratio because it usually takes a long time to convert inventory into cash. Prepaid expenses are also not included because they are not convertible into cash, and as such are not capable of covering current liabilities.

The Ratio Company had a quick ratio of 1.3 in 19X2 and 1.26 in 19X3, computed as ($30,000 + $20,000 + $20,000) ÷ $55,400. The ratio has been fairly constant over the years.

11.4 ACTIVITY RATIOS

Activity ratios, also called *turnover ratios*, measure the firm's use of assets to generate revenue and income. The higher the turnover, the more efficiently the firm is managing its assets. The turnover ratios are described below.

ACCOUNTS RECEIVABLE RATIOS

Accounts receivable ratios consist of the accounts receivable turnover and the collectiom period, which is the number of days the receivables are held. The *accounts receivable turnover* gives the number of times accounts receivable are collected during the year. The turnover is found by dividing net credit sales (if not available, then total sales) by the average accounts receivable. Average accounts receivable is typically found by adding the beginning accounts receivable to the ending accounts receivable and dividing by 2. Average accounts receivable may be computed more accurately on a monthly or quarterly basis, but this information is usually known only to management. Using data from the shortest period available will give the most accurate ratio. The higher the accounts receivable turnover, the better, since this means the company is collecting quickly from customers. These funds can then be invested for a return. Ratio Company's average accounts receivable for 19X3 are $17,500 ($15,000 plus $20,000, divided by 2) and the accounts receivable turnover is 4.57 times ($80,000/$17,500). For 19X2, the accounts receivable turnover is 8.16. The drop in the accounts receivable turnover ratio is significant, indicating a serious problem in collecting from customers. Therefore, a careful analysis of the company's credit policy is required.

The average *collection period*, or the number of days sales remain in accounts receivable, is found by dividing the accounts receivable turnover into 365 days. In 19X3, the Ratio Company's collection period was 79.9 days (365/4.57). This means that it took almost 80 days for a sale to be converted to cash. In 19X2, the collection period was 44.7 days. The materially higher collection period in 19X3 indicates a danger that customer balances may become uncollectible. Perhaps the company is now selling to highly marginal customers.

INVENTORY RATIOS

Two major ratios to look at are the inventory turnover and average age of inventory. *Inventory turnover* is computed by dividing the cost of goods sold by the average inventory. Average inventory is determined by adding the beginning and ending inventories and dividing by 2. The inventory turnover for Ratio Company in 19X3 was 1.05 times ($50,000/$47,500), and in 19X2 it was 1.26 times.

The decline in the inventory turnover indicates the stocking of more goods. An attempt should be made to determine whether specific inventory categories are not selling well and the reasons therefor. However, a decline in the turnover rate would not cause concern if it was due primarily to the introduction of a new product line for which the advertising effects were not yet felt.

Average age of inventory is computed by dividing 365 days by the turnover rate. The result indicates the length of time needed to buy, sell, and replace inventory. For Ratio Company, the average age of inventory in 19X3 was 347.6 days (365/1.05), and in 19X2 it was 289.7 days. The increase in the holding period suggests greater risk of obsolescence.

TOTAL ASSET TURNOVER

Total asset turnover is sales divided by total assets. It measures the level of capital investment relative to sales volume. It tells the firm how well it manages its overall assets. For Ratio Company, the total asset turnover in 19X3 was 0.45 times ($100,000/$220,000), and in 19X2 it was 0.55 times. The decrease in total asset turnover indicates that too much money was being built up in total assets.

11.5 LEVERAGE RATIOS

Long-term creditors are interested in the long-term solvency of the firm, which is the ability to meet its long-term obligations as they become due. The analysis concentrates on the long-term financial and operating structure of the business. The degree of long-term debt in the capital structure is also considered. Further, solvency is dependent on profitability, since in the long run a firm will not be able to meet its debts unless it is profitable.

TIMES INTEREST EARNED

The *times interest earned ratio* reflects the number of times before-tax earnings cover interest expense. This is found by dividing income before interest and taxes by interest expense. It is a safety margin indicator in the sense that it shows how much of a decline in earnings a company can absorb. In 19X3, interest of Ratio Company was covered 9 times ($18,000/$2,000), while in 19X2 it was covered 11 times. The decline in the coverage is a negative indicator, since less earnings are available to meet interest charges.

THE DEBT–EQUITY RATIO

The *debt–equity ratio* is a significant measure of solvency, since a high degree of debt in the capital structure may make it difficult for the company to meet interest charges and principal at maturity.

Further, with a high debt position comes the risk of running out of cash under conditions of adversity. Also, excessive debt will result in less financial flexibility in the sense that it will be difficult to obtain funds during tight money markets. For Ratio Company the ratio was 1.60 in 19X3 ($135,400/$84,600) and 1.67 in 19X2. The ratio remained fairly constant. A desired ratio depends on many variables, including the rates of other companies in the industry, access to further debt financing, and the stability of earnings.

11.6 PROFITABILITY RATIOS

An indication of good financial health is the company's ability to earn a satisfactory profit and return on investment. Investors will be reluctant to associate themselves with an entity that has poor earning potential, since the market price of stock and dividend potential will be adversely affected. Creditors will shy away from companies with deficient profitability, since the amounts owed to them may not be paid.

Some major ratios that measure operating results are summarized below.

PROFIT MARGIN

The ratio of net income to net sales is termed the *profit margin*. It indicates the profitability generated from revenue and hence is an important operating performance measure. In 19X3 the ratio for our company was 12 percent ($9,600/$80,000), and in 19X2 it was 12 percent. The profit margin was constant, indicating that the earning power of the business remained static.

RETURN ON INVESTMENT

Return on investment is a key measure because it shows the earnings achieved by the investment made in the business. Basically, two ratios evaluate the return on investment. One is the *return on total assets* and the other is the *return on owners' equity*.

The return on total assets indicates the efficiency with which management has used its available resources to generate income. It is found by dividing the sum of the net income and the interest expense adjusted for the tax rate by the average total assets. In 19X3, the return on total assets for Ratio Company was 0.05 {$9,600 + ($2,000)(0.6) ÷ [($220,000 + $200,000)/2]}. In 19X2, the return was 0.07. The productivity of assets in deriving income deteriorated in 19X3.

The return on owners' equity measures the return applicable to stockholders after the deduction of interest payments to creditors. It is found by dividing the net income by the average stockholders' equity. In 19X3, Ratio Company's return on owners' equity was 0.12 {$9,600 ÷ [($84,600 + $75,000)/2]}, and in 19X2 it was 0.17. There has been a significant drop in the return earned by the owners of the business.

EARNINGS PER SHARE

Earnings per share indicate what the earnings are for each common share held. When preferred stock is included in the capital structure, net income must be reduced by the preferred dividends to determine the amount applicable to common stock. When preferred stock does not exist, as is the case with the Ratio Company, earnings per share are equal to net income divided by common shares outstanding. Earnings per share are a useful indicator of the operating performance of the company, as well as of the dividends that may be expected. In 19X3, earnings per share for Ratio Company were $2.13 ($9,600/4,500 shares). In 19X2, they were $2.67. The decline in earnings per share should be of concern to investors.

All of the aforementioned profitability ratios have declined for Ratio Company in 19X3 relative to 19X2. This is a very negative sign.

PRICE–EARNINGS RATIO

Some ratios appraise the enterprise's relationship with its stockholders. The often-quoted price–earnings ratio, or P–E ratio, is equal to the market price per share of stock divided by the earnings per share. A high P–E ratio is good because it indicates that the investing public considers the company in a favorable light.

EXAMPLE 11.1 Let us assume that the market price per share of Ratio Company's stock was $20 on December 31, 19X3, and $22 on December 31, 19X2. Therefore, the P–E ratio in 19X3 was 9.39 ($20/$2.13) and the ratio in 19X2 was 8.24 ($22/$2.67). The rise in the P–E multiple indicates that the stock market had a higher opinion of the company in 19X3.

DIVIDEND RATIOS

Many stockholders are interested primarily in receiving dividends. The dividend yield of a stock is the dividends per share divided by tthe market price per share. Another ratio is the *dividend payout*, which is equal to the dividends per share divided by the earnings per share. A decline in dividends will cause concern on the part of stockholders.

BOOK VALUE PER SHARE

Book value per share is net assets available to common stockholders divided by shares outstanding, where net assets is stockholders' equity minus preferred stock. Comparing it with market price per share tells you whether the stock is overpriced or underpriced.

EXAMPLE 11.2 Assume the market price per share of Ratio Company's stock is $22 on December 31, 19X2, as in Example 11.1. The book value per share is ($84,600 − $0)/4,500 = $18.80 per share. The stock may be overvalued.

11.7 SUMMARY OF RATIOS

LIQUIDITY RATIOS

1. Working capital = Current assets − Current liabilities

2. $$\text{Current ratio} = \frac{\text{Current assets}}{\text{Current liabilities}}$$

3. $$\text{Quick (acid-test) ratio} = \frac{\text{Cash} + \text{Marketable securities} + \text{Accounts receivable}}{\text{Current liabilities}}$$

ACTIVITY RATIOS

1. Accounts receivable ratios:

   (*a*) $$\text{Accounts receivable turnover} = \frac{\text{Net credit sales}}{\text{Average accounts receivable}}$$

   (*b*) $$\text{Average collection period} = \frac{365}{\text{Accounts receivable turnover}}$$

2. Inventory ratios:

   (*a*) $$\text{Inventory turnover} = \frac{\text{Cost of goods sold}}{\text{Average inventory}}$$

(*b*) Average age of inventory $= \dfrac{365}{\text{Inventory turnover}}$

3. Total asset turnover $= \dfrac{\text{Sales}}{\text{Total assets}}$

LEVERAGE RATIOS

1. Times interest earned $= \dfrac{\text{Income before interest and taxes}}{\text{Interest expense}}$

2. Debt-to-equity ratio $= \dfrac{\text{Total liabilities}}{\text{Stockholders' equity}}$

PROFITABILITY RATIOS

1. Profit margin $= \dfrac{\text{Net income}}{\text{Net sales}}$

2. Return on investment:

   (*a*) Return on total assets $= \dfrac{\text{Net income + Interest expense (net of tax)}}{\text{Total assets}}$

   (*b*) Return on owners' equity $= \dfrac{\text{Net income}}{\text{Average stockholders' equity}}$

3. Earnings per share $= \dfrac{\text{Net income} - \text{Preferred dividends}}{\text{Number of common shares outstanding}}$

4. Price–earnings ratio $= \dfrac{\text{Market price per share}}{\text{Earnings per share}}$

5. Book value per share $= \dfrac{\text{Stockholders' equity} - \text{Preferred stock}}{\text{Number of common shares outstanding}}$

6. Dividend ratios:

   (*a*) Dividend yield ratio $= \dfrac{\text{Dividends per share}}{\text{Market price per share}}$

   (*b*) Dividend payout ratio $= \dfrac{\text{Dividends per share}}{\text{Earnings per share}}$

11.8 STATEMENT OF CASH FLOWS

The statement of cash flows shows the sources and uses of cash, which is a basis for cash flow analysis for financial managers. The statement aids in answering vital questions such as "Where was money obtained?" and "Where was money put and for what purpose?" Following is a list of specific questions that can be answered by the statement of cash flows and cash flow analysis.

1. Is the company growing or just maintaining its competitive position?
2. Will the company be able to meet its financial obligations?
3. Where did the company obtain funds?
4. What use was made of net income?

5. How much of the required capital was generated internally?
6. How was the expansion in plant and equipment financed?
7. Is the business expanding faster than it can generate funds?
8. Is the company's dividend policy in balance with its operating policy?
9. Is the company's cash position sound, and what effect will it have on the market price of stock?

Cash is vital to the operation of every business. How management utilizes the flow of cash can determine a firm's success or failure. Financial managers must control their company's cash flow so that bills can be paid on time and extra dollars can be put into the purchase of inventory and new equipment or invested to generate additional earnings.

11.9 FASB REQUIREMENTS

Management and interested external parties have always recognized the need for a cash flow statement. Therefore, in recognition of the fact that cash flow information is an integral part of both investment and credit decisions, the Financial Accounting Standards Board (FASB) has issued *Statement No. 95*, "Statement of Cash Flows." This pronouncement requires that enterprises include a statement of cash flows as part of the financial statements. A statement of cash flows reports the cash receipts, payments, and net change in cash on hand resulting from the *operating*, *investing*, and *financing* activities of an enterprise during a given period. The presentation reconciles beginning and ending cash balances.

11.10 ACCRUAL BASIS OF ACCOUNTING

Under *generally accepted accounting principles* (GAAP), most companies use the *accrual basis* of accounting. This method requires that revenue be recorded when earned and that expenses be recorded when incurred. Revenue may include credit sales that have not yet been collected in cash and expenses incurred that may not have been paid in cash. Thus, under the accrual basis of accounting, net income will generally not indicate the net cash flow from operating activities. To arrive at net cash flow from operating activities, it is necessary to report revenues and expenses on a cash basis. This is accomplished by eliminating those transactions that did not result in a corresponding increase or decrease in cash on hand.

EXAMPLE 11.3 During 19X1, the Eastern Electric Supply Corporation earned $2,100,000 in credit sales, of which $100,000 remained uncollected as of the end of the calendar year. Cash that was actually collected by the corporation in 19X1 can be calculated as follows:

Credit sales	$2,100,000
Less: Credit sales uncollected at year end	100,000
Actual cash collected	$2,000,000

11.11 CASH AND CASH EQUIVALENTS

FASB *Statement No. 95* also requires that the cash flow statement explain the changes during the period in cash and cash equivalents. *Cash equivalents* are defined as short-term, highly liquid investments that are both readily convertible to known amounts of cash and so near maturity that it is appropriate to refer to them as being equivalent to cash. Investments may or may not meet the definition of a cash equivalent. The statement indicates that only those investments with remaining maturities of three months or less at the date of their acquisition can qualify as cash equivalents.

For example, if a company bought a three-month United States Treasury Bill two months ago, it would be treated as cash equivalent because it was purchased within three months of its maturity date. However, a one-year bill purchased a year ago does not become a cash equivalent when its remaining maturity becomes three months or less. Other items commonly considered to be cash equivalents include commercial paper and money market funds.

11.12 PRESENTATION OF NONCASH INVESTING AND FINANCING TRANSACTIONS

A statement of cash flows focuses only on transactions involving the cash receipts and disbursements of a company. Noncash investing and financing transactions, such as the acquisition of land in return for the issuance of bonds, preferred stock, or common stock, should not be presented in the body of the statement. These noncash transactions must, however, be disclosed elsewhere in the cash flow statement.

11.13 OPERATING, INVESTING, AND FINANCING ACTIVITIES

As stated previously, a statement of cash flows focuses only on transactions involving the cash receipts and disbursements of a company. The statement of cash flows classifies cash receipts and cash payments into operating, investing, and financing activities.

OPERATING ACTIVITIES

Operating activities include all transactions that are not investing or financing activities. They relate only to income statement items. Thus, cash received from the sale of goods or services, including the collection or sale of trade accounts and notes receivable from customers, interest received on loans, and dividend income are treated as cash from operating activities. Cash paid to acquire materials for the manufacture of goods for resale, rental payments to landlords, payments to employees as compensation, and interest paid to creditors are classified as cash outflows for operating activities.

EXAMPLE 11.4 For the year ended December 31, 19X9, the net income of the Forbes Picture Frame Corporation was $60,000. Depreciation on plant assets for the year was $25,000. The balances of the current asset and current liability accounts at the beginning and end of 19X9 are as follows:

	Beginning	End
Cash	$ 70,000	$ 65,000
Short-term investments	0	9,000
Accounts receivable	90,000	100,000
Inventories	155,000	145,000
Prepaid expenses	9,500	7,500
Accounts payable	59,000	51,000

What is the amount to be reported for cash flows from operating activities for 19X9?

Net income		$60,000
Add: Depreciation	$25,000	
Decrease in inventories	10,000	
Decrease in prepaid expenses	2,000	37,000
Deduct: Increase in short-term investments	$ 9,000	
Increase in accounts receivable	10,000	
Decrease in accounts payable	8,000	27,000
Cash inflows from operating activities		$70,000

INVESTING ACTIVITIES

Investing activities include cash inflows from the sale of property, plant, and equipment used in the production of goods and services, debt instruments or equity of other entities, and the collection of principal on loans made to other enterprises. Cash outflows under this category may result from the purchase of plant and equipment and other productive assets, debt instruments or equity of other entities, and the making of loans to other enterprises.

EXAMPLE 11.5 During 19X9, the Zandex Altimeter Corporation sold its plant and equipment for $9,000,000 and sold all of its stock investment in Trunk Realty Corporation, an unrelated entity, for $8,000,000. It bought a new plant for $7,000,000 and made a loan of $5,500,000 to another company. Net cash provided by the corporation's investing operations for the year 19X9 is calculated as follows:

Cash received:		
Sale of plant and equipment	$9,000,000	
Sale of stock investment	8,000,000	
Total		$17,000,000
Cash paid:		
Purchase of new plant	$7,000,000	
Loan to another entity	5,500,000	
Total		12,500,000
Net cash provided by investing activities		$ 4,500,000

FINANCING ACTIVITIES

The financing activities of an enterprise involve the sale of a company's own preferred and common stock, bonds, mortgages, notes, and other short- or long-term borrowings. Cash outflows classified as financing activities include the repayment of short- and long-term debt, the reacquisition of treasury stock, and the payment of cash dividends.

EXAMPLE 11.6 In 19X9, the Hanniford Ore Processing Corporation sold 2,000 shares of its own common stock for $2,000,000 cash and $10,000,000 of 10 percent, ten-year bonds. It also issued another $50,000,000 in preferred stock in return for land and buildings. Hanniford then reacquired 10,000 shares of its own common stock for $8,800,000 and paid a cash dividend of $4,000,000. Net cash provided by the corporation's investing operations for the year 19X9 is calculated as follows.

Cash received:		
Sale of common stock	$ 2,000,000	
Sale of bonds	10,000,000	
Total		$12,000,000
Cash paid:		
Reacquisition of common stock	$ 8,800,000	
Cash dividend paid	4,000,000	
Total		12,800,000
Net cash used in financing activities		$ 800,000

The issuance of the preferred stock in exchange for the land and buildings is a noncash transaction that would be disclosed in supplementary form at the end of the statement.

11.14 PRESENTATION OF THE CASH FLOW STATEMENT

A cash flow statement can be presented in either the direct or indirect format. The investing and financing sections will be the same under either format. However, the operating section will be different.

DIRECT METHOD

Enterprises that utilize the direct method should report separately the following classes of operating cash receipts and payments:

1. Cash collected from customers, including lessees, licensee, and other similar items
2. Interest and dividends received
3. Other operating cash receipts, if any
4. Cash paid to employees and other suppliers of goods or services, including supplies of insurance, advertising, and other similar expenses
5. Interest paid
6. Income taxes paid
7. Other operating cash payments, if any

Companies that use the direct method must provide a reconciliation of net income to net cash flow from operating activities in a separate schedule in the financial statements.

INDIRECT METHOD

The indirect method starts with net income and reconciles it to net cash flow from operating activities. The cash flow from operating activities is found by adjusting net income for (1) changes in current assets and current liabilities and (2) depreciation expense. Depreciation expense is not a cash flow. Because it decreases net income, it is added back to net income in order to arrive at the operating cash flow. The following summarizes the process:

Change	Adjustment to Net Income
Decrease in a current asset	Add
Increase in a current asset	Subtract
Decrease in a current liability	Subtract
Increase in a current liability	Add

The indirect method is more widely used, since it shows the relationship between the income statement and the balance sheet and therefore aids in the analysis of these statements.

EXAMPLE 11.7 A comparative balance sheet and income statement of Banner Cord Corporation for the year ended December 31, 19X8, was presented as follows.

BANNER CORD CORPORATION

Comparative Balance Sheet
December 31, 19X9

	19X9	19X8	Change Increase/Decrease
ASSETS			
Cash	$ 74,000	$ 98,000	$ 24,000 Decrease
Accounts Receivable	52,000	72,000	20,000 Decrease
Prepaid Expenses	12,000	0	12,000 Increase
Long-Term Investments	1,000	2,000	1,000 Decrease
Land	140,000	0	140,000 Increase
Building	400,000	0	400,000 Increase
Accumulated Depreciation—Building	(22,000)	0	22,000 Increase
Equipment	136,000	0	136,000 Increase
Accumulated Depreciation—Equipment	(20,000)	0	20,000 Increase
Total	$773,000	$172,000	
LIABILITIES AND STOCKHOLDERS' EQUITY			
Accounts Payable	$ 81,000	$ 12,000	$ 69,000 Increase
Bonds Payable	300,000	0	300,000 Increase
Common Stock	120,000	120,000	0
Retained Earnings	272,000	40,000	232,000 Increase
Total	$773,000	$172,000	

BANNER CORD CORPORATION

Income Statement
For the Year Ended December 31, 19X9

Revenues		$984,000
Operating Expenses (excluding depreciation)	$538,000	
Depreciation Expense	42,000	580,000
Income from Operations		$404,000
Income Tax Expense		136,000
Net Income		$268,000

During 19X9, Banner Cord paid $36,000 in cash dividends.
Prepare a statement of cash flows using (*a*) the direct method and (*b*) the indirect method.
(*a*) The statement of cash flows, using the *direct method*, would be presented as follows.

BANNER CORD CORPORATION

Statement of Cash Flows
For the Year Ended December 31, 19X9

Cash Flows from Operating Activities:		
Cash Received from Customers	$1,004,000	
Cash Payments for Operating Expenses	(469,000)	
Cash Payments for Prepaid Expenses	(12,000)	
Cash Payments for Taxes	(136,000)	
Net Cash Provided by Operating Activities		$387,000
Cash Flows from Investing Activities:		
Cash Paid to Purchase Land	$ (140,000)	
Cash Paid to Purchase Building	(400,000)	
Cash Paid to Purchase Equipment	(136,000)	
Sale of Long-Term Investment	1,000	
Net Cash Used in Investing Activities		(675,000)
Cash Flows from Financing Activities:		
Cash Received from the Issuance of Bonds	$ 300,000	
Cash Paid for Dividends	(36,000)	
Net Cash Provided by Financing Activities		264,000
Net Decrease in Cash and Cash Equivalents		(24,000)
Cash and Cash Equivalents at the Beginning of the Year		98,000
Cash and Cash Equivalents at the End of the Year		$ 74,000

Under this method, the $1,004,000 in cash received from customers represents $984,000 in sales increased by a reduction in accounts receivable of $20,000. Accounts receivable was reduced due to a conversion into cash. The cash outflow of $469,000 was determined by reducing the $538,000 in expenses by the increase to accounts payable of $69,000. All other amounts were obtained either directly from the balance sheet or from the income statement.

Under the direct method, a separate schedule reconciling net income to net cash would be presented as follows.

BANNER CORD CORPORATION

Statement of Cash Flows
For the Year Ended December 31, 19X9

Cash Flows from Operating Activities:		
Net Income		$268,000
Add: Adjustments to Reconcile Net Income to Net Cash:		
Depreciation Expense	$42,000	
Decrease in Accounts Receivable	20,000	
Increase in Prepaid Expenses	(12,000)	
Increase in Accounts Payable	69,000	119,000
Net Cash Provided by Operating Activities		$387,000

(*b*) If the indirect method were utilized, the cash flow statement would be presented as follows.

BANNER CORD CORPORATION

Statement of Cash Flows
For the Year Ended December 31, 19X9

Cash Flows from Operating Activities:		
Net Income		$268,000
Add: Adjustments to Reconcile Net Income to Net Cash Earnings		
Depreciation Expense	$ 42,000	
Decrease in Accounts Receivable	20,000	
Increase in Prepaid Expenses	(12,000)	
Increase in Accounts Payable	69,000	119,000
Net Cash Flow Provided by Operating Activities		$387,000
Cash Flows from Investing Activities:		
Cash Paid to Purchase Land	$(140,000)	
Cash Paid to Purchase Building	(400,000)	
Cash Paid to Purchase Equipment	(136,000)	
Sale of Long-Term Investments	1,000	
Net Cash Used in Investing Activities		(675,000)
Cash Flows from Financing Activities		
Cash Received from the Issuance of Bonds	$300,000	
Cash Paid for Dividends	(36,000)	
Net Cash Provided by Financing Activities		264,000
Net Decrease in Cash and Cash Equivalents		$(24,000)
Cash and Cash Equivalents at the Beginning of the Year		$ 98,000
Cash and Cash Equivalents at the End of the Year		$ 74,000

Summary

(1) ____________ is the ability of a company to meet its current liabilities out of current assets.

(2) The current ratio is equal to ____________ divided by ____________.

(3) ____________ is included in computing the current ratio but not the quick ratio.

(4) The accounts receivable turnover is equal to ____________ divided by ____________.

(5) The number of times interest is earned is equal to ____________ divided by ____________.

(6) Return on owners' equity is found by dividing ____________ by ____________.

(7) The price–earnings ratio is equal to the ____________ per share divided by the ____________ per share.

(8) Two measures that are of interest to stockholders in evaluating the dividend policy of the firm are the dividend ____________ and the dividend ____________ ratios.

(9) The statement of cash flows seeks to explain the changes in ____________ and ____________ rather than ambiguous terms such as ____________.

(10) The ____________ is the breakdown of the return on total assets into the profit margin and ____________.

(11) Depreciation expense is one of the items that must be ____________ to net income to determine the cash flows from ____________.

(12) The three major categories of the statement of cash flows are cash flows associated with ____________ activities, investing activities, and ____________ activities.

(13) The return on equity is the return on total assets multiplied by the ____________.

(14) A stock dividend (is/is not) shown in the statement of cash flows.

(15) Financial statement analysis should combine ____________ and industry comparisons.

Answers: (1) liquidity; (2) current assets, current liabilities; (3) inventory; (4) net credit sales, average accounts receivable; (5) income before interest and taxes; (6) net income, average stockholders' equity; (7) market price, earnings; (8) yield, payout; (9) cash, cash equivalents, funds; (10) Du Pont formula, total asset turnover; (11) added back, operating activities; (12) operating, financing; (13) equity multiplier; (14) is not; (15) trend analysis.

Solved Problems

11.1 Charles Corporation's balance sheet at December 31, 19A, shows the following:

Current Assets	
Cash	$ 4,000
Marketable Securities	8,000
Accounts Receivable	100,000
Inventories	120,000
Prepaid Expenses	1,000
Total Current Assets	$233,000
Current Liabilities	
Notes Payable	$ 5,000
Accounts Payable	150,000
Accrued Expenses	20,000
Income Taxes Payable	1,000
Total Current Liabilities	$176,000
Long-Term Liabilities	$340,000

1. Determine (*a*) working capital, (*b*) current ratio, and (*c*) quick ratio.
2. Based on the answers to part 1, does Charles Corporation have good or poor liquidity if the industry averages are a current ratio of 1.29 and a quick ratio of 1.07?

SOLUTION

1. (*a*)

$$\text{Working capital} = \text{Current assets} - \text{Current liabilities}$$
$$\$233{,}000 - \$176{,}000 = \$57{,}000$$

(*b*)

$$\text{Current ratio} = \frac{\text{Current assets}}{\text{Current liabilities}} = \frac{\$233{,}000}{\$176{,}000} = 1.32$$

(*c*)

$$\text{Quick ratio} = \frac{\text{Cash} + \text{Marketable securities} + \text{Accounts receivable}}{\text{Current liabilities}}$$
$$= \frac{\$4{,}000 + \$8{,}000 + \$100{,}000}{\$176{,}000} = \frac{\$112{,}000}{\$176{,}000} = 0.64$$

2. While the company's current ratio is slightly better than the industry norm, its quick ratio is significantly below the norm. Charles Corporation has more in current liabilities than in highly liquid assets. It therefore has a poor liquidity position.

11.2 The Rivers Company reports the following data relative to accounts receivable:

	19X2	19X1
Average accounts receivable	$ 400,000	$ 416,000
Net credit sales	2,600,000	3,100,000

The terms of sale are net 30 days.

1. Compute the accounts receivable turnover and the collection period.
2. Evaluate the results.

SOLUTION

1.

$$\text{Accounts receivable turnover} = \frac{\text{Net credit sales}}{\text{Average accounts receivable}}$$

$$\text{19X2:} \quad \frac{\$2{,}600{,}000}{\$400{,}000} = 6.5 \text{ times} \qquad \text{19X1:} \quad \frac{\$3{,}100{,}000}{\$416{,}000} = 7.45 \text{ times}$$

$$\text{Collection period} = \frac{365 \text{ days}}{\text{Accounts receivable turnover}}$$

$$\text{19X2:} \quad \frac{365}{6.5} = 56.2 \text{ days} \qquad \text{19X1:} \quad \frac{365}{7.45} = 49 \text{ days}$$

2. The company's management of accounts receivable is poor. In both years, the collection period exceeded the terms of net 30 days. The situation is getting worse, as is indicated by the significant increase in the collection period in 19X2 relative to 19X1. The company has significant funds tied up in accounts receivable that could be invested for a return. A careful evaluation of the credit policy is needed. Perhaps sales are being made to marginal customers.

11.3 Utica Company's net accounts receivable were $250,000 at December 31, 19A, and $300,000 at December 31, 19B. Net cash sales for 19B were $100,000. The accounts receivable turnover for 19B was 5.0. What were Utica's total net sales for 19B?

(AICPA, adapted)

SOLUTION

$$\text{Average accounts receivable} = \frac{\text{Beginning accounts receivable} + \text{Ending accounts receivable}}{2}$$

$$= \frac{\$250{,}000 + \$300{,}000}{2} = \$275{,}000$$

$$\text{Accounts receivable turnover} = \frac{\text{Net credit sales}}{\text{Average accounts receivable}}$$

$$= \frac{\text{Net credit sales}}{\$275{,}000}$$

$$\text{Net credit sales} = 5 \times \$275{,}000 = \$1{,}375{,}000$$

Since the cash sales were $100,000, the total net sales must be $1,475,000.

11.4 On January 1, 19D, the River Company's beginning inventory was $400,000. During 19D, River purchased $1,900,000 of additional inventory. On December 31, 19D, River's ending inventory was $500,000.

1. What is the inventory turnover and the age of inventory for 19D?
2. If the inventory turnover in 19C was 3.3 and the age of the inventory was 110.6 days, evaluate the results for 19D.

SOLUTION

1.

Cost of Goods Sold	
Beginning Inventory	$ 400,000
Purchases	1,900,000
Cost of Goods Available	$2,300,000
Ending Inventory	500,000
Cost of Goods Sold	$1,800,000

$$\text{Average inventory} = \frac{\text{Beginning inventory} + \text{Ending inventory}}{2}$$

$$= \frac{\$400{,}000 + \$500{,}000}{2} = \$450{,}000$$

$$\text{Inventory turnover} = \frac{\text{Cost of goods sold}}{\text{Average inventory}} = \frac{\$1{,}800{,}000}{\$450{,}000} = 4$$

$$\text{Age of inventory} = \frac{365 \text{ days}}{\text{Inventory turnover}} = \frac{365}{4} = 91.3 \text{ days}$$

2. River Company's inventory management improved in 19D, as evidenced by the higher turnover rate and decrease in the days that inventories were held. As a result, there is less liquidity risk. Further, the company's profitability will benefit by the increased turnover of merchandise.

11.5 A condensed balance sheet and other financial data for Alpha Company appear below.

ALPHA COMPANY
Balance Sheet
December 31, 19X1

ASSETS	
Current Assets	$100,000
Plant Assets	140,000
Total Assets	$250,000
LIABILITIES AND STOCKHOLDERS' EQUITY	
Current Liabilities	$100,000
Long-Term Liabilities	75,000
Total Liabilities	$175,000
Stockholders' Equity	75,000
Total Liabilities and Stockholders' Equity	$250,000

Income Statement Data

Net Sales	$375,000
Interest Expense	4,000
Net Income	22,500

The following account balances existed at December 31, 19X0: Total Assets, $200,000; Stockholders' Equity, $65,000. The tax rate is 35 percent.

Industry norms as of December 31, 19X1 were:

Debt–equity ratio	1.75
Profit margin	0.12
Return on total assets	0.15
Return on stockholders' equity	0.30
Total asset turnover	1.71

Calculate and evaluate the following ratios for Alpha Company as of December 31, 19X1:

(*a*) Debt–equity ratio
(*b*) Profit margin
(*c*) Return on total assets
(*d*) Return on stockholders' equity
(*e*) Total asset turnover

SOLUTION

(*a*)
$$\frac{\text{Total liabilities}}{\text{Stockholders' equity}} = \frac{\$175{,}000}{\$75{,}000} = 2.33$$

Alpha's debt–equity ratio is considerably above the industry norm, indicating a solvency problem. Excessive debt may make it difficult for the firm to meet its obligations during a downturn in business. A high debt position will also make it difficult for the entity to obtain financing during a period of tight money supply.

(*b*)
$$\text{Profit margin} = \frac{\text{Net income}}{\text{Net sales}} = \frac{\$22{,}500}{\$375{,}000} = 0.06$$

Alpha's profit margin is far below the industry norm. This indicates that the operating performance of the entity is poor because the profitability generated from revenue sources is low.

(*c*)
$$\text{Return on total assets} = \frac{\text{Net income} + \text{Interest expense (net of tax)}}{\text{Average total assets}}$$
$$= \frac{\$22{,}500 + \$4{,}000\ (1 - 0.35)}{(\$200{,}000 + \$250{,}000)/2} = \frac{\$25{,}100}{\$225{,}000} = 0.11$$

Alpha's ratio is below the industry norm. Therefore, the company's efficiency in generating profit from assets is low. Profit generation is, of course, different from revenue (sales) generation because for the former, corporate expenses are deducted from sales.

(*d*)
$$\text{Return on stockholders' equity} = \frac{\text{Net income}}{\text{Average stockholders' equity}}$$
$$= \frac{\$22{,}500}{(\$65{,}000 + \$75{,}000)/2} = \frac{\$22{,}500}{\$70{,}000} = 0.32$$

Since the return earned by Alpha's stockholders is slightly more than the industry norm, investment in the firm relative to competition was advantageous to existing stockholders. This may be due to a currently low stockholders' equity investment in the firm.

(*e*)
$$\frac{\text{Net sales}}{\text{Average total assets}} = \frac{\$375{,}000}{\$225{,}000} = 1.67$$

Alpha's ratio is about the same as the industry norm. Therefore, the company's ability to utilize its assets in obtaining revenue is similar to the competition's. The utilization of assets has a bearing upon the ultimate profitability to stockholders.

11.6 The Format Company reports the following balance sheet data:

Current liabilities	$280,000
Bonds payable, 16%	120,000
Preferred stock, 14%, $100 par value	200,000
Common stock, $25 par value, 16,800 shares	420,000
Premium on common stock	240,000
Retained earnings	180,000

Income before taxes is $160,000. The tax rate is 40 percent. Common stockholders' equity in the previous year was $800,000. The market price per share of common stock is $35. Calculate (*a*) net income, (*b*) preferred dividends, (*c*) return on common stock, (*d*) times interest earned, (*e*) earnings per share, (*f*) price–earnings ratio, and (*g*) book value per share.

SOLUTION

(*a*)

Income before taxes	$160,000
Taxes (40% rate)	64,000
Net income	$ 96,000

(*b*)
$$14\% \times \$200{,}000 = \$28{,}000$$

(*c*) Common stockholders' equity:

Common stock	$420,000
Premium on common stock	240,000
Retained earnings	180,000
Common stockholders' equity	$840,000

$$\text{Return on common stock} = \frac{\text{Net income} - \text{Preferred dividends}}{\text{Average common stockholders' equity}}$$

$$= \frac{\$96{,}000 - \$28{,}000}{(\$800{,}000 + \$840{,}000)/2}$$

$$= \frac{\$68{,}000}{\$820{,}000} = 0.08$$

(*d*) Income before interest and taxes:

Income before taxes	$160,000
Interest expense (16% × $120,000)	19,200
Income before interest and taxes	$179,200

$$\text{Times interest earned} = \frac{\text{Income before interest and taxes}}{\text{Interest expense}} = \frac{\$179{,}200}{\$19{,}200} = 9.33 \text{ times}$$

(*e*)

$$\text{Earnings per share} = \frac{\text{Net income} - \text{Preferred dividends}}{\text{Common stock outstanding}}$$

$$= \frac{\$96{,}000 - \$28{,}000}{16{,}800 \text{ shares}} = \$4.05$$

(*f*)

$$\text{Price–earnings ratio} = \frac{\text{Market price per share}}{\text{Earnings per share}} = \frac{\$35.00}{\$4.05} = 8.64 \text{ times}$$

(*g*)

$$\text{Book value per share} = \frac{\text{Stockholders' equity} - \text{Preferred stock}}{\text{Common stock outstanding}}$$

$$= \frac{\$840{,}000}{16{,}800 \text{ shares}} = \$50 \text{ per share}$$

11.7 Wilder Corporation's common stock account for 19B and 19A showed $45,000 of common stock at $10 par value. Additional data are

	19B	19A
Dividends	$2,250.00	$3,600.00
Market price per share	20.00	22.00
Earnings per share	2.13	2.67

1. Calculate the dividends per share, dividend yield, and dividend payout.
2. Evaluate the results.

SOLUTION

1.

$$\text{Dividends per share} = \frac{\text{Dividends}}{\text{Outstanding shares}}$$

$$\text{19B:} \quad \frac{\$2{,}250}{4{,}500 \text{ shares}} = \$0.50 \qquad \text{19A:} \quad \frac{\$3{,}600}{4{,}500 \text{ shares}} = \$0.80$$

$$\text{Dividend yield} = \frac{\text{Dividends per share}}{\text{Market price per share}}$$

$$\text{19B:} \quad \frac{\$0.50}{\$20.00} = 0.025 \qquad \text{19A:} \quad \frac{\$0.80}{\$22.00} = 0.036$$

$$\text{Dividend payout} = \frac{\text{Dividends per share}}{\text{Earnings per share}}$$

$$\text{19B:} \quad \frac{\$0.50}{\$2.13} = 0.23 \qquad \text{19A:} \quad \frac{\$0.80}{\$2.67} = 0.30$$

2. The decline in dividends per share, dividend yield, and dividend payout from 19A to 19B will cause concern to stockholders.

11.8 Jones Corporation's financial statements appear below.

JONES CORPORATION
Balance Sheet
December 31, 19B

ASSETS		
Current Assets		
Cash	$100,000	
Marketable Securities	200,000	
Inventory	300,000	
Total Current Assets		$ 600,000
Noncurrent Assets		
Plant Assets		500,000
Total Assets		$1,100,000
LIABILITIES AND STOCKHOLDERS' EQUITY		
Current Liabilities	$200,000	
Long-Term Liabilities	100,000	
Total Liabilities		$ 300,000
Stockholders' Equity		
Common Stock, $1 par value, $100,000 shares	$100,000	
Premium on Common Stock	500,000	
Retained Earnings	200,000	
Total Stockholders' Equity		800,000
Total Liabilities and Stockholders' Equity		$1,100,000

JONES CORPORATION
Income Statement
For the Year Ended December 31, 19B

Net Sales	$10,000,000
Cost of Goods Sold	6,000,000
Gross Profit	$ 4,000,000
Operating Expenses	1,000,000
Income before Taxes	$ 3,000,000
Income Taxes (50% rate)	1,500,000
Net Income	$ 1,500,000

Additional information available is a market price of $150 per share of stock and total dividends of $600,000 for 19B, and $250,000 of inventory as of December 31, 19A. Compute the following ratios:

(*a*) Current ratio
(*b*) Quick ratio
(*c*) Inventory turnover
(*d*) Average age of inventory
(*e*) Debt–equity ratio
(*f*) Book value per share
(*g*) Earnings per share
(*h*) Price–earnings ratio
(*i*) Dividends per share
(*j*) Dividend payout

SOLUTION

(*a*) $$\text{Current ratio} = \frac{\text{Current assets}}{\text{Current liabilities}} = \frac{\$600{,}000}{\$200{,}000} = 3$$

(*b*) $$\text{Quick ratio} = \frac{\text{Cash + Marketable securities}}{\text{Current liabilities}} = \frac{\$300{,}000}{\$200{,}000} = 1.5$$

(*c*) $$\text{Inventory turnover} = \frac{\text{Cost of goods sold}}{\text{Average inventory}} = \frac{\$6{,}000{,}000}{(\$250{,}000 + \$300{,}000)/2} = 21.82$$

(*d*) $$\text{Average age of inventory} = \frac{365}{\text{Inventory turnover}} = \frac{365}{21.82} = 16.7 \text{ days}$$

(*e*) $$\text{Debt–equity ratio} = \frac{\text{Total liabilities}}{\text{Stockholders' equity}} = \frac{\$300{,}000}{\$800{,}000} = 0.375$$

(*f*) $$\text{Book value per share} = \frac{\text{Stockholders' equity} - \text{Preferred stock}}{\text{Common shares outstanding}} = \frac{\$800{,}000}{100{,}000 \text{ shares}} = \$8$$

(*g*) $$\text{Earnings per share} = \frac{\text{Net income}}{\text{Outstanding common shares}} = \frac{\$1{,}500{,}000}{100{,}000 \text{ shares}} = \$15$$

(*h*) $$\text{Price–earnings ratio} = \frac{\text{Market price per share}}{\text{Earnings per share}} = \frac{\$150}{\$15} = 10$$

(*i*) $$\text{Dividends per share} = \frac{\text{Dividends}}{\text{Outstanding shares}} = \frac{\$600{,}000}{100{,}000 \text{ shares}} = \$6$$

(*j*) $$\text{Dividend payout} = \frac{\text{Dividends per share}}{\text{Earnings per share}} = \frac{\$6}{\$15} = 0.4$$

11.9 The Konrath Company is considering extending credit to the Hawk Company. It is estimated that sales to the Hawk Company would amount to $2 million each year. The Konrath Company is a wholesaler that sells throughout the midwest. The Hawk Company is a retail chain operation that has a number of stores in the midwest. The Konrath Company has had a gross margin of approximately 60 percent in recent years and expects to have a similar gross margin on the Hawk Company order. The Hawk Company order is approximately 15 percent of the Konrath Company's present sales. Recent statements of the Hawk Company are given below.

HAWK COMPANY
Balance Sheet
As of December 31
(000,000 omitted)

ASSETS	19A	19B	19C
Current Assets			
Cash	$ 2.6	$ 1.8	$ 1.6
Government Securities (Cost)	0.4	0.2	–
Accounts and Notes Receivable (Net)	8.0	8.5	8.5
Inventories	2.8	3.2	2.8
Prepaid Assets	0.7	0.6	0.6
Total Current Assets	$14.5	$14.3	$13.5
Property, Plant, and Equipment (Net)	4.3	5.4	5.9
Total Assets	$18.8	$19.7	$19.4
EQUITIES			
Current Liabilities			
Notes Payable	$ 3.2	$ 3.7	$ 4.2
Accounts Payable	2.8	3.7	4.1
Accrued Expenses and Taxes	0.9	1.1	1.0
Total Current Liabilities	$ 6.9	$ 8.5	$ 9.3
Long-Term Debt; 6%	3.0	2.0	1.0
Total Liabilities	$ 9.9	$10.5	$10.3
Shareholders' Equity	8.9	9.2	9.1
Total Equities	$18.8	$19.7	$19.4

HAWK COMPANY
Income Statement
For the Year Ended December 31
(000,000 omitted)

	19A	19B	19C
Net Sales	$24.2	$24.5	$ 24.9
Cost of Goods Sold	16.9	17.2	18.0
Gross Margin	$ 7.3	$ 7.3	$ 6.9
Selling Expenses	$ 4.3	$ 4.4	$ 4.6
Administrative Expenses	2.3	2.4	2.7
Total Expenses	$ 6.6	$ 6.8	$ 7.3
Earning (Loss) before Taxes	$ 0.7	$ 0.5	$ (0.4)
Income Taxes	0.3	0.2	(0.2)
Net Income	$ 0.4	$ 0.3	$ (0.2)

HAWK COMPANY

Statement of Changes in Financial Position
For the Year Ended December 31
(000,000 omitted)

	19A	19B	19C
Sources of Funds:			
Net Income (loss)	$ 0.4	$ 0.3	$(0.2)
Depreciation	0.4	0.5	0.5
Funds from Operations	$ 0.8	$ 0.8	$ 0.3
Sale of Building	0.2	—	—
Sales of Treasury Stock	—	0.1	0.1
Total Sources	$ 1.0	$ 0.9	$ 0.4
Uses of Funds:			
Purchase of Property, Plant, and Equipment	$ 1.2	$ 1.6	$ 1.0
Dividends	0.1	0.1	—
Retirement of Long-Term Debt	—	1.0	1.0
Total Uses	$ 1.3	$ 2.7	$ 2.0
Net Increase (Decrease) in Working Capital	$(0.3)	$(1.8)	$(1.6)

1. Calculate for the year 19C the following ratios:
   (*a*) Return on total assets
   (*b*) Acid-test ratio
   (*c*) Profit margin
   (*d*) Current ratio
   (*e*) Inventory turnover

2. As part of the analysis to determine whether Konrath should extend credit to Hawk, assume that the ratios below were calculated from Hawk Company statements. For each ratio, indicate whether it is a favorable, unfavorable, or neutral statistic in the decision to grant Hawk credit. Briefly explain your choice in each case.

	19A	19B	19C
(*a*) Return on total assets	1.96%	1.12%	(0.87)%
(*b*) Profit margin	1.69%	0.99%	(0.69)%
(*c*) Acid-test ratio	1.73/1	1.36/1	1.19/1
(*d*) Current ratio	2.39/1	1.92/1	1.67/1
(*e*) Inventory turnover (times)	4.41	4.32	4.52
(*f*) Equity relationships:			
Current liabilities	36.0%	43.0%	48.0%
Long-term liabilities	16.0	10.5	5.0
Shareholders	48.0	46.5	47.0
	100.0%	100.0%	100.0%
(*g*) Asset relationships:			
Current assets	77.0%	72.5%	69.5%
Property, plant, and equipment	23.0%	27.5%	30.5%
	100.0%	100.0%	100.0%

3. Would you grant credit to Hawk Company? Support your answer with facts given in the problem.
4. What additional information, if any, would you want before making a final decision?

(CMA, adapted)

SOLUTION

1. (*a*) Return on total assets $= \dfrac{\text{Net income} + \text{Interest expense}}{\text{Average assets}} = \dfrac{-\$0.2 + \$0.045^*}{(\$19.7 + \$19.4)/2} = -1\%$

   * $\dfrac{(\$2.0 + \$1.0)0.06}{2} = \$0.09$ interest; \$0.45 net of taxes

   (*b*) Acid-test ratio $= \dfrac{\text{Cash} + \text{Accounts and notes receivable (net)}}{\text{Current liabilities}} = \dfrac{\$1.6 + \$8.5}{\$9.3} = 1.086$

   (*c*) Profit margin $= \dfrac{\text{Net income}}{\text{Sales}} = \dfrac{-\$0.2}{\$24.9} = -0.8\%$

   (*d*) Current ratio $= \dfrac{\text{Current assets}}{\text{Current liabilities}} = \dfrac{\$13.5}{\$9.3} = 1.45$

   (*e*) Inventory turnover $= \dfrac{\text{Cost of goods sold}}{\text{Average inventory}} = \dfrac{\$18.0}{(\$3.2 + \$2.8)/2} = 6$

2. (*a*) Return on total assets: Unfavorable—the rate is low and has been declining.
   (*b*) Profit margin: Unfavorable—the rate is low and has been declining.
   (*c*) Acid-test ratio: Favorable—the direction of change is unfavorable, but it is probably more than adequate.
   (*d*) Current ratio: Unfavorable—the decline has been sharp and the ratio is probably too low.
   (*e*) Inventory turnover: Neutral—inventory turnover has been fairly constant and we do not know enough about the business to determine if the turnover is adequate.

3. The facts available from the problem are inadequate to make a final judgment; additional information as listed in part 4 would be necessary. However, the facts given do not present an overall good picture of Hawk. The company does not appear to be in serious trouble at the moment, but most of the trends reflected in figures are unfavorable. The company appears to be developing liquidity problems:
   (*a*) Cash and securities are declining.
   (*b*) Inventories and plant and equipment are an increasing portion of the assets.
   (*c*) Current liabilities are an increasing portion of capital.

   The operations of the company also show unfavorable trends:
   (*a*) Cost of goods sold is increasing as a percent of sales.
   (*b*) Administrative expenses are increasing as a percent of sales.
   (*c*) Recognizing that prices have risen, it appears that physical volume at Hawk might have actually decreased.

   On the basis of these observations and the fact that Hawk would be a very large customer (thus a potentially large loss if the accounts became uncollectible), credit should be extended to Hawk only under carefully controlled and monitored conditions.

4. Additional information would be:
   (*a*) Quality of management of the Hawk Company
   (*b*) Locations of the Hawk stores
   (*c*) Current activities of Hawk which have increased plant and equipment but not inventories

(*d*) Industry position of the Hawk Company
(*e*) Credit rating of the Hawk Company
(*f*) Current economic conditions
(*g*) Capacity of the Konrath Company to handle such a large single account
(*h*) Normal ratios for the industry

11.10 Charles Corporation reports net income of $47,000. Amortization expense is $12,000, depreciation expense is $20,000, and interest expense is $8,000. There is a gain on the sale of an auto of $5,000. Determine the cash flows provided from operations.

SOLUTION

Net income		$47,000
Add: Nonworking capital expenses		
Amortization expense	$12,000	
Depreciation expense	20,000	32,000
Less: Nonworking capital revenue		
Gain on the sale of an auto		(5,000)
Cash flows from operations		$74,000

11.11 Classify each of the following transactions as an operating activity, an investing activity, or a financing activity. Also indicate whether the activity is a source of cash or a use of cash.

(*a*) A plant was sold for $550,000.
(*b*) A profit of $75,000 was reported.
(*c*) Long-term bonds were retired.
(*d*) Cash dividends of $420,000 were paid.
(*e*) Four hundred thousand shares of preferred stock were sold.
(*f*) A new high-tech robotics was purchased.
(*g*) A long-term note payable was issued.
(*h*) A 50 percent interest in a company was purchased.
(*i*) A loss for the year was reported.
(*j*) Additional common stock was sold.

SOLUTION

(*a*) Investing—source of cash
(*b*) Operating—source of cash
(*c*) Financing—use of cash
(*d*) Financing—use of cash
(*e*) Financing—source of cash
(*f*) Investing—use of cash
(*g*) Financing—use of cash
(*h*) Investing–use of cash
(*i*) Operating–use of cash
(*j*) Financing—source of cash

11.12 Indicate whether each of the events described below will be added to or deducted from net income in order to compute cash flow from operations.

(*a*) Gain on sale of an asset
(*b*) Increase in accounts receivable
(*c*) Decrease in prepaid insurance
(*d*) Depreciation expense
(*e*) Increase in accounts payable
(*f*) Uncollectible accounts expense
(*g*) Decrease in wages payable
(*h*) Increase in inventory
(*i*) Amortization of a patent

SOLUTION

(*a*) Deducted from
(*b*) Deducted from
(*c*) Added to
(*d*) Added to
(*e*) Added to
(*f*) Added to
(*g*) Deducted from
(*h*) Deducted from
(*i*) Added to

11.13 Classify each transaction in the first three columns by its correct cash flow activity.

	Types of Activity			
	Operating	Investing	Financing	Not Applicable
Payments to acquire materials for manufacturing				
Payments to acquire stock of other companies				
Proceeds from the issuance of equity instruments				
Acquisition of land for the corporation's common stock				
Receipt of interest and dividends				
Payment of dividends				
Issuance of corporate bonds				
Issuance of corporate mortgage				
Receipts from sale of corporate plant				
Exchange of corporate bonds for the corporation's preferred stock				

SOLUTION

	Type of Activity			
	Operating	Investing	Financing	Not Applicable
Payments to acquire materials for manufacturing	X			
Payments to acquire stock of other companies		X		
Proceeds from the issuance of equity instruments			X	
Acquisition of land for the corporation's common stock				X
Receipt of interest and dividends	X			
Payment of dividends			X	
Issuance of corporate bonds			X	
Issuance of corporate mortgage			X	
Receipts from sale of corporate plant		X		
Exchange of corporate bonds for preferred stock				X

11.14 O'Hara Bus and Terminal Lines, Inc.'s transactions for the year ended December 31, 19X9, included the following:

(1) Purchased real estate for $500,000, which was borrowed from a bank.
(2) Sold investment securities worth $600,000.
(3) Paid dividends of $300,000.
(4) Issued 500 shares of common stock for $350,000.
(5) Purchased machinery and equipment for $175,000.
(6) Paid $750,000 toward a bank loan.
(7) Accounts receivable outstanding of $100,000 were paid.
(8) Accounts payable were increased by $190,000.

Calculate O'Hara's net cash used in its (*a*) investing activities and (*b*) financing activities.

SOLUTION

(*a*) Investing activities:		
Cash inflows:		
Sale of investment securities		$ 600,000
Less cash outflows:		
Purchase of real estate	$ 500,000	
Purchase of machinery and equipment	175,000	675,000
Net cash used in investing activities		$(75,000)

(*b*) Financing activities:

Cash inflows:		
Borrowed from bank to purchase real estate		$ 500,000
Issued common stock		350,000
		$ 850,000
Less cash outflows:		
Paid dividends	$ (300,000)	
Paid bank loan	(750,000)	1,050,000
Net cash used in investing activities		$(200,000)

11.15 Ace Pipeline and Transmission Corporation's transactions for the year ended December 31, 19X9, included the following:

(1) Cash sales of $2,300,000.
(2) Taxes, fines, and penalties of $80,000.
(3) Sold investment securities for $980,000.
(4) $330,000 in cash was borrowed from a bank.
(5) Cash paid for inventory totaled $940,000.
(6) Issued 10,000 shares of its preferred stock for land with a fair market value of $750,000.
(7) Purchased a secret formula for $100,000.
(8) Purchased land for $230,000.
(9) Paid $225,000 toward a bank loan.
(10) Sold 600 of its 10 percent debenture bonds due in the year 2000 for $600,000.

Calculate Ace's net cash inflows or outflows for (*a*) operating, (*b*) investing, and (*c*) financing activities. (*d*) Which of the transactions are not reported as part of the operating, investing, or financing activities of the corporation, but rather are reported separately on the statement of cash flows?

SOLUTION

(*a*) Operating activities:

Cash inflows:		
Cash sales		$2,300,000
Less: Cash outflows:		
Cash paid for inventory	$(940,000)	
Taxes, fines, and penalties	(80,000)	1,020,000
Net cash inflows from operating activities		$1,280,000

(*b*) Investing activities:

Cash inflows:		
Sold investment securities		$ 980,000
Less: Cash outflows:		
Purchase of secret formula	$(100,000)	
Purchase of land	(230,000)	330,000
Net cash inflows from investing activities		$ (650,000)

(*c*) Financing activities:

Cash inflows:	
Borrowing from bank	$ 330,000
Sold debenture bonds	600,000
	$ (930,000)
Less: Cash outflows:	
Paid bank loan	(225,000)
Net cash inflow from investing activities	$ (705,000)

(*d*) The issuance of 10,000 shares of Ace's preferred stock for land with a fair market value of $750,000 does not involve an exchange of cash and must be reported separately on the statement of cash flows.

11.16 Newport Steam Corporation's balance sheet accounts as of December 31, 19X8, and December 31, 19X9, and the information relating to the 19X9 activities, are presented below.

	December 31	
	19X9	19X8
ASSETS		
Cash	$ 230,000	$ 100,000
Short-Term Investments	300,000	0
Accounts Receivable (net)	550,000	550,000
Inventory	680,000	600,000
Long-Term Investments	200,000	300,000
Plant Assets	1,700,000	1,000,000
Accumulated Depreciation	(450,000)	(450,000)
Goodwill	90,000	100,000
Total Assets	$3,300,000	$2,200,000
LIABILITIES AND STOCKHOLDERS' EQUITY		
Accounts Payable	$ 825,000	$ 720,000
Long-Term Debt	325,000	0
Common Stock, $1 Par	800,000	700,000
Additional Paid-in Capital	370,000	250,000
Retained Earnings	980,000	530,000
Total Liabilities and Stockholders' Equity	$3,300,000	$2,200,000

Information relating to 19X9 activities is as follows:

(1) Net income for 19X9 was $700,000.

(2) Purchase of short-term investments for $300,000, which will mature on June 30, 20X0.

(3) Cash dividends declared and paid in 19X9 worth $250,000.

(4) Equipment costing $400,000, having accumulated depreciation of $250,000, was sold in 19X9 for $150,000.

(5) Plant assets worth $1,100,000 were purchased for cash.

(6) A long-term investment costing $100,000 was sold for $135,000.

(7) 100,000 shares of $1-par-value common stock were sold for $2.20 a share.

(8) Amortization of goodwill for 19X9 was $10,000.

Calculate Newport's net cash inflows or outflows for (*a*) operating, (*b*) investing, and (*c*) financing activities. Discuss whether or not the short-term investments are cash equivalents.

SOLUTION

(*a*) Operating activities:

Net income	$ 700,000
Depreciation	250,000
Increase in inventory	(80,000)
Increase in accounts payable	105,000
Gain on sale of investment	(35,000)
Amortization of goodwill	10,000
Total cash provided from operating activities	$ 950,000

(*b*) Investing activities:

Sale of equipment	$150,000
Sale of investment	135,000
Purchase of short-term investments	(300,000)
Purchase of plant assets	(1,100,000)
Total cash used for investing activities	$(1,100,000)

(*c*) Financing activities:

Dividends paid	$ (250,000)
Long-term debt	325,000
Common stock issued	220,000
Total cash provided from financing activities	$ 295,000

Only short-term investments acquired within three months of their maturity date may be treated as cash equivalents. The short-term investments acquired by Newport are due at the end of six months and therefore are not cash equivalents.

11.17 Acme Manufacturing has provided the following financial statements:

ACME MANUFACTURING

Comparative Balance Sheets

For the Years Ended December 31, 19X8 and 19X9

ASSETS	19X8	19X9
Cash	$ 112,500	$ 350,000
Accounts Receivable	350,000	281,250
Inventories	125,000	150,000
Plant and Equipment	1,000,000	1,025,000*
Accumulated Depreciation	(500,000)	(525,000)
Land	500,000	718,750
Total Assets	$1,587,500	$2,000,000
LIABILITIES AND EQUITY		
Accounts Payable	$ 300,000	$ 237,500
Mortgage Payable	—	250,000
Common Stock	75,000	75,000
Contributed Capital in Excess of Par	300,000	300,000
Retained Earnings	912,500	1,137,500
Total Liabilities and Equity	$1,587,500	$2,000,000

*Beginning Equipment	$ 1,000,000
Purchases	250,000
Less Sales	(225,000)
Ending Equipment	$ 1,025,000

ACME MANUFACTURING
Income Statement
For the Year Ended December 31, 19X9

Revenues	$1,200,000
Gain on Sale of Equipment	50,000
Less: Cost of Goods Sold	(640,000)
Less: Depreciation Expense	(125,000)
Less: Interest Expense	(35,000)
Net Income	$ 450,000

Other information:

(*a*) Equipment with a book value of $125,000 was sold for $175,000 (original cost was $225,000).

(*b*) Dividends of $225,000 were declared and paid.
Prepare a statement of cash flows.

SOLUTION

ACME MANUFACTURING
Statement of Cash Flows
For the Year Ended December 31, 19X9

Cash Flows from Operating Activities:		
Net Income	$450,000	
Add (Deduct) Adjusting Items:		
Gain on Sale of Equipment	(50,000)	
Decrease in Accounts Receivable	68,750	
Increase in Inventory	(25,000)	
Depreciation Expense	125,000	
Decrease in Accounts Payable	(62,500)	
Net Operating Cash		$ 506,250
Cash Flows from Investing Activities:		
Sale of Equipment	$175,000	
Purchase of Equipment	(250,000)	
Purchase of Land	(218,750)	
Net Cash from Investing Activities		(293,750)
Cash Flows from Financing Activities:		
Mortgage Received	$250,000	
Dividends	(225,000)	
Net Cash from Financing Activities		25,000
Net Increase in Cash		$ 237,500

11.18 Motel Enterprises operates and owns many motels throughout the United States. The company has expanded rapidly over the past few years, and company officers are concerned that they may have overexpanded.

The following financial statements and other financial data have been supplied by the controller of Motel Enterprises.

MOTEL ENTERPRISES

Income Statement
For Years Ending October 31
(unaudited)
(000 omitted)

	19A	19B
Revenue	$1,920	$2,230
Cost and Expenses		
Direct Room and Related Services	$ 350	$ 400
Direct Food and Beverage	640	740
General and Administrative	250	302
Advertising	44	57
Repairs and Maintenance	82	106
Interest Expense	220	280
Depreciation	95	120
Lease Payment	73	100
Total Costs and Expenses	$1,754	$2,105
Income before Taxes	$ 166	$ 125
Provision for Income Tax	42	25
Net Income	$ 124	$ 100

MOTEL ENTERPRISES

Balance Sheet
as of October 31
(Unaudited)
(000 omitted)

ASSETS	19A	19B
Current Assets		
Cash	$ 125	$ 100
Accounts Receivable (net)	200	250
Inventory	50	60
Other	5	5
Total Current Assets	$ 380	$ 415
Long-Term Investments	$ 710	$ 605
Property and Equipment		
Buildings and Equipment (net)	$2,540	$3,350
Land	410	370
Construction in Progress	450	150
Total Property and Equipment	$3,400	$3,870
Other Assets	$ 110	$ 110
Total Assets	$4,600	$5,000

LIABILITIES AND STOCKHOLDERS' EQUITY		
Current Liabilities		
Accounts Payable	$ 30	$ 40
Accrued Liabilities	190	190
Notes Payable to Bank	10	30
Current Portion of Long-Term Notes	50	80
Total Current Liabilities	$ 280	$ 340
Long-Term Debt		
Long-Term Notes	$2,325	$2,785
Subordinated Debentures (due May 1989)	800	800
Total Long-Term Debt	$3,125	$3,585
Total Liabilities	$3,405	$3,925
Stockholders' Equity		
Common Stock ($1 par)	$ 300	$ 300
Paid-In Capital in Excess of Par	730	730
Net Unrealized Loss on Long-Term Investments	—	(105)
Retained Earnings	165	150
Total Stockholders' Equity	$1,195	$1,075
Total Liabilities and Stockholders' Equity	$4,600	$5,000

1. Compute the following ratios for 19A and 19B:
   (*a*) Debt–equity ratio
   (*b*) Times interest earned
   (*c*) Return on total assets
   (*d*) Current ratio
   (*e*) Return on common stock equity
   (*f*) Accounts receivable turnover
2. Evaluate the financial condition based on the trend analysis.

(CMA, adapted)

SOLUTION

1. (*a*) Debt–equity ratio:

$$19A: \frac{\$3,405}{\$4,600} = 74.0\% \qquad 19B: \frac{\$3,925}{\$5,000} = 78.5\%$$

(*b*) Times interest earned:

$$19A: \frac{\$386}{\$220} = 1.75 \qquad 19B: \frac{\$405}{\$280} = 1.45$$

(*c*) Return on total assets:

$$19A: \frac{\$124}{\$4,600} = 2.7\% \qquad 19B: \frac{\$100}{(\$4,600 + \$5,000)/2} = 2.1\%$$

(*d*) Current ratio:

$$19A: \frac{\$380}{\$280} = 1.36 \qquad 19B: \frac{\$415}{\$340} = 1.22$$

(*e*) Return on common stock equity:

19A estimated: $\dfrac{\$124}{\$1{,}195} = 10.4\%$ 19B: $\dfrac{\$100}{(\$1{,}195 + \$1{,}075)/2} = 8.8\%$

(*f*) Accounts receivable turnover:

19A estimated: $\dfrac{\$1{,}920}{\$200} = 9.6$ 19B: $\dfrac{\$2{,}230}{(\$200 + \$250)/2} = 9.91$

2. Based on the trend analysis for 19A and 19B, the company's financial condition has deteriorated to some degree in this period and there is going to be a serious liquidity problem, as is evidenced by the decline in the current ratio and the decline of net working capital.

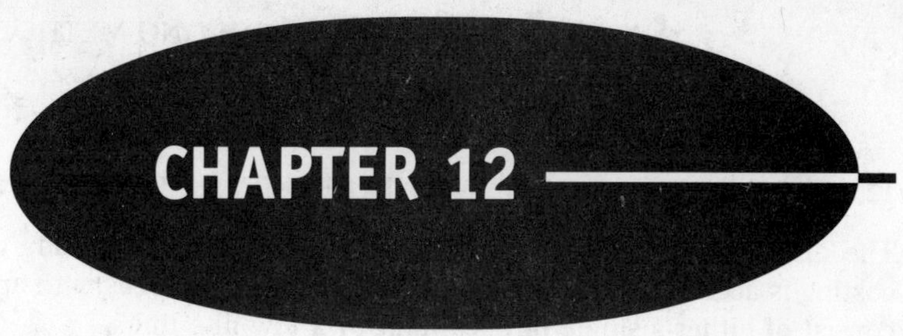

CHAPTER 12

Product Costing Methods (Job-Order Costing, Process Costing, Cost Allocation, and Joint-Product Costing)

12.1 COST ACCUMULATION SYSTEMS

A cost accumulation system is a product costing system. This process accumulates manufacturing costs such as materials, labor, and factory overhead and assigns them to cost objectives, such as finished goods and work in process. Product costing is necessary not only for inventory valuation and income determination but also for establishing the unit sales price.

We will discuss the essentials of the cost accumulation system that is used to measure the manufacturing costs of products. This is essentially a two-step process: (1) the measurement of costs that are applicable to manufacturing operations during a given accounting period; and (2) the assignment of these costs to products.

There are two basic approaches to cost accounting and accumulation:

(1) Job-order costing

(2) Process costing

12.2 JOB-ORDER COSTING AND PROCESS COSTING COMPARED

The distinction between job-order costing and process costing centers largely around how product costing is accomplished. With job-order costing, the focus is to apply costs to specific jobs, which may consist of either a single physical unit or a few like units.

Under process costing, accounting data are accumulated by the production department (or cost center) and averaged over all of the production that occurred in the department. There is mass production of like units which are manufactured on a continuous basis through a series of uniform production steps known as *processes*. Table 12-1 summarizes the basic differences between these two methods.

Table 12-1 Differences Between Job-Order Costing and Process Costing

	Job-Order Costing	Process Costing
1. Cost unit	Job, order, or contract	Physical unit
2. Costs are accumulated	By jobs	By departments
3. Subsidiary record	Job cost sheet	Cost-of-production report
4. Used by	Custom manufacturers	Processing industries
5. Permits computation of	(*a*) A unit cost for inventory costing purposes (*b*) A profit or loss on each job	A unit cost to be used to compute the costs of goods completed and work in process

12.3 JOB-ORDER COSTING

Job-order costing is the cost accumulation system under which costs are accumulated by jobs, contracts, or orders. This costing method is appropriate when the products are manufactured in identifiable lots or batches or when the products are manufactured to customer specifications. Job-order costing is widely used by custom manufacturers such as printing, aircraft, and construction companies. It may also be used by service businesses such as auto repair shops and professional services. Job-order costing keeps track of costs as follows: Direct material and direct labor are traced to a particular job. Costs that are not directly traceable—factory overhead—are applied to individual jobs using a predetermined overhead (application) rate.

12.4 JOB COST SHEET

A *job cost sheet* is used to record various production costs for work-in-process inventory. A separate cost sheet is kept for each identifiable job, accumulating the direct materials, direct labor, and factory overhead assigned to that job as it moves through production. The form varies according to the needs of the company. This is the key document in the system. It summarizes all of the manufacturing costs—direct materials, direct labor, and applied factory overhead (to be discussed in detail later)—of producing a given job or batch of products. One sheet is maintained for each job, and the file of job cost sheets for unfinished jobs is the subsidiary record for the Work-in-Process Inventory account. When the jobs are completed and transferred, the job cost sheets are transferred to a "completed jobs" file and the number of units and their unit costs are recorded on inventory cards supporting the Finished Goods Inventory account.

EXAMPLE 12.1 Chiphard Works collects its cost data using the job-order cost system. For Job 123, the following data are available:

Direct Materials		Direct Labor	
7/14 Issued	$1,200	Week of July 20	180 hours @ $6.50
7/20 Issued	650	Week of July 26	140 hours @ $7.25
7/25 Issued	350		
	$2,200		

Factory overhead is applied at the rate of $4.50 per direct labor hour.

We will compute (*a*) the cost of Job 123 and (*b*) the sales price of the job, assuming that it was contracted with a markup of 40 percent of cost.

(*a*) The cost of the job is:

Direct material		$2,200
Direct labor:		
180 hours × $6.50	$1,170	
140 hours × $7.25	1,015	2,185
Factory overhead applied:		
320 hours × $4.50		1,440
Cost of Job 123		$5,825

(*b*) The sales price of the job is:

$$\$5,825 + 40\% \ (\$5,825) = \$5,825 + \$2,330 = \$8,155$$

12.5 FACTORY OVERHEAD APPLICATION

Many items of factory overhead cost are incurred for the entire factory and for the entire accounting period and cannot be identified specifically with particular jobs. Furthermore, the amount of actual factory overhead costs incurred is not usually available until the end of the accounting period. However, it is often critical to make cost data available for pricing purposes as each job is completed. Therefore, in order for job costs to be available on a timely basis, it is customary to apply factory overhead by using a *predetermined factory overhead rate.*

PREDETERMINED FACTORY OVERHEAD RATE

Regardless of the cost accumulation system used (i.e., job order or process), factory overhead is applied to a job or process. The predetermined overhead rate is determined as follows:

$$\text{Predetermined overhead rate} = \frac{\text{Budgeted annual overhead}}{\text{Budgeted annual activity (or cost driver) units (direct labor hours, direct labor dollars, direct material dollars, or production volume)}}$$

Budgeted activity units used in the denominator of the formula, more often called the *denominator activity* level, are measured in direct labor hours, machine hours, direct labor costs, production units, or any other representative surrogate of production activity.

DISPOSITION OF UNDER- AND OVERAPPLIED OVERHEAD

Inevitably, actual overhead cost incurred during a period and factory overhead costs applied will differ. Conventionally, at the end of the year, the difference between actual overhead and applied overhead is closed to Cost of Goods Sold if it is immaterial. On the other hand, if a material difference exists, Work in Process, Finished Goods, and Cost of Goods Sold are adjusted on a proportionate basis based on units or dollars at year-end for the deviation between actual and applied overhead. Underapplied overhead and overapplied overhead results as follows:

$$\text{Underapplied overhead} = \text{Applied overhead} < \text{Actual overhead}$$
$$\text{Overapplied overhead} = \text{Applied overhead} > \text{Actual overhead}$$

EXAMPLE 12.2 Two companies have prepared the following budgeted data for the year 19X8:

	Company X	Company Y
Predetermined rate based on	Machine hours	Direct labor cost
Budgeted overhead	\$200,000 (1)	\$240,000 (1)
Budgeted machine hours	100,000 (2)	
Budgeted direct labor cost		\$160,000 (2)
Predetermined overhead rate (1)/(2)	\$2 per machine hour	150% of direct labor cost

Assume that actual overhead costs and the actual level of activity for 19X8 for each firm are shown as follows:

	Company X	Company Y
Actual overhead costs	\$198,000	\$256,000
Actual machine hours	96,000	
Actual direct labor cost		176,000

Note that for each company, the actual cost and activity data differ from the budgeted figures used in calculating the predetermined overhead rate. The computation of the resulting underapplied and overapplied overhead for each company is provided below.

	Company X	Company Y
Actual overhead costs	\$198,000	\$256,000
Factory overhead applied to Work in Process during 19X8:		
96,000 actual machine hours × \$2	192,000	
\$176,000 actual direct labor cost × 150%		264,000
Underapplied (overapplied) factory overhead	\$ 6,000	\$ (8,000)

EXAMPLE 12.3 A company uses a budgeted overhead rate in applying overhead to production orders on a labor cost basis for Department A and on a machine hour basis for Department B. At the beginning of the year, the company made the following predictions:

	Department A	Department B	Total
Budgeted factory overhead	\$72,000	\$75,000	\$147,000
Budgeted direct labor cost	64,000	17,500	81,500
Budgeted machine hours	500	10,000	10,500

The predetermined overhead rates for each department are:

$$\text{Department A:} \quad \frac{\$72,000}{\$64,000} = \$1.125 \text{ per labor dollar or } 112.5\%$$

$$\text{Department B:} \quad \frac{\$75,000}{\$10,000} = \$7.50 \text{ per machine hour}$$

During the month of January, the cost record for a job order, No. 105, which was processed through both departments, shows the following:

	Department A	Department B	Total
Materials issued	$30	$45	$75
Direct labor cost	36	25	61
Machine hours	6	15	21

The total applied overhead for job order No. 105 follows:

Department A: $36 × 1.125	$ 40.50
Department B: 15 × $7.50	112.50
	$153.00

Assume that job order No. 105 consisted of 30 units of product. What is the total cost and unit cost of the job?

	Department A	Department B	Total
Direct material	$ 30.00	$ 45.00	$ 75.00
Direct labor	36.00	25.00	61.00
Applied overhead	40.50	112.50	153.00
Total	$106.50	$182.50	$289.00

Hence, the total cost of the job is $106.50 + $182.50 = $289; the unit cost is $9.63 ($289/30 units).

EXAMPLE 12.4 Refer to Example 12.3 and assume that the company uses a single plant-wide rate based on direct labor costs. What is (*a*) the total applied overhead for job order No. 105 and (*b*) the total cost and unit cost of the job?

The predetermined overhead rate is:

$$\frac{\$147,000}{\$81,500} = 180\% \text{ of direct labor cost}$$

Then the total applied overhead for the job is:

$61 × 180% = $109.80 (as compared to $153.00 under a department rate system)

Therefore, the total cost of the job is $245.80 ($75.00 + $61.00 + $109.80); the unit cost is $8.19 ($245.80/30 units).

Notice the difference in the unit cost, $8.19 vs. $9.63.

EXAMPLE 12.5 Refer to Example 12.3 and assume, at the end of the year, that actual factory overhead amounted to $80,000 in Department A and $69,000 in Department B. Assume further that the actual direct labor cost was $74,000 in Department A and the actual machine hours were 9,000 in Department B.

Then, the overapplied or underapplied overhead for each department is:

Department A:	Applied overhead (1.125 × $74,000)	$83,250
	Actual overhead	80,000
	Overapplied overhead	$3,250
Department B:	Applied overhead ($7.50 × 9,000)	$67,500
	Actual overhead	69,000
	Underapplied overhead	$ (1,500)

12.6 PROCESS COSTING

Process costing is a cost accumulation system that aggregates manufacturing costs by departments or by production processes. Total manufacturing costs are accumulated by two major categories, direct materials and conversion costs (the sum of direct labor and factory overhead applied). Unit cost is determined by dividing the total costs charged to a cost center by the output of that cost center. In that sense, the unit costs are averages.

Process costing is appropriate for companies that produce a continuous mass of like units through a series of operations or processes. Process costing is used in such industries as petroleum, chemicals, oil refining, textiles, and food processing.

12.7 STEPS IN PROCESS COSTING CALCULATIONS

There are basically five steps to be followed in accounting for process costs. They are summarized below.

Step 1 *Summarize the flow of physical units.* The first step of the accounting provides a summary of all units on which some work was done in the department during the period. *Input must equal output.* This step helps to detect lost units during the process. The basic relationship may be expressed in the following equation:

$$\text{Beginning inventory} + \text{Units started for the period} = \text{Units completed and transferred out} + \text{Ending inventory}$$

Step 2 *Compute output in terms of equivalent units.* In order to determine the unit costs of the product in a processing environment, it is important to measure the total amount of work done during an accounting period. A special problem arises in processing industries in connection with how to deal with work still in process, that is, work partially completed at the end of the period. The partially completed units are measured on an equivalent whole-unit basis for process costing purposes.

Equivalent units are a measure of how many whole units of production are represented by the units completed plus the units partially completed. For example, 100 units that are 60 percent completed are the equivalent of 60 completed units in terms of conversion costs.

Step 3 *Summarize the total costs to be accounted for by cost categories.* This step summarizes the total costs assigned to the department during the period.

Step 4 *Compute the unit cost per equivalent unit.* The unit cost per equivalent unit is computed as follows:

$$\text{Unit cost} = \frac{\text{Total costs incurred during the period}}{\text{Equivalent units of production during the period}}$$

Step 5 *Apply total costs to units completed and transferred out and to units in ending Work in Process.*

12.8 COST-OF-PRODUCTION REPORT

The process costing method utilizes a *cost-of-production report.* This report summarizes both total and unit costs charged to a department and indicates the allocation of total costs between work-in-process inventory and units completed and transferred out to the next department or the finished goods inventory.

The cost-of-production report covers all five steps described above. It is also the source for monthly journal entries as well as a convenient compilation from which cost data may be presented to management.

PROCESS COST COMPUTATION: NO BEGINNING INVENTORY

The first illustration of unit cost computations under a process system assumes for simplicity that there is no beginning work-in-process inventory. A company produces and sells a chemical product that is processed in two departments. In Department A the basic materials are crushed, powdered, and mixed. In Department B the product is tested, packaged, and labeled, before being transferred to finished goods inventory.

EXAMPLE 12.6 Assume the following for Production Department A for May. Materials are added when production is begun; therefore, all finished units and all units in the ending work-in-process inventory will have received a full complement of materials.

Actual production costs:	
Direct materials used, 18,000 gallons costing	$27,000
Direct labor and factory overhead	$25,000
Actual production:	
Completed and transferred to Production Department B, 8,000 gallons	
Ending work in process, 10,000 gallons, 20% complete as to conversion	

1. Summarize the flow of physical units.

To be accounted for:	
Added this period	18,000 gallons
Accounted for as follows:	
Completed this period	8,000 gallons
In process, end of period	10,000
Total	18,000 gallons

2. Compute output in terms of equivalent units.

	Materials	Conversion Cost
Units completed	8,000 gallons	8,000 gallons
Ending work in process (10,000 gallons)		
100% of materials	10,000	
20% of conversion cost		2,000
Equivalent units produced	18,000 gallons	10,000 gallons

3–5. ***Cost of Production***

	Total Cost	Equivalent Production	Unit Cost
Material	$27,000	18,000 gallons	$1.50
Conversion cost	25,000	10,000	2.50
To be accounted for	$52,000		$4.00
Ending work in process:			
Materials	$15,000	10,000 gallons	$1.50
Conversion cost	5,000	2,000	2.50
Total work in process	$20,000		
Completed and transferred	32,000	8,000	$4.00
Total accounted for	$52,000		

12.9 WEIGHTED AVERAGE VS. FIRST-IN, FIRST-OUT (FIFO)

When there is a beginning inventory of work in process, the production completed during the period comes from different batches, some from work partially completed in a prior period and some from new units started in the current period. Since costs tend to vary from period to period, each batch may carry different unit costs. There are two ways to treat the costs of the beginning inventory. One is weighted average costing and the other is first-in, first-out (FIFO).

Under the weighted average method of costing, both unit costs of work in process at the beginning of the period are combined with current production unit costs started in the current period and an average cost is computed. In determining equivalent production units, no distinction is made between work partially completed in the prior period and units started and completed in the current period. Thus, there is only one average cost for goods completed. Equivalent units under weighted average costing may be computed as follows:

$$\text{Units completed} + [\text{Ending work in process} \times \text{Degree of completion } (\%)]$$

Under FIFO, on the other hand, beginning work-in-process inventory costs are separated from added costs applied in the current period. Thus, there are two unit costs for the period: (1) beginning work-in-process units completed and (2) units started and completed in the same period. Under FIFO, the beginning work in process is assumed to be completed and transferred first. Equivalent units under FIFO costing may be computed as follows:

$$\text{Units completed} + [\text{Ending work in process} \times \text{Degree of completion } (\%)] - [\text{Beginning work in process} \times \text{Degree of completion } (\%)]$$

EXAMPLE 12.7 To illustrate, the following data relate to the activities of Department A during the month of January:

	Units
Beginning work in process (all materials; 66.67% complete as to conversion)	1,500
Started this period	5,000
Available	6,500
Completed and transferred	5,500
Ending work in process (all materials; 60% complete as to conversion)	1,000
Accounted for	6,500

Equivalent production in Department A for the month is computed, using weighted average costing, as follows:

	Materials	Conversion Costs
Units completed and transferred	5,500	5,500
Ending work in process:		
Materials (100%)	1,000	
Conversion costs (60%)		600
Equivalent production	6,500	6,100

Equivalent production in Department A for the month is computed, using FIFO costing, as follows:

	Materials	Conversion Costs
Units completed and transferred	5,500	5,500
Ending work in process:		
Materials (100%)	1,000	
Conversion costs (60%)		600
Equivalent production for weighted average	6,500	6,100
Minus: Beginning work in process:		
Materials (100%)	1,500	
Conversion costs (66.67%)		1,000
Equivalent production for FIFO	5,000	5,100

In the following example, we will illustrate, step by step, the weighted average and FIFO methods.

EXAMPLE 12.8 The Portland Cement Manufacturing Company, Inc., manufactures cement. Its processing operations involve quarrying, grinding, blending, packing, and sacking. For cost accounting and control purposes, there are four processing centers: Raw Material No. 1, Raw Material No. 2, Clinker, and Cement. Separate cost-of-production reports are prepared in detail with respect to these cost centers. The following information pertains to the operation of Raw Material No. 2 Department for July 19A:

	Materials	Conversion
Units in process July 1:		
800 bags	Complete	60% complete
Costs	$12,000	$ 56,000
Units transferred out:		
40,000 bags		
Current costs	$41,500	$521,500
Units in process July 31:		
5,000 bags	Complete	30% complete

Using weighted average costing and FIFO costing, we will compute (*a*) equivalent production units and unit costs by elements; (*b*) cost of work in process for July; and (*c*) cost of units completed and transferred.

(*a*) Computation of output in equivalent units:

	Physical Flow	Materials	Conversion
Work in process, beginning	800 (60%)		
Units transferred in	44,200*		
Units to account for	45,500		
Units completed and transferred out	40,000	40,000	40,000
Work in process, ending	5,000 (30%)	5,000	1,500
Units accounted for	45,000		
Equivalent units used for weighted average costing		45,000	41,500
Less: Old equivalent units for work done on beginning inventory in prior period		800	480
Equivalent units used for FIFO		44,200	41,020

*(40,000 + 5,000) − 800 = 45,000 − 800 = 44,200.

RAW MATERIAL NO. 2 DEPARTMENT

Cost-of-Production Report, Weighted Average
For the Month Ended July 31, 19A

	Work-in-Process Beginning	Current Costs	Total Costs	Equivalent Units	Average Unit Cost
Materials	$12,000	$ 41,500	$ 53,500	45,000	$ 1.1889
Conversion costs	56,000	521,500	577,500	41,500	13.9156
	$68,000	$ 563,000	$631,000		$ 15.1046

Cost of goods completed ($40,000 × $15.1046)		$604,184
Work in process, ending:		
Materials 5,000 × $1.1899	$ 5,944.50	
Conversion 1,500 × $13.9156	20,873.55	26,818.05
		(rounded) $631,000

RAW MATERIAL NO. 2 DEPARTMENT

Cost-of-Production Report, FIFO
For the Month Ended July 31, 19A

	Total Costs	Equivalent Units	Unit Costs
Work in process, beginning	$ 68,000		
Current costs:			
Materials	41,500	44,200	$ 0.9389
Conversion costs	521,500	41,020	12.7133
Total costs to account for	$631,000		$ 13.6522

Cost of goods completed, 40,000 units:	
Work in process, beginning, to be transferred out first	$ 68,000
Additional costs to complete: 800 × (1 − 0.6)* × $12.7133	4,068.26
Cost of goods started and completed this month: 39,200 × $13.6522	535,166.24
	$607,234.50
Work in process, end:	
Materials: 5,000 × $0.9389	$ 4,694.50
Conversion: 1,500 × $12.7133	19,069.95
	$ 23,764.45
Total costs accounted for	(rounded) $631,000

*(1 − 0.6) = 0.4 means that it takes an additional 40% work to complete 800 work-in-process units.

A summary follows:

		Weighted Average		FIFO	
		Materials	Conversion	Materials	Conversion
(*a*)	Equivalent units	45,000	41,500	44,200	41,020
	Unit costs	$1.1889	$13.9156	$0.9389	$12.7133
(*b*)	Cost of work in process	$ 26,818.05		$ 23,764.45	
(*c*)	Cost of units completed and transferred	$604,184		$607,234.50	

Note the difference in unit costs between the weighted average and FIFO methods. From the perspective of cost control, FIFO costing is superior to the weighted average method because of its focus on current-period costs.

12.10 ALLOCATION OF SERVICE DEPARTMENT COSTS TO PRODUCTION DEPARTMENTS

There are two basic types of departments in a manufacturing company: production departments and service departments. A production department (such as assembly or machining) is where the production or conversion occurs. A service department (such as engineering or maintenance) provides support to production departments. Before departmental factory overhead rates are developed for product costing, the costs of a service department should be allocated to the appropriate production departments (as part of factory overhead).

BASIS OF ASSIGNING SERVICE DEPARTMENT COSTS

Some service department costs are direct. Examples are the salaries of the workers in the department. Other service department costs are indirect—that is, they are incurred jointly with some other department. An example is building depreciation. These indirect costs must be allocated on some arbitrary basis. The problem is selecting appropriate bases for assigning the indirect costs of service departments to other departments. Service department costs should be allocated on a basis that reflects the type of activity in which the service department is engaged. The ideal basis should be logical, have a high cause-and-effect relationship between the service provided and the costs of providing it, and be easy to implement. The basis selected may be supported by physical observation, by correlation analysis, or by logical analysis of the relationships between the departments. A list of some service departments and possible bases for allocation is given below.

Service Department	Allocation Basis
Supplies	Number of requisitions
Power	Kilowatt-hours used
Buildings and grounds	Number of square or cubic feet
Maintenance and repairs	Machine hours or number of calls
Personnel	Number of employees
Cafeteria	Number of employees
Purchasing	Number of orders

12.11 PROCEDURE FOR SERVICE DEPARTMENT COST ALLOCATION

Once the service department costs are known, the next step is to allocate the service department costs to the production departments. This may be accomplished by one of the following procedures:

(1) Direct method
(2) Step method
(3) Reciprocal method

DIRECT METHOD

The direct method allocates the costs of each service department directly to production departments, with no intermediate allocation to other service departments. That is, no consideration is given to services performed by one service department for another. This is perhaps the most widely used method because of its simplicity and ease of use.

EXAMPLE 12.9 Assume the following data:

	Service Departments		Production Departments	
	General Plant (GP)	Engineering (E)	A Machining	B Assembly
Overhead costs before allocation	$20,000	$10,000	$30,000	$40,000
Direct labor hours by General Plant (GP)	15,000	20,000	60,000	40,000
Engineering hours by Engineering (E)	5,000	4,000	50,000	30,000

Using the direct method yields:

	Service Departments		Production Departments	
	GP	E	A	B
Overhead costs	$20,000	$10,000	$30,000	$40,000
Reallocation:				
GP (60%, 40%)*	(20,000)		12,000	8,000
E (⅝, ⅜)†		(10,000)	6,250	3,750
			$48,250	$51,750

*Basis is (60,000 + 40,000 = 100,000); 60,000/100,000 = 0.6; 40,000/100,000 = 0.4.
†Basis is (50,000 + 30,000 = 80,000); 50,000/80,000 = ⅝; 30,000/80,000 = ⅜.

STEP METHOD

The step method allocates services rendered by service departments to other service departments using a sequence of allocation; it is also called the *step-down method* or the *sequential method*. The sequence normally begins with the department that renders service to the greatest number of other service departments; the sequence continues in step-by-step fashion and ends with the allocation of costs of service departments that provide the least amount of service. After a given service department's costs have been allocated, it will not receive any charges from the other service departments.

EXAMPLE 12.10 Using the same data as in Example 12.9, the step allocation method yields:

	Service Departments		Production Departments	
	GP	E	A	B
Overhead costs	$20,000	10,000	$30,000	$40,000
Reallocation:				
GP (⅙, ½, ⅓)*	(20,000)	3,333	10,000	6,667
E (⅝, ⅜)†		(13,333)	8,333	5,000
			$48,333	$51,667

*Basis is (20,000 + 60,000 + 40,000 = 120,000); 20,000/120,000 = ⅙; 60,000/120,000 = ½; 40,000/120,000 = ⅓.
†Basis is (50,000 + 30,000 = 80,000); 50,000/80,000 = ⅝; 30,000/80,000 = ⅜.

RECIPROCAL METHOD

The reciprocal allocation method, also known as the *reciprocal service method*, the *matrix method*, and the *simultaneous allocation method*, is a method of allocating service department costs to production departments, where reciprocal services are allowed between service departments. The method sets up simultaneous equations to determine the allocable cost of each service department.

EXAMPLE 12.11 Using the same data as in Example 12.9, we set up the following equations:

$$GP = \$20{,}000 + \frac{50}{85}E$$

$$E = \$10{,}000 + \frac{1}{6}GP$$

Substituting E from the second equation into the first:

$$GP = \$20{,}000 + \frac{5}{85}\left(\$10{,}000 + \frac{1}{6}GP\right)$$

Solving for GP gives GP = \$28,695. Substituting GP = \$28,695 into the second equation and solving for E gives E = \$14,782.

Using these solved values, the reciprocal method yields:

	Service Departments		Production Departments	
	GP	E	A	B
Overhead costs	\$20,000	\$10,000	\$30,000	\$40,000
Reallocation:				
GP ($\frac{1}{6}$, $\frac{1}{2}$, $\frac{1}{3}$)	(28,695)	4,782	14,348	9,565
E ($\frac{50}{85}$, $\frac{30}{85}$, $\frac{5}{85}$)	8,695	(14,782)	5,217	870
	0	0	\$49,565	\$50,435

12.12 JOINT-PRODUCT AND BY-PRODUCT COSTS

When two or more types of products result from a single production process, the outputs are referred to as either joint products or by-products, depending on their relative importance. Joint products are those that have a relatively significant sales value, while by-products are those whose sales value is relatively minor in comparison with the value of the main, or joint, products.

Joint costs are the cost of inputs that are required for the joint products as a group. They cannot be identified directly with any of the joint products that emerge from the process. An example of a joint cost is the price paid by a packing house for a steer. Various joint products emerge, such as different cuts of meat, hides, glue, and fertilizer. (The last two might be classified as by-products if their value is relatively small.) It is impossible to tell how much of the cost of each steer pertains to T-bone steaks, hamburger, hides, and so forth. Any assignment of the joint cost to the joint products is arbitrary. The point in the production process at which joint products are separated is the *split-off point.* After the split-off point, each type of product can be separately identified and is independent of the others. Separate decisions can be made as to whether to sell the joint products as they are or to process them further before sale.

ACCOUNTING FOR JOINT PRODUCTS

Three different bases of allocating joint costs to products have sometimes been advocated:

(1) The physical unit basis
(2) The sales value basis
(3) The net realizable value basis

We will discuss only the physical unit basis. The physical unit basis of allocating joint costs to the resulting joint products assigns an equal share of the joint costs to the outputs on the basis of some physical measure, such as gallons or pounds, contained in each output.

Assume that two chemical products result from a single production process. During a given period, the total input costs of the joint process amounted to \$400,000. The output consisted of 200,000 gallons of Product A and 300,000 gallons of Product B.

The total cost allocated to each type of product can be computed as follows:

$$\frac{\text{Quantity of each product}}{\text{Total output quantity}} \times \text{Joint cost} = \text{Total cost allocated to each joint product}$$

Thus:

$$\text{Product A total cost} = \frac{200{,}000 \text{ gallons}}{500{,}000 \text{ gallons}} \times \$400{,}000 = \$160{,}000$$

$$\text{Product B total cost} = \frac{300{,}000 \text{ gallons}}{500{,}000 \text{ gallons}} \times \$400{,}000 = \$240{,}000$$

METHODS OF ACCOUNTING FOR BY-PRODUCT COSTS

By-products have already been defined as products resulting from a single production process but whose sales value is relatively minor in comparison with the value of the main, or joint, products. Because the relative value of the by-products is not very important, it is usually considered undesirable to use a refined accounting method in dealing with by-product costs. Thus the methods used to allocate joint costs to joint products (physical unit basis, sales value basis, and net realizable value basis) are not used in accounting for by-products, because the value of the resulting information would not be worth the cost of obtaining it.

Several different methods of accounting for by-products are in use. Their main difference lies in whether or not they assign an inventoriable cost to by-products in the period in which they are produced.

There are two methods that do not assign a cost to by-product inventory in the period of production:

(1) Revenue from by-product sales is treated as sales revenue, or miscellaneous revenue, in the period in which the by-product is sold.

(2) Revenue from by-product sales is treated as a deduction from cost of goods sold in the period in which the by-product is sold.

Summary

(1) There are two basic approaches to cost accounting and accumulation. They are ______________ and ______________.

(2) With ______________, the focus is to apply costs to specific jobs, which may consist of either a single physical unit or a few like units. Under process costing, accounting data are accumulated by the ______________ and averaged over all of the production that occurred in the department.

(3) The fundamental record in a job-order cost system is the ______________.

(4) In order for job costs to be available on a timely basis, it is customary to apply factory overhead by using a ______________.

(5) Overhead is applied to jobs using a ______________ multiplied by ______________.

(6) Possible cost drivers include direct labor hours, ____________, ____________, direct material dollars, or production volume.

(7) Process costing is appropriate for companies that produce a continuous mass of ____________ through a series of ____________.

(8) When there are no beginning ____________ inventories, equivalent units produced are the same as ____________.

(9) When there are no beginning ____________ inventories, total equivalent units produced using the weighted average method are computed by ____________.

(10) The five steps in the analysis of process costing are: (*a*) ____________, (*b*) ____________, (*c*) ____________, (*d*) ____________, and (*e*) ____________.

(11) In process costing, 100 units that are 60 percent completed are the equivalent of ____________ completed units in terms of conversion costs.

(12) There are two ways to treat the costs of the beginning inventory: ____________ and ____________.

(13) Allocation of the service department costs to the production departments may be accomplished by one of the following procedures: ____________, ____________, or ____________.

(14) ____________ are those that have a relatively significant sales value, while ____________ are those whose sales value is relatively minor in comparison with the value of the main, or joint, products.

Answers: (1) job-order costing, process costing; (2) job-order costing; production department (or cost center); (3) job cost sheet; (4) predetermined factory overhead rate; (5) predetermined factory overhead rate, actual cost driver usage; (6) machine hours, direct labor dollars; (7) like units, operations or processes; (8) work in process, the current equivalent units; (9) the sum of equivalent units started and completed plus equivalent units in ending work in process; (10) summarize the flow of physical units, compute output in terms of equivalent units, summarize the total costs to be accounted for by cost categories, compute the unit costs per equivalent unit, apply total costs to units completed and transferred out and to units in ending work in process; (11) 60; (12) weighted average costing, first-in, first-out (FIFO); (13) direct method, step method, reciprocal method; (14) joint products, by-products.

Solved Problems

12.1 Thunderbird uses a job-order cost system and applies factory overhead to production orders on the basis of direct labor costs. The overhead rates for 19X9 are 200 percent for Department A and 50 percent for Department B. Job 123, started and completed during 19X9, was charged with the following costs:

	Department	
	A	B
Direct materials	$25,000	$ 5,000
Direct labor	?	30,000
Factory overhead	40,000	?

Determine the total manufacturing costs assigned to Job 123.

SOLUTION

	Department A	Department B	Total
Costs assigned to Job 123:			
Direct materials	$25,000	$ 5,000	$ 30,000
Direct labor	20,000*	30,000	50,000
Factory overhead	40,000	15,000†	55,000
Total	$85,000	$50,000	$135,000

*$40,000/2.00 = $20,000
†$30,000 × 0.50 = $15,000

12.2 The Helper Corporation manufactures one product. You have obtained the following information for the year ended December 31, 19X9, from the corporation's books and records:

(1) Total current manufacturing costs were $1,000,000.

(2) The 19X9 cost of goods manufactured was $970,000.

(3) Current factory overhead costs were 75 percent of current direct labor costs and 27 percent of total current manufacturing costs.

(4) Beginning work in process, January 1, was 80 percent of ending work in process, December 31.

Prepare a formal statement of goods manufactured for the year ended December 31, 19X9.

SOLUTION

HELPER CORPORATION
Statement of Cost of Goods Manufactured
For the Year Ended December 31, 19X9

		Possible Solution Sequence
Cost of Raw Materials Placed in Production	$ 370,000	3
Direct Labor ($270,000/0.75)	360,000	2
Factory Overhead ($1,000,000 × 0.27)	270,000	1
Total Costs Placed in Production	$1,000,000	
Work in Process, Beginning ($150,000 × 0.8)	120,000	5
Total Costs in Process	$1,120,000	6
Work in Process, Ending*	−150,000	4
Cost of Goods Manufactured	$ 970,000	

*Let x = Work in Process, Ending. Then

$$\$1{,}000{,}000 + 0.8x - x = \$970{,}000$$
$$0.2x = 30{,}000$$
$$x = 150{,}000$$

12.3 Golden Bear Company is a manufacturing company with a fiscal year that runs from July 1 to June 30. The company uses a normal job-order accounting system for its production costs. A predetermined overhead rate based on direct labor hours is used to apply overhead to individual jobs. For the 19X8–19X9 fiscal year, the predetermined overhead rate is based on an expected level of activity of 120,000 direct labor hours and the following cost–volume (or flexible budget) formula:

$$T = \$216{,}000 + \$3.25x$$

where T = estimated total overhead
x = direct labor hours

The following information presented is for November 19X8. Jobs 87-50 and 87-51 were completed during November.

Inventories November 1, 19X8:	
Raw materials and supplies	$ 10,500
Work in process (Job 87-50)	54,000
Finished goods	112,500
Purchases of raw materials and supplies:	
Raw materials	$135,000
Supplies	15,000
Materials and supplies requisitioned for production:	
Job 87-50	$ 45,000
Job 87-51	37,500
Job 87-52	25,500
Supplies	12,000
Total	$120,000
Factory direct labor hours:	
Job 87-50 3,500 DLH	
Job 87-51 3,000 DLH	
Job 87-52 2,000 DLH	
Labor costs:	
Direct labor wages	$51,000
Indirect labor wages (4,000 hours)	15,000
Supervisory salaries, factory	6,000
Building occupancy costs (heat, light, depreciation, etc.):	
Factory facilities	$6,500
Sales offices	1,500
Administrative offices	1,000
Total	$9,000
Factory equipment costs:	
Power	$4,000
Repairs and maintenance	1,500
Depreciation	1,500
Other	1,000
Total	$8,000

(*a*) Determine the predetermined overhead rate to be used to individual jobs during the 19X8–19X9 fiscal year.

(*b*) Determine the total cost of job 87-50.

(*c*) Determine the over- or underapplied overhead for November 19X8.

SOLUTION

(*a*)

$$\text{Estimated total overhead} = \$216{,}000 + \$3.25\ (120{,}000) = \$606{,}000$$

$$\text{Predetermined overhead rate} = \frac{\$606{,}000}{120{,}000} = \$5.05 \text{ per direct labor hour}$$

(*b*)

		Job 87-50
Balance, 11/1/X8		$ 54,000
Costs to complete:	$45,000	
Direct labor (3,500 × $6.00*)	21,000	
Applied overhead (3,500 × $5.05)	17,675	83,675
Total cost of job		$137,675

*Direct labor rate = $51,000/(3,500 + 3,000 + 2,000) = $6.00

(*c*) Actual overhead for November 19X8:

Supplies	$12,000	
Indirect labor	15,000	
Supervisory salaries	6,000	
Building occupancy, factory	6,500	
Factory equipment costs	8,000	$47,500
Applied overhead for November 19X8 (8,500 direct labor hours × $5.05 =)		−42,925
Underapplied overhead for November 19X8		$ 4,575

12.4 Camp Company uses a job-order costing system. The company has two departments through which most jobs pass. Selected budgeted and actual data for the past year follow:

	Department A	Department B
Budgeted overhead	$100,000	$500,000
Actual overhead	$110,000	$520,000
Expected activity (direct labor hours)	50,000	10,000
Expected machine hours	10,000	50,000
Actual direct labor hours	51,000	9,000
Actual machine hours	10,500	52,000

During the year, several jobs were completed. Data pertaining to one such job follows:

	Job 310
Direct materials	$20,000
Direct labor cost:	
Department A (5,000 hours @ $6)	$30,000
Department B (1,000 hours @ $6)	$ 6,000
Machine hours used:	
Department A	100
Department B	1,200
Units produced	10,000

Camp Company uses a plant-wide predetermined overhead rate to assign overhead to jobs. Direct labor hours (DLH) is used to compute the predetermined overhead rate.

(1) Compute the predetermined overhead rate.

(2) Using the predetermined rate, compute the per-unit manufacturing cost of Job 310.

(3) Recalculate the unit manufacturing cost for Job 310 using departmental overhead rates. Use direct labor hours for Department A and machine hours for Department B.

SOLUTION

(1) Predetermined overhead rate = $600,000/60,000 = $10 per DLH. Add the budgeted overhead for the two departments and divide by the total expected direct labor hours (DLH = 50,000 + 10,000).

(2)

Direct materials	$ 20,000
Direct labor	36,000
Overhead ($10 × 6,000 DLH)	60,000
Total manufacturing cost	$116,000
Unit cost ($116,000/10,000)	$ 11.60

(3) Predetermined rate for Department A: $100,000/50,000 = $2 per DLH. Predetermined rate for Department B: $500,000/50,000 = $10 per machine hour.

Direct materials	$20,000
Direct labor	36,000
Overhead:	
Department A: $2 × 5,000	10,000
Department B: $10 × 1,200	12,000
Total manufacturing cost	$78,000
Unit cost ($78,000/10,000)	$ 7.80

Overhead assignment using departmental rates is more accurate because there is a higher correlation with the overhead assigned and the overhead consumed. Notice that Job 310 spends most of its time in Department A, the least overhead-intensive of the two departments. Departmental rates reflect this differential time and consumption better than plant-wide rates do.

12.5 The quantity schedule for Department 2 at the Jelenick Transport Company for the month of June 19X2 is shown below.

	Quantities
Units in process at beginning (all materials; ½ conversion)	8,000
Units started	76,000
Units transferred to next department	78,000
Units still in process (all materials; ⅔ conversion)	6,000

Compute the equivalent production units for material and conversion costs (labor and factory overhead) for the month, under (*a*) FIFO, and (*b*) weighted average cost.

SOLUTION

Weighted average cost:

	Materials	Conversion
Units completed and transferred out	78,000	78,000
Add: Ending work in process amount completed (all materials; ⅔ conversion costs)	6,000	4,000
Equivalent production units	84,000	82,000

FIFO:

	Materials	Conversion
Units completed and transferred out	78,000	78,000
Add: Ending work in process amount completed (all materials; ⅔ conversion costs)	6,000	4,000
Equivalent production units	84,000	82,000
Less: Beginning work in process (all materials; ½ conversion costs)	8,000	4,000
	76,000	78,000

12.6 Texas Texturizing is a texturizer of polyester yarn. On June 1, 19A, an inventory of 10,000 pounds was complete as to materials, but only three-quarters complete as to conversion. During the period, 160,000 pounds were completed. The inventory at the end of the period consisted of 40,000 pounds that were complete as to materials but only one-quarter complete as to conversion. Costs for materials and conversion are as follows:

	Materials	Conversion	Total
Work in process, beginning	\$ 10,000	\$ 5,000	\$ 15,000
Current costs	140,000	76,600	216,600

Prepare a cost-of-production report for Texas Texturizing using the weighted average method.

SOLUTION

TEXAS TEXTURIZING

Cost-of-Production Report
For the Month of June
(Weighted Average)

Physical Flow:

Work in Process, Beginning	10,000 (75%)
Started	190,000
In Process	200,000
Completed	160,000
Work in Process, Ending	40,000 (25%)
Accounted for	200,000

Equivalent Units in Process:

	Materials	Conversion
Units Completed	160,000	160,000
Equivalent Units, Ending Work in Process	40,000	10,000
Equivalent Units in Process	200,000	170,000

Total Costs to Be Accounted for:
Cost per Equivalent Unit:

	Materials	Conversion	Total
Work in Process, Beginning	$ 10,000	$ 5,000	$ 15,000
Current Costs	140,000	76,600	216,600
Total Costs in Process	$150,000	$ 81,600	$231,600
Equivalent Units in Process	200,000	170,000	
Cost per Equivalent Unit	$ 0.75	$ 0.48	$ 1.23
Accounting for Total Costs:			
Completed and Transferred out (160,000 × $1.23)			$196,800
Work in Process, Ending:			
Materials (40,000 × $0.75)	$ 30,000		
Conversion (10,000 × $0.48)		$ 4,800	34,800
Total Costs Accounted for			$231,600

12.7 Using data from Problem 12.6, prepare a cost-of-productiion report using the FIFO method.

SOLUTION

TEXAS TEXTURIZING
Cost-of-Production Report
For the Month of June
(FIFO)

Physical Flow:

Work in Process, Beginning	10,000 (75%)
Started	190,000
In Process	200,000
Completed	160,000
Work in Process, Ending	40,000 (25%)
	200,000

Equivalent Units in Process:

	Materials	Conversion
Units Completed	160,000	160,000
Equivalent Units, Ending Work in Process	40,000	10,000
Equivalent Units in Process	200,000	170,000
Less: Equivalent Units, Beginning Work in Process	10,000	7,500
	190,000	162,500

Total Costs to Be Accounted for:			
Cost per Equivalent Unit Manufactured:			
	Materials	Conversion	Total
Work in Process, Beginning			$ 15,000
Current Costs	$140,000	$ 76,600	216,600
Total Costs in Process	$140,000	$ 76,600	$231,600
Equivalent Units	190,000	162,500	
Cost per Equivalent Unit	$ 0.7368	$ 0.4714	$ 1.2082
Accounting for Total Costs:			
Completed and Transferred out			
First Batch:			
Beginning Inventory		$15,000.00	
Costs to Complete:			
Materials	$ 0.00		
Conversion $(1 - 0.75) \times 10{,}000 \times \$0.4714$		1,178.50	$16,178.50
Second Batch:			
$(160{,}000 - 10{,}000) \times \$1.2082$			181,230.00
			$197,408.50
Work in Process, Ending:			
Materials $(40{,}000 \times \$0.7368)$	$29,472.00		
Conversion $(10{,}000 \times \$0.4714)$	4,714.00		34,186.00
Total Costs Accounted for			$231,594.50*

*$5.50 rounding error.

12.8 A toy manufacturer has two departments, forming and finishing. Consider the finishing department, which processes the formed toys through the addition of hand shaping and metal. Although various direct materials might be added at various stages of finishing, for simplicity we will suppose that all additional direct materials are added at the end of the process.

The following is a summary of the April operations in the finishing department:

Units:
- Work in process, March 31, 5,000 units, 60% completed for conversion costs
- Units transferred in during April, 20,000
- Units completed during April, 21,000
- Work in process, April 30, 4,000 units, 30% completed for conversion costs

Costs:
- Work in process, March 31 (transferred-in costs, $17,750; conversion costs, $7,250), $25,000
- Transferred-in costs from forming department during April, $104,000
- Direct materials added during April, $23,100
- Conversion costs added during April, $38,400
- Total costs to account for, $190,500

Using the weighted average method, prepare a cost-of-production report for the finishing department for April.

SOLUTION

Weighted Average Method

Flow of Production	Physical Units	Transferred-in Costs	Direct Materials	Conversion Costs
Beginning Work in Process, March 31 (50%)	5,000			
Transferred in	20,000			
Total Units to Account for	25,000			
Completed and Transferred out	21,000	21,000	21,000	21,000
Ending Work in Process, April 30 (30%)	4,000			12,000
Total Units to Account for	25,000			
Work Done to Date		25,000	21,000	22,200

Costs in Detail				
Costs of Work Done on Beginning Work in Process	$ 25,000	$ 17,750	0	$ 7,250
Current Costs to Account for	165,600	104,000	$ 23,100	38,400
Total Costs to Account for	$190,500	$121,750	$231,000	$45,650
Divide by Equivalent Units to Obtain Unit Cost		$ 25,000	$ 21,000	$22,200
Unit Cost	$ 8.0263			

Application of Costs		
Costs of Completed and Transferred out	$168,552	21,000 × $8.0263
Ending Work in Process		
Transferred-in Costs	$ 19,480	4,000 × $4.87
Direct Materials	0	
Conversion Costs	2,468	(4,000 × 0.3) × $2.0563
Ending Work in Process	$ 21,948	
Total Costs to Account for	$190,500	

12.9 Using FIFO costing, repeat the requirements in Problem 12.8.

SOLUTION

Flow of Production	Physical Units	Transferred-in Costs	Direct Materials	Conversion Costs
Beginning Work in Process, March 31 (50%)	5,000			
Transferred in	20,000			
Total Units to Account for	25,000			
Completed and Transferred out	21,000	21,000	21,000	21,000
Ending Work in Process, April 30 (30%)	4,000			12,000
Total Units to Account for	25,000			
Work Done to Date		25,000	21,000	22,200

		Work Done in This Period Only		
Work Done in the Previous Period		5,000		$ 3,000
Work Done in This Period Only		20,000	$ 21,000	19,200
Costs of Work Done on Beginning Work in Process	$ 25,000			
Current Costs to Be Added	165,000	$104,000	23,000	$38,400
Total Costs to Account for	$190,500			
Divide by Equivalent Units to Obtain Unit Costs		20,000	21,000	19,200
Unit Cost	$ 8.3000	$ 5.2000	$ 1.1000	$2.0000

Costs of Completed and Transferred out:		
Beginning Work in Process	$ 25,000	
Additional Costs:		
Direct Materials	5,500	5,000 × $1.1
Conversion Costs	4,000	5,000 (1 − 0.6) × $2
Costs of Started and Completed	132,800	(21,000 − 5,000) × $8.30
	$167,300	
Ending Work in Process		
Transferred-in Costs	$ 20,800	4,000 × $5.2
Direct Materials	0	
Conversion Costs	2,400	(4,000 × 0.3) × $2
Ending Work in Process	$ 23,200	
Total Costs to Account for	$190,500	

12.10 Angelo Trucking is divided into two operating divisions: Perishable Foods and Household Goods. The company allocates personnel and accounting costs to each operating division. Personnel costs are allocated on the basis of employees. Accounting costs are allocated on the basis of the number of transactions processed. Allocations for the coming year are based on the following data:

	Service Departments		Operating Divisions	
	Personnel	Accounting	Perishable Foods	Household Goods
Overhead costs	$100,000	$205,000	$80,000	$50,000
Number of employees	20	60	60	80
Transactions processed	2,000	200	3,000	5,000

(*a*) Allocate the service costs using the direct method.

(*b*) Allocate the service costs using the step method.

(*c*) Allocate the service costs using the reciprocal method.

SOLUTION

(*a*) *Direct Method:*

	Foods	Goods
Proportion of:		
Number of employees	0.429	0.571
Transactions processed	0.375	0.625
Personnel:		
(0.429 × 100,000)	$ 42,900	
(0.571 × 100,000)		$ 57,100
Accounting		
(0.375 × $205,000)	76,785	
(0.625 × $205,000)		128,125
Direct costs	80,000	50,000
	$199,775	$235,225

(*b*) *Step method:*

	Personnel	Accounting	Foods	Goods
Transactions	0.2	—	0.300	0.500
Employees	—	—	0.429	0.571
Direct cost	$100,000	$205,000	$ 80,000	$ 50,000
Accounting				
(0.2 × $205,000)	41,000	(41,000)		
(0.3 × $205,000)		(61,500)	61,500	
(0.5 × $205,000)		(102,500)		102,500
Personnel				
(0.429 × $141,000)	(60,489)		60,489	
(0.571 × $141,000)	(80,511)			80,511
	0	0	$201,989	$233,011

(*c*) *Reciprocal method:*

	Personnel	Accounting	Foods	Goods
Transactions	0.2	—	0.3	0.5
Employees	—	0.3	0.3	0.4

$$A = 205{,}000 + 0.3P \qquad P = 100{,}000 + 0.2A$$
$$A = 205{,}000 + 0.3(100{,}000 + 0.2A) \qquad P = 100{,}000 + 0.2(250{,}000)$$
$$A = 205{,}000 + 30{,}000 + 0.06A \qquad P = 150{,}000$$
$$0.94A = 235{,}000$$
$$A = 250{,}000$$

	Total Cost	Foods	Goods
From Accounting	$250,000		
(0.3 × $250,000)		$ 75,000	
(0.5 × $250,000)			$125,000
From Personnel	150,000		
(0.3 × $150,000)		45,000	
(0.4 × $150,000)			60,000
Direct cost		80,000	50,000
		$200,000	$235,000

12.11 Total Mining Company produces two products from ore, copper and zinc. The following events took place in May:

	Copper	Zinc	Total
Units produced	40,000	60,000	100,000
Unit selling price	$2.00	$1.00	

Joint costs incurred were $110,000.

(*a*) Allocate the joint costs to the two products using the physical measures method.

(*b*) Allocate the joint costs to the two products using the relative sales value method.

(*c*) Explain the difference in unit costs using the two methods.

(*d*) Which method do you think better allocates joint costs? Why?

SOLUTION

(*a*) *Physical measures method:*

	Units	Ratio		Joint Costs		Allocated Joint Costs
Copper	40,000	40,000/100,000	×	$110,000	=	$ 44,000
Zinc	60,000	60,000/100,000	×	110,000	=	66,000
	100,000					$110,000

(*b*) *Relative sales value method:*

	Sales Value at Split-off	Ratio		Joint Costs		Allocated Joint Costs
Copper	$ 80,000	$80,000/$140,000	×	$110,000	=	$ 62,857
Zinc	60,000	$60,000/$140,000	×	110,000	=	47,143
	$140,000					$110,000

(*c*) Both the physical measures method and the relative sales value method are acceptable ways to allocate joint costs. Under the physical measures method, joint costs are allocated based on the relative number of units produced. The product with the most units will be allocated the most costs. Under the relative sales value method, joint costs are allocated based on the relative sales value of the units produced. Since copper has a higher relative sales value, it will be allocated more of the joint costs under the relative sales value method even though fewer units are produced.

(*d*) The major advantage of the relative sales value method is that it allocates joint costs according to the relative revenue-generating ability of the individual products. This can avoid wide swings in gross margin percentages of the two products.

CHAPTER 13

Activity-Based Costing (ABC), Just-in-Time (JIT), Total Quality Management (TQM), and Quality Costs

13.1 ACTIVITY-BASED COSTING

Many companies use a traditional cost system such as job-order costing or process costing, or some hybrid of the two. Using the traditional methods of assigning overhead costs to products using a single predetermined overhead rate based on any single activity measure can produce distorted product costs. The growth in the automation of manufacturing (such as increased use of robotics, high-tech machinery, and other computer-driven processes) has changed the nature of manufacturing and the composition of total product cost. The significance of direct labor cost has diminished and that of overhead costs has increased. In this environment, overhead application rates based on direct labor or any other volume-based cost driver may not provide accurate overhead charges, since they no longer represent cause-and-effect relationships between output and overhead costs.

Activity-based costing (ABC) attempts to get around this problem. An ABC system assigns costs to products based on the product's use of activities, not product volume. An activity-based cost system is one which first traces costs to activities and then to products. Traditional product costing also involves two stages, but in the first stage costs are traced to departments, not to activities. In both traditional and activity-based costing, the second stage consists of tracing costs to products.

The principal difference between the two methods is the number of cost drivers used. Activity-based costing uses a much larger number of cost drivers than the one or two volume-based cost drivers typical in a conventional system. In fact, the approach separates overhead costs into overhead cost pools, where each cost pool is associated with a different cost driver. Then a predetermined overhead rate is computed for each cost pool and each cost driver. In consequence, this method has enhanced accuracy.

13.2 HOW DOES ABC WORK?

ABC is not an alternative costing system to job costing or process costing. It starts with the detailed activities required to produce a product or service and computes a product's cost using the following three steps:

1. Identify the activities or transactions that cause costs to be incurred. These activities are called *cost drivers.* Cost drivers are causes of costs incurred. Table 13-1 lists possible cost drivers.
2. Assign a cost to each cost driver.
3. Sum the costs of the cost drivers that make up the product.

Table 13-1 Cost Drivers

Manufacturing:

Number of setups	Square footage
Weight of material	Number of vendors
Number of units reworked	Asset value
Number of orders placed	Number of labor transactions
Number of orders received	Number of units scrapped
Number of inspections	Number of parts
Number of material handling operations	Replacement cost
Number of orders shipped	Machine hours
Design time	Direct labor hours

Nonmanufacturing:

Number of hospital beds occupied
Number of take-offs and landings for an airline
Number of rooms occupied in a hotel

EXAMPLE 13.1 Global Metals, Inc., has established the following overhead cost pools and cost drivers for their product:

Overhead Cost Pool	Budgeted Overhead Cost	Cost Driver	Predicted Level for Cost Driver	Predetermined Overhead Rate
Machine setups	$100,000	Number of setups	100	$1,000 per setup
Material handling	100,000	Weight of raw material	50,000 pounds	$2.00 per pound
Waste control	50,000	Weight of hazardous chemical used	10,000 pounds	$5.00 per pound
Inspection	75,000	Number of inspections	1,000	$75 per inspection
Other overhead costs	200,000	Machine hours	20,000	$10 per machine hour
	$525,000			

Job No. 107 consists of 2,000 special-purpose machine tools with the following requirements:

Machine setups	2
Raw material required	10,000 pounds
Waste material required	2,000 pounds
Inspections	10
Machine hours	500

The overhead assigned to Job No. 107 is computed below:

Overhead Cost Pool	Predetermined Overhead Rate	Level of Cost Driver	Assigned Overhead Cost
Machine setups	$1,000 per setup	2 setups	$ 2,000
Material handling	$2.00 per pound	10,000 pounds	20,000
Waste control	$5.00 per pound	2,000 pounds	10,000
Inspection	$75 per inspection	10 inspections	750
Other overhead cost	$10 per machine hour	500 machine hours	5,000
Total			$37,750

The total overhead cost assigned to Job No. 107 is $37,750, or $18.88 per tool ($37,750/2,000).

Compare this with the overhead cost that is assigned to the job if the firm uses a single predetermined overhead rate based on machine hours:

$$\frac{\text{Total budgeted overhead cost}}{\text{Total predicted machine hours}} = \frac{\$525{,}000}{20{,}000}$$

$$= \$26.25 \text{ per machine hour}$$

Under this approach, the total overhead cost assigned to Job No. 107 is $13,125 ($26.25 per machine hour × 500 machine hours). This is only $6.56 per tool ($13,125/2,000), which is about one-third of the overhead cost per tool computed when multiple cost drivers are used.

The reason for this wide discrepancy is that these special-purpose tools require a relatively large number of machine setups, a sizable amount of waste materials, and several inspections. Thus, they are relatively costly in terms of driving overhead costs. Use of a single predetermined overhead rate obscures that fact.

Inaccurately calculating the overhead cost per unit to the extent illustrated above can have serious adverse consequences for the firm. For example, it can lead to poor decisions about pricing, product mix, or contract bidding.

The fundamental differences in the traditional and ABC cost systems are summarized in Table 13-2.

Table 13-2 Cost System Comparison

	Traditional	ABC
Cost pools	One or a limited number	Many, to reflect different activities
Applied rate	Volume-based, financial	Activity-based, nonfinancial
Suited for	Labor-intensive, low-overhead companies	Capital-intensive, product-diverse, high-overhead companies
Benefits	Simple, inexpensive	Accurate product costing, possible elimination of non-value-added activities

13.3 BENEFITS OF AN ABC SYSTEM

Benefits of an ABC system are numerous. They include:

1. Improved product or service cost data.
2. Improved decisions about pricing, service mixes, and product strategies based on more accurate cost information.
3. Cost reduction by eliminating the non-value-added activities. These are activities that are inefficient, wasteful, and do not add value. Examples are scheduling, moving, waiting, inspecting, and storing.
4. Greater control of costs because of its focus on the behavior of costs at their origination, both short-term and long-term.
5. More accurate evaluation of performance by programs and responsibility center.

13.4 JUST-IN-TIME MANUFACTURING

Just-in-time (JIT) is a demand-pull system. Demand for customer output (not plans for using input resources) triggers production. Production activities are "pulled," not "pushed," into action. JIT production, in its purest sense, is buying and producing in very small quantities, just in time for use. As a philosophy, JIT targets inventory as an evil presence that obscures problems that should be solved, and declares that, by contributing significantly to costs, large inventories keep a company from being as competitive or profitable as it otherwise might be. Practically speaking, JIT has as its principal goal the elimination of waste, and the principal measure of success is how much or how little inventory there is.

Furthermore, the little inventory that exists in a JIT system must be of good quality. This requirement has led to JIT purchasing practices that are uniquely able to deliver high-quality materials.

13.5 JIT COMPARED WITH TRADITIONAL MANUFACTURING

JIT manufacturing is a demand-pull, rather than the traditional "push" approach. The philosophy underlying JIT manufacturing is to produce a product when it is needed and only in the quantities demanded by customers. Demand pulls products through the manufacturing process. Each operation produces only what is necessary to satisfy the demand of the succeeding operation. No production takes place until a signal from a succeeding process indicates a need to produce. Parts and materials arrive just in time to be used in production.

Reduced Inventories. The primary goal of JIT is to reduce inventories to insignificant or zero levels. In traditional manufacturing, inventories result whenever production exceeds demand.

Manufacturing Cells and Multifunction Labor. In traditional manufacturing, products are moved from one group of identical machines to another. Typically, machines with identical functions are located together in an area referred to as a department or process. JIT replaces this traditional pattern with a pattern of manufacturing cells or work centers. Manufacturing cells contain machines that are grouped in families, usually in a semicircle. The machines are arranged so that they can be used to perform a variety of operations in sequence. Each cell is set up to produce a particular product or product family. Products move from one machine to another from start to finish. Workers are assigned to cells and are trained to operate all machines within the cell. Thus, labor in a JIT environment is multifunction labor, not specialized labor. Each manufacturing cell is basically a minifactory or a factory within a factory.

Total Quality Control. A strong emphasis on quality control goes along with JIT. A defective part will bring production to a grinding halt. Poor quality simply cannot be tolerated in a stockless manufacturing environment. In other words, JIT cannot be implemented without a commitment to *total quality management (TQM)*. TQM is essentially an endless quest for perfect quality. This approach to quality is opposed to the traditional belief, called *acceptable quality level (AQL)*, which allows defects to occur provided they are within a predetermined level.

Suppliers as Outside Partners. In JIT, suppliers should be viewed as "outside partners" who can contribute to the long-run welfare of the buying firm rather than as outside adversaries.

Better Cost Management. Cost management differs from cost accounting in that it refers to the management of cost, whether or not the cost has direct impact on inventory or the financial statements. The JIT philosophy simplifies the cost accounting procedure and helps managers manage and control their costs, as will be discussed in detail later in the chapter. JIT recognizes that with simplification comes better management, better quality, better service, and better cost control. Traditional cost accounting systems have a tendency to be very complex, with many transactions and reporting of data.

The major differences between JIT manufacturing and traditional manufacturing are summarized in Table 13-3.

Table 13-3 Comparison of JIT and Traditional Manufacturing

JIT	Traditional
1. Pull system	1. Push system
2. Insignificant or zero inventories	2. Significant inventories
3. Manufacturing cells	3. "Process" structure
4. Multifunction labor	4. Specialized labor
5. Total quality management (TQM)	5. Acceptable quality level (AQL)
6. Complex cost accounting	6. Simple cost accounting

13.6 BENEFITS OF JIT

The potential benefits of JIT are numerous, including:

1. JIT practice reduces inventory levels, which means lower investments in inventories.
2. Since purchasing under JIT requires a significantly shorter delivery lead time, lead time reliability is greatly improved.
3. Reduced lead times and setup times increase scheduling flexibility.
4. Improved quality levels have been reported by many companies.
5. The costs of purchased materials may be reduced through more extensive value analysis and cooperative supplier development activities.
6. Other financial benefits include:
   (*a*) Lower investments in factory space for inventories and production
   (*b*) Less obsolescence risk in inventories
   (*c*) Reduction in scrap and rework
   (*d*) Decline in paperwork
   (*e*) Reduction in direct material costs through quantity purchases

13.7 JIT COSTING SYSTEM

The cost accounting system of a company adopting JIT will be quite simple compared to job-order or processing costing. Under JIT, raw materials and work-in-process (WIP) accounts are typically combined into one account called "Resources in Process (RIP)" or "Raw and In-process." Under JIT, materials arrive at the receiving area and are whisked immediately to the factory area. Thus, the Stores Control account vanishes. The journal entries that accompany JIT costing are remarkably simple as follows:

Raw and In-process (RIP) inventory	45,000	
Accounts Payable or cash		45,000
To record purchases.		
Finished Goods	40,000	
RIP Inventory		40,000
To record raw materials in completed units.		

As can be seen, there are no Stores Control and WIP accounts under JIT.

In summary, JIT costing can be characterized as follows:

1. There are fewer inventory accounts.
2. There are no work orders. Thus, there is no need for detailed tracking of actual raw materials.
3. With JIT, activities can be eliminated on the premise that they do not add value. Prime targets for elimination are storage areas for WIP inventory and material-handling facilities.
4. Direct labor costs and factory overhead costs are not tracked to specific orders.

13.8 TOTAL QUALITY MANAGEMENT

In order to be globally competitive in today's world-class manufacturing environment, firms place an increased emphasis on quality and productivity. *Total quality management (TQM)* is an effort in this direction. Simply put, TQM is a system for creating competitive advantage by focusing the organization on what is important to the customer. Total quality management can be broken down into: "total"—that is, the whole organization is involved and understands that customer satisfaction is everyone's job; "quality"—the extent to which products and services satisfy the requirements of internal and external customers; and "management"—the leadership, infrastructure, and resources that support employees as they meet the needs of those customers.

TQM is essentially an endless quest for perfect quality. It is a *zero-defects* approach. It views the optimal level of quality costs as the level where zero defects are produced. This approach to quality is opposed to the traditional belief, acceptable quality level (AQL), which allows a predetermined level of defective units to be produced and sold. AQL is the level where the number of defects allowed minimizes total quality costs. The rationale behind the traditional view is that there is a trade-off between prevention and appraisal costs and failure costs. Quality experts maintain that the optimal quality level should be about 2.5 percent of sales.

13.9 QUALITY COSTS

Costs of quality are costs that occur because poor quality may exist or actually does exist. More specifically, quality costs are the total of the costs incurred by (1) investing in the prevention of nonconformances to requirements; (2) appraising a product or service for conformance to requirements; and (3) failure to meet requirements.

Quality costs are classified into three broad categories: prevention, appraisal, and failure costs. *Prevention costs* are those costs incurred to prevent defects. Amounts spent on quality training programs, researching customer needs, quality circles, and improved production equipment are considered in prevention costs. Expenditures made for prevention will minimize the costs that will be incurred for appraisal and failure. *Appraisal costs* are costs incurred for monitoring or inspection; these costs compensate for mistakes that are not eliminated through prevention. *Failure costs* may be internal (such as scrap and rework costs and reinspection) or external (such as product returns due to quality problems, warranty costs, lost sales due to poor product performance, and complaint department costs). Market shares of many U.S. firms have eroded because foreign firms have been able to sell higher-quality products at lower prices.

Studies indicate that costs of quality for American companies are typically 20 to 30 percent of sales. Quality experts maintain that the optimal quality level should be about 2.5 percent of sales.

13.10 QUALITY COST AND PERFORMANCE REPORTS

The principal objective of reporting quality costs is to improve and facilitate managerial planning, control, and decision making. Potential uses of quality cost informatioin include:

1. Quality program implementation decisions.
2. Evaluation of the effectiveness of quality programs.
3. Strategic pricing decisions. (For example, a reduction in quality costs might enable a firm to reduce its selling price, improve its competitive position, and increase market share.)

The control process involves comparing actual performance with quality standards. This comparison provides feedback that can be used to take corrective action if necessary. The first step in a quality cost reporting system is to prepare a detailed listing of actual quality costs by category. Furthermore, each category of quality costs is expressed as a percentage of sales. This serves two purposes: (1) it permits managers to assess the financial impact of quality costs, and (2) it reveals the relative emphasis currently placed on each category.

Performance reports to measure a company's quality improvement include:

1. *Quality performance report.* This report measures the progress achieved within the period relative to the planned level of progress for the period (see Fig. 13-1).
2. *One-year quality trend report.* This report compares the current year's quality cost ratio with the previous year's ratio. More specifically, it compares the current year's variable quality cost ratio with the previous year's variable quality cost ratio, and the current year's actual fixed quality costs with the previous year's actual fixed quality costs (see Fig. 13-2).
3. *Long-range quality performance report.* This report compares the current year's actual quality costs with the firm's intended long-range quality goal (see Fig. 13-3).

13.11 ACTIVITY-BASED COSTING AND OPTIMAL QUALITY COSTS

Activity-based costing (ABC) supports the zero-defect view of quality costs. ABC classifies activities as: (1) value-added activities and (2) non-value-added activities. Quality-related activities can be classified as value-added and non-value-added. Internal and external failure activities and their associated costs are non-value-added and should be eliminated. Prevention activities that are performed efficiently are value-added. (Costs caused by inefficiency in prevention activities are non-value-added costs.) Appraisal activities may be value-added or non-value-added, depending on the activity. For example, quality audits may serve a value-added objective.

Once the quality-related activities are identified for each category, resource drivers can be used to improve cost assignments to individual activities. Root or process drivers can also be identified and used to help managers understand what is causing the cost of the activities.

Quality Performance Report
For the Year Ended March 31, 19X9

	Actual Costs	Budgeted Costs*	Variance	
Prevention costs:				
Quality training	$ 30,000	$ 30,000	$0	
Reliability engineering	79,000	80,000	1,000	(F)
Total prevention	$109,000	$110,000	$ 1,000	(F)
Appraisal costs:				
Materials inspection	$ 19,000	$ 28,000	$ 9,000	(F)
Product acceptance	10,000	15,000	5,000	(F)
Process acceptance	35,000	35,000	0	
Total appraisal	$64,000	$ 78,000	$14,000	(F)
Internal failure costs:				
Scrap	$ 40,000	$44,000	$ 4,000	(F)
Rework	34,000	36,500	2,500	(F)
Total internal failure	$ 74,000	$ 80,500	$ 6,500	(F)
External failure costs:				
Fixed:				
Customer complaints	$ 24,000	$ 25,000	$ 1,000	(F)
Variable:				
Warranty	24,000	20,000	(4,000)	(U)
Repair	15,000	17,500	2,500	(F)
Total external failure	$ 63,000	$ 62,500	($ 500)	(U)
Total quality costs	$310,000	$331,000	$21,000	(F)
Percentage of actual sales	10.62%	11.34%	0.72%	(F)

*Based on actual sales of $2,920,000.

Fig. 13-1

Summary

(1) Activity-based costing (ABC) traces costs to ______________ and then ______________.

(2) ABC is not an alternative costing system to ______________ or ______________.

(3) ______________ are causes of costs incurred. They may be volume-based, such as direct labor hours or machine hours, or ______________, such as number of setups or number of inspections.

(4) An ABC system is suited for ______________, ______________, and/or ______________ companies.

(5) Major benefits of using ABC include ______________ and ______________.

One-Year Quality Trend Report
For the Year Ended March 31, 19X9

	Actual Costs 19X9*	Actual Costs 19X8	Variance	
Prevention costs:				
Quality training	$ 30,000	$ 36,000	$ 6,000	(F)
Reliability engineering	79,000	120,000	41,000	(F)
Total prevention	$109,000	$156,000	$47,000	(F)
Appraisal costs:				
Materials inspection	$ 19,000	$ 33,600	$14,600	(F)
Product acceptance	10,000	16,800	6,800	(F)
Process acceptance	35,000	39,200	4,200	(F)
Total appraisal	$64,000	$89,600	$25,600	(F)
Internal failure costs:				
Scrap	$ 40,000	$ 48,000	$8,000	(F)
Rework	34,000	40,000	6,000	(F)
Total internal failure	$74,000	$ 88,500	$14,000	(F)
External failure costs:				
Fixed:				
Customer complaints	$ 24,000	$ 33,000	$ 9,000	(F)
Variable:				
Warranty	24,000	23,000	(1,000)	(U)
Repair	15,000	16,400	1,400	(F)
Total external failure	$ 63,000	$ 72,400	$ 9,400	(F)
Total quality costs	$310,000	$406,000	$96,000	(F)
Percentage of actual sales	10.62%	13.90%	3.29%	

*Based on actual sales of $2,920,000.

Fig. 13-2

(6) Just-in-time (JIT) manufacturing is a ____________, rather than the traditional "push" approach.

(7) The primary goal of ____________ is to reduce ____________ to insignificant or zero levels.

(8) JIT cannot be implemented without a commitment to ____________.

(9) The cost accounting system of a company adopting JIT will be quite simple compared to ____________.

(10) Under JIT, ____________ accounts are typically combined into one account called "Resources in Process (RIP)" or "Raw and In-process."

Long-Range Quality Performance Report
For the Year Ended March 31, 19X9

	Actual Costs	Target Costs*	Variance	
Prevention costs:				
Quality training	$ 30,000	$14,000	$ (16,000)	(U)
Reliability engineering	79,000	39,000	(40,000)	(U)
Total prevention	$109,000	$53,000	$ (56,000)	(U)
Appraisal costs:				
Materials inspection	$ 19,000	$ 7,900	$ (11,100)	(U)
Product acceptance	10,000	0	(10,000)	(U)
Process acceptance	35,000	12,000	(23,000)	(U)
Total appraisal	$ 64,000	$19,900	$ (44,100)	(U)
Internal failure costs:				
Scrap	$ 40,000	$0	$ (40,000)	(U)
Rework	34,000	0	(34,000)	(U)
Total internal failure	$ 74,000	$0	$ (74,000)	(U)
External failure costs:				
Fixed:				
Customer complaints	$ 24,000	$0	$ (24,000)	(U)
Variable:				
Warranty	24,000	0	(24,000)	(U)
Repair	15,000	0	(15,000)	(U)
Total external failure	$ 63,000	$0	$ (63,000)	(U)
Total quality costs	$310,000	$72,900	$(237,100)	(U)
Percentage of actual sales	10.62%	2.50%	−8.12%	(U)

*Based on actual sales of $2,920,000. These costs are value-added costs.

Fig. 13-3

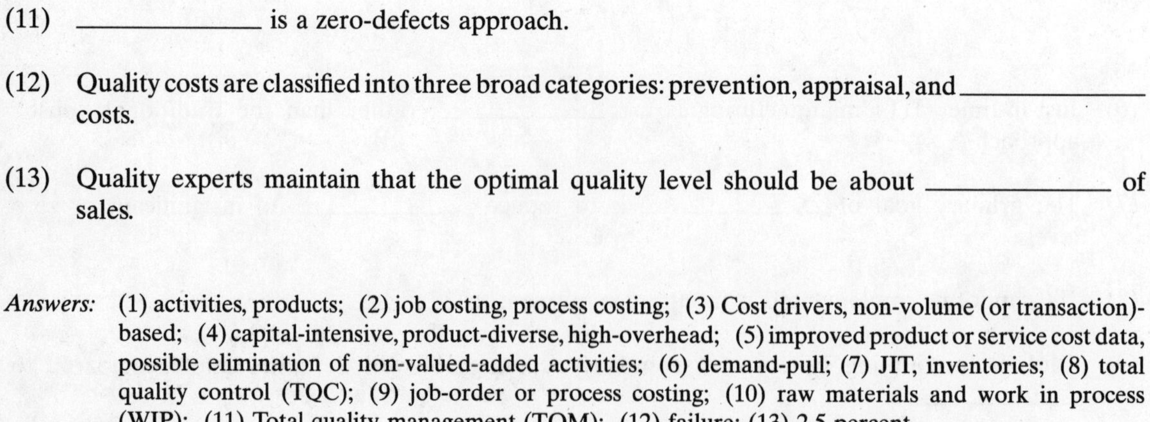

(11) ____________ is a zero-defects approach.

(12) Quality costs are classified into three broad categories: prevention, appraisal, and ____________ costs.

(13) Quality experts maintain that the optimal quality level should be about ____________ of sales.

Answers: (1) activities, products; (2) job costing, process costing; (3) Cost drivers, non-volume (or transaction)-based; (4) capital-intensive, product-diverse, high-overhead; (5) improved product or service cost data, possible elimination of non-valued-added activities; (6) demand-pull; (7) JIT, inventories; (8) total quality control (TQC); (9) job-order or process costing; (10) raw materials and work in process (WIP); (11) Total quality management (TQM); (12) failure; (13) 2.5 percent.

Solved Problems

13.1 Assume that a plant has two categories of overhead: material handling and quality inspection. The costs expected for these categories for the coming year are as follows.

Material handling	$100,000
Quality inspection	300,000

The plant currently applies overhead using direct labor hours and expected actual capacity. This figure is 50,000 direct labor hours.

The plant manager has been asked to submit a bid and has assembled the following data on the proposed job:

	Potential Job
Direct materials	$3,700
Direct labor (1,000 hours)	$7,000
Overhead	$?
Number of material moves	10
Number of inspections	5

The manager has been told that many competitors use an ABC approach to assign overhead to jobs. Before submitting his bid, he wants to assess the effects of this alternative approach. He estimates that the expected number of material moves for all jobs during the year is 1,000; he also expects 5,000 quality inspections to be performed.

(*a*) Compute the total cost of the potential job using direct labor hours to assign overhead. Assuming the bid price is full manufacturing cost plus 25 percent, what would be the manager's bid?

(*b*) Compute the total cost of the job using the number of material moves to allocate material-handling costs and the number of inspections to allocate the quality inspection costs. Assuming a bid price of full manufacturing cost plus 25 percent, what should be his bid using this approach?

(*c*) Which approach do you think best reflects the actual cost of the job? Explain.

SOLUTION

(*a*) Total overhead is $400,000. The plant-wide rate is $8 per direct labor hour ($400,000/50,000).

(*b*) In the ABC approach, the consumption ratios are different for all two-overhead activities, so overhead pools are formed for each activity. The overhead rates for each of these pools are as follows:

Material moves:	$100,000/1,000 = $100/move
Quality inspections:	$300,000/5,000 = $60/inspection

This produces the following job costs and bid prices:

Volume-based approach:		
Prime costs	$10,700	
Overhead costs	8,000	(1,000 × $8)
Total costs	$18,700	
Plus 25%	$ 4,675	($18,700 × 25%)
Bid price	$23,375	
Activity-based approach:		
Prime costs	$10,700	
Overhead costs:		
Material moves	1,000	(10 × $100)
Inspections	300	(5 × $60)
Total costs	$12,000	
Plus 25%	$ 3,000	($12,000 × 25%)
Bid price	$15,000	

(*c*) The volume approach overestimates the overhead and would cause the company to overbid the job.

13.2 Alfred Autoparts, Inc., previously used a cost system that allocated all factory overhead costs to products based on 350 percent of direct labor cost. The company has just implemented an ABC system that traces indirect costs to products based on consumption of major activities as indicated below. Compare the total annual costs of Product X using both the traditional volume-based and the new ABC systems.

Activity	Annual Cost Driver Quantity	Cost	Product X Cost Driver Consumption
Labor	$300,000	$ 30,000	$10,000
Machining	20,000 hours	$500,000	800 hours
Setup	10,000 hours	$100,000	100 hours
Production order	2,000 orders	$200,000	12 orders
Material handling	1,000 requisitions	$ 20,000	5 requisitions
Parts administration	12,000 parts	$480,000	18 parts

SOLUTION

Cost Systems	Pool Rate	Cost Driver Consumption	Cost Assignment
Traditional cost system	350%	$10,000	$35,000
ABC system			
Labor	10%	$10,000	$ 1,000
Machining	$25/hour	800 hours	20,000
Setup	$10/hour	100 hours	1,000
Production order	$100/order	12 orders	1,200
Material handling	$20/requisition	5 requisitions	100
Parts administration	$40/part	18 parts	720
Total costs			$24,020

13.3 Hangover Manufacturing has four categories of overhead. The four categories and expected overhead costs for each category for next year are listed below.

Maintenance	$200,000
Material handling	32,000
Setups	100,000
Inspection	120,000

Currently, overhead is applied using a predetermined overhead rate, based on budgeted direct labor hours. Fifty thousand direct labor hours are budgeted for next year.

The company has been asked to submit a bid for a proposed job. The plant manager feels that getting this job would result in new business in future years. Bids are based on full manufacturing cost plus 20 percent.

Estimates for the proposed job are as follows:

Direct materials	$ 6,000
Direct labor (1,000 hours)	$10,000
Number of material moves	12
Number of inspections	10
Number of setups	2
Number of machine hours	500

In the past, full manufacturing cost has been calculated by allocating overhead using a volume-based cost driver, direct labor hours. The plant manager has heard of a new way of applying overhead that uses cost pools and cost drivers.

Expected activity for the four activity-based cost drivers that would be used are:

Machine hours	20,000
Material moves	1,600
Setups	2,500
Quality inspections	41,000

1. (*a*) Determine the amount of overhead that would be allocated to the proposed job if direct labor hours is used as the volume-based cost driver.
   (*b*) Determine the total cost of the proposed job.
   (*c*) Determine the company's bid if the bid is based on full manufacturing cost plus 20 percent.
2. (*a*) Determine the amount of overhead that would be applied to the proposed project if activity-based cost drivers are used.
   (*b*) Determine the total cost of the proposed job if activity-based costing is used.
   (*c*) Determine the company's bid if activity-based costing is used and the bid is based on full manufacturing cost plus 20 percent.

SOLUTION

1. (*a*)

$$\text{Total overhead} = \$200{,}000 + \$32{,}000 + \$100{,}000 + \$120{,}000 = \$452{,}000$$

$$\text{Overhead rate} = \$452{,}000/50{,}000 \text{ direct labor hours} = \$9.04 \text{ per direct labor hour}$$

$$\text{Overhead assigned to proposed job} = \$9.04 \times 1{,}000 \text{ direct labor hours} = \$9{,}040$$

(*b*) Total cost of proposed job:

Direct materials	$ 6,000
Direct labor	10,000
Overhead applied	9,040
Total cost	$25,040

(*c*) Company's bid = Full manufacturing cost × 120% = $25,040 × 120% = $30,048

2. (*a*)

Maintenance:	$200,000/20,000 = $10 per machine hour
Materials handling:	$32,000/1,600 = $20 per move
Setups:	$100,000/2,500 = $40 per setup
Inspection:	$120,000/4,000 = $30 per inspection

Overhead assigned to proposed job:

Maintenance ($10 × 500)	$5,000
Material handling ($20 × 12)	240
Setups ($40 × 2)	80
Inspection ($30 × 10)	300
Total overhead assigned to job	$5,620

(*b*) Total cost of proposed project:

Direct materials	$ 6,000
Direct labor	10,000
Overhead applied	5,620
Total cost	$21,620

(*c*) Company's bid = Full manufacturing cost × 120% = $21,620 × 120% = $25,944
The bid price of $25,944 was determined as follows:

Direct materials		$ 6,000
Direct labor		10,000
Overhead assigned:		
Maintenance ($10 × 500)	$5,000	
Material handling ($20 × 12)	240	
Setups ($40 × 2)	80	
Inspections ($30 × 10)	300	
Total overhead assigned to job		5,620
Total cost		$21,620
Markup		120%
Bid price		$25,944

13.4 The following information pertains to Omni, Inc., for 19X8:

Sales	$30,000,000
External failure costs	900,000
Internal failure costs	1,800,000
Prevention costs	400,000
Appraisal costs	600,000

1. Calculate each category of quality costs as a percentage of sales.
2. Calculate total quality costs as a percentage of sales.
3. If quality costs were reduced to 2.5 percent of sales, determine the increase in profit that would result.

SOLUTION

1.

External failure costs:	$900,000/$30,000,000 = 3.0%
Internal failure costs:	$1,800,000/$30,000,000 = 6.0%
Prevention costs:	$400,000/$30,000,000 = 1.3%
Appraisal costs:	$600,000/$30,000,000 = 2.0%

2. Total quality costs: $3,700,000/$30,000,000 = 12.3%

3.

Current quality costs	$3,700,000
Goal (2.5% × $30,000,000)	750,000
Increase in profit	$2,950,000

13.5 At the beginning of the year, Donjuan Company initiated a quality improvement program. The program was successful in reducing scrap and rework costs. To help assess the impact of the quality improvement program, the following data were collected for the current and preceding years:

	Preceding Year	Current Year
Sales	$4,000,000	$4,000,000
Quality training	10,000	15,000
Materials inspection	25,000	35,000
Scrap	200,000	180,000
Rework	250,000	200,000
Product inspection	40,000	60,000
Product warranty	300,000	250,000

1. Classify each of the costs as prevention costs, appraisal costs, internal failure costs, or external failure costs: (*a*) quality training; (*b*) materials inspection; (*c*) scrap; (*d*) rework; (*e*) product inspection; (*f*) product warranty.

2. Compute each category of quality costs as a percentage of sales:

	Preceding Year	Current Year
Prevention costs		
Appraisal costs		
Internal failure costs		
External failure costs		

3. (*a*) How much has profit increased as a result of quality improvement?
   (*b*) If quality costs can be reduced to 2.5 percent of sales, how much additional profit will result?

SOLUTION

1. (*a*) Quality training: Preventive cost
   (*b*) Materials inspection: Appraisal cost
   (*c*) Scrap: Internal failure cost
   (*d*) Rework: Internal failure cost
   (*e*) Product inspection: Appraisal cost
   (*f*) Product warranty: External failure cost

2.

	Preceding Year		Current Year	
Preventive costs:				
Quality training	$10,000	0.25%	$15,000	0.38%
Appraisal costs:				
Materials inspection	$25,000		$35,000	
Product inspection	40,000		60,000	
Total appraisal costs	$65,000	1.63%	$95,000	2.38%
Internal failure costs:				
Scrap	$200,000		$180,000	
Rework	250,000		200,000	
Total internal failure costs	$450,000	11.25%	$380,000	9.50%
External failure costs:				
Product warranty	$300,000	7.50%	$250,000	6.25%

3. (*a*)

Total quality costs: preceding year	$825,000
Total quality costs: current year	740,000
Increase in profit	$85,000

(*b*)

Total quality costs: current year	$740,000
Goal (2.5% × $4,000,000)	100,000
Increase in profit	$640,000

13.6 In 19X9, Allison Foods Company instituted a quality improvement program. At the end of 19X9, the management of the corporation requested a report to show the amount saved by the measures taken during the year. The actual sales and actual quality costs for 19X8 and 19X9 were:

	19X8	19X9
Sales	$500,000	$600,000
Scrap	15,000	15,000
Rework	20,000	10,000
Training program	5,000	6,000
Consumer complaints	10,000	5,000
Lost sales, incorrect labeling	8,000	—
Test labor	12,000	8,000
Inspection labor	25,000	24,000
Supplier evaluation	15,000	13,000

Prepare the one-year trend report that corporate management requested. How much did profits increase because of quality improvements made in 19X9 (assuming that all reductions in quality costs are attributable to quality improvements)?

SOLUTION

ALLISON FOODS COMPANY
Performance Report: Quality Costs
One-Year Trend
For the Year Ended December 31, 19X9

	Actual Costs 19X9	Actual Costs 19X8	Variance	
Prevention Costs:				
Training Program	$ 6,000	$ 5,000	$ 1,000	U
Supplier Evaluation	13,000	15,000	2,000	F
Total Prevention Costs	$19,000	$20,000	$ 1,000	F
Appraisal Costs:				
Test Labor	$ 8,000	$ 14,400	$ 6,400	F
Inspection Labor	24,000	30,000	6,000	F
Total Appraisal Costs	$32,000	$44,400	$12,400	F
Internal Failure Costs:				
Scrap	$15,000	$ 18,000	$ 3,000	F
Rework	10,000	24,000	14,000	F
Total Internal Failure Costs	$25,000	$ 42,000	$17,000	F
External Failure Costs:				
Consumer Complaints	$ 5,000	$ 12,000	$ 7,000	F
Lost Sales, Labeling	0	9,600	$ 9,600	F
Total External Failure Costs	$ 5,000	$ 21,600	$16,600	F
Total Quality Costs	$81,000	$128,000	$47,000	F
% of Actual Sales	13.5%	21.33%	7.83%	F

Based on sales of $600,000, profits increased by $47,000

Examination III

Chapters 8–13

Part I For each of the following statements, enter a T or an F in the blank to indicate whether the statement is true or false.

_____ **1.** Capital turnover multiplied by margin is equal to residual income (RI).

_____ **2.** Return on investment (ROI) divided by margin is equal to turnover.

_____ **3.** The IRR and the NPV methods always produce the identical ranking.

_____ **4.** The modified accelerated cost recovery system (MACRS) abandons the concept of useful life.

_____ **5.** The shorter the payback period, the greater is the liquidity and the less risky the project.

_____ **6.** Transfer prices are prices for goods and services sold by subunits to outside customers.

_____ **7.** Market price is the best transfer price under any circumstance.

_____ **8.** In business, the word *funds* generally refers to working capital.

_____ **9.** Amortization is a source of funds.

_____ **10.** In determining "funds provided by operations," it is necessary to add depreciation back to net income.

_____ **11.** A high inventory turnover means too much money is tied up in inventory.

_____ **12.** The acid-test ratio is a more stringent test of short-term liquidity than the current ratio.

_____ **13.** The objective of linear programming is to control the quality of production by means of computer programming.

_____ **14.** The EOQ is the order quantity that would minimize the annual ordering cost.

_____ **15.** The quantity of the safety stock plus expected usage during lead time is equal to the optimal reorder point.

_____ **16.** Dividends per share are generally regarded as an indication of whether a stock is overpriced or underpriced.

_____ **17.** The profitability index is commonly used in ranking investment projects competing for limited funds.

_____ **18.** The general formula for computing a transfer price is: Transfer price = Fixed cost per unit + Opportunity costs for the company as a whole.

Part II Answer the following questions.

1. Charles Corporation reports the following for 19X1:

Accounts receivable—1/1	$100,000
Accounts receivable—12/31	150,000
Inventory—1/1	40,000
Inventory—12/31	55,000
Net credit sales	800,000
Cost of goods sold	450,000

Compute (*a*) accounts receivable turnover, (*b*) average collection period, (*c*) inventory turnover, and (*d*) average age of inventory.

2. Ace Corporation reports the following information:

Net income	$57,000
Loss on the sale of fixed assets	2,000
Depreciation expense	6,000
Amortization expense	3,000
Amortization of deferred income	4,000
Salaries expense	20,000

Determine the funds provided from operations.

3. The Winchell Corporation manufactures and markets two products, A and B. Each product is processed through two phases—machining and finishing—before it is sold. The following unit information is provided:

	A	B
Selling price	$10.00	$14.00
Direct labor	4.00	6.00
Direct materials	1.50	0.50
Variable overhead	1.00	1.20
Fixed overhead	0.80	0.62
Materials requirements in pounds	20	10
Labor requirements in hours:		
Machining	$\frac{2}{3}$	$\frac{1}{6}$
Finishing	$\frac{1}{6}$	$\frac{1}{3}$

Six thousand pounds of materials are available each week. The machining department has 240 hours of labor available each week, while the finishing department has 180 hours of labor available per week. No overtime is allowed. The company wishes to determine the mix of products A and B so as to maximize weekly contribution margin. Formulate the objective function and constraints.

4. The following information is given for the Starr Company:

Total annual demand	360,000 units
Carrying costs per unit	$2
Costs per order	$100
Lead time	5 weeks

Assume 50 weeks per year.
Find the following:

(*a*) EOQ ____________

(*b*) Optimum number of orders ____________

(*c*) Total carrying and ordering costs ____________

(*d*) Optimal reorder point ____________

5. The following data pertain to Division XYZ of the United Republic Company:

Operating assets	$260,000
Operating income	$ 44,200
Minimum required rate of return	11%

(*a*) What is the division's ROI?

(*b*) What is the division's RI?

(*c*) The division is presented with a project which returns 15 percent on its investment. Would the division accept this project

(1) If ROI were used to evaluate performance? Why?

(2) If RI were used to evaluate performance? Why?

6. Mahony Company is considering the purchase of a new machine which will cost $7,370. The machine will provide revenues of $4,000 per year. The cash operating costs will be $2,000 per year. The new machine will have a useful life of six years. The company's cost of capital is 12 percent. Ignore income taxes.

(*a*) What is the machine's NPV?

(*b*) What is the machine's IRR?

(*c*) Should the company buy the new machine?

7. K-Parks Industries, Inc., used to assign factory overhead costs to products based on 800 percent of direct labor cost. The company just implemented an ABC system that traces overhead to products based on consumption of major activities as indicated below. Compare the total overhead costs of Product X using the traditional labor-based and the new ABC system.

Activity Pool	Annual Cost Driver Quantity	Traceable Overhead Costs	Cost Pool Rate	Product X Cost Driver Consumption
Labor	$300,000	$ 30,000		$2,000
Machining	20,000 hours	$500,000		800 hours
Setup	10,000 setups	$100,000		100 setups
Production order	2,000 orders	$200,000		12 orders
Material handling	1,000 requisitions	$ 20,000		5 requisitions

Answers to Examination III

Part I

1. F **2.** T **3.** F **4.** T **5.** T **6.** F **7.** F **8.** T **9.** T **10.** T **11.** F **12.** T **13.** F **14.** F **15.** T **16.** F **17.** T **18.** F

Part II

1. (*a*)

$$\text{Accounts receivable turnover} = \frac{\text{Net credit sales}}{\text{Average accounts receivable}} = \frac{\$800{,}000}{\$125{,}000} = 6.4 \text{ times}$$

(*b*)

$$\text{Average collection period} = \frac{365 \text{ days}}{\text{Accounts receivable turnover}} = \frac{365}{6.4} = 57 \text{ days}$$

(*c*)

$$\text{Inventory turnover} = \frac{\text{Cost of goods sold}}{\text{Average inventory}} = \frac{\$450{,}000}{\$47{,}500} = 9.47 \text{ times}$$

(*d*)

$$\text{Average age of inventory} = \frac{365 \text{ days}}{\text{Inventory turnover}} = \frac{365}{9.47} = 38.5 \text{ days}$$

2.

Net income		$57,000
Add: Nonworking capital expenses		
Depreciation expense	$6,000	
Amortization expense	3,000	
Loss on the sale of fixed assets	2,000	11,000
Less: Nonworking capital revenue		
Amortization of deferred income		(4,000)
Funds provided from operations		$64,000

3. Let A = number of units of product A to be produced
B = number of units of product B to be produced

	A	B
Selling price	$10.00	$14.00
Variable costs:		
Direct labor	4.00	6.00
Direct materials	1.50	0.50
Variable overhead	1.00	1.20
Contribution margin per unit	$ 3.50	$ 6.30

Therefore, the objective function would be:

$$\text{Maximize:} \quad TCM = \$3.50A + \$6.30B$$

The constraints are:

— *Labor constraints*

Machining department: $\frac{2}{3}A + \frac{1}{6}B \leqq 240$ hours

Finishing department: $\frac{1}{6}A + \frac{1}{3}B \leqq 180$ hours

— *Material constraints*

$$20A + 10B \leqq 6{,}000 \text{ pounds}$$

– *Non-negativity constraints*

$$A, B \geqq 0$$

4. (*a*) $$EOQ = \sqrt{\frac{2\,(100)\,(360{,}000)}{\$2}} = \sqrt{36{,}000{,}000} = 6{,}000 \text{ units}$$

(*b*) $$\text{Optimum number of orders} = \frac{360{,}000}{6{,}000} = 60 \text{ times}$$

(*c*) Total carrying and ordering costs:

$$(\$2)\left(\frac{6{,}000}{2}\right) + (\$100)\left(\frac{360{,}000}{6{,}000}\right) = \$6{,}000 + \$6{,}000 = \$12{,}000$$

(*d*) $$\text{Optimum reorder point} = 5 \text{ weeks} \times \frac{360{,}000}{50 \text{ weeks}} = 36{,}000 \text{ units}$$

5. (*a*) $$ROI = \frac{\$44{,}200}{\$260{,}000} = 17\%$$

(*b*) $$RI = \$44{,}200 - (11\% \times \$260{,}000) = \$44{,}200 - \$28{,}600 = \$15{,}600$$

(*c*) (1) No, because the additional project would bring down the division's overall ROI.
(2) Yes, because the additional project would raise the division's overall RI.

6. (*a*) $NPV = (\$2{,}000)\,(4.111) - \$7{,}370 = \$8{,}222 - \$7{,}370 = \$852$

(*b*) *IRR:*

At *IRR*, $$I = PV$$

Thus, $$\$7{,}370 = \$2{,}000 \text{ (PV factor for 6 years)}$$

$$\frac{\$7{,}370}{\$2{,}000} = 3.685 \text{ gives IRR} = 16\%$$

(*c*) The company should buy the machine because

(1) NPV = \$852 is positive, or

(2) IRR = 16 percent exceeds the cost of capital of 12 percent.

7.

Cost Systems	Cost Pool Rate	Product X Cost Driver Consumption	Cost Assignment
Traditional system:	800%	$2,000	$16,000
ABC system:			
Labor	10%	$2,000	$ 200
Machining	$25 per hour	800 hours	20,000
Setup	$10 per setup	100 setups	1,000
Production order	$100 per order	12 orders	1,200
Material handling	$20 per requisition	5 requisitions	100
			$22,500

Index